To forgive is generous
To forget is unthinkable
Stand up for justice.

Journey to Happily Ever After

Journey to Happily Ever After

ॐ

Rita B. Ross

ISBN-13: 9781545029664
ISBN-10: 1545029660
Library of Congress Control Number: 2017905082
CreateSpace Independent Publishing Platform
North Charleston, South Carolina

Dedication

To the righteous : To my family members: aunts, uncles, cousins, grand-parents and friends who were murdered by the Nazis, while the "good people" stood by and did nothing. To the Gentiles who saved countless persons at the risk of losing their own lives.

To the courageous and outspoken few who fight genocide, igno-rance, prejudice even today, because so many have not learned the futility of war and the need for tolerance.

Acknowledgements

I AM DEEPLY indebted to many people who helped and encouraged me in this endeavor. My husband, Dan, the love of my life urged me on, researched and corroborated my memories, checked for historical accuracy, took me on a trip to Poland to validate my early impressions, made all the computer adjustments, resurrected old documents and photographs, and stood by me encouragingly while I went back to explore my painful past.

My editor, shrink, teacher, and mentor, Melinda Blau, who was relentless in getting me to do the best I was capable of, forced me to go back to my past to dig further than I wanted to, kept me focused, and was always available for consultations. She empowered and encouraged me by saying "I know you can do better than that." In the process, she helped me tackle the destructive roots lodged in my heart, bring them to light and give up my ongoing chronic bouts with depression.

To my loyal readers, I thank you from the bottom of my heart. Your eager willingness to read through this manuscript helped, encouraged and validated my effort: Leora Chalow, who read through the manuscript several times, making suggestions, telling me what was confusing and needed to be addressed to make more sympathetic and to Daniel Belmondo for editing, correcting and pointing our inconsistencies.

Prologue

ALL MY LIFE I have fought anxiety, depression and fear of abandonment. After much soul searching and help I came to realize that my problems are rooted in the real life nightmare of my early childhood experiences.

Before I reached the age of three, my father left our home in Vienna with the promise that my mother, brother and I would soon join him in a wonderful country, America, where we would live happily ever after. My mother kept that "happily ever after" myth alive as we hid in dark factories, cold churches, cemeteries and parks; while danger, terror, loss, hunger and cold chased us relentlessly. My mother repeated the fairy tale assuring my younger brother and myself, that this nightmare soon would be over and that we were bound for a happy life with my father in America. When I felt pangs of hunger she told me that as soon as we got we arrived in America we would have more food than was possible to eat. When I shivered in the unrelenting cold of the Polish winter she informed me that my father was building a warm, safe beautiful home for us in America. She would be forced to leave us alone in the ghetto to forage for food outside its walls and all I could think of was that she was captured, tortured and murdered by the Nazis. And I had good reason to feel that way because every day someone would report the atrocities that were taking place; the murders, shootings torture. It didn't take much imagination to see her trapped, beaten, bleeding and dehumanized. She tried to reassure me, tell me I was safe, that my father was waiting for us and we would be seeing him in a matter of days. She kept telling me of this place called "happily ever after" and how happy we would all be there.

In spite of my skepticism, I believed her when she told me that my father was alive in America. In my mind I imagined that my father was a handsome, protective man who would anticipate all my desires and grant them before I had a chance to express them. He would be rich, funny, generous, indulgent, kind and smart. He would rescue us and bring into the land of "happily ever after."

No human being could possibly deliver on my mother's promises and my father fell short of them. I had grand ideas of what he would be like and how lovely my life would become.

He had his own set of expectations. We fell short on both ends. My brother and I certainly were not the children he had last seen in Vienna in 1939, nor was he the father who left us. We were all super-optimistic and we were all disappointed. He expected gratitude, we expected indulgence. He wanted respect, we wanted unconditional love, acceptance and lots of toy. He envisioned a smart son, Michael couldn't read (he was only seven years old and had not attended school) and I wanted a happily ever after childhood. He harbored visions of me as a quiet, demure little lady and I was a feisty child, used to arguing to get my own way.

By the age of nine, I had spent most of my life fleeing from the Nazis, but well into adulthood I tried to convince myself that I had a normal childhood. My blond, blue-eyed, Aryan-looking (but Jewish) mother, wanting to spare my brother and me from the horrifying truth of our reality invented a make believe childhood couching real danger with myth defying adventure.

Well into adulthood I kept her fictitious tales alive. I did not consider myself a "Holocaust survivor." Certainly I had been in hiding, hungry, scared and freezing cold, but I never experienced starvation, beatings, mutilation and didn't have a number tattooed on my forearm. When the German government began offering monetary reparations to victims of the Holocaust, I refused to apply, claiming that I had a normal childhood and was not going to claim something I wasn't entitled to. More recently, my experience was videotaped by Steven Spielberg's Foundation and again I found myself repeating over and over again the wonderful childhood myth.

Incredible as it seems now, I didn't link my depression or anxieties to the atrocities I witnessed as a young child. Of course, I wondered about the nightmares that to this day invade my sleep regularly and leave me with the feeling of impending doom and danger, but I was unwilling or unable to link them to any experience I might have had.

Neither I nor the several therapists I worked with were able penetrate the armor of denial I had polished over the years. I was so committed to my version of my childhood, that at one point, after reading the book, *Many Lives, Many Masters*, by Brian LWeiss I became convinced that the bouts of depression that began to plague me in early adolescence were rooted in a former existence, maybe a hundred or even a thousand years ago.

I consulted a past life regression therapist to look for a past life. The dimly lit office, with New Age music playing in the background and the scent of incense seemed to be the perfect setting to play out my past. I was ready to go back in time to a previous unhappy life.

"Not so fast," the therapist cautioned me. "First, tell me about your present life, your childhood, your parents and family."

I launched into my story, the one drilled into my head by my mother, stressing, as I always did, that I had a happy, normal childhood in spite of living through that hell referred to as the Holocaust. I was one of the lucky ones, alive and able to leave that chapter of my life behind. I was a high- functioning adult--a good mother, an esteemed teacher, an active member of my temple, a volunteer in many worthy organizations. Whenever I was asked to lecture young people about that time of my life, I titled my talk, "A Happy Childhood in Spite of the Holocaust."

The therapist listened carefully to my story, jotting down notes on a yellow legal pad. When I finished, I thought he'd offer to put me in a trance so that I could revisit earlier lives. Instead, he sat up straight in his chair, shaking his head.

"You are convinced that your childhood did not affect you?" he exclaimed incredulously. "That's bullshit!" The word shot out his mouth like a spit ball. "Unless you're some kind of a zombie you had to be affected by your early years. Do you really think you had a *normal* childhood? Go home. If you decide to work with me, be prepared to examine your present life before going off on some past life expedition."

Post-traumatic stress disorder is a relatively new diagnosis. It certainly was not in use when I began storing my little cache of trauma in the early 1940s. PTSD came into the vernacular only after the post Viet-Nam veterans retuned home and began re-experiencing harrowing events that had taken place in the jungles of Asia, now re-appearing in their dreams and stressful moments. PTSD invites unwelcome episodes that invade lives and cannot be let go of, like pit bulls clutching prey in their clamped jaws.

The persistent anxieties that invaded my sub-conscious gradually worked their way into the present moment. No amount of reasoning, examining and dialogue with professionals lessened my abiding fears of abandonment, betrayal and doom. In my desperate search for solution and dissolution of the ghosts that hovered around my psyche I decided to write down my experiences and try to gain an understanding of their origins. The result was a wider understanding and acceptance of the fact that PTSD experiences almost never leave one alone, and too often insert themselves into the present.

Photo of my mother, brother and myself taken at a fourth of July celebration in the POW camp in Liebenau, Germany, in 1943

Alexander Schmelkes
1931

Freda Perlberger
1933

Rita, Freda, Michael Wielizka, Poland

Cousin Ruth Birnbaum
Age 15 Killed in Krakow Poland

Identification Photo
Michael, Freda, Rita

Liebenau
Rita, Freda, Michael
1943

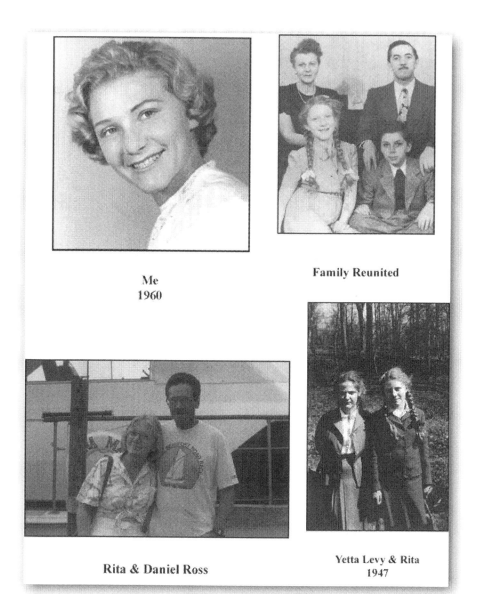

Me
1960

Family Reunited

Rita & Daniel Ross

Yetta Levy & Rita
1947

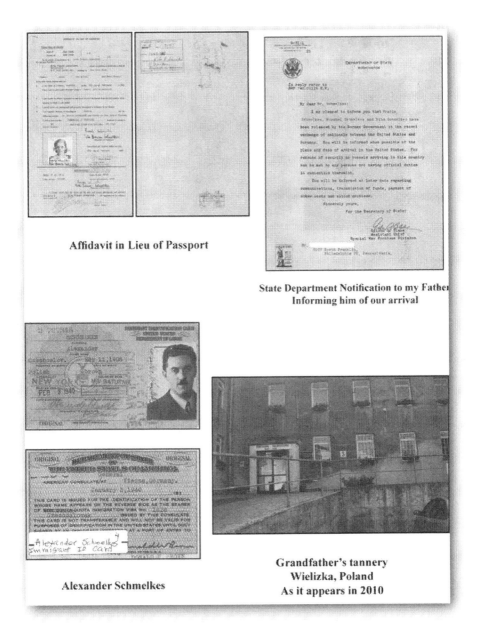

Affidavit in Lieu of Passport

**State Department Notification to my Father
Informing him of our arrival**

Alexander Schmelkes

**Grandfather's tannery
Wielizka, Poland
As it appears in 2010**

HAMILTON BOOKS

"Ross writes in a compelling narrative voice that conveys childlike innocence and honesty while unflinchingly describing acts of ineffable cruelty. Her style gives the story an immediacy that draws the reader into the world of the child who struggles to understand the events of her life. *Running from Home* speaks eloquently of the fragility of life while also celebrating the resiliency of the human spirit."

—Patricia Sack, English department chairperson, Merion Mercy Academy

"A deeply insightful memoir, skillfully written and, at times, painfully honest in depicting a child's terror created by anti-Semitism, the loss of loved ones, and years of running away. Unlike other stories of survival, this account helps those of us, fortunate not to have lived during the Holocaust, to understand the horror, the fortitude, the courage required as well as the lasting impact of these events on the lives of those who lived through them."

—Rabbi Neil S. Cooper, Temple Beth Hillel-Beth El, Wynnewood, PA and honorary doctorate, Jewish Theological Seminary

"A most unusual and harrowing Holocaust tale. Because she suffered every inhumanity *except* a concentration camp, she spent a lifetime in denial, believing that hers was a 'happy childhood.' Rita's discovery of the truth and her eventual acceptance of reality is a story that will resonate with anyone who has ever survived any kind of adversity—and who among us hasn't?"

—Melinda Blau, journalist and best-selling author

Running from Home chronicles Rita's flight from the Nazis as it was perceived by a young child. The sense of bewilderment, loss of home, and suffering from hunger and cold create an indelible mark upon her mind and do not leave when she eventually comes to America. Raised in different cultures, she never feels at home but is always the outsider, trying to reconcile her old life and experiences with her new surroundings. Her youth and adolescence are assaulted by the demons that have been imprinted on her young brain. Furthermore, Rita's father suffers from his own demons: financial insecurity, disenfranchisement, and constant poverty serve to reestablish her old fears and sense of loss. For Rita, the war is not over when the peace treaties have been signed.

Rita B. Ross was born in Vienna, Austria, two years before Hitler's troops stormed the country. She spent the war years hiding her Jewish identity and came to America in 1945. She taught at the Perlman Jewish Day School in Wynnewood, Pennsylvania, for twenty-seven years and is a frequent lecturer on her Holocaust experiences and the need for tolerance.

For orders and information please contact the publisher
HAMILTON BOOKS
A member of the Rowman & Littlefield Publishing Group, Inc.
4501 Forbes Boulevard, Suite 200
Lanham, Maryland 20706
1-800-462-6420
www.hamilton-books.com

ISBN 978-0-7618-4562-1
90000
9 780761 845621

Part I

CHAPTER 1

———— ❦ ————

THE NAZI OFFICER thrusts his high beam flashlight into the car and peers inside. Fat raindrops slide from the visor of his captain's hat to his dripping nose. He is on duty rounding up Jews who are violating the recently imposed curfew in Vienna and this is a routine stop at the check-point. My father tells me years later that he has taken me along on this little journey to visit his parents because he hopes that my blond hair and blue eyes will distract the Nazi from checking his own identity too closely.

The SS officer squints into the car. He sees a blond, blue-eyed little girl accompanied by a man. He asks me who the man next to me is and I reply confidently that he is my father. He looks at me and tells me he has a little girl like me at his home and that I remind him of her. He misses her and he asks me, "Are we going on holiday with this lucky man?"

"We are going to visit my *oma and opa.*"

The officer chuckles, "have a good time." I lean out of the window, raise my right arm in the Nazi salute, "*Heil Hitler*," I shout. He smiles and waves us on.

The Nazi hates standing here in the freezing rain and fog. But he is doing this for the Fatherland, his beloved Deutschland. He loves the *Fuhrer*, a man with a vision. He sees what it will take to make Germany a leading power in Europe and eventually in the world. Hitler doesn't waste any time. He tackles each problem as it arises. The officer is assigned to help rid Germany, Austria and eventually all of Europe of the Jews. He tells himself that he is not an unkind man. He does as he is told. The Jews are draining the economy of all its resources. He knows the Jews, has seen them going and returning from their synagogues. Stooped little men dressed in black, carrying velvet bags containing the prayer shawls, their long noses pointed to the ground. He's seen their women, wearing unsightly wigs and unfashionable clothes. They have plenty of money. They are the only ones who have any money during this period of recession. Some of the women wear expensive jewelry, pearl necklaces and diamond rings. Their nerve is astonishing. His very own mother worked for one of them, as a maid. Imagine the humiliation! A German housewife forced into menial work for a dirty little Jewess; yes forced, because those very same Jews are bleeding Germany of her resources. He has no use for them and neither does anyone else.

We climb the shaky wooden stairs at my *opa's* house.

"*Maidi!*" *oma* and *opa* exclaim, and I look up to see them smiling at us from the top of the dark stairs. They live one flight up in a simple, small apartment that has a large dining room table in the parlor and a small bedroom in the back. They are dressed in dull, shapeless clothing. *opa* is wearing a black velvet *kippa* on his head and *oma*'s head is covered with an ill-fitting, brown, everyday *sheytl*, the wig that all pious Jewish women wear.

We are so happy to see each other. They hug me tightly and exclaim over my growth.

"You are already a young lady, a *fruelein*." They are delighted to see me. *Oma* and *opa* are my favorite people, and I know I am theirs.

"One, two, three," they count before taking my hands, and swinging me up into the air. The apartment smells sweet, full of chocolates and cookies, baked especially for our visit. *Opa* and I play our usual game, a pony ride. He sits on a chair and crosses his legs, while I straddle his shoe as he bounces his leg up and down. "*Schneller, schneller,* (faster, faster)" I urge. I am happy that my little brother, Bubbi, isn't with us. I hate to share the spotlight with him. He can't even talk yet and already gets plenty of recognition that he doesn't deserve. I know that I am the most adored grandchild from the youngest child in my mother's family and the first grandchild in my father's family. I am happy to have everyone vying for my attention. I learn to hum little songs before I talk, dance as soon as I am steady enough on my feet know how to get smiles of approval from loving relatives.

I go into *oma's* bedroom. Two beds separated by a night table and a large black dresser occupy most of the room. Two wooden dummy heads stand next to each other on the dresser; twins with no faces. My grandmother uses them her hold her *sheytls* when she is not wearing them. I love looking at the bald heads, bereft of their wigs. Their wooden contours are polished to a high gloss as they look at me with sightless eyes. I reach up to pat the bare one, wondering if my *oma* removes her own head every night when she goes to sleep to place it on the dresser next to the wig stands. The imagined ritual has a magical quality to it. My own *mutti* does not wear a wig, but perhaps she will when she gets old like my *oma*.

It is a loving reunion with no hint of what is to come. I eat *oma's* cookies, generously wrapping up a few to take home for Bubbi. I make silver balls and shiny rings out of the tinfoil wrappers used to package chocolate and sing my repertoire of German songs to lots of enthusiastic applause and encouragement. My *oma* gives me two red hats, and *opa* calls me *"Rotkopchen"* (Red Riding Hood). They wave good-bye from the top of the steps, beaming. Only much later do I realize how painful this good-bye must have been for them, yet they never betray any hint of impending danger.

Shortly after our visit *oma* and *opa* will disappear.

CHAPTER 2

—— ❦ ——

BRIGHT PATCHES OF sunlight cast golden beams across the parquet floor of our apartment in Vienna. It is 1939, three years after I came into the world. Now, I am a toddler, marching in my mother's high heeled shoes, avoiding the oriental rugs strewn about the floor. I want to be noisy, to be heard. I sing at the top of my lungs, one of the many Nazi anthems I've come to love, *"Haute gehert uns Deutschland, morgen die ganse velt....Sig heil, Sig heil."* I raise my pudgy arm straight into the air as I have seen soldiers doing on the streets. My mother does not try to stop me. A long time from now I will wonder whether she was amused at her little girl's innocence or she believed that sometime in the future my affinity for things German might be useful.

Vienna is in a frenzy of hysteria, welcoming their compatriots the conquering Nazis. Even with the windows closed we can hear the excited shouting. German soldiers have crossed the border and on the very next day, Hitler announces the *Anshluss* (annexation) of Austria into the Third Reich. The Austrians don't cower like a conquered nation. They are ecstatic, elated at belonging to the conquering heroes. Celebrations take place all over Vienna. Triangular flags, green, black, red and white wave frantically in the wind welcoming the soldiers of the Third Reich. Young men wearing green uniforms are followed by others in black knickers ballooning above their polished boots, proud to be wearing the uniforms of the infamous SS. All sport the red armbands displaying the black swastika in a white circle. Goose stepping and singing in unison, unsmiling, unbending and ramrod straight, they march as one individual entity. No one blinks, twitches, or moves any part of his body without the central force that seems to controls them all. Their eyes are fixed straight ahead, while the crowds go wild with excitement. In spite of the cheering crowd, the waving flags, the loud singing, in spite of the raised arms and loud salutations to Hitler, nothing distracts them. Every so often they stop, turn to the right, turn to their left, raise their right arms and shout, "Heil Hitler" saluting the huge posters of their hero, Adolf Hitler. All this is done with the precision of wind-up toys- the army of conquering heroes.

The spectators, a thrilled excited crowd, shout encouragement to the soldiers. Strangers hug each other like family members, tears of joy glide down their cheeks as children are lifted onto shoulders by enthusiastic fathers. I, from the vantage point of a three year old am enthralled. I am caught up by the drama, the music, the festiveness of the moment. I love the pink cheeked soldier boys, singing in unison as they march. It is a rousing, exciting time for a three year-old.

Several days later my *mutti* takes me to the park as she often does. We go for a walk with the music still reverberating in my head exhorting me to march like a soldier. I raise my arm to greet everyone on the street, loudly imitating what I have heard so many times. "Heil Hitler," I salute an old man carrying a gnarled walking stick, dressed in knickers, and wearing a Tyrolean hat on top of his white hair, his pink cheeks and bushy moustache rest on his face as though they were painted on.

"Heil Hitler," he responds enthusiastically, and then turns to my mother, "What a sweet little girl." He hands me a lollypop and I curtsy and thank him.

I get warm smiles of encouragement from strangers and soldiers alike. They seem delighted by my spirit, my blue eyes and blond hair; a perfect child, a representation of the master race. I am delighted by their attention and encouragement. Later, when I am an adult and can discuss this time with my mother, I will understand that she cringed at such moments and wondered how long our appearance would protect us.

My father comes into our apartment in tears. I have never seen him so distraught. He sobs loudly. I feel a shock go through my body. I have discovered where my heart is and I am scared.

"They're coming after all the old and helpless people," he tells us. "It won't be much longer before no Jew will be safe here."

He continues between sobs, "I was walking on the street. It was early in the morning when I saw several Hassidim walking back from *shul*, carrying their *tallis* (prayer shawls) bags. Out of nowhere, young hoodlums came running and started pulling them by their and their beards. They knocked the old men to the ground and started kicking them and shouting insults. They pulled out handfuls of hair. One of them kicked an old man who was lying on the ground, kicked him in the face, knocked out several teeth. The poor old man tried to stand up as he spit out mouthfuls of blood and broken teeth. These thugs are not human beings. They're not even animal. Animals kill for food. These monsters kill for pleasure. And what are the civilized Austrians doing when all of this is taking place?" he asks no one in particular. "Nothing," he answers his own question. "Nothing at all! They stand by watching, not even talking to each other." My father looks helpless and frightened. He too has *peyis*, (earlocks that all religious Jews wear) although his are hidden behind his ears. It would not take long to discover them if anyone was looking. He knows that he is not exempt from this kind of terrorism even though his German is perfect and he wears modern clothing, not the black garb of the Hassidim.

"I watched the whole attack and I stood by just like all the others, like puppets. I knew that there was nothing I could do to protect the Hassidim without unleashing violence toward myself. When the hooligans left, I tried to help the Hassidim up. They were so broken. These dignified old men, humiliated, covered in blood and dirt with their clothing torn. What is going to happen to us?" He rocks back and forth, clutching his elbows as if to safeguard his own body.

"We can't stay here any longer," he tells my *mutti*. "We have to find a way to get out of Austria before we're all victims of this new regime."

CHAPTER 3

THE LASH OF anti-Semitism was not new to my father. Born in May of 1906 near a border town that was constantly shifting between Czechoslovakia and Austria, he attended public elementary school in his town that at that time was designated as a part of Austria. Long before Hitler's rise to power, hating the Jews was widespread in the region, even in the little school he attended. Every day when attendance was taken, and his name was called, little Alex Schmelkes was required to stand and respond by stating his religion. While most students answered *Romish Catolish,* Alex and the few other Jewish boys were forced to say "*Hebraish,*" inviting the majority to bully and curse them.

"Hey Jew boy, what you got under your little hat?" one of the boys taunts him when during recess when the teacher was not looking or listening.

"Probably chicken fat and a piece of that dried cardboard that the Jews eat on Easter!" another responds. They roar with glee as they harass him.

Sometimes, their ridicule would takes on a more menacing turn. A group of boys follows him home from school and threatens him.

"Here he comes, the little Jew," one of them shouts.

"Get him, get him," says another. Suddenly, one of his classmates grabs him from behind while his buddy rubs pork into Alex's face.

"Here's a little treat for you, Christ killer!"

Alex spits and rubs his arm across his mouth to rid himself of the putrid smell and taste. He can do nothing more. Telling the authorities would only enrage the offenders, and since none of them would get punished for beating up a Jew boy they were likely to do it again, only more viciously. They hate him for being smart, for being Jewish and for being alive. He made a decision right there that he would never tolerate being ridiculed and humiliated again. He promises himself that he will fight back, if not with his body, then with his brains.

My father's family did not have material wealth. Alex who was 8 years older than his sister grew up with their parents in a modest Jewish neighborhood in Bartfeld, an outskirt of Vienna. His family traced their lineage back to the middle ages. They were descended from a long line of learned and respected Talmudic scholars. Dark and intensely serious, Alex was an excellent student, studying mathematics, art and science in public school and Judaic studies at the tiny synagogue with teachers of the Torah as well as his own father, a respected Torah scholar. The rabbis who guided him predicted that he would follow in the family tradition and become a Torah scholar himself. He loved the Talmud, the analyzing, comparing, reasoning, questioning of the great abstract thinkers.

He did not, however, want to become a professional student of the sacred books. He dreamed of becoming a doctor or a professor of languages. Torah study was a noble calling, but he was a practical person. Even as a ten-year old boy, he knew that he could never make a living as a scholar.

After elementary school, my father became eligible for "gymnasium," the equivalent of secondary school. Motivated and curious, he yearned for a broader education in addition to his study of ancient Jewish texts. Although he qualified academically, Saturday attendance was mandatory. Some of his Jewish friends attended class, but they did not write or take notes. He was eager to join them. However, Alex's father did not permit him to break with the ancient tradition of observing the Sabbath, going to the synagogue and doing no work on the Sabbath. "No one in our family ever took the easy way out," his father said to him. "Besides, all the boys who go to gymnasium and university come out of there behaving and living like 'goyim.'(yidddish term for gentiles).

My father tried to console himself by remembering the Jewish martyrs of earlier times who had accepted torture and death rather than renounce their religious beliefs. Forgoing higher education was a small price to pay for not defiling his religion he told himself. But for all his rationalizations he felt conflicted. He regretted that a secular life would be permanently closed to a man totally immersed in study of the holy books. He desperately wanted to, no, needed to learn about the world outside that circumscribed circle of Hassidism. And so, in secret, on his own, he began to study music, history and the arts. He taught himself French and English and attended concerts in Vienna before Hitler prohibited Jews from going. He read extensively, went to museums and was knowledgeable about cultural and political events. For all his hard work, he would never gain entry to the university or to the professional world he so desperately wanted to be part of. Even though his self-education ultimately made it possible for him to journey to America and bring his family over. Until the day he died, he never got over the disappointment of being forced to make do with less.

CHAPTER 4

MY MOTHER FREDA Perlberger was born into a wealthy business family in Wieliczka, Poland, a small village famous for its salt mines. My grandfather owned a successful tannery that supplied the Polish army with leather for coats, boots and saddles. Although they were more worldly than my father's family, interested in music, the arts, literature and travel, the Perlbergers had deep reverence and respect for religion and had produced great Torah scholars, as well. Few Jewish families had the money, the leisure time, the creativity and commitment to the arts that the Perlbergers had. One of my mother's first cousins, Artur Schnabel, became a world- famous concert pianist who set a record by being the first artist to perform Beethoven's 32 sonatas on consecutive evenings in Carnegie Hall.

Freda, the youngest of eleven children was the beautiful, adored baby of many doting relatives. Two of her brothers and one sister were already married when she was born and she was an aunt as soon as she was born with nephews and nieces who were older than she was. In fact, out of deference and respect to age, she couldn't bring herself to call her oldest brother by his given name, and referred to him as "Uncle" Moshe.

My mother had the education of many upper class girls of her generation, taking piano lessons, embroidery, and painting and elocution lessons to augment her formal education. She would travel by train to the nearby large city of Krakow to take advantage of these opportunities. Her parents were elderly by the time she reached adolescence and it was Freda who was the primary nurse when her father became ill and disabled with arteriosclerosis. She often talked about her father, whom she adored, and how very privileged she felt when he called upon her for help. He had a beautiful singing voice and often sang in order to distract himself from his pain. He died in 1925 before anyone heard of Hitler.

Freda was in her mid-twenties when she met Alex. They were introduced to each other by my aunt who lived in Vienna.

She was a tall, slender, graceful, blue-eyed, fun-loving young woman who played the piano, and appreciated art. Alex, my father was twenty-eight, dark and handsome, spoke perfect German, French and English, was self- taught and could speak about any current topic. His seriousness was offset by her sense of humor. They were married in August of 1934 and moved to the fairy tale city of Vienna, where the boots of Hitler's soldiers would soon be shaking the continent.

My mother loved Vienna, an enchanting city; a dream come true especially to a small town girl with so many interests. The excitement of living in a large apartment building, with neighbors across the hall, and above, and below were a novelty for her. These people were nothing like the superstitious peasants, her neighbors in Wieliczka.

The first two years of their marriage were idyllic. They had many friends, and my mother had family living close by. Alex and Freda went to concerts every Sunday, and to coffee houses with friends discussing politics, arts, and the latest news about their community. She was able to go to museums whenever she pleased, browse through the fashionable shops and take advantage of all that the large, beautiful city of Vienna offered. She had become a bona-fide Viennese hausfrau. The first thing my father bought for the new apartment was a surprise for her; a gleaming ebony baby grand piano, a highly prized Bechstein. It dominated the empty living room like a queen on her throne. Life, she thought, could not get any better than this.

CHAPTER 5

———— ✥ ————

IN MAY OF 1935, my mother becomes pregnant. She and my father are thrilled. She does not know what to do to prepare for this event since buying things or even decorating a nursery is not done before the baby is actually born. Superstition, which she never got rid of entirely, forbids it. She enrolls in a *mutter schule*, a school for expectant mothers run by the government. She finds the classes very informative; the modern techniques, so different from the way things were done in Wieliczka. She learns how to diaper a baby, how and why to burp it, what kind of behavior warrants punishment and what needs to be rewarded.

She is determined to be the best mother in Vienna. I finally arrive on a snowy day, February 2, 1936. Later my mother ells me that initially she was disappointed in having given birth to a girl. She so badly wanted a son whom she could name Reuven after her beloved father. They name me Rita Bianca, after my grandfather, a man I would think of as my guardian angel, because although dead for many years before my birth, the use of his name in a fake birth certificate will save our lives.

My mother quickly gets over her disappointment and loves me like she has never loved before. Liselle, a young woman who my parents hire to be my nanny, has two long blond braids, broad shoulders, strong hands, an easy forthcoming smile which reveals a huge space between her teeth, causing her to lisp. She is an experienced nanny and helps my mother by changing diapers, pureeing food for me, and staying at home with me while my parents go out. Liselle lives with us and between her and my mother, I get lots of loving attention, am taught many German songs, and am played with like a doll which belongs to my mother, but whom she is willing to share with Liselle. Two years later my brother Moschel, arrives. His nick name is Bubbi and I am not particularly thrilled with him. My mother tells of the time she came into the nursery to hear him screaming while I was forcing a knife into his mouth.

"*Was machs du den?* (What are you doing)?" she asks me in a frightened and angry voice.

"The child wants to have some butter," I calmly respond.

CHAPTER 6

ALTHOUGH MOST JEWISH people in Austria feel that the rest of the world will come to its senses, my father does not believe this. He has experienced anti-Semitism all his life and knows its appetite for Jewish scapegoats. He is determined to leave the hotbed of Europe and save whomever he can. Years before meeting my mother, years before Hitler was a threat, my father had thought of visiting America. He taught himself English and became fluent. If he ever had the time and the money, he reasoned, he might go on a tour of America; visit places he had only read about, The Grand Canyon, The Badlands of South Dakota, The Great Salt Lake and Hollywood. He acquired a visa and a permit for himself and his younger sister to travel to the United States. Sari, his sister went to America on her eighteenth birthday and remained there. His visa and travel permit are tucked in a desk drawer, almost forgotten, until he starts making plans to rescue his family.

He examines his visa. It is still valid. Now he faces a serious dilemma: since he only has one visa, he will have to abandon us in order to save us. If he stays in Vienna, he fears, no, he is convinced that the whole family will perish. If he leaves, he has a chance of sending for us once he arrives in the United States. It is a wrenching decision and he agonizes over his plans. He can't bear to leave us, yet he is convinced that staying in Europe and waiting Hitler out will have dire consequences. My mother does not know how to advise him. She will miss him terribly if he leaves, but she is a realistic person and is fully aware of the hostile climate in Austria.

I understand nothing of this, of course, as I am only three, but I remember the good-bye visit to *oma* and *opa* and the packing up of wicker baskets. When I question the packing, my mother tells me that we are going to America, not explaining that only my father is going. I dance around the baskets singing, "*Wir fahren nach America.*" No one tries to disabuse me of my conviction.

A few days later, my father comes into the living room. He is dressed to go out, wearing his long overcoat and a brown fedora. He hugs Bubbi and me, holding onto us for a long time in an embrace so tight that I have trouble breathing.

"I'm going away for a little while, but soon we will all be together and happier than you ever imagined." I don't understand. "Why are you going Papa?" I ask. My *mutti* talks to me but does not answer my question, "We'll be together soon," she promises. He nods in agreement, stands up and I see the tears in his eyes. He walks to the front door, swallows hard and turns around to look at us, sighs deeply and picks up his valise. *Mutti* goes out with him leaving us with Liselle while she accompanies him to the train that will take him to the ship. When I am a grown woman, my mother tells me that as the train was pulling out of the station, she was running after it, and she heard two German soldiers comment to one another, "The poor woman is saying good-bye to her husband who is going to the front."

I am much too young to understand what is happening around me or why it is occurring. I am only aware of how drastically our lives are changing. The house feels cold and empty. The rugs are gone from the shiny parquet floors, the paintings and photographs have been removed from the walls, a few blankets are rolled up in a basket and our clothing is packed up. Bubbi and I stomp around the rooms making loud echoing noise on the bare floors.

"When will we be going to America?" I ask my mother again and again.

As always, she's vague in her response. Today she seems especially distracted and distant. "I don't know."

I am relentless in my pursuit of an answer. "What do you mean you don't know? You and papa promised that it would be soon."

There is a knock on the door. It is our upstairs neighbor, Frau Yaeger. She does not answer my friendly *"Heil Hitler"* greeting, but looks at me through small, red rimmed eyes. She is accompanied by two miniature white poodles, yapping and sliding all over our uncarpeted floor. She is tall, skinny as a broomstick, wearing a long, brown, satin dressing gown that hangs from her skinny shoulders like a dress on a hanger. Her matted blond hair looks like it is painted on her head, resembling yesterday's scrambled eggs. Her thin lips are compressed, a visible line on her scowling face. She shuffles over to my mother's china closet and opens it without permission, picks up a plate and runs her skeletal finger over the back of it. *"Das gafehlt mir,* (I like this,)" she says to no one in particular, picking up our good china serving platter. She turns it over and examines the stamp on the back and proceeds to carefully take the rest of the china out of the cabinet. She takes all the dinner plates, soup bowls, cups and saucers belonging to the set and places them on the table. She never takes her eyes off them. She shrugs and without looking at my mother starts to talk to her.

"The Germans are already here, practically on our doorstep. They will take all of your precious possessions." She holds a large dinner plate up to the light, focusing her eyes on the china, she says, "I might as well take these. If I don't, they will. You can have your things back when times are better. You know where to find me. My maid will be picking these up in a few minutes. Please don't let anyone else take them," she adds as an afterthought and leaves.

My mother sighs. She examines her hands as if she has never seen them before, turning them over and over again in her lap. The other neighbors come to our apartment and start fighting over our silver, linens and crystal as if we are already dead and they the crows pick the carcasses. I can't stand watching this. I shout at them. *"Heraus,*

heraus,(Out, out) get out, get out!" I scream. "Get out of our house, you stealers!"

One of the women looks at me sadly, shaking her head. She gets on her knees to achieve eye contact with me. "*Leibchen,* I promise you that when all this is over, your mama and papa will have their things back. At least your family knows where their things are. If we don't take them, the Nazis will come here and break what they do not take. They are safe with us."

My mother overhears her. "Yes, yes," she agrees. "Our things are safe here in Vienna with you." Then I hear her whisper to herself, "but what will become of us?" What is the use of another person reassuring us, telling us how safe our possessions will be in their care when she knows that we are in mortal danger.

After they leave, our apartment is emptier and colder than before. My mother tells me that we are leaving Vienna. Naturally, I assume that we will be going to meet my father and go off to America.

In a matter of days, we are packed and a taxi is waiting for us downstairs. Our remaining things, clothing, bedding and a few toys are piled into the trunk. Liselle is standing next to the taxi. She holds a large white handkerchief to her face sobbing loudly, shaking her head from side to side. She has come to say good-bye to us and she and my mother hug, weeping, burying their heads in each other's shoulders as if they will never let go. Then they step apart and the two look at each other for a long time as if to memorize the other's faces. We speed off in the taxi. I am convinced that we are going to America. Anticipation and joy fill my little heart. "Finally we are going to America." I announce.

My mother feels compelled to answer. She seems vague and distracted. "Well sort of. First we are going to Wieliczka, the town where I was born and lived when I was a little girl like you. We'll stay there for a while with all your aunts, uncles and cousins, and then we will go to America." I persist with my questions.

"How long will we stay with the aunts and the uncles? Where is papa right now? Will the aunts and the uncles come with us to America?"

My mother has had enough of my questions, she breaks down.

"Papa is already on his way to America. He has taken a train to the ship that will take him and we will join him there soon."

"What?" I demand, outraged. "He went to America without me?"

"Yes, but you'll see. We will be going there soon ourselves."

"Papa promised to take me," I cry.

"He never promised to take you. He said we would all be going there soon, and we will," she tries to reason with me.

"Why, why, why didn't he take me along?" I wail, shrugging my shoulders, my cupped palms facing upward. "He made a promise. He made a promise and now he broke it. That's like telling a lie. Papa lied to me. Papa made a sin." I start sobbing, big, wet tears.

"Stop it," my mother says harshly. "Stop sniveling and don't you ever accuse your father of lying to you," she warns me. "Your papa is a truthful man. He never told a lie."

I let out a long grief stricken wail, "Papa lied to me."

I start kicking the seat of the taxi, "My papa lied to me!" My sobbing gets louder and louder and my mother becomes embarrassed and impatient. We are in the taxi cab and she doesn't want to attract the attention of the pedestrians the street look at the noisy taxi every time it stops. My mother is afraid of the attention. She tries to hush me.

Unexpectedly, a new fear grabs my stomach. Why are we going without our papa? What if he comes back and sees that we are not at home? How will he find us? What if our mother leaves us just as papa did? Will Bubbi and I be just like Hansel and Gretel, orphans? I surrender my anger and anguish permitting terror to plant itself in my heart. What if we end up all alone?

CHAPTER 7

———— ✿ ————

MY MOTHER HAS many reasons for going back to Poland. It is March of 1939 and Poland is not yet under German occupation. Moreover, my mother has a large and prosperous family there and we can buy some time until my father is ready to send for us.

We travel by airplane from Vienna to Krakow, a large city that is about fifteen kilometers from Wieliczka. When we land, the three of us take a train to the station in Krakow. I have never been on a train. This one is filled with many people. Some of them, like us, carry luggage, some of them hold on to young children, there are couples clinging to each other and several families traveling together. One young man stands up and offers his seat to my mother. She thanks him in Polish and tries to maneuver both Bubbi and me onto her lap. There are many German soldiers talking loudly to each other. The noisy, shaking train does little to distract me from my fear. In fact the icy terror spreads to other parts of my body. I find that I cannot take a breath because I fear that I have lost my Papa forever and dare not ask my mother about him. The train lurches and stops with most of the passengers, including ourselves getting off.

My mother looks around trying to get her bearings, and then she spots him! A smile of recognition wipes the apprehension off her face. An old man, wearing a shapeless sheepskin coat rushes towards her.

"*Pani Freda*, how wonderful to see you again. We are so happy to have you home at last." My mother clasps him warmly. She turns to me. "Stanislav," she says, "is our faithful friend. He takes care of all the horses and cows on the farm. He is going to take us to my old home- your new

21

home." I don't know what to say, so I curtsy to Stanislav. After all, he is my mother's friend. Stanislav smiles at us; his face creased like an accordion. His blue eyes sparkle at us under bushy brows that look as though they were formed by falling snow. "So *Pani* Freda, these are the famous Maidi and Bubbi we've all been hearing so much about."

We follow Stanislav to the street. Two chestnut horses, their tails braided and interwoven with red ribbons are harnessed to a shiny, polished sled. I have never seen anything like this. Stanislav lifts me and Bubbi and helps my mother onto the soft leather seats. We snuggle under the warm fur blankets while he tosses our luggage in the back and mounts the high seat in front. He clicks his tongue and the horses respond, dragging the sled with us and our possessions.

They plod along, heads bobbling up and down in time to their feet while the little silver bells strung around their necks tinkle. The snow covered countryside passes us like in a dream. It looks like an illustration in a book of fairy tales. The few houses we pass are small, nestled under thatched roofs piled high with snow. They look like a Viennese dessert, giant gingerbread cakes topped with mountains of whipped cream. The scenery is captivating. Little houses under layers of snow appear all along the way. Being familiar with fairy tales, I half expect to see little old, hunchbacked witches emerging from their cottages, leaning on their canes, heads covered by colorful babushkas, and all wearing long aprons protecting their dresses.

In spite of the anguish I feel, I love this sleigh ride; being pulled along by two horses on a giant sled. My mother looks all around. "Nothing has changed here on the road from Krakow to Wieliczka," she shouts up to Stanislav. "I haven't seen a Wieliczka winter in several years and it feels like it was only yesterday that you took me to Krakow for my piano lessons." She tears up, "yet so much has happened since."

Stanislav nods his head, but remains silent. We start climbing the big slippery hill leading to the gates that guard my mother's old home. The horses begin to lose their footing under the heavy load of luggage and passengers. They whinny loudly and start sliding backwards toward the sled. I am scared and excited. The horses' hooves hover in the air while Stanislav clutches the reins. We seem to be going backwards down the snow-packed hill. But Stanislav is persistent. He's done this many times before and he halts the horses, giving them time to catch their breath. After a few minutes he tightens the reins, clicks his tongue three times and the horses once again resume their ascend. We slow down in front of iron gates that are left open in anticipation of our arrival. There are several houses behind the gates. A door opens and a noisy throng of people come flooding out. I know many of them because they have come to see us in Vienna, but some of them are new to me.

"Freda is here with the children!" I am being passed around, hugged and kissed by many people who are speaking Polish, a strange language to my ears, that I feel frightened and start to scream. I have lost sight of my mother. "*Nein, nein. Horen sei auf. Wo ist meine Mutti? Sie hat verschwinden!* (No, no. Stop. Where is my mommy? She's disappeared)!" My mother rushes over to me, scoops me up in her arms and comforts me. She dries my tears with her pink embroidered handkerchief, smoothing my damp hair off my worried forehead. She holds me tightly, stroking my back, "You're fine, and it's alright. I will never, never, never leave you. We are with my brothers, sisters, all your uncles, aunts and cousins. They are all so happy to see you. Don't be frightened, Maidi. We are safe here."

My mother's birthplace in Wieliczka is a farm/estate/factory. Many of my aunts, uncles and cousins live there. They run the tanning factory, fill orders for the Polish army and other customers and reside in the living quarters. Each of the siblings has their own apartment on the estate grounds and we are soon ushered into ours. It has always been there for my mother and father as though waiting for our return. It is a large, beautiful, bright suite of rooms. Tall windows, framed in white lace curtains overlook the gates we passed through. In the corner of the bedroom are two large closets one containing men's clothing, the other empty awaiting our arrival. Since we all eat our meals together in the main house, the apartment contains no kitchen.

Bubbi and I are the youngest children on the estate and everyone tries hard to please us. A rocking horse made of real leather, stuffed animals, coloring books and crayons are waiting for us in our room.

CHAPTER 8

WHEN WE FIRST get there, life in Wieliczka is pleasant and peaceful. I am encouraged to be myself, to explore and to learn. My aunts and uncles never pass by me without giving me a loving tap or if they have time, they bend down to plant a kiss on my head. The farm is certainly an exciting place for Bubbi and me. We have never had so much freedom. We are allowed to explore as we wish since there are always people around to supervise us if we get into trouble. The barnyard is full of noisy chickens and one angry rooster.

"Shoo, shoo," I say, my arms flapping, frightening the poor chickens into a frenzy of activity.

Large, snorting horses and fat, lazy cows who are constantly chewing live in the stable. The horses frighten me. They appear like monsters. They are noisy and restless, pawing the ground and neighing.

The cows, on the other hand, though big, are quiet and look bored. They stand around, munching, not making a sound and hardly ever moving, except to swing their tails at annoying flies. I am awed by their size yet not frightened by their bulk. They are serene and contented and I want to overcome my reticence. I stand near them, and occasionally pat their black hides, not risking more than three fingers.

The young stable boy, Kasper, wearing knee length pants, a white shirt and black cap, comes into the barn carrying a short stool. He claps the stool down, sits at the rear of the cow, and slaps a bucket between his legs and chewing nonchalantly on a blade of grass starts pulling on the cow's udders. He pulls the udders rhythmically and each yank produces a squirt of milk. I watch, fascinated. "Want some fresh milk?" he grins at me.

"Sure," I respond eagerly.

"Come here then." He positions my head below the cow's udders. "Open your mouth wide." I do as I am told and feel a shot of warm milk enter my mouth. "It's hot," I exclaim.

"Of course, what did you expect, refrigerated milk straight from the cow?" He laughs with me. He moves on to another cow and repeats the process. I would love to try it but am too shy to ask.

"Wanna try? It's not as easy as it looks," he tells me.

"I really would. I can do it," I say.

"Here," he moves off the stool and invites me to try my luck with a cow. I pull on the warm, slippery teats but my small hands can't get a grip and they slide quickly from my hands.

On a warm day in April, the sun is shining and the sky is full of puffy, cotton ball clouds. I am four years old, sitting on a stone step in front of our house, my chin is resting on the navy blue pinafore covering my knees. Today I have undertaken a mission; I am going to learn to speak proper Polish. The patriotic Poles, whose love of their country is almost as great as their hatred for Germany and Austria, encourage me to speak only in Polish. I am learning quickly but need to get rid of my rolling Austrian "r" and master the hard Polish "r." I spend days sitting in the sun and practicing, but today I am determined to get it right.

I practice it over and over again and suddenly I've got it! "Mutti, Mutti," I shout, running to her eagerly, "I can say it. Listen: *kurrra, Krakow, crrravatka,*" I feel powerful and Polish, just like everyone around me. The Polish farm workers applaud. I am finally one of them.

Life is good on the farm, full of surprises. Nothing is expected of us. All we have to do is play and be happy. There are no loud voices, band music or marching boots. I miss the excitement of Vienna but enjoy the freedom of Wieliczka. Little do I know that this will be the happiest period of my childhood.

Bubbi and I attend a pre-school for Jewish children. We have very few toys but make up for that with much imaginative play in the sandbox, dressing up, telling stories, singing, and putting on shows. In the spring and early summer we pick flowers and replant them in our little sand garden. I love the attention I get when I do something special and am soon bossing everyone around.

I am always surrounded by loving people who seem to want nothing more than to please Bubbi and me. There are many children on the farm, both cousins and the sons and daughters of the farm workers.

CHAPTER 9

———— ✂ ————

"A LETTER, A letter for Freda," my Aunt Angie announces. She comes into the library breathless. "Fredel," she says, trying to catch her breath, "You have a letter from Alex." The whole family trudges in behind my aunt. A letter from my father is a cause for the family to gather around and listen to my mother read.

"Open it, open it at once," My Uncle says peering over her shoulder. My mother puts down the beige linen tablecloth she is embroidering, wipes her hands on her apron and opens the letter.

She reads it quietly to herself, takes a deep breath as though inhaling the contents of the letter and reads aloud. "My darling Freda," the letter begins. "I arrived in Genoa and only have to get on board the ship to go to America. The salami we packed up was delicious!" My aunts and uncles laugh and applaud.

The salami was a plan for my father to get my mother's diamond engagement ring out of Austria. Before leaving for America my father gently pried open one end of a small salami and stuffed the ring deep inside before sealing it. He hoped to keep the diamond safely hidden from the prying, greedy eyes of the customs officials who scrutinized every Jewish passenger's belongings. No gentile customs officer would question the reason for a Jew to be carrying kosher salami smelling of garlic.

A few days after the letter, a small package arrives. We excitedly rip the paper off and to my astonishment the package contains two small, flat, rectangular tin cans. Bubbi and I are surprised, and delighted.

"What's in there?" I ask my mother, "a toy?"

"No *maidchen*, these are sardines."

"Sardines? What are sardines? Do you make things with them?" I stroke the shiny, smooth surface of one of the cans, rubbing it across my cheek. It is perfectly formed. My mother laughs, again. "No *schatzie*, they are little fish packed in oil."

"What do we do with such flat little fish?"

"We eat them, of course," she answers.

I am eager to try them. I can't believe that a real fish can be shrunken to fit such small, flat cans. "Open them," I beg, "let's at least see them."

"Not now, we have to save them for a special occasion," she insists, as she carefully hides them between two tablecloths in the huge linen closet belonging to the estate.

Every day after that, I pull a chair over to the closet, climb up and look at the sardine cans. I caress them lovingly, holding their glossy, cool sides against my face. "Is today the day we open the sardines?" I ask my mother hopefully. "How can a fish be made so small and flat?" My pleading does little to convince her to open a can. She is holding out. She's waiting for a special day to come that warrants the opening of a can of sardines. She ignores my pleading. As it turns out, the special day never arrives. The sardines, along with all her belongings remain in Wieliczka along with most of her siblings and relatives.

CHAPTER 10

MY EIGHT YEAR old cousins, Gizelle and Miriam are taking me for a walk in the village. It is the first time I am allowed off the premises without an adult to supervise. We admire the colorful wares displayed on the ground of the market and hold on to the coins each of us has in her pocket. We are going to buy something but haven't decided what.

We are standing on a plot of grass trying to decide what to purchase when several Polish girls come up to us snickering, "*Zyidoweczki*, little Jew girls." No one is watching. "What do you have there in your pockets? Come on. Let us see." They pull at our dresses trying to peer inside the pockets.

"Nothing," my cousin Giselle replies. She pulls out a handkerchief and waves it at the strangers. "Just a handkerchief."

"Na, na, na," one of them taunts. "You got money. All the Jews have money. Come on, hand it over." She grabs a handful of Giselle's hair while another one pulls my arm. They hit us with sticks. Why are they hitting us, I wonder? We did nothing to them. They take our money and run away laughing. We run home crying to our parents, but there is nothing anyone can do to protect us even though our families know who these girls are. In fact, some of their parents work for our family: the men as tannery and farmhands, the women as cooks, laundresses, and housekeepers. Jewish children are fair game for bullying Polish kids who make a sport out of taunting us. They hide around corners and in doorways surprising and scaring us with sticks and rocks.

It is getting more and more difficult to stay in Poland. The political climate is turning against the Jews. New laws are enacted daily and now all Jewish adults have to wear an armband with the Star of David on it to identify their religion. The war is coming to Poland, and few Polish people need encouragement to vent their age old resentments towards the Jews. A sense of approaching doom, suspended like a heavy mist hangs between what was and what is coming.

One evening, in early September, 1939 my mother's older brother, Hertzel, comes into the house. He tells us that he was in Krakow and had gone to visit one of his friends who had just come out of prison. "It was terrible," he cries, "The guards have dogs and Yaakov was bitten on his arms and legs. He was chained and unable to defend himself from the wild beasts. And for what?" he asks with indignation. He answers his own question with another question. "For speaking out against the Nazis who are occupying Krakow! The Poles hate the Nazis and yet they imprisoned Yaakov, a Polish citizen for speaking out against their enemy, for defending Poland. Why, why, I ask myself. Why are the Jews so loathsome?" He shrugs his shoulders, his open palms are level with his shoulders, he shakes his head from side to side. "We've done so much for the Poles. Whenever someone in the village needs something, money, food for a wedding feast or a funeral supper, this is the first place they come. We give them money when they are in need and medicine when they are sick, and yet they despise us.

Krakow isn't safe anymore. Many Poles are collaborating with the Nazis against their own citizens; the few decent ones who have morals and ethics are scorned and ridiculed by the others. Mind you, last week, alone, several professors from Jagiellonian University were executed, right in the town square, together with the Jews."

I do not understand what he is saying, but his tone and my aunts and uncles reactions frighten me. They are wringing their hands, looking desperate. I want to know what they are talking about, but am afraid to ask. "No Jew should remain in Krakow," Hertzel declares, shaking his head in disbelief.

My uncle Moshe claps his hands to his cheeks, "How can this be? The Nazis haven't even attacked Krakow. Who is doing the shooting?"

"I thought Krakow would be spared," my aunt wails, "such a beautiful city, so many historic sites!"

A few days later Uncle Herzel does not come home. We wait for him all night and on the following day question anyone who might know his whereabouts, but no one is able to help. We contact his friend Yaakov in Krakow, but he too has disappeared. My grandmother and all her children and grandchildren sit up night after night waiting for his return. He doesn't come home. He is gone, blown away as dust. We mourn his disappearance. "Where could he have gone to?" we ask each other? There are no answers. Every official who has ever done business with my grandfather or uncles shrugs his shoulders when we ask about Hertzel. He has vanished.

Where is my Uncle Hertzel? How does a grown man disappear without leaving a trace of himself? I still have a picture of him in my mind. He is tall, slender, wears a beige suit with a waistcoat, his brown hair is combed straight back, off his high forehead and light eyebrows and lashes frame the bluest of eyes. A slow smile spreads across his whole face when he sees me, making his cheeks crinkle at the corners of his eyes. He is the only one of my uncles who does not have a beard. He carries a watch in his vest pocket and squints to read the dial. How can such a real person vanish? All I have to do to see him is close my eyes and imagine he is in the room. I love him. He gives us rides on his broad shoulders and makes the most unbelievable folk and fairy tales ring true by changing his voice and his accent. But most of all I love him for his gentle manner. He never raises his voice, always looks into my eyes when I have something to say to him, he makes me feel as important as a grown up and he never laughs at my questions. He is a safe person to be around. I feel a paralysis in my throat much like the one I felt when I realized that I might never see my Papa again. I can't even take a breath, afraid that it might make me cry and that if I cry I will never be able to stop. If I start crying I might make his disappearance real. If I can just control my tears, keep them in check, he might come walking in through the door with chocolate for us, telling us he was delayed by the weather. We will have a joyful reunion, if only

I don't cry. If only I don't cry it won't be real. But the pain in my chest is pressing against my heart. I can control my tears, but I can't control my fear, my pain and my paralysis.

My mother has gone to Krakow to buy some medicine for my Aunt Paula and chemicals for the factory. The tannery is now running twenty-four hours a day. The army needs leather for saddles, boots, jackets, coats and belts. The reason she was the one sent is because she looks totally Aryan, won't have to wear the Star of David on her sleeve and her command of the Polish and German language is flawless. She will be able to go to a pharmacy, order the medicine in German and no one is likely to question her. She will go to the chemist for the tanning chemicals, speak to him in Polish and no one will be likely to ask her for identity papers. She kisses us and promises to bring us a toy when she returns. "I'll be back before supper," she tells Bubbi and me. The morning passes uneventfully. Bubbi and I play in the fields with our cousins. Right after lunch, we are told to take a nap and as soon as I wake up, without wanting to, or planning, I start the process of "waiting," doing nothing but straining my eyes towards the road home. I am waiting for my mother and I am hoping she will be early.

When my mother isn't home by late afternoon, the old fear takes up a defined space inside of me. The sun sets and, suddenly, to my horror I forget what my mother looks like. I quickly rummage through a night table drawer and find an old photograph of her. I tuck the picture into a window pane in our room and continue waiting. "Good," I say to the picture I inserted into the pane. "Now I'll recognize her." But the panic and sense of danger overtake my spirit and are shooting painful arrows around my heart. I can't help myself. I am determined to sit it out, staring at her picture until I see her coming up the walk. I start to pray, "*Shma Yisroel*, Please God, let my mother come home. I will never ask You for anything again, just let my mother please come home." I refuse to eat supper. I am waiting, and nothing will move me from my vigil at the window. My ritual takes on an obsessive dimension.

"If I stop looking out for her," I tell myself, "I might not see her coming up the walk and then she might not come home." In a child's magical way I believe that I am able to draw her home with my prayers and the power of my eyes. It has gotten dark, and I refuse to budge. At the age of four, I have developed my own ritual of compulsive waiting. I will practice it for the rest of my life. It is always accompanied by catastrophic thinking, as if the thinking will ward off the disaster from occurring. I pace, I sweat and I feel breathless. I cannot be distracted. When I am waiting I am too busy to do anything to pass the time. I press my fingertips hard into my palms, am alert for the slightest sound or movement. I am prey, waiting for the predator.

"Please Maidi," my aunt Angie implores, "come and eat your supper. Your *mutti* will not be happy to see that you haven't eaten." I can see by the double crease between her eyes that she too is beginning to worry. I don't answer her. I'm afraid that if I talk, I might cry, and if I cry, my mother's disappearance will become real. I sit in silence on the window seat. By now, everyone is peering out. Finally, long after darkness has blackened the sky I see her trudging up the walkway to our house. She is walking slowly, shuffling her feet; so unlike my mother's usual confident stride.

"Where were you so long?" everyone asks her.

"You know," she replies, "everything takes longer. First, I had to wait in the pharmacy. Then I had to wait for the train, which was late" she sighs. She is so tired and disheartened. "When it got there, I couldn't get on it was so crowded. Finally, I went outside and begged a driver with a horse and carriage to take me to Wieliczka, I paid him in advance, of course, he wouldn't move otherwise, but when we got out of Krakow, he told me to get out. He wouldn't take me all the way. I had to walk several kilometers." She collapses on a chair, totally exhausted. It is not safe to be walking in Wieliczka alone, at night. Even I know that. Now that I see her, it is safe to cry. I am inconsolable. I sob convulsively until I exhaust myself and finally go to sleep without having eaten supper.

CHAPTER 11

— ❧ —

WE ARE SITTING in the dining room eating dinner when insistent pounding at the front door drowns the adult conversation. "Open up. Open up, before we knock the door down," a loud, threatening voice shouts. Before my uncle has a chance to reach the door, it bursts open. Four Polish army officers storm into our house. They push my uncle aside and proceed directly into the parlor. They are dressed in identical uniforms, with lots of brass buttons, colorful insignias pinned to their chests and shoulders, shiny high boots, and thick leather belts encircling waists, with tall peaked officer hats adding height and arrogance to their haughty stance.

"Bring in all the furs," one of them snarls. He tells us he is here on behalf of the Polish army. He is fat, with a large scar across his upper lip that gives his face a perpetual smirk, nothing like the pink cheeked German soldier boys who sang and marched with dancers' precision. "And don't think you can hide any of your treasures, you filthy Jews."

"We know your tricks," the younger man hisses, baring his large crooked teeth. He hooks his thumbs into his belt, rocks back on his heels, "we're going to search everywhere before we leave. And heaven help you if we find any fur, even a dead mouse." He laughs at his joke and turns to face his comrades anticipating their approval.

From behind the china closet I watch, terrified, as my mother, her siblings, and their spouses clear the dining room table. My aunt Angela picks up a long shiny sable collar and runs it lovingly across her cheek, eyes closed remembering the last time she wore it.

"Make it fast," the fat one hollers. "We don't have all night." The coats, jackets, stoles and hats slide down the long dining room table while the soldiers collect them quickly stuffing them with their gloved hands into burlap sacks. One of the younger men, his face covered with red angry acne cysts picks up my grandmother's sable hat and plops it on his head. "How do I look boys?" he asks, swiveling his hips and mincing around the table. "Am I elegant? Would one of you kiss me?" They laugh at him.

In happier times, transactions between the Polish officers and our family were marked with smiles and handshakes. And when the deal was closed, a toast with a glass of whiskey would bind the agreement.

"*Na-zdrowie,* to your health," they would say lightheartedly.

"*L'chaim,*" my uncles would respond good-naturedly. Everyone would be laughing and joking.

But this time the very same officers are terrifying. "Filthy Jews," one of them hisses spitting on the red oriental carpet. "You won't be needing furs where you're going!" He and the others pick up the bulging sacks. There are no smiles, no pats on the back, no handshakes, no whiskey, only our tears. They walk out with their spoils. I hear them talking. They are not joking now. Their voices sound angry.

"The dirty Jews" one of them says to the other. "Where the hell do they come off with these furs while good, Polish citizens are freezing to death? And did you see the inside of that house? Two pianos! Two! As if one isn't enough. No wonder we're going hungry. They've taken everything that should be ours." He stomps off the property shaking mud from his black boots. "It's about time to get back what is rightfully ours. They want us to have pity on them. Where is the pity for us? We live in cold shacks while they live like royalty in palaces! Two pianos, what else do they want?"

Within days, strange workmen come to the estate and start building concrete huts. They are not high enough for an adult to stand up in, but to me they look sturdy and protective. They have iron gates that open and shut smoothly and no windows. Although they are bleak and cold looking, they are perfectly sized playhouses for Bubbi and me.

"Are these going to be our new houses?" I ask one of the workmen.

"Nah," he answers. "Not unless you start barking and baring your teeth. They're for the dogs."

"What dogs?" I ask.

"The police dogs. As soon as we're finished building here, the police are bringing their dogs over here to train them."

A shudder runs down my spine as I recall Uncle Hertzel's sad news about the dogs that attacked his friend Yaakov. "Police are training dogs in our fields? Why?" I ask trembling.

He shrugs, "Who knows. Maybe Wieliczka is joining the rest of the world." He and the others laugh, but I feel nothing but dread and anxiety. I have no idea what is happening and no one wants to tell me.

C H A P T E R   1 2

ON A LOVELY spring day in May of 1940, my mother takes Bubbi, me and a baby grand- niece to Krakow. We are going to have our pictures taken and we are noisy and excited. It is a great adventure to travel to Krakow by train. The hard wooden benches on the train, polished to a high sheen by the many backsides that have rubbed against them and the steam coming off the engine are promises of a wonderful day. My mother has become quite bold about going to Krakow without her Star of David armband and she knows her way around. She is wearing a tiny, silly looking hat made of two squares of stiff black lace, held together by a large, pink silk rose, with a spider web of a veil, and a black silk dress. I am wearing a black velvet dress with a white lace collar. A huge pink, puffy taffeta ribbon is tied in a bow in my hair. Bubbi, whose hair has not yet been cut in a grown up style, wears black velvet short pants held up by suspenders, and a white shirt. He looks like a girl. I tease him along the way. On a sudden impulse, my mother has taken her one year old little grandniece Halinka along for the photo session. She will have her picture taken with us. My mother hopes to pass her off as her own child, should the need arise. Halinka who is dark with curly hair and an olive complexion is dressed in a white knit sweater and matching skirt. We are laughing and joking. It is such a beautiful day, the air is fragrant, and Krakow, to my delight, is filled with handsome German speaking soldiers, not the menacing, angry Polish officers, but good-natured laughing young men who push each other around and pound each other on the back, blond, clean-cut, joking and well fed.

We walk around Krakow to the famous town square, *Sukiennice,* Clothe Hall, a covered stone structure dating back to the time of Kazimierz the Great in the thirteenth century. Hundreds of stalls are filled with all kinds of merchandise. Farmers, artists, tailors, shoemakers and jewelers all sorts of craftsmen bring their wares to sell.

My mother stops to admire some colorful blankets and buys two of them impulsively. They are dark mustard yellow with bright red lines running horizontally and vertically creating large, colorful window-like squares.

We leave the market and continue walking around the cobblestone square my mother clutching the package of blankets on one arm and carrying Halinka in the other. Bubbi and I trudge behind careful not to lose sight of her. Horses with colorful ribbons entwined into their braided tails and harnesses adorned with matching reigns are hitched to brightly painted wagons. The drivers wear costumes that match the adornments on the horses and buggies: white shirts with voluminous sleeves, beaded, vests and top hats all embroidered in the same colors as the ribbons in the horses' tails. They are lined up waiting for clients. Musicians play at every corner. We stop to listen to three accordionists. They play sad songs and are so engrossed in their music that they don't even look at the many people who surround them. My mother drops a few *zlotys* on the towel in front of them and we continue walking.

We stop at a tailor shop and walk inside. A little bent over man, wearing a skullcap stands, facing a dress dummy. His mouth is full of pins as he adjusts a long swath of green silk on the dummy's body. The floor is covered with scraps of material and the slanting sunlight from the window lights up a shaft of dancing dust particles. I hear the sound of a sewing machine coming from behind a curtain.

The man walks over to us and removes the pins from between his lips. *"Ahh, Panna Perlbergeruvna,"* he addresses my mother by her maiden name, "Nice to see you again. Are you interested in having something made?"

My mother produces the blankets and tells him that she would like to have coats made for the children.

"Oh yes," he shakes out the blankets, inspecting them. "These will make beautiful winter coats. We try to stand still while he takes our measurements. Bubbi, Halinka and I will have identical coats to wear in the winter. When he is finished measuring, he tells her that he's going to rush the coats. "Times are bad," he says, "and I want you to have these coats before the cold weather gets here." My mother agrees and tells him that she is in a hurry to have them. They never mention the threatening political climate that might interfere with the transaction. They shake hands and he assures her that the coats will be ready before the end of summer, in time for the High Holidays.

We leave the little tailor and continue walking until we come to a small dark shop containing no wares. This, my mother tells us is the photographer's studio. It is in a small dimly lit shop positioned between a shoemaker and milliner. Several props stand in various places: a table with flowers on it, a tall cardboard column that looks like it's made of marble, a mural of a lake with trees bordering it with a real bench in front of the painted scenery and a hat rack with several articles of clothing hanging from its arms: a black cape, a colorful shawl, a peasant vest and several hats. The photographer comes to the front of the store.

She is a young woman, dressed in a man's white shirt, with a red scarf tied beneath her collar and black trousers cuffed at the bottom. She has dark curly hair, pulled back severely from her face defining her sharp widow's peak. Her black eyebrows, perfectly arched, rise and fall with every syllable she utters, and a crimson slash outlines her narrow lips.

"Yes, how can I help you?" she asks in a husky voice.

"We would like to have some family photos taken."

"You've come to the right place. Do you want a formal portrait or maybe some casual pictures?"

Mutti wants some of each, she tells the photographer.

She poses us in front of the column, standing around my mother who is sitting on the bench with Halinka on her lap. Then she hands me a bouquet of fake flowers and tells me to hold it in front of my chest, underneath my chin. I do as I am told. She puts her head under a black cloth, snaps a picture and comes out. She decides to take another picture. This time, she has me sit on a stool in front of my mother and hold Halinka on my lap. She makes small talk with my mother.

"So," she asks casually, addressing my mother, "why are you having pictures taken? For a special occasion?"

"Well, yes and no," my mother answers her. "My husband is in the army, on the front, and I want to send him pictures of our family. He hasn't seen a recent photo of the baby yet."

The photographer nods her head and then scrutinizes us with a practiced eye. "Hmm," she muses, "Your husband is on the front? That must be hard on you with three children to look after." They continue making small talk, about the weather, the many German officers wandering around Krakow, how difficult it is to buy sugar and eggs. She never takes her eyes off my mother's face. She looks carefully at each of us, walks around her studio, stops and addresses my mother. "Stop me if I am out of line," she says, her eyebrows almost reaching her hairline, "but is this a second marriage for you?"

"Why would you ask such a question?" *Mutti* blushes.

"No. No reason. I was just wondering," she answers.

"Come on now," my mother says to her, "You must have a reason to ask such a question."

"It's just, …it's just," she seems to be searching for a word.

"Look madam," she sighs facing my mother squarely, "Times are hard and people are doing things they would never have considered in the past. This is none of my business but if it helps you in any way it's worth speaking up. There is no way that this baby has the same set of parents as your older children." My mother acts shocked.

"Listen, if your husband is fooled into thinking that this is his child, it's alright with me," she continues while adjusting a lens. "But I'm a professional. I worked in Warsaw in the cinema industry before returning to

Krakow. I was a casting director. It was my job to secure the right actors to look convincing in their roles. Often the parts required actors who resembled each other to play the parts of relatives, look-alike actors, young actresses as daughters who resembled the actresses who played the mothers, roles for actors who could pass as siblings, dark skinned people to act the parts of Gypsies. That is my profession and I am good at it. There is no way that this small boned, dark skinned, black- eyed baby has the same parents as your older, fair skinned, large boned children. They resemble you and the baby looks nothing like them. I would cast her as a child of Italian, Greek or Spanish descent. You and the boy and older girl look like Saxons, Irish, German, maybe even Polish."

My mother is worried. The photographer might have the idea that the baby my mother is holding on to might be the result of an illicit affair she had while her husband was on the front fighting. She hopes the photographer does not suspect her real motives for having the picture taken. She wants to have Halinka in our family portrait which she will send to my father to have American citizenships forged. But what is she to do if some other less friendly person were to spot the difference? She takes the photographer's warning seriously. She knows that if the photographer is able to tell the difference so might other people, less kindly disposed. Her offhand observation frightens my mother who later tells us the real motive for including Halinka. She sits quietly, thinking and then realizes that she is probably putting the rest of us into a dangerous position without benefitting anyone. She shrugs her shoulders. She does not trust the photographer but realizes that her judgment is probably good. She laughs self-consciously, and agrees with her.

"You know what?" she says, "Why don't you take one more picture of just my older children and me?"

She shrugs her shoulders and looks at her knowingly, "my husband will just have to wait until he comes home. If he asks about the baby, I'll just write and tell him she was sick when we had the pictures taken. There's time for discussion later, when he returns."

The photographer nods and winks, "I don't blame you."

Weeks later another letter arrives from my father. "Read it, read it," we all beg her. It is the only news we receive that doesn't include loss and death. My mother clears her throat and begins, "My darling Freda and my sweet children, I am happy to tell you that I am having some wonderful coats made for you with the material you sent me from Krakow. As soon as they are ready, I will send them to you. I hope they fit and protect you from the harsh climate in Poland." Everyone applauds.

"Coats? What coats?" I ask. "Aren't we having coats made in Krakow, by that old man with all those pins in his mouth? Papa had coats made for us in America? Why do we need so many coats?" Everyone laughs at me. Later, I will find that out "coats" is the code word for the papers and documents, "cover-ups" that we will use to try to pass for Americans and that the pictures my mother sent him are the "material" used to produce the "coats." Much later, when we get to America, my father will tell Bubbi and me about all the ploys he used in order to secure our safety. First, he tried to enlist in the US Army because that would have granted him immediate American citizenship and protect our family by giving us status as American citizens. He was rejected because he had a hernia. He then contacted American officials and government workers who, although extremely sympathetic were powerless to help him. He was desperate. He went to printing shops and requested all kinds of counterfeit documents, with gold insignias and official looking seals, because the Nazis were impressed by papers bearing many official-looking signatures and seals.

Later on, in a desperate ploy, he bought an old Jewish Bible in a used book shop, the pages were brittle and yellow with age and the binding was frayed. He asked a chemist friend of his how to make ink appear old and created a family tree including the birth of my maternal grandfather. Taking advantage of the fact that before the twentieth century families recorded important events in family Bibles he created a family tree comprised of many relatives, both real and imaginary. He took the precaution of changing my grandfather's name. Instead of

Reuven Perlberger he wrote in Richard Prauser, with the birth date of July 13, 1875. He was hoping for that with a less Jewish sounding name our chances for survival might be better. With this Bible in hand, he went to City Hall in Philadelphia, and approached a clerk in the statistics office.

"My father-in-law needs a birth certificate to put in a claim for Social Security," he told her, "and all he has to prove his birth is this old Bible. Would it be possible to apply for a birth certificate with this Bible?"

"Sure," the clerk complies as she inserted a blank birth certificate into the typewriter. "We get these requests all the time. Now how do you spell his name?"

My father sends this document along with the other notarized official looking papers, bearing our photographs to my mother in Wieliczka.

I hear talk among the grown- ups. It is time for us to leave Wieliczka. Poland is overrun with Germans who are encouraging anti-Semitic, zealous Poles not to tolerate the hated Jews. It doesn't take much prodding to unleash the open anti-Semitism. Wieliczka is becoming a dangerous place for us where everyone know that we Jewish, and where my mother has to wear the Star of David on her arm every time she leaves the house because she is well known in the village. The family is talking about retreating to a bunker underneath the factory that has been there since 1914 when our family hid during World War I.

"Fredel, listen," my aunt Angela says, looking sad and worried. "You take the children and go hide in Krakow. No one will suspect you of being Jewish, and if you stay here with us in the bunker, Bubbi may cry and give away our hiding place." *Mutti* agrees that young children can be very dangerous for people who are hiding. She makes plans to leave. She packs only a few things for us in a leather bag; a change of underwear and socks, toothbrushes and pajamas. She forgets about the sardines-- and so do I until years later when I allow myself to recall the darkness and disappointments of a childhood spent in fear.

CHAPTER 13

———— ♍ ————

MUTTI KNEELS ON the floor in front of Bubbi and me, gathers us into her arms and tells us, "Forget Jewish. You were never Jewish. It was just your imagination. Like Little Red Riding Hood, this is not a true story and it is not true that you were ever Jewish." It is August of 1940, I am four years old. *Mutti* is serious. A crease forms between her eyebrows as she tells us that we will be leaving Wieliczka very soon.

"Now look, Bubbi and Maidi," *mutti* instructs us. "We are going to live in Krakow and we have to be very sure of what we are. We are not and never have been Jewish. Do you understand how important it is for you to remember this?" My *mutti* knows that if she does not engage us and make us take this seriously Bubbi might betray us and endanger all our lives. I nod my head enthusiastically. Who wants to be Jewish? I think to myself. All you get for being Jewish is beat up and stolen from. I don't want to be Jewish. I would be happy to be like everyone else; to genuflect in front of a church, to wear a crucifix around my neck.

Bubbi is not as compliant as I. He insists on being Jewish. "I was a Jew, I am a Jew and I will always be a Jew."

"No, no Bubbi, you don't know what you are saying," my mother tries to impress him, holding on tightly to his little arms. She must convince him or there will be no use trying to keep ourselves safe. He is three and very sure of himself. He loved going to the little *shul* with my uncles on Friday evenings and Saturday mornings. He couldn't wait to wind *tefillin*, leather prayer straps around his left arm and place the small box, phylactery, on his forehead. He wants to become a Jewish man.

"It was all a game," she presses on, "We were never Jews and we are not Jews now. We only did it so we could live on this farm. Now we are leaving and it is no longer necessary to pretend we are Jewish" How could she make him understand the importance accepting a new identity, that of being Catholic? She is adamant. She must convince him that we are not Jewish. But Bubbi does not relent. Mutti crouches down to his eye level. "Listen Bubbi, what do you want to be when you grow up?" Without a moment's hesitation he replies. "A blacksmith," *kowal* in Polish.

"Alright Bubbi, your new name is *Tomek Kowalczik,* Tommy the Blacksmith. Now, you know that a blacksmith can't be Jewish," she implores. "Let's just be Catholic so that you can become a blacksmith when you grow up. But for now we are Catholic. Then, when you are grown up, you can be anything you want to be. Right now, you cannot and are not Jewish." She gives me a new name, Maria, puts small crucifixes around our necks, shows us how to cross ourselves and how to genuflect when we pass a cathedral.

We leave for Krakow on a sunny August morning. *Pan* Janowski, who delivers mail to us in Wieliczka drives us in his truck. He is a kind, sympathetic man who recently got married and now has a two year old boy. He tells my mother that he will save us. It is his dream, his conviction to do something noble in his lifetime to make him worthy. He is young and idealistic. He takes us to his home in Krakow, tells his wife that we are his distant cousins from Gdynia, Helena, Tomek and Maria Kowalczik, and that we will be staying with them for a little while. My mother, "Helena," has fake Polish identification papers made with our new surname, Kowalczik. *Pani* Ewa, his wife, is very welcoming and pleasant to us. She has a warm, sincere smile, a dimple on her cheek, and dark brown eyes. She feels familiar to me, like one of my aunts. *Pani* Ewa takes us to a small room where, she tells us we can stay for as long as we like. She is kind and she hugs my mother and gives Bubbi and me sweets.

Krakow is a medieval city, filled with beautiful cathedrals and elegant stores. At first it is an exciting place for us. There are many people on the streets and all seem to be in a hurry to get somewhere else. After a week or so in the Janowski home Bubbi and I tire of the daily routine and are bored. We have visited all the interesting places and suddenly our lives seem empty. We have nowhere to go and nothing to do. We have no friends, relatives or cousins to play with and there are very few toys for us to play with at the Janowskis, only baby pull toys for two year old Stefan, their little boy.

Sometimes we go down to the Vistula River and walk along its banks, and at other times we go to the *Sukiennice*, the marketplace and look at all the things there that we cannot own: soft warm slippers, bright peasant shawls, dolls with real hair and funny wind-up monkeys. We stop at a bakery and buy some bread, which we eat on the way back to the little apartment. Once there, we know we must be on our best behavior. Even though *Pani* Ewa is very kind, smiles a lot and tries to engage my mother in conversation, my mother is sad and does not tell us stories or play games with us as she used to. Instinctively I know to keep quiet, behave, and not to pester anyone with my questions. Bubbi takes his cues from me. He becomes practically mute.

We stay with the Janowski family in Krakow for about two months. We go to church with them every Sunday and behave "Catholic," genuflecting at the proper times and crossing ourselves. We eat non-kosher food and say grace before and after meals. Bubbi and I have become obedient little Catholics. One day, *Pani* Ewa beckons my mother into the parlor. She says she has to speak with her, alone. I am told to play in the kitchen. I watch them from a small hallway in the front of the apartment. I have made myself thin, like a piece of paper, a butterfly, or a moth, and insert myself between the wall and the credenza. I cannot be seen and I certainly cannot be heard for I have almost stopped breathing. They sit facing each other, my mother on the couch, and *Pani* Ewa across from her on a straight backed chair. *Pani* Ewa pulls the chair close to the couch before speaking. She takes my mother's hands into her own, kisses them and does not let go of them as she speaks. "Please, please, dear Jesus, forgive me, and you, Helena, you please, also forgive me. I am so frightened." She rubs her eyes, absent-mindedly pulls her hair away from her face and crushes her left hand in her right. "The neighbors are asking me questions about you, and they do not believe me when I tell them you are a relative of my husband. They nod their heads, but I know they are talking about me. They are saying that I am hiding a Jewess and her children and that I am collecting a fortune to keep you here." She sobs, pulls a handkerchief out of her sleeve and blows her nose.

She sighs deeply and goes on, "I would be so happy to have you stay here for free. It would buy us a place in heaven for my whole family, but I am so scared. You have no idea what my neighbors are like. For two *zlotys* they would sell your family and mine down the river of hell." She gets on her knees in front of my mother. She crosses herself and says, "I know that my Lord Jesus would never act this way, He would hide you even if it would cost Him His life." Sobbing, she adds, "It is not myself. I'm worried about my little boy, my son. He is so little and so innocent and I feel I must protect him from the mean gossips who pretend to be my friends." She turns away from my mother and looks towards the ceiling. Huge tears slide down her cheeks. "Please, sweet Jesus, try to understand me." She implores her God and bows her head in prayer.

My mother tries to comfort her, while she herself weeps and nods her head as if in agreement. "I understand the danger you are in. You were good to us and kind, I will never forget you," she adds. Both women look at each other and weep. "Give me a few minutes to collect our things and we will go." I watch and listen terrified. My heart feels like a basket of unraveling yarn that a kitten has been playing with. Where will we go? What will become of us? How could life have changed so quickly for us? A short while ago I was playing in the barn surrounded by people who loved and took care of me and now we have to leave this new home that I've only known for a short time.

Pani Ewa bows her head and continues weeping. "You don't have to leave right now. Spend the night here, eat supper with us and then tomorrow you will have a whole day to prepare yourself." She blows her nose, and continues weeping. "I wish things were different, that there was some way I could help you." She pauses, sniffs twice and tries to gather her thoughts. She repeats herself, "I do so wish that there were some way I could help you but I will make some suggestions, if you don't mind. I have an acquaintance, a Turk, he owns a furniture factory not very far from here. He has helped several Jews hide in his ware-house and he doesn't ask any questions." She goes over to a desk and writes something down on a small piece of paper. "Here is his address. Tell him that I sent you. He will help you if he is at all able. He is dark skinned and remember, the Nazis are not partial to anyone who does not look like they do. The Nazis don't have much to do with him but that is an advantage for you. They mostly ignore his comings and goings." My mother takes the address and looks at it quickly before tucking it into her pocket. "Try not to live in the ghetto," *Pani* Ewa goes on. "I hear that the conditions in the ghetto are very bad. There are many people crowded into one room and there is a lot of sickness there, typhus, consumption, all kinds of skin infections. I also heard that rats the size of cats brazenly scurry in the streets, into and out of the sew-ers." She hugs my mother and holds her close. "I will always love you," she whispers into her ear. "And I will pray for you forever."

We leave the next morning. *Mutti* has all our things in the brown leather bag she took when we left Wieliczka. It is the last piece of the family's tannery that we will ever own.

We spend a few nights in a small hotel near the river, but our days again are without purpose. In order to avoid the suspicion of the Germans and the nosey Poles milling about we pretend to have some-where to go. We leave every morning, with a seeming destination. It is early autumn, the leaves are collecting on the ground and there is a crisp feel in the air. We go into churches because they provide indoor shelter and no one bothers us there. I know I am supposed to pray, but I know only one prayer, and that one is in Hebrew. I kneel in the pew and silently recite the "*Shma*" over and over again. "Listen Oh Israel.

The Lord our God, the Lord is One." But in reality I am asking God to help us get to America and make my *mutti* happy again. Although no one tells me I can sense danger and sadness all around me. Sometimes I see stooped old men and women walking on the streets burdened by huge bundles on their backs. Every now and then they stop, drop their bundles and look around, as if not sure where to go next.

Carts pulled by horses and open trucks filled with people are everywhere. I can tell the passengers are Jewish because some of the men have *peyes* and beards, and the women wear *sheytls*. We stop and look. I pause and try to look into their faces to see if I recognize any of them, to try to understand what they are feeling. Of course, I have no idea where they are going and neither have they, but all look anguished and forlorn. We all know they are not going to a good place.

Suddenly, I spy my old nanny, Bella, from Wieliczka standing near the edge of the wagon. I recognize her long black braids. A sad frown has replaced her laughing face and rosy cheeks. She was only fifteen years old when she took care of us, but to me she was a grown-up. I break away from my mother and run into the street after the truck.

"Bella, Bella, where are you going? Stop, jump off the wagon!" I shout following the transport of unhappy people. She sees me and reaches out her arms to me, "Maidi, Maidi, I thought I'd never see you again." My mother grabs me and pulls me away angrily.

"Don't ever do that again!" My mother shakes me, "If they catch you, you'll be shipped to a bad, bad place."

"But that was Bella, our Bella. We love her," I whine, not understanding. "She should be with us. Why is she on that wagon?"

Mutti ignores my protests and cautions me again, "Bella is Jewish. We never knew her," my mother states through compressed lips "We would never have had a Jewish nanny. We don't have anything to do with Jews. Do you understand me? We are not Jewish, and we don't know anyone who is. She shakes me in fear, but what I feel is her anger. Bubbi and I nod our heads. We have never seen my mother so agitated.

We continue wandering the streets for a few more days and by that time my mother realizes that we need to make other plans. We can try to live on the outside as Catholics, find Ewa's acquaintance who owns a furniture company, or enter the ghetto.

"We can't really stay here at the hotel any longer," she tells us. "There are too many German soldiers and I don't want them to notice me. We will go to see the man *Pani* Ewa told us about." The owner of the furniture factory turns out to be a Turkish man who wears a red fez and speaks with an accent. A small crescent moon is pinned in his lapel. His skin is swarthy. He is so fat that his eyes look like they are buried inside his cheeks. He and my mother talk for a long time. He seems to be agreeing and nodding his head to whatever my mother tells him. He smiles at her and I catch sight of a mouthful of gold teeth, glinting from behind his thin lips. He is friendly, and puts his arm on my mother's elbow, guiding the three of us into a large furniture storage area. Bubbi, who has no recollection of my father, lights up, "Is this our Papa?" he asks *mutti* tugging at her sleeve urgently. She smiles sadly, "no schatzie," she tells him. This nice man is going to let us live in this big room." My mother gestures towards the warehouse filled with furniture. She thanks him graciously and slips something into his palm.

"You are welcome to stay here," he assures her taking the money and smoothly sliding it into his breast pocket.

"Well," my mother sighs, "at least we have a roof over our heads. And look at all this beautiful furniture." Despite her enthusiasm about our new arrangements, she looks tired and her shoulders sag.

The factory is filled with new furniture. Every piece is protected, wrapped in bundles of shiny straw. Even the mattresses are covered with straw. There is a small bathroom in the factory. It contains one disgusting brown toilet bowl and a small sink that drips cold, rusty water into a dirty bowl. "Oooooh, disgusting. Worse, far worse than the outhouse in Wieliczka." I complain. My mother quiets my protests about the toilet. "Now stop it," she admonishes me. "We are lucky to have a toilet and a sink to wash up in."

At first, we each choose a different mattress to sleep on, making sure that we are not too far apart from one another. The factory is easy to get lost in, especially since much of the furniture is taller than we are and everything is wrapped in identical straw covers. When we go to sleep, we brush the straw off the surface and use it to cover ourselves instead. We cannot stay in the factory during the day when customers begin to arrive so we leave promptly at nine every morning.

Again, we have nowhere to go. It is getting colder and we spend most of our time in a church. On warm sunny days we hide out at the cemetery. Bubbi and I play around the headstones. Sometimes we play hide and seek; other times we play tag. Mutti sits nearby on a stone bench watching us. When we become too noisy, she warns us to keep quiet. I notice a difference in her. She is impatient with us, scolds us for things that never bothered her before.

When someone comes to the cemetery, she says, "Pray, pray for your grandmother." And quickly we sink to our knees in front of the nearest gravesite, cross ourselves and fold our hands in front of our chests, mumbling to the headstone.

One day, a young family, a mother, father and two little girls come quietly into the cemetery. The parents silently carry a small white coffin with angels engraved on its side. A young man with swollen eyes and running nose is holding onto the front of the coffin. He is followed by his wife who holds onto the rear and two young daughters. She is dressed in black with a heavy veil covering her face. She holds the casket with one hand and a handkerchief to her mouth with the other. The two girls are staring straight ahead, stone faced, their lips moving in silent prayer. I stand close by, watching sadly. They carry the little casket to a grave- site, and the man takes a shovel that is leaning against a tree, and starts digging vigorously. The girls and their mother sink to their knees, fold their hands in front of their chests, bow their heads and start to pray. I drop to my knees next to them, and weep and pray with them. "Please God, please let the world be happy," I pray. "Please let all this sadness stop."

CHAPTER 14

⟡

THE WEATHER IS turning colder and the warehouse is unheated, dark and damp. We shiver in our summer clothes. Because we fled Wieliczka in warm weather and expected to return shortly we took only the summer clothes we had on our backs and the sandals we were wearing. There is no protective layer between our bodies and the relentless cold of a Polish winter. As grim as the factory is, it is even colder outside, and we have no place to go. The churches are unheated and I wonder where the "coats" that my father promised are. Not only do they not arrive, but when *mutti* takes us to the tailor shop to get them a few months later, the tailor shop is boarded up and there is no sign of the tailor. A huge white swastika is painted on the door.

We try to keep warm by sleeping on one mattress and huddling close to each other. My mother lies between Bubbi and me with a protective arm around each of us. We snuggle under her sheltering wings. I hear her pray, quietly in Polish. She thinks I am sleeping and can't hear her, but I am well- trained in the art of eavesdropping. I listen carefully to her intimate whispers to God. "Please God. Let me bring my children to safety. I don't care what happens to me. Let my children live then You can take me. I don't mind dying," she cries quietly, tears sliding off her face into her ears.

I don't want God to take her. What is she talking about? I resolve that I won't ever tell her how cold I am. I will keep all my bad feelings locked up. My mother touches my forehead. She can tell by feeling it that I am running a high fever. My throat hurts, I can't swallow without a spasm of pain and I can hardly speak. The roof of my mouth feels as though it is caving onto my tongue, closing off my breathing. I sweat and shiver at the same time. Before long, I begin to hallucinate. "Look *mutti*," I shout, "we are in a castle, in a palace. The furniture is gold. We are finally safe." The fever makes me shake. My mother holds me all night long. She knows that we have to leave the freezing factory, to move on. But where to? The danger of the cold is only overshadowed by the danger from the Poles and Germans. When my temperature subsides, we leave. My mother locks the iron gates that bar intruders from entering. She looks straight ahead, never turning back.

We walk around Krakow looking for lodgings. The cold penetrates my bones. It is worse by far than the hunger and more intense than the fear. My toes, fingertips and nose hurt the most, then my ankles, wrists and knees. It is relentless, uncompromising and when the frost numbs my senses, the wind picks up. It slaps my face with the back of a bony hand, it burns my skin and makes my eyes water. It is worse than every pain I've ever felt and it never, ever stops.

We trudge along the streets, going nowhere, with not even a sweater to protect our shoulders and arms. Suddenly, my mother stops in the middle of the street. She gasps with a sharp intake of air and does not exhale for a long time. When she does I hear her moan quietly. There, on the opposite side of the street is a woman, walking with her two daughters who are wearing identical coats. They are made of the blankets that my mother had bought only last summer and taken to the tailor to have coats made for us. Right there, on the streets of Krakow, someone is wearing our stolen coats.

"*Mutti,*" I shout, tugging at her sleeve, "they stole our coats. Run after them. Let's get our coats back." She is stunned, horrified. Everything shifts. She looks up at the sky and addressing the clouds and patches of blue she implores the heavens. "God, God, what have we done that You abandon us so completely? That You take away everything we have ever had, my brothers, my sisters, my mother, nephews, nieces, even our clothing? That You let us freeze and starve while others take our things." She looks up into the sky as though invoking her God to finally reveal Himself: daring Him to give her a reason. She cries softly, her sobs tear through her body and mine as well. I am frightened, more of her crying than of the terrible cold that penetrates to our very bones. My mother hardly ever cries, at least not in front of me. If she gives in to the terror that has gripped us then I know everything will be gone. It feels as though the world has shifted.

She stands up, holding her hands to her eyes and shaking her head from side to side. "Hurry *mutti*, hurry, the lady with our coats is disappearing." I tug at her arm, urging her to move. I don't understand why she is letting them get away. "They're thieves. Don't let them get away with our coats."

"No *schatzie*," she says sadly. "If I run after the coats, the police will come after us. Those coats no longer belong to us." She looks to the sky one more time as though giving God one last chance to redeem Himself. "Nothing belongs to us anymore."

We walk from house to house, looking for lodgings. Is there no place in this big city for us? Is there no place in this big world for us? I ask myself these questions as we are turned away from one house after another. One small home has a sign in the window offering a room for rent. My *mutti* taps the door and it is opened before she finishes knocking. An elderly woman comes to the door, "Are you interested in renting the room?" She looks us up and down, then she smiles revealing two eye-teeth in an otherwise toothless mouth gleaming with red gums. Before my mother can answer her she goes on, "This house belongs to my daughter, but times are bad now, we have to take in boarders. Have you seen that flour and eggs are not available at any price?" She beckons us into a hallway with a sharp, skinny index finger and without stopping to take a breath, continues, "I'll only rent to nice, decent people like you. I can tell a person's character just by looking into their eyes. I can tell by your eyes that you are good people. Here," she opens a door onto a small room opposite a bathroom. "This is the room my daughter is renting." It is bright, with two cots on each side of a wall, a small night table between them and a crucifix above each cot. Jesus is staring mournfully down at us and I wonder how He feels with all that is going on. Does He see that the world He gave His life for is so bad? What would He do if He was here on earth?

The room is warm and inviting. The woman has not stopped talking, "We are charging ten *zlotys* a week. A low price for you, because I can tell that you'll keep the room nice and clean and that you won't be inviting any riffraff." She turns to us and asks, "What brings you to Krakow?" *Mutti* is well prepared.

"We're from Gdynia, in the north, but you know that the Germans invaded Gdynia and we wanted to get out of there before they discovered that my husband was in our Polish Army, at the front," she adds to assure her of our respectability.

The woman utters sympathetic noises, "Such bad times," she says shaking her head from side to side. "So, tell me" she asks, "do you want to take the room? My daughter insists for me to tell you that you can have no visitors, and that you have to pay one week in advance."

My mother assures her. "There'll be no visitors here. It is all I can do to keep my children safe and warm."

She waits until my mother hands her the money. She counts it carefully and tucks it into the sleeve of the green cardigan with ripped elbows that she is wearing. "Welcome to our home. Oh," she adds, "my name is *Pani* Sciepka."

CHAPTER 15

———— ⁊ ————

THE ROOM IS more than we bargained for. It is clean, it is warm and there is a nice bathroom across the hallway. A burlap sack containing flour is propped up against a wall in the corner of the room under the window. Because of the cold, we remain indoors almost all the time playing and looking out of the window. When Bubbi and I are very hungry, we go to the sack of flour and scoop out handfuls. When mixed with our saliva it actually begins to taste good. Occasionally, when it isn't too cold we go out to get some food: rolls, an apple or a jar of yogurt which we sneak back into the room. We are not allowed to use the kitchen. By the time we return, we are so happy to have a cozy, warm room that we don't want to go anywhere.

Mutti spots a familiar silhouette one afternoon when we are outside on one of our food runs. She moves toward her. "Matilda?" she whispers and then exclaims joyfully, "Matilda!" It is my aunt Matilda. They hug each other, in tears and exchange whatever news they have. "How did you get to Krakow?" my mother asks. My aunt pauses, takes a breath and starts sobbing. "The Germans came to the farm. Well, to the factory actually. You know the factory was taken over by the Poles. Everyone was hiding in the bunker. We had no food, and we couldn't even whisper." She pauses, looks around as if to check that no one is listening and continues, haltingly. "I heard their boots above my head. I was so frightened. We had already lost so much, and *mamuncha*, our beloved mother was taken a few days before, when she stepped out to get some air. She was sent on a transport to Siberia." She stops for air, sniffles and goes on. "Imagine our dear mother, seventy years old, grabbed by a bunch of hooligans and pushed onto a wagon. She couldn't even grab a sweater. My little Miriam, my only child, I sent her away before we started hiding. I only hope she is safe. She went on a children's transport to Hungary, to a cloister and is living there with the nuns. The last I heard she was christened and living as a Catholic child among the nuns. What else could I do?" she asks no one in particular. "The police were everywhere. I knew it would only be a matter of time before they discovered us. So early in the morning, before the sun came up, I snuck upstairs into the factory and jumped out the window. Of course, one of them spotted me and started chasing me. But he was fat, and out of breath, and I was running for my life. I ran into the village." She pauses and tries to catch her breath, blow her nose and wipe the tears away, as she continues. "I ran into Shumsky's barn. You remember Shumsky?" she asks my mother. My mother nods. "Well, they transported him long ago to God knows where. Anyway, I ran into his barn, there was nothing alive in it any more. I covered myself up with straw and waited until it was dark, then I jumped on a train, and here I am." Aunt Matilda goes on, "The Nazis and the Polish police flooded the area. I know that they got to our bunker because I met Rysek, our nephew at the train station in Wieliczka. He was hiding in the church cellar. He got away and so did a few others. Shalom (my uncle, her husband) was caught and sent to a labor camp. I don't know if he's dead or alive," she bursts out crying.

Mutti too is crying at this point. "Matilda, Matilda," she says, embracing her, "we must not let go of our hope. That's the only thing they can't take from us. I never thought that I would see my sister again, on the street in Krakow no less, and here you are." She has not grasped the dreadful truth of what Matilda is telling her. It will take years before she is able to accept it. "It is such a comfort to know that at least you and Miriam are safe." Then *mutti* laughs cynically at her own words, "Safe indeed. As if anyone of us can be safe"

My mother tells Matilda to follow us home. Once we arrive, she begs our landlady to let her sister stay in our room. "I'll have to ask my daughter. It's her house, you know. If it were up to me, I wouldn't care." She shuffles out of the room in her felt house slippers. Her daughter appears, scowling, "I said no guests, and I certainly didn't even think of people staying overnight."

My mother takes a safe tactic. "My sister has money. She'll be happy to pay you. If you don't want her to stay with us she will surely find someone else who will gladly take her *zlotys*. "Who knows," she says, pushing her luck, "maybe we'll find a place for all of us,"

At the mention of money, the landlady's small, yellowish eyes light up. "It's against my rules," she tells my mother. "And I hope I'm not making a mistake but mind you I'm not putting in any more beds, she can stay but I'll have to charge you more than you are paying now, an extra seven *zlotys*. After all," she goes on, "there'll be four of you and you'll be using more water and the wear and tear on my furniture…"

We all pack into the tiny room. It is wonderful having Aunt Matilda with us, someone who knows us and loves us, someone we love. For the first time since coming to Krakow, *mutti's* shoulders don't sag. She is turning to her old pleasant self again. She too is comforted by her sister's presence.

Unfortunately her revived spirit does not last long. The landlady's mother starts behaving strangely. She avoids us and her daughter comes to collect the rent, seventeen *zlotys*. A cigarette dangles loosely from her mouth as she counts the money. She puts it in her pocket, and saying nothing walks away.

A few days later, two tall men, in civilian clothes barge into the little room.

"Here, here they are," the daughter points to our little group. "Don't blame me for being suspicious but I'm not going to take any chances harboring Jews. Not for the few *zlotys* they pay. Beside, aren't the Germans paying us some money for turning in the Jews. Not that I'm doing it for the money," she quickly assures them. "I would never harbor filthy, disgusting Jews in my nice, clean Catholic, home." She talks to the officers standing at the door, her arms crossed, watching us as if we were cats ready for mischief. "This is a respectable house and I'm not going to tarnish its image, not for any amount of money." She wears a smug, satisfied look on her face, catching the ashes from her cigarette in her palm. She shrugs her skinny shoulders. "I'm only doing my duty," she tells everyone.

The men are big and noisy. One of them has a huge black mole next to his upper lip. It quivers when he shouts at my mother and my aunt. "Show me your identity papers," he yells. He rocks back and forth on his heels as my mother rushes to get them. She gives him the Polish identity papers, but withholds the ones my father had sent her about our American connection. The man with the mole scrutinizes them and hands them over to his companion who is wearing glasses, which he removes from his pale, colorless eyes, in order to read. They converse in conspiratorial whispers. "Madam, there's something wrong here. These papers state that you are from Krakow and you clearly told *Pani* Sciepka that you are from Gdynia. And if your husband is at the front, why are you staying here and paying for lodging? Don't you have some other place to stay where you wouldn't have to pay for lodgings?" Something doesn't ring true. "Why are you here?"

Mutti trembles as the officers comes menacingly close to her. Bubbi walks boldly up to the men. "Leave my mommy alone," he starts punching their legs and kicking their boots. "Get away from my mommy, you bad, bad men." The men have no patience for the little boy. The one with the mole shoves him away, while the other one knocks him to the floor. Two grown men overpower the three-year-old Bubbi. He never cries. He stands up and makes for their legs again. This time my mother picks him up and holds him tightly. She doesn't know what kind of anger Bubbi might provoke in them if he attacks them again. Mutti pales; her lips are trembling. My aunt sits on the edge of the cot, gripping her thighs. She gets up quickly, goes to the closet and from a pocket extracts a gold bracelet and two gold rings. She gives the rings to one to one man, the bracelet to the other. They make the jewelry disappear like a magic trick. *Pani* Sciepka looks stunned. She has no idea that my mother and aunt have valuable jewelry. If she had known, instead of reporting us she would have held out for more money.

"Let's find out about these papers." The man with the glasses says. He sounds much more amenable, almost friendly. "You stay here, but we'll take the documents. We'll look them over at the station, discuss what to do with them, and then we will return them to you. Right Woczek?" he turns to his companion for confirmation. *Pani* Sciepka's daughter looks unhappy even though she thinks she will profit for turning in two Jewish women and children. She regrets not having held out for more money from her Jewish tenants.

Mutti is desperate because the documents they took not only are counterfeit, but they also have her picture. She keeps crying, "My picture, now they have my picture." I do not understand her dilemma, because in my mind nothing worse than losing her picture has taken place. I try to reassure her by telling her that we can get more pictures of her when we are in America.

"Do you think he'll leave us alone?" my aunt asks my mother, "after all, he did take the jewelry."

"We can't take a chance. For the bracelet and the ring, they gave us the gift of not taking us with them. Let's not take any chances about their feelings towards us."

Pani Sciepka asks my mother if she has any other jewelry. "Maybe we could arrange for you to go to the farm where my sister lives. She would be glad to hide you there and you wouldn't be in danger so far away from the city." She stands in front of the door, guarding it with her body, her greedy eyes blazing.

Mutti and Aunt Matilda push her away, grab a few items and tear out of her house. We are sprinting down the street while she is screaming for us to stop. We run for about ten minutes until we can no longer hear her voice and stop several blocks further down the street where we sit down in a café and try to catch our breath. Aunt Matilda and *mutti* speak in whispers. Later, my aunt tells us that she is going to try to get to Hungary to be with Miriam. We have nowhere to go. It is too dangerous for us to live as Catholics. My mother tells us. "We are going to go to a place called the ghetto, where we will be with many other Jews. The life here on the outside is too dangerous for us.

"Can we still be Catholic? I ask in a small voice. One thing I know, being Jewish is being scared, being cold, being hungry and having to leave one place after another. I don't want to go to the ghetto. We've passed by many times, and even *Pani* Ewa says no one wants to be there. There is sickness and misery in the ghetto and I am sure we won't survive there.

CHAPTER 16

"Yisgadal ve-yiskadish sh'mei raba," An old man paces back and forth on a street where people sit hunched over like so many piles of debris. Wailing the *Kaddish*, the ancient prayer of Jewish mourners, with palms open towards the heavens and eyes tightly shut. His ripped black coat and dirty ritual fringes slap sharply at the backs of his legs on this cold, gray day. The cold sky looks down on us, steely, unyielding.

We have passed the ghetto many times while walking the streets of Krakow seeking food and shelter. My mother would always pull us across the street trying to shield us from the sight of brick walls shaped like tombs, crowned with rolled barbed wire, and the cries of the hopeless coming from behind the walls. "Don't look there," she would say, shielding our eyes protectively afraid that we might retain some of the ghastly images; images that are made for nightmares. She made us keep our eyes on the ground and no wonder. This place is terrifying. And now we are here, part of this terrifying scene.

The ghetto is located in the section in Podgorze, an industrial part of Krakow. Three thousand people lived there before it was turned into the ghetto. By 1941, when we arrive, 6,500 Jews are crammed into its miserable quarters, between eight and ten people into one room. The ghetto is mostly ignored by the citizens of Krakow, but passers-by can hear gunshots daily as new groups of Jews are rounded up and massacred on the streets. The Jews are divided into two groups: the able bodied who will be deported to work in the work camps and the frail, elderly, women and children, deemed useless who will be sent to the death camps..

The noise, garbage and decay invade all of my senses. An old man wearing rags rambles around in the street. He is mumbling to himself and seeming to be having an argument with some inner demon who is making him weep. He is dazed, confused. His soul appears to have departed and yet he walks around. He approaches us, grabs my mother by the lapels on her jacket and pulls her close to him.

" Chanya? Are you Chanya?" he asks desperately.

"No, I'm not," she answers him, recoiling instinctively. He takes hold of her hands, pulls them towards his mouth and starts to kiss them. "You are not Chanya? Are you sure? Didn't you see her?" My mother tries to be gentle with him.

"I'm so sorry." She looks at his face while pulling her hands slowly away from his grasp. He is repulsive but she can see his suffering and wants to be kind. "When did you last see her?" she asks.

He shrugs his shoulders. He doesn't remember. He starts to cry, "Everybody is gone. Everyone in my family is gone. I just feel that Chanya is still alive. Are you sure you haven't seen her?" he asks again. My mother shakes her head sadly, her eyes filling with tears. He sinks to the sidewalk slowly, as if his bones are dissolving. He buries his head in his knees, and sobs like a small boy. My heart feels so full of pain that I fear I won't be able to contain it in my body. A hard rock has lodged itself deep in my throat: I cannot swallow and I cannot talk, I cannot even cry.

A young woman dressed in rags holding a baby close to herself stops everyone she meets. "My milk dried up and my baby is hungry," she pleads. "Can you help me with a small amount of milk, or maybe tea?" No one pays attention to her. All around me, people are weeping, begging for food, scratching their bodies and the red sores that infest them. So much pain and suffering around me. I can't stay here I tell myself. I don't want to know why these people are being tortured. I just want it to stop. "Please *muttii*," I say, "why can't we do anything for these poor people?" I look into her face and see that she too is crying.

She stops a pale young man in a black jacket that resembles some kind of uniform. His trousers are ripped, his shoes are scuffed and he wears no socks. He bears no resemblance to the well- dressed officers I am used to seeing. "*Prosze bartzo*, please, excuse me," she says to the young man. "Can you tell me where I can find a room?" He looks at her and laughs without smiling. His pale, thin face twitches. He has the unhealthy pallor of someone who hardly ever goes outdoors.

"*Pani zartuye*, the lady is joking," he tells her. "This place is so full you can't get an empty paper bag into this space. Anyway, finding space isn't up to me. Go knock on doors. Maybe someone died and there is room in one of the flats." My mother nods, "*rozumye*, I understand."

Later on *mutti* tells me that he was a safe person to talk to as he was part of the *Judenrat*, the Jewish police that the Gestapo has rounded up. A few of the able- bodied Jewish young men they have assigned the job of policing their fellow inmates. It is their duty to enforce the rules imposed on their fellow Jews, to report any infractions and to act as agents for the Gestapo against their fellow Jews. For this service, they are rewarded with a black uniform jacket and the illusion of power and control. While many of them are protective of the ghetto dwellers, others become zealous enforcers of the rules, eager to catch their fellow Jews transgressing, hoping to score points with the Gestapo. Life in the ghetto is filled with suspicions and humiliation.

A cocky teenager, swaggering in his new uniform stops an old man and makes him empty his pockets. He squares his shoulders insolently, hikes up his pants, and speaks in Yiddish. "Just because you are old, doesn't mean you can't smuggle." The old man shakes his head in disbelief, "Such behavior from a *Yiddishe bocher*, a Jewish boy. That I had to live to experience such rudeness, such *chutzpah*!" This breakdown in order, authority and respect encourages suspicion and paranoia among the dwellers of the ghetto.

We continue walking and looking around before approaching one of the buildings. My mother knocks on the door and a woman peers out cautiously. Her head tightly swathed in a colorless kerchief. She is gaunt, like a pencil and her threadbare housedress hangs on her like a shroud but her eyes are on fire, and she recognizes my mother. "Freda," she exclaims, "why are you here?" She embraces my mother. It turns out that she is from Wieliczka, the rabbi's wife. "We thought you were on your way to America by now."

Mutti, although frightened, seems relieved to see a familiar face. She sighs, "It's a long story but believe me it feels so good to finally be among my own people, to know that there are still some who are alive, if you can call this being alive." She remembers the purpose of her visit and looks around the dark corridor. "Is there any room for us in your flat?"

"What do you mean is there any room for us? You are us. Do you think we can't make room for one of ours? It will be an honor and a privilege to have you in our little room, although, I must warn you, it isn't what you're used to."

"What I'm used to?" my mother asks no one in particular. "What I'm used to is an unheated furniture warehouse and a room in the home of an anti-Semite, who couldn't wait to turn us over to the Polish Gestapo." She follows the rabbi's wife up the narrow staircase, littered with foul smelling garbage.

"This is it," she exclaims, flinging one of the doors open. "It isn't much, but you are so very welcome." A dark, narrow room with little light that is filtered through one grimy window is to be our new home. The bare wooden floor is strewn with people of all ages, some sitting, others standing while a few are actually lying down. Everyone packed so close together that it is almost impossible to get from one end of the room to the other without stepping over a sleeping body or bumping into someone sitting or standing and praying. Two men, wearing black hats and *tzitzis*, fringed ritual garments are standing, facing the wall, swaying vigorously to- and- fro, their eyes tightly shut, praying to their unresponsive God. A red-headed young woman sits on a frayed velvet chair, rocking her baby to sleep. A woman lies on a cot next to the wall, coughing uncontrollably into a blood- soaked handkerchief. A teenaged boy leans against a window, his hands covering his eyes, not moving. Everyone seems to be his or her own world. No wonder! The reality is ghastly.

The rabbi's wife seems to be in charge. "Move over, please, we have new guests," she tells a woman who is lying on the floor, staring at the ceiling. "We have to make room." Everyone stops what they are doing to look at us.

"God, I don't belong here," I say to myself. "I am a Catholic girl, Maria Kowalsczik." I drop to my knees. "Hail Mary, full of grace...." I intone the matriarch of the religion I have chosen.

Why am I here? I hate this room with its awful sounds and putrid smells. I hate the dying people, the coughers, the weepers, the oozing sores, and the hopeless visions. I would rather be back in the furniture warehouse, burning up with fever and hallucinating. *I want to be anywhere but here.* All of us in this room are together only because we are Jews. In spite of my beliefs, in spite of my longings, I am subject to all the suffering and humiliations of my people. Aside from the rabbi's wife, we don't know anyone. We have nothing in common yet we are all staying here in one room, together. Those who have given up hope sit and stare into vacant space. Others, wait for the Messiah. Still others, the so called enlightened ones are waiting for the world to come to its senses and stop this outrageous torture. The foolish ones are convinced that they will be freed. They are making plans, trading gloves for socks, scarves for caps. No one's prayers are answered.

The room has one cot and several chairs. The adults sign a list and are given a specific time to use the cot. Each person sleeps for about an hour and then the next one in turn wakes the sleeping one up by gentle nudging or assertive pushing, demanding the space. No one cares that the bedding is never changed, that lice and bedbugs are crawling over the blankets, that the smell of the person who just got up is rank and clinging. All they want is an hour of uninterrupted sleep, an hour to escape from hell. Two chairs are placed facing each other, and it is on these chairs that the children take turns sleeping. Sometimes, when one of us is active, the chairs slide apart, and then we find ourselves on the floor. After this happens to me twice, I decide that it is easier to sleep on the floor. The children never leave the room. We play indoors, under the table, constructing a make-believe world, blotting out our surroundings.

Once again, *mutti*, because of her Aryan looks is pressed into service by the rabbi's wife. She hands her a black wool coat, "don't ask where it comes from," she says. "Just take it and wear it. The owner will never use it again." *Mutti* is sent out to forage for food for the rest of the residents in our little room, a trip she will make several times in the coming weeks. She removes her Star of David armband from the sleeve and is escorted by one of the Jewish guards to the gate. She trudges bravely, her back straight, her eyes forward through the snow covered Krakow streets. She is the daughter of a successful business man and knows how to strike a bargain and to haggle with the shopkeepers for a few moldy potatoes, half rotten carrots and anything else she can get for the few *zlotys* she has acquired from her roommates. She wants to pay for the food herself. She has brought money with her from Wieliczka and can well afford to feed her room mates. But they won't hear of it. "We still have our dignity," one woman says, pressing two *zlotys* into her hand. My mother agrees. She understands the need for pride and dignity and, she doesn't want to take it from them when they have so little. She tries gathering as much food as she can. She is not particular about quality. We are many and we are hungry, but we share everything equally. The rabbi's wife tries to press some of her rations onto a nursing mother. "Come on," she urges, "you have to eat to nourish two lives."

While my mother is away, Bubbi and I stay in the room playing under the table with the other children. In that small space we feel safe and protected. Suddenly darkness descends and with it comes panic and fear for me. It is dark and she isn't back. I take up my vigil at the dirty window, waiting with her picture tucked up in a corner of the pane. I experience unimaginable terror; she has been caught, she is being tortured, mutilated. In my mind, I see her beaten and bloodied. I am preparing for the worst. Even though I am not yet six, I have been listening to adult conversations for a long time and know all about the things that happen to Jews who are found outside the ghetto. I have already had first- hand experience with people I love never being seen again.

It doesn't take long for my active imagination to take root and transport me to the forest of "Hansel and Gretel." My mother is gone. We are alone, lost in the woods, surrounded by all kinds of danger. The horror of this reality is much more frightening than any fairy tale I have heard. "What if she never returns?" I will not be able to survive that. Bubbi and I are alone with no relatives to turn to. Dangerous shadows hide in behind every door, just as they do in the illustrations of the frightening stories read aloud to us before the horror of our reality set in. Now that my mother is gone it is difficult for me to separate my harsh world from the fairy tale. I sit on the floor biting my lips to keep myself from crying. Everyone around me is going about their own business. Even Bubbi is playing train on two overturned chairs. I am caving into myself, folding up like an accordion, holding my breath. No one notices me, and if they do, no one has the patience to comfort me. No one thinks about reassuring a small frightened child. I am dreadfully alone, afraid that I will never see my *mutti* again. What will happen to us? I ask myself again and again. So many people disappear. I see myself as a *sierota*, an orphan, a word I hate the very sound of. Alone in the world with no one to take us in, a fate that so many children I know are now facing. I cover my eyes and start to pray, *shma Yisroel.*

Suddenly, the door bursts open. She's here. She's safe and beautiful and smelling of snow. She has had an exceptional day outside the ghetto, she tells all who gather around her eagerly, hungry for anything. She managed to get a loaf of bread, three tiny potatoes, a jar of yogurt and a maggot- infested slab of meat. The kosher people won't eat the meat, but we do. "This is war," my mother tells us "You eat whatever you can." She reaches underneath her coat and to our astonishment produces two small jackets for Bubbi and me.

As long as my *mutti* is nearby, I feel safe and protected. She never tires of sheltering us from devastating realities that occur all around us. She tries to keep us full of hope and promises that things will get much better when we get to America. "You'll see," she tells us, "we will have so much food that you are going to beg me to stop feeding you. You'll each have a beautiful room with your own beds to sleep in, many toys and a closet full of warm clothing."

"Will Papa play ball with me?" Bubbi asks hopefully.

"Everyday," she answers emphatically.

"And will Papa take us to the circus?" I ask hopefully.

"Not only will he take you to the circus, he will take you to shake hands with the dancing tigers." She assures us.

"Will we be able to go to school?"

"Able?" she asks incredulously. "You *have* to go to school. In America everyone goes to school."

"Can I be Jewish in America?" Bubbi asks anxiously.

"Yes, of course you'll be Jewish. You will always be Jewish. In America, there is no anti-Semitism."

"Can I be Catholic?" I ask hopefully.

I want to be like everyone else. I've been Jewish longer than I wanted to be. "What if I don't want to be Jewish? If America is a free country, will I be able to go to church?"

She doesn't answer. I know what I want. I want to be a Catholic,

"I don't want to live in a ghetto with nothing but Jews, these sad people, taking turns sleeping on a bed for one hour each night, listening to that sick woman coughing, seeing dead people taken out onto the streets slumping against walls, their heads rolling onto their chests. I hate the Jews. I don't want to be Jewish, not now, not ever." I am in tears quickly forgetting the promises my mother has just made to us about the wonderful life in America. In no time, I am back to reality and the sordid life we are living only because we are Jews.

"Maidi, Maidi," *mutti* rocks me gently. "When we get to America none of that will be happening. You can be Jewish and live in a beautiful house, with a nice big garden. Your Papa will buy you anything you want, and you will never have to see people suffering because they are Jewish."

I don't believe her. I resolve that when I am free and grown up I will become a Catholic again. I comfort myself, promising myself that I will never be Jewish and suffer like this. But Bubbi buys into her promises. Her stories about my father are so real for Bubbi that he thinks my father is just around the corner. Every time my mother talks to a man Bubbi tugs at her sleeve impatiently, "Ask him," he lisps, "Ask him. Maybe this is our father."

Mutti realizes that I am becoming aware of what is going on around me. She knows I no longer believe the stories she tells me to assuage my longings and fears. The conditions in the ghetto are deteriorating and no amount of magic and make believe can make me deny what I am seeing around me. There is no longer enough food left to share and people are sick, starving and dying all around us. The illness, starvation and hopelessness of the ghetto are closing in on the living.

Even I can see that the ghetto is a dangerous place. Those who don't starve or succumb to illness, vanish. People are disappearing daily, dragged away from the few loved ones left and taken to God knows where. Children and older people are dying in the streets and no one is strong enough to pick them up and bury them. All this I see with my own eyes open wide. My mother, who likes to attribute all the unpleasant things I hear and see to my imagination has stopped trying to cheer me up. She knows that she cannot erase the present with fairy tales of the future. She has had enough. One night, she collapses on the cot. She covers her face with her hands and sobs quietly.

The coughing woman has not awakened. She hasn't coughed or moved since early morning, and even I can tell that something is terribly wrong. The rabbi's wife, though weak and starving herself, takes charge. "Her body can't stay in the room with us. We have to have it removed. Let me see what we can do." She leaves the room and returns minutes later with three of the Jewish guards. They are going to remove her body. I am not going to watch. I hide under the table and wait for them to take the coughing woman away. I don't ask where they are taking her. I'm afraid that the truth may be more frightening than not knowing.

Later on that very night, without telling anyone of her plans, my mother quietly packs our few possessions, takes us with her and leaves the ghetto with the men who are taking away the body of the coughing woman; we never find out what her name was. *Mutti* can't bear to say good-bye to any of our roommates. Saying good-bye to people she knows are not going to live to the end of the month is too much for her to bear. We have already lost too many people.

CHAPTER 17

THE SNOW IS coming down quickly, landing on our eyelashes and clinging for a short moment on our hair before melting into icy puddles and streaming onto our neck. We are again outside with no prospects of a room, shelter or protection. The howling wind bares its hungry fangs and attacks us unmercifully. My mother tells us that we are once again Catholic, Maria and Tomek Kowalczik. Even my brother doesn't question her. He accepts his new assignment without the protest he usually makes. We haven't eaten since our evening meal of cold potatoes the night before in the ghetto. Before us, the window of a delicatessen store displays its wares: hanging racks of smoked meat, and fat, pink sausages dangle from the ceiling, long, thin salamis suspended like light fixtures sway as the door is opened or closed, thick cylinders of bologna lie in the showcase emitting aromas more fragrant than the most exotic perfumes. Two German officers come out with steaming sandwiches, thin slices of moist, pink meat are hanging over the edges of fresh white rolls. They are laughing and conversing loudly. We watch them playfully nudging each other, horsing around playfully, acting like young boys.

My mouth is watering. I loved deli even before I experienced hunger. The Germans seem happy, oblivious to the suffering around them. They take several bites and carelessly toss the uneaten remains into a trash can. I am immobilized, fascinated by the discarded food. Bubbi scrambles up the can and joyfully retrieves the uneaten sandwiches; a meal for us, big red sausages on fresh white rolls: still warm. Nothing has ever tasted better.

The afternoon sun slowly sinks behind the cold clouds. Evening comes quickly and with it more cold icy air. In spite of our new jackets our teeth are chattering. We walk around in the harsh descending night looking for lodging, a place to lie down and maybe feel the gentle caress of warmth. Hotels are out of the question, all are filled with soldiers from the German army. The streets are full of German officers boisterous and noisy, shoving each other, laughing at each other's antics, enjoying the freedom of living in an occupied country. I remember the soldiers from Vienna, the Nazis marching in unison, somber and dignified in their stiff new uniforms. I make no connection between these soldiers here in Krakow and the marching SS in Vienna. I don't realize that these happy, free going soldiers are in any way related to the horrors of the ghetto, the suffering and pain of the Jews. I am glad to see the soldiers again. They are familiar to me and I salute them, raising my arm. "Heil Hitler," I say. They smile warmly at me, probably thinking that my blond mother is the wife of some high ranking officer.

We board a tram. When we are ready to get off, *mutti* takes us by the hand and prepares to disembark. A courteous German soldier pops out of his seat and offers his arm helping her get off the trolley. He lifts Bubbi and me off the tram as if we weigh nothing and bows his head courteously to my mother. This, I think, is how a German gentleman behaves.

"*Gruss Gott, und danke schon.*" I thank him and curtsy as all well-bred girls are taught to do.

He turns to my Mutti, "*Wie schon, sie spricht Deutch* how beautifully she speaks German," he tells her, smiling happily at us.

I quickly add in German, "Yes, right now I can speak German and Polish, but soon we are going to America, where I'll see my Papa and learn to speak English."

The soldier laughs heartily.

"The fantasy of a child," he exclaims to my mother. She smiles and thanks him in German.

Mutti knocks on many doors before finding a Polish woman willing to take in boarders in exchange for a gold necklace my mother has taken with her from Wieliczka. We spend a few nights with her. She is kind and even brings us hot soup. But my mother is afraid. She doesn't trust any Poles, even the ones who are kind. She won't spend more than a week with her. If the woman is sincere, then we will be putting her into jeopardy. If not, then she will betray us. We leave, thanking the woman for her hospitality. *Mutti* takes us to a jewelry store, digs into her pocket and produces a gold bracelet with some colorful stones in it. "I know how much this bracelet is worth," she tells the jeweler. "I paid two hundred *zlotys* for it only one year ago."

He examines it through a funny little glass placed close up to his eye. "It is beautiful, the stones are real, and I can tell you that if you paid only two hundred *zlotys* you got a bargain. But these are hard times and I don't have many customers. Hungry people don't have buy jewelry, even at bargain prices I'll be lucky if I can sell this bracelet to some Nazi who wants to buy his sweetheart a present. I won't get more than a hundred *zlotys* for it, if I'm lucky." He buys it for sixty *zlotys*. My mother agrees to the price. She knows she can't hold out for what the bracelet is worth. She confides in me, as though I am a grown up: "This bracelet is only good for getting us what we need to stay alive, for one day at a time." She quickly adds. "It doesn't protect us from the cold and it doesn't put food in our stomachs, but it will help us acquire both." I listen carefully. Her tone toward me has changed from playful mother to one adult confiding to another. I nod my head. I understand even though I am only six years old.

We approach another house and this time my mother offers the woman three *zlotys* for a room for one night. At first the woman argues with her. She wants more. But my mother has some money now and she feels a bit more secure. She refuses to pay more than three *zlotys* and the woman grudgingly agrees.

The next morning, there is a loud banging on the door and again a police officer flings it open. "I am here to inspect your papers. Please show them to me now!" He is arrogant, disdainful. He runs his red tongue over his lips, squares his shoulders and inhales deeply. Clearly he is enjoying his role. He plans to prolong the moment. His uniform has granted him power, status and he is going to make the most of it. Once again, *mutti* realizes we were betrayed by a landlady who is getting even with her for not giving her more money. *Mutti* looks the policeman squarely in the eye, assuming her full stature and acting confident, aware of her blond hair, blue-eyes and aristocratic beauty. She feels she has nothing left to lose.

"I have no papers now," she asserts with self-confidence. There is no point in acting scared "All my identity papers were taken away from me by your Polish officers and they were never returned to me as promised. Your police have them and the officer who promised to return them to me never showed up. Now I am stuck here with no identity," she adds, feigning anger in hope of diverting his attention.

"All they left me with is my father's birth certificate, and I doubt that it will be of any use to you, since it is written in English." She thrusts the birth certificate at him and the Polish officer scrutinizes it and sizes her up. He observes her dispassionately: her stance, her haughty arrogance. He is fully aware of the loathing and contempt she harbors for him.

He puts on a pair of glasses and tries to interpret the document she has just given him. "It's a birth certificate," she tells him. "It's my father's birth certificate. It is written in English because he was born in America."

The officer feels bested. It is hard for him to maintain his composure in the presence of my mother's apparent scorn. He tries to act as though this is nothing new for him, as if he has seen hundreds of American birth certificates. But his lack of experience is not lost on my mother. She recognizes an amateur when she sees one. "Come with me," he beckons to her, trying to regain his self-confidence. "I'm going to deliver you to the German authorities. Let the German devils deal with you. They'll know what to do." He looks at my mother, shrugs his shoulders and leads us out of the house.

We follow him while he flags down an open truck. I am trembling, whether it is with fear or with cold, or maybe both, I do not know. We climb up into the open truck. There are several other people on it, and stops are made along the way picking up additional passengers. An old man boards the truck protesting loudly in German that he is a diplomat. A gray fedora sits squarely on his head and he is wearing a long gray overcoat. I look at him trying to see if he looks familiar but he refuses to acknowledge me. I wonder if we are to be taken away as all the other people I have seen on trucks in the streets of Krakow. Bubbi and I huddle under the black coat *mutti* acquired in the ghetto. We are shivering even though we are wearing jackets. She protects us with her body. We have no idea of where we are going even though *mutti,* as always, reassures us by telling us that we are on our way to America. She knows we no longer believe her but she can't stop herself.

"Just one of the stops on the road to see your Papa," she says optimistically.

Years later after we have gotten to America, she will answer when I ask her why she never told us the truth; "Why frighten little children with the truth? You had enough to cope with. If a little lie was going to make you less fearful, why should I deny it? Deprive you a bit of hope?" she wisely asks, adding "besides it certainly wasn't going to harm you if you felt there would be a happy ending to this ordeal. Whatever was going to happen would happen, whether you were frightened for a long time or just for a moment."

CHAPTER 18

———— ❧ ————

THE TRUCK FINALLY stops in front of an imposing iron gate surrounded by a stone wall topped with barbed wire. I look up to see a bird fly over the horizon. A piercingly blue sky looks down indifferently on our little family. We have arrived at what I later learn is a huge prison, Montelupi, administered by the Gestapo. In addition to the Jews who are processed before being sent to Auschwitz and Birkenau, the prison also includes political prisoners, British and Soviet spies, priests and nuns, soldiers who have deserted the *Waffen,* SS, and liberal minded Polish professors from Jagiellonian University. All are subject to medieval torture which the Nazis practice without discrimination.

The Polish officer who brought us walks over to the Gestapo officer guarding the gate. He talks to him quietly and gives him a big envelope containing all kids of documents, including my grandfather's birth certificate. The hallway is filled with officers patrolling the corridors wearing helmets and carrying rifles, ready for battle. Their tall leather boots echo loudly on the bare tile floors. The atmosphere is tense. Because we lack of proper identification, we are placed in an empty room containing no furniture, not even a chair. It is a holding station for political prisoners and persons whose status has not yet been determined. The rooms are separated by stainless steel bars and tall gates that lock with jangling keys. Every sound is amplified, whether a slight cough or a gate banging shut. The overhead lights brightly reflect off the steel bars. I will later find out that Montelupi is an infamous prison known for torturing its detainees. Between 1940 and 1945, fifty thousand prisoners passed through its gates, most of them met their death there or in the concentrations camps they were dispatched to.

A tall Gestapo officer enters our waiting area. Suddenly the atmosphere grows tense. He looks at no one. He is scrutinizing some papers that he is holding. "Freda Schmelkes?" his voice echoes off the walls of the bare room. We are singled to come out and follow him, leaving all the others behind, waiting in the small room.

He ushers us into a dark office, salutes the officer behind the desk, clicks his heels, nods his head and disappears. A German officer is seated at a large imposing desk. He motions with one hand for us to sit down opposite him never uttering a word or looking up from the paper before him. His green officer's cap rests on his massive desk with the eagle and swastika mounted above the visor, gleaming as though polished. He hunches over the birth certificate of my grandfather, holding it close to his face and squinting at it. His glasses are resting close to the end of his pinched nostrils and he peers above them. He pays no attention to us. He studies the paper, concentrating, as he chews his lower lip. He looks at the front, turns it over and then holds it up to the light. I notice that his fingernails are neatly trimmed and polished, just like a lady's. Finally he puts the paper down on the green blotter in front and without looking up he addresses my mother in hesitant, schoolboy English.

"And, …um, how did you, ahhh…, come into possession, um…., acquire this uh, birth certificate?" he asks in haltingly, mentally translating from the German to the English, pausing between words trying to retrieve enough of the foreign language to make himself understood.

She answers him in perfect German and she sits up tall in her chair. Whatever small advantage she has in the language department gives her courage. Besides, she has lost her fear. She has nothing left to lose. They have already taken everything from everyone. She doesn't expect to get any special treatment nor does she seek it. She takes a deep breath, has become another person. Instinctively she knows that it will go better for her if she commands respect rather than pity. They have no pity, she knows that well.

I clutch her black dress so hard that my nails make deep crescents in my palm long after I let go. She attempts to make eye contact with him, engage him in German conversation and force him to look her in the eye. She pulls her chair close to his desk, rests her elbow on its edge and cradles her chin in her palm, attempting to establish an air of informality, equality. He resists the temptation to look her way. He cannot afford to, he never looks at the victims. He is afraid that if he looks at her she might become a person rather than the vermin that all Jews are. Looking at them would establish an identity for them, which, in turn, could lead to compassion and he knows that will destroy his resolve and cost him this miserable job.

"It was in a family photo album," she tells him indifferently. "I don't know why I took it with me, perhaps as a souvenir to remember my father by."

He looks down at his blotter, concentrates on it as if it holds a secret message he must see. He must keep his eyes averted even as he struggles with the impulse to look at this woman, this American who speaks German better than many Germans he knows. He is determined to keep this encounter as simple as all the others, but it's no use. Her voice, something about her demeanor breaks his resolve and compels him to take a risk, look her in the face. He is moved by what he sees and suddenly feels. He didn't expect the rush of anticipation that always floods his inner core when he sees a beautiful woman. He takes note of her clothes, her poise, the way she tilts her head when she speaks to him, the way she twirls a strand of her hair around an index finger and the way she runs her tongue across her lips. He knows he must fight that familiar urge to make a conquest, impress her, arouse her interest and flirt with her. He wishes he had resisted the urge to look, doesn't know what to make of this woman, her cockiness, her low lidded blue eyes and her air of supreme confidence.

She knows the effect she has on him, is familiar with men who get flustered in her presence. Men who want favors she will never grant.

She knows how to make her beauty work for her. He also knows that he needs to maintain his edge, keep her in her place, make her frightened, but he is at a loss.

"Hmmm," he muses and in German, almost like he's talking to himself, "this certificate says your father was born in America, but your German sounds Austrian, Viennese, actually. Where are you from? Austria?" He doesn't wait for a response; doesn't want one. He is squirming inwardly not liking the direction this encounter is taking. She is nothing like the people who come into his office, cowering, compliant, some even hopeful. He wishes she was ugly, repulsive, and then he wouldn't have to battle this inner war that he will not win.

He hates his job. The old resentment slowly creeps into his body. He doesn't know what he is doing here, in this dungeon, waiting for the forlorn, forsaken, broken Jews to pass through his office. He is bored to the bones. He was a hero in the last war Germany fought, a winner of many medals, honors and rewards. Even though Germany lost the war, his achievements did not go unrecognized. He is a soldier, trained to fight on a battlefield, kill the enemy, capture territory, acquire land for his country, not to sit in a Polish prison trying to frighten the frightened, take hope from the hopeless, menace these undefended, the elderly, the hungry, the children, the lice infested dregs of society, some begging for mercy, others afraid to speak.

He doesn't understand what the Third Reich is doing. Well he understands, but he cannot make sense of it. Of what purpose is it to hunt down all these Jews and send them to death camps? He doesn't like the Jews. He finds them as repulsive and despicable as any other Nazi does. But why spend all this this time, money and manpower keeping them here in Europe? What's this obsession with the Jews? It's useless, he tells himself. This Nazi propaganda is destroying the very ideals it is trying to foster: a strong Germany, wealthy, powerful incorruptible. Instead they are wasting their time rounding up the frightened Jews, Gypsies and cripples and incarcerating them in ghettos or sending them to gas chambers.

Who is to say that the typhoid, dysentery, cholera, typhus, diphtheria, hepatitis and all sorts of ailments can are contained within the ghetto walls can't spread to the outside? He hates the Jews, everyone does, but there must be a more rational way for his countrymen to behave. One escaped Jew walking through the city could conceivably infect an entire population. For Heaven's sake stop wasting all this time on them. Send them to the jungles of Africa, to Australia -anywhere. By all means get rid of them, but why should Germany have to bear all the expense and responsibility for ridding Europe of this malignant dirt.

He continues ruminating. He has lost faith in the *Fuhrer*. In his opinion these Jews are not the enemy. The Nazi party should be concentrating its energy on Russia not on some decrepit people. They're not dangerous, have no weapons, and aren't planning to overthrow the government, have not done anything to undermine the Third Reich. Yet Hitler and his Gestapo, the SS and Hitler's advisors don't see beyond their noses.

He retraces the events that brought him here; they are laughable. A sixteen year old adolescent, rebels against his hypocrite of a father and this is where he ends up. His father, the pastor of a small Lutheran church in southwestern Germany preaches love and peace on Sunday mornings, comes home, drinks all afternoon and beats the hell out of his son at night. Young Georg shows his father. He enlists in the German army in 1917 just as the war is winding down. He is a daredevil, almost single handedly he manages to capture a small village outside of Namu, France He brings the citizens to their knees and wins decorations and medals for heroism from his superiors but no recognition or admiration from his father. His father disowns him. He has unmasked him. By joining the army he has defied his father's posturing and preaching. He is not welcome in his house by the preacher and his cowering wife, Georg's mother who feels she has to take sides in this patriarchal drama. If his father had so much as lifted a finger to assault him Georg would show him a thing or two that he learned as a soldier. What reward does he finally win with his heroism in this new war, a desk and a chair in Montelupi Prison dispensing fear and panic to a pack of mice?

He feels the white sword of anger insert itself between his ribs, sending waves of resentment along every nerve in his body, consuming him. He is furious at his at his commanding officer for putting him in this position, this young snot nose of twenty-something with a university education but no battle experience. He despises the system for demeaning his stature and outwardly disrespecting his achievements, furious at the Third Reich that turned his career as a soldier into a terrorist whose mission it is to kill the undefended. He is out of breath and feeling the familiar wave of nausea sweep over him.

He is still young and strong, capable of fighting the real enemy. However, here, in Montelupi he has been stripped of his drive, his thirst for blood, his pride and sense of honor. The Germans are swatting at flies while the Russian lions are massing at the borders getting ready for the kill. But the Nazis are so wrapped up in their ridiculous agenda that they don't see what is really happening around them. All they seem to want to do is follow orders; orders issued by a demented demagogue. Georg Schmidt is a trained strategist, can see all the scenarios at play. But no one is interested in his expertise and knowhow. All they have to do is to look over their shoulders and see the real enemy gaining on them. Anyway, no one is interested in his opinion.

He bemoans his fate. This is the reward the Nazis give to war heroes. Make them useless eunuchs, force them to interview people whose fates are already decided, inflict suffering and send the broken ones to certain death and the able-bodied to slave labor camps. He has lost all desire to enforce the rules that have been entrusted to him, he has lost all interest in the direction that the war is taking and worst of all, and he has lost the spirit that made him such an excellent soldier.

He steals one more glance at the woman in front of him. Can she really be a Jewess? She has none of the desperation that the others have. He doesn't smell the stench of fear that envelops them. He sees and recognizes composure, an attitude that is unsettling him. She reminds him of his sister Annalisa. Same age, same arrogance, Annalisa, with her two children about the same age as these two. She is a ferocious tigress of a mother when it comes to protecting her cubs. Long ago she swore that she would never sit idly and watch anyone, including her husband abuse her children the way her mother had.

Bah, he had better stop thinking while he still has a shred of dignity left. He checks his watch, yawns, stretches, shakes his head to rouse himself. It is almost 5:30 and he's had enough. He doesn't want to invite the demons to parade through his sleep tonight. He is ready to take his young Polish *panienka* to dinner, enjoy some wine, have some fun and forget the pathetic people trudging through his office. He looks at the certificate once more, blows his nose and beckons the waiting guard.

"Take them to room 22. And, oh yes. Here is your father's birth certificate," he leans over his desk and returns the document to my mother, lightly, almost as if by accident he brushes her cool fingers "You might need it in the future." He stands up, places the officer's cap on this head and adjusts his uniform. We have been dismissed.

We follow a guard through several corridors separated from each other by heavy clanging gates. Each gate is unlocked and bangs shut behind us with finality and menace. Finally, he opens one of the doors and we enter a large room, crowded with women and children. Bubbi and I stand at the entranceway holding on tightly to my mother's hands while the lock behind us slides smoothly into its resting place. We look around our strange new quarters.

Some of the women are sitting at a long narrow table others have brought chairs over to the window where they sit and talk to one another. No one looks up when we enter. No one even approaches us. We will have no friends here. My mother looks around the room. She takes a deep breath and walks over to one of the women. They talk briefly before she returns to us. "Montelupi is just a stopping off place. We won't be here long." I nod my head knowingly. Again, she is talking to me as an adult and not a child. "Apparently, no one stays here very long," she tells me. Still, we are scared. We are surrounded by strangers, and no one makes a move towards us.

We quickly learn the routine of the prison. Everyone sleeps on mats on the floor. In the morning the mats are picked up and stacked against a wall. A long table is brought in and stays in place until it is time to put the mats on the floor again and go to sleep.

At that table, we eat breakfast which consists of black coffee and a saccharine tablet served in a chipped enameled bowl. The only other meal is served in midafternoon when we receive the same bowl, only this time it is filled with sloppy, unrecognizable, slippery, greasy pieces of discarded fat. It is called *Eintopf,* "one pot." It consists of every piece of garbage that no one else will eat, heated up and served to us. Because I am so desperately hungry I put it in my mouth and try to chew. I can't swallow. I gag and choke before spitting it out.

Other amenities in Montelupi include a closet containing one sink with a slow leaking faucet, where all the women and their children wash up as best they can with the cold rusty water. Sometimes one manages to rinse out a pair of socks or underwear.

The first time I need to use the bathroom, I ask one of the women where it is. She takes me over to the closet and points to an enormous garbage can. "This is it," she tells me nonchalantly. I gasp. It is tall and reaches my waist. "How do I climb up? What if I fall in?" I ask, seeing myself floating on top of the excrement. "Oh, you'll get used to it," she tells me. "Everyone hates it at first, but you get used to it." I peer inside the disgusting garbage can. I weigh the options. I can't bring myself to attempt to climb up the side of the can, but I am desperate. I run for my mother. She picks me up and holds me over the can. Still scared of landing inside, I grab onto her arms tightly. I am repulsed by the smell and use the can as seldom as possible. I try to stop going to the bathroom all together and only use it to pee. Several times a day the can is emptied by the women, who take turns with this unpleasant task. Emptying it does little to alleviate the stench and sight of it.

To supplement our daily food, the Red Cross occasionally sends burlap bags of onions to be distributed to each of the inmates. We look forward to receiving them. We peel them, sprinkle left over saccharine tablets which we've ground down to a powder on them and eat them like apples. Strangely enough, they begin to taste good, almost like apples. We elect officers, people from our ranks to be spokespersons, and things are run in an orderly manner. The Gestapo officers inspect our quarters each morning. They bark orders in loud, threatening tones. *"Achtung, achtung,"* they demands angrily," how many prisoners, how many children, what are their origins?" The thundering voice and terrifying demeanor makes goose bumps crawl up my arms. Our room captain, a German speaking prisoner with short hair and a quiet, clear voice answers in German. " *Zimmer tzwei und twatznig, funfzehn Amerikaner, funf und twatzig Englender, neun kinder und ein samlung von andere Lande."* Room twenty-two, fifteen Americans, twenty-five British women, nine children, and a collection of other nationalities." We all spring to attention and stand ramrod straight in front of our mats, not daring to move. All are frightened as the Germens take a head count, click their boots, take two military quarter turns and stiff as an iron rod exits the room. The women breathe a sigh of relief.

With *mutti* in the same quarters, I feel sheltered and protected. I know exactly where she is. She is not allowed out of there, so she cannot leave us alone. For the first time in a long time I do not have to wait for her return. For me, it is a huge improvement over the long waiting periods I had to endure in Wieliczka and the ghetto and I decide that Montelupi is a good place to be in.

Several days after our arrival in Montelupi a girl my age and her mother join us. Monica has short black hair and beautiful blue eyes. On her first evening with us, Monica's mother announces that Monica will entertain us. Her mother puts rouge circles on her cheeks and Monica is encouraged to sing her repertoire of songs. She sings a few songs; one in French the other in English. No one seems to be impressed by Monica's talents except her mother who encourages her to sing "one more song." All the kids here think Monica is a big show off and we all walk around imitating her pretending to be singing in foreign languages. Nothing could have made her less popular than what is about to happen.

Amazingly huge favors are bestowed on some of the prisoners, Monica and her mother in particular. Chicken, grapes, salad, almond cookies and other delicacies from the outside arrive with china plates, linen napkins and silverware. Monica and her mother eat their meals on the window sill away from the rest of us, never sharing a morsel, while the rest of us choke down our slop.

The other kids and I stand around watching them eat, despising Monica for her greed and bounty, never sharing one morsel of food, to say nothing of her showing off. Our gazes never stray from their food and we never miss an opportunity to tease her. "How were your grapes today, Monica? Were they fresh and tasty, or were they a bit on the sour side?" Monica looks away. She doesn't give us so much as a glance. I later wonder if the chicken, the linens and the silverware were worth the taunting we kids inflicted upon her over our next several years in captivity.

One morning, after we put away our sleeping mats, three Gestapo officers march into our room, stiff as lead soldiers. We spring to attention expecting a head count and prepared for a catastrophe. They are carrying briefcases and papers, not a good sign.

"Take out your identifications, passports, whatever papers you have," they bark, "and line up against the wall please." Panic ensues. Will this be a prelude to our disappearance? No one knows for sure but everyone knows that it won't be good. The grown-ups as well as the children are terrified. We've all heard stories of people who disappeared and were never heard from again.

We are ordered to get in line, many of the women praying and some of them crying and trembling; all except my mother. She is standing calmly, examining a loose thread on her sleeve. In the coming years, she will recall how she had a dream the night before the Gestapo appeared in which my grandmother wearing her old green sweater with white angora trim around the collar had come to her and spoken.

"Stand tall," she told my mother. "Do not be afraid. Stand tall and act arrogant. Look everyone directly in the eye and use whatever charm you have. Remember, you are young, you are beautiful, you are smart and you are rich."

That day, even as the Gestapo prowl the room, growling at the frightened women, the dream is stunningly vivid in my mother's mind, and when it's her turn to present her papers, she stands her full height and makes direct eye contact with a young, pink cheeked officer. He holds the fake birth certificate, pretending to be studying it, but I can see he's really looking at *mutti*, sizing her up; her legs, her hair, her poise, the tilt of her head.

She smiles at him and raises one eyebrow flirtatiously. He returns her smile and winks. She is only thirty-three years old and beautiful. They smile at each other, as if sharing a secret. He nods his head. He's made a decision. *"Alles ist im ordnung,"* he motions with his head, directing us to one of several lines.

CHAPTER 19

ONCE AGAIN WE are on an open truck with other passengers. Fellow emigrants from Montelupi including, Monica and her mother are with us. Two elderly drivers take turns at the wheel. The snow is pristine and the air feels pure and clean. Everything seems is so clear that it appears to be outlined with a thick black crayon. Elongated shadows lead or follow us depending on the time of day. The snow insulates all sounds, even our voices are muffled. There is a strange air of hope in our little group. Here outside the prison life seems bright and promising. If only for the moment calm settles and people speak, recalling the good lives they once led.

We have been traveling for days through a hushed, still landscape. "*Mutti*, where are we going?" I ask my mother again and again, knowing well what her answer will be. "We are going to America to be with your Papa." I don't believe it, but somehow feel reassured when she repeats the same answer to the same question. It's almost a game.

I persist. "But where are we now?"

"On our way to America, but first we have to make a few stops."

Darkness drops suddenly with no hint of twilight and even though there is no wind, the air turns frigid. Sleep overtakes us, covers our bodies as soon as it gets dark. We huddle together, close to each other to conserve every bit of warmth we can generate. When I awaken I wiggle my fingers to make sure they are still all there. They are always cold. I don't remember ever being warm. The drivers change places every time we come to a village. Our little transport attracts lots of attention: old men, young women, children and a few dogs line the roads of the villages we pass through. We wave to them and they wave back to us and smile. These towns have very little in the way of diversion and whenever a vehicle passes through they run out of their houses to stare and wave. Petrol is scarce and no one is going anywhere. A truck coming through the town is a notable event. Often when we pass through a village we stop and one of the drivers jumps off the truck and returns with some food, bread, a bottle of water, turnips, potatoes and whatever else can be scrounged from the villagers. We take a bite and a swallow and pass it on to the others.

Several times a day we stop along the way and many of us get off. We stretch our legs. We paint the fresh snow yellow with splotches of urine, or slink off among some trees, relieving ourselves in the cold. The virgin snow is a welcome change from the loathsome cans of Montelupi. No one on the truck has any feeling of shame or embarrassment. We do what we have to do. The trip is monotonous but in a way reassuring. I find myself wishing it would never end. The falling snowflakes drift like butterflies floating to the waiting earth. So quiet is the air around us that at times people are reluctant to disturb the silence by talking.

It feels as though our journey will go on forever: the eternal voyage. It is comforting. Time is standing still. We are no longer running from the unknown. We are being driven through friendly villages by nice old men. These drivers tell us that they had been imprisoned by the British during the First World War and they remember how well they were treated. Although they are now working for the Gestapo, they are polite and kind to us.

Early one morning, just as the sun unfurls a pink gauze curtain across the sky announcing her arrival, four large buildings appear behind a gated wall. Our convoy arrives on a fairy tale set, complete with castles and towers. Somewhere in the distance we hear the chime of church bells. I count seven gongs. We get off the truck and stretch. Nothing is moving. No birds are chirping to complain of our intrusion, no icicles are melting from the branches, no leaf is stirring. The huge evergreen trees, standing like snow covered giants, their arms, although weighted down with heavy blankets of snow extend toward the sky. The whole world is sleeping. It is an illustration from one of my fairy tale books.

We stand outside the truck hovering in the magical landscape. Suddenly, the gates open to a flurry of activity. German officers greet the drivers. They shake hands, talk to each other, check some papers, and count us.

Several nuns come out like a flurry of penguins to greet us. They tell us to follow them. Our contingent of women and children is taken to communal baths. We are told to undress and, to my delight, take long hot baths. It is part of the delousing process. The steam and hot water thaw my freezing fingertips, and toes. I discover parts of my body that have been numb ever since I can remember. My body comes alive and defrosts. The seemingly endless supply of clean hot water and strong smelling soap make for an unforgettable bath. It warms my very soul and makes me feel whole again, warmly welcomed to my new home!

CHAPTER 20

THE CONVENT AT Liebenau was and still is an operating mental health facility, known as "The Asylum." It is located in a German town not far from the Swiss border and consists of four buildings, The Clara House, Josef House, Cathedral and *Der Schloss,* the palace. By 1940, several hundred agitated and violent patients were gassed in order to make room for the British women and children trapped in Europe when Germany invaded Great Britain. The American prisoners of war do not join them until the U.S. enters the conflict. The remaining patients are for the most part, docile, compliant and often mentally challenged. The POWs are supervised by the Swiss who visit periodically to make certain that all the rules of the Geneva Convention are observed. It is home to 600 prisoners of war, all women and children. Boys are permitted to stay in the camp with their mothers until they reach the age of fourteen at which time they are sent to a men's internment camp. By some miracle of fate we, Austrian-Polish Jews, have ended up in an American and British POW camp, all at the whimsy of one Gestapo officer who was smitten by my mother's beauty and a fake birth certificate. Our lives are spared. The birth certificate automatically, though false, makes my mother, an American citizen, thereby entitling her to POW status. We are not persecuted for being Jewish, but we are a minority compared to the British and American POWs and the mental patients whom the sisters of the convent still care for.

Miss Crew, a brisk British woman is in charge of all the children in the camp. She is thin, sharp-featured, with rosy pink skin and thick black eyebrows which meet over her nose, framing piercing blue eyes which seem to be able to look into your heart. Her lips are narrow and barely move when she speaks, but her word is law and her manner is brusque. She hardly ever smiles and scolds us over silly for little things, like using a sleeve for a handkerchief.

Before she was captured, Miss Crew, a British governess, worked for Polish royalty, the Potowskis and the Radziwills. Her job was to teach their children proper English and good manners. She lets us know that we, common children, are a major step down for her and she reminds us constantly how unlike those well behaved children we are. All of us are scared of Miss Crew.

She holds our fate in her hands, telling us what to wear and how to speak. She can see whether or not we've brushed our teeth and washed our faces just by looking at us. But worst of all, she makes us go out in all kinds of weather. No matter how cold it is outside, when Miss Crew is in charge she enforces her rule that "children must have fresh air in order to survive." And if that isn't enough, she won't permit us to wear warm clothes. I wear short skirts and light jackets on the coldest after-noons. I come inside, teeth chattering, fingers stiff, thighs red, com-plaining. Miss Crew's passion cannot be penetrated. She would prefer for us to freeze rather than risk the possibility of becoming overheated. "Becoming overheated," she says authoritatively, "is inviting all sorts of diseases and germs to attack our bodies. We need to keep mov-ing around outdoors to stimulate our circulation and keep ourselves healthy." She tells us this, although she hardly ever goes out in the cold. I wonder how those royal children managed to survive in the freezing cold of a Polish winter.

All the children sleep in the Clara House, in what is "the nursery." At night Miss Crew sits in a corner of the nursery, near the black-shaded window, knitting in the dark, not leaving until she is sure everyone is sleeping. We hear her needles clicking rhythmically. She is knitting a blue jumper which she will rip as soon as she finishes it only to start another one using the same wool.

One of the children pretends to be snoring, making the rest of us laugh.

"Stop that at once," Miss Crew hisses angrily.

We try to stay quiet, but we can't stop laughing. Every now and then another brave soul snores, and soon half the kids are snoring and the other half are laughing. Miss Crew is furious. For security reasons, lights may not be turned on after dark, not even by Miss Crew. She walks from bed to bed trying to catch the culprits. She stubs her toe on the edge of a chair and quietly curses, "Darn it!" She is determined to figure out who the snorers are. The minute she comes near one of us, we feign sleep. The room is dark and noisy and Miss Crew is furious. She is going to punish us all.

"Very well, then," she says, "since you are all misbehaving and not sleeping, you may as well stay up all night long." And with that she pulls off all our blankets and opens the tall windows to the blasting gusts of cold air. She is determined that none of us will be allowed to sleep as long as some of us are misbehaving. We curl up to stay as warm as possible and the noise subsides gradually. Before long the only sound is the even breathing of fourteen sleeping children. She is able to keep us from snoring and laughing, but she cannot take away the pleasure, the joy and the fun we have by just being children.

The food, prepared by the nuns, tastes good and is, for the most part nutritious. We are fed whatever the patients and the sisters eat. The vegetables grown in the camp gardens are fresh in the summer and canned for the winter. Eggs are only served once a year, on Easter. When we get meat, it is usually inedible: tough, stringy, fatty, not anything I am able to swallow. There is plenty of bread and potatoes and we never have to go hungry. We also receive generous supplements from the American Red Cross.

The packages are meant for the soldiers on the front and sent to us because we are American POWs. We each receive a parcel every month containing cans of Spam, condensed milk, coffee, cigarettes, warm socks, playing cards, tiny chess sets, shaving kits, toothbrushes and toothpaste. We eat the Spam and enjoy teaspoons of the sweet condensed milk. We trade the coffee and cigarettes for luxuries. Cigarettes are like money.

We keep the cards and small chess sets with tiny holes on the board that hold the chess pieces. The shaving kits are exchanged for special favors from the guards: a newspaper, magazine, or a fountain pen. The cigarettes are the most valuable items in the packages. They will buy us anything we want or need. Packages of Old Gold, Chesterfields and Lucky Strikes are exchanged daily for luxuries. Because our family consists of three people we receive three packages. Since the packages are identical and each contains two cartons of cigarettes, we are especially lucky because my mother has so much to barter with.

Every internee is supplied with one aerogram per month; letters to send to relatives or friends outside the camp. Again luck strikes us. Because Bubbi and I each get an aerogram of our own my mother is able to send out three letters a month. She writes to my father, sews several photos of us onto the inside of the aerogram sheet and tells him that we are still alive, and doing very well in a protected internment camp. The first letter he receives fills him with boundless hope and joy. The unexpected letter telling him of our safety fills him with hope and renewed energy he has not experienced in years. He quickly sends us huge packages full of treats we never dreamed of. He's making good money, he writes to my mother. He works as a cutter in a leather factory making jackets for pilots and other officers. The pay is higher than anything he earned in Vienna and he has been able to set aside money for our arrival.

He sends packages as often as possible and they are generously filled with necessities as well as luxuries: pajamas, snowsuits, underwear, socks, colorful striped polo shirts, dresses, trousers, games, books, candy bars, sweaters, shoes, combs and brushes, paper dolls with fabulous wardrobes, coloring books and crayons. When a package arrives for us, everyone in my mother's room gathers around exclaiming over our good fortune. Suddenly we are rich! My mother knows how to share. She gives some things to her friends and roommates, but Miss Crew takes over Bubbi's and my windfall immediately. She appropriates all of our new, "American" clothing and distributes it to other children.

"We have to share," she tells everyone not bothering to tell them who is doing the sharing. "This is war and we cannot afford to be greedy." Before long, all the children in the camp are wearing the striped polo shirts and socks that my father sent to us. One of my snowsuits goes to Monica, the chicken- eater from Montelupi. Monica never acknowledges my unintended generosity. As far as she's concerned, the snowsuit is a gift from Miss Crew. Now I resent Miss Crew almost as much as Monica.

When we are away from Miss Crew's scrutiny we do what children all over the world have been doing since time immemorial. We run around outdoors, play hopscotch, hide and seek, jump rope and throw snowball at each other. We talk to and play with the patients, whom we call "the loonies." Many of them are friendly and childlike. They join us in our games. Most of them are allowed to roam freely around the camp when they aren't working in the kitchen or tending the gardens. I am fascinated by them and watch as they walk around the garden whispering, arguing, gesticulating, and nodding their heads to unseen companions. One old fellow roams around the camp cursing and shouting at the kids. We know he's harmless so we delight in his behavior. He can't stop yelling out bad words, and he enjoys the attentive, encouraging audience we make.

But not all the loonies are always harmless and naive. Luther, a gaunt, dark patient, unshaven, silently menacing who stalks around the camp has suddenly become aggressive. He is threatening to kill Gunther, one of the other inmates because he claims he's heard him talking to the devil, making plans to kill him. He tells the sisters that Gunther has been poisoning his food and stealing his ideas right out of his head. Luther is spitting and flailing his arms, punching the air around him. "As soon as I get him, as soon as I get his head in my grip he will be dead, pfft, just like that. Soon as I get him…"

"Calm down, Luther," the gentle Sister Hortense tries to talk to him. "Take a deep breath. You know you do not mean what you are saying. Gunther is your good friend. He does not try to harm you"

"Oh, is that so, sister? Is that why I hear him talking to Satan every night. He doesn't know, but I can hear everything they say. As soon as I fall asleep they plan to stick the knife in my throat. I hear them talking and laughing at me. "

"You must stop," Sister Hortense says softly, trying to reassure him. She is a tiny woman, with a ruddy complexion and light eyebrows. She is not afraid of the raging Luther. "Gunther is your friend. He would never harm you."

Luther ignores her. "I've got to get him first, otherwise he and his devil friends are going to kidnap me and take me to hell, to burn eternally. I heard him making plans." He is ranting and kicking the sisters who surround him.

Sister Hortense tries again to soothe him. She has a gentle, calming voice, even though Luther is thrashing about and trying to bite her. "Shhh, Luther, no one is going to hurt you while you are here."

He grabs the sleeves of her habit and starts shaking her. "Shut up, Sister, or I'll be coming for you at night with my knife," he shouts at her, "and I'll cut your heart out."

We watch, awestruck, mesmerized and scared, as he throws himself around uncontrollably. Several nuns run out of the cloister with long strips of knotted sheets. They attempt to immobilize him by dancing around him and trying to wrap his body in the sheets, like a mummy. But it becomes impossible for the nuns to restrain him, so one of the sisters runs to the guardhouse at the entrance of the camp. She returns with two German guards who grab Luther by his armpits, under his shoulders and by his feet and drag him off. This is a routine occurrence and we know that Luther will end up in one of the two cells reserved for such misbehavior; an isolated, escape proof cell, with thick, painted windows that no one can see through.

When that happens we can hear the desperate raging through the thick wall. Some of us try to peek in through a hole that has been scratched in the thick painted glass. Others taunt the unfortunate souls trapped in the isolation cells, threatening them with new demons and increasing their fury and fear. I don't join in the teasing. I'm scared I might be caught by the loony when he is released from his cell.

"I'm going to get you. I'm going to tear your arms off your bodies. I'm going to kill you and rip your bloody hearts out," Luther screams and then whimpers. "Let me out, let me out. Oh please, let me out. I'll be good."

His agony launches my own catastrophic fantasies. I become desperately frightened that the mad Luther might escape and punish us for tormenting him. I picture him at night, climbing up the doorway, squeezing through the transom and choking me. He won't know that I am not one of their tormentors. "You made fun of me? You made fun of me? Here Here's what you get."

I am also fearful that if I talk to myself I am just one step away from madness myself. "Isn't that what the loonies do? Talk to themselves?" So I force myself to stop thinking, and try never ever plan or practice anything in my head. I'm rarely successful in quieting my mind and when I catch myself thinking, I am convinced that I'm going crazy myself. When we are not taunting the patients we entertain ourselves by playing store, school, house, and prison. Too many of us know about prison. We have been incarcerated and know what that is like. At more sane moments we put on shows for each other and the adults.

A spectacular production has been prepared for Easter. It is a musical comedy, written and directed by a professional actress who happens to be one of the internees, Miss Thompson from England. The main roles are to be played by grownups but the children are given parts of singing chickens and roosters. I have the glorious distinction of having a solo and being the only rabbit in the play. We rehearse daily, cavorting on the makeshift stage that is erected at the far end of a large hall. It is spring time and we are ready to shine.

The scenery, painted by a professional artist, consists of a red barn, with a real door that swings open and shut, surrounded by a large barnyard. The costumes are made by a real fashion designer. My costume is constructed from old terry cloth towels and pink flannel ears from someone's discarded pajamas. The chickens and roosters wear bonnets made of crepe paper, with wings attached to their arms over the striped polo shirts supplied unknowingly by my father. Six chickens and roosters enter the stage through the barn door and they stomp their chicken feet and dance while singing loudly, *"Run rabbit, run rabbit, run, run, run. Don't give the farmer his fun, fun, fun….."* I come on stage and sing my solo, the chickens and the roosters continue dancing while I jump up and down trying to scare them.

The farmer comes onstage and shoots me and a few of the chickens as well. We flop over while trying to stifle our giggles and he drags us off the stage to make his rabbit pie. The curtain comes down to the enthusiastic applause of everyone in the audience. I am thrilled with my performance and determined that I want to be an actress, singer and dancer. Everyone is invited to the show: the sisters, the internees, the loonies, even the camp commandant. He comes with one of his fellow officers and they watch the entire performance never once smiling.

CHAPTER 21

I WAKE UP early on weekday mornings. I want to be the first one ready for school. I wash up slowly and carefully, brush my hair back firmly, not allowing one wisp to escape the tight braids *mutti* has made for me the night before. School is my passion. I sit up straight in our one room, multi grade classroom. My hands are folded in front of me as if in prayer. I focus carefully on the teacher's face. I long for a notebook, a sharpened pencil and a backpack to carry my belongings. I want to be a real pupil with homework, text books covered with brown paper and a small assignment pad. Somewhere in my mind there's a picture of a school girl and I want to be her.

Our instructors are the British nuns and teachers imported and employed by exclusive private schools and wealthy households prior to the war. They were trapped in Germany and Poland when Great Britain was invaded. They are strict, but fair: rewarding the "good" and punishing the "bad." I feel safe in our little schoolroom where I know what is expected, can follow the rules and receive praise for work well done. This is the first time since I was three years old that my life is ruled by predictable, reasonable boundaries and rules that are easily followed. School supplies are sparse. Several English texts are brought to the camp by the teachers who could not bear to part with them. Paper is scarce and the only way we are going to learn anything is by rote, repetition and memorization. There are about twenty students from many countries; Holland, Greece, Italy, Belgium, Germany and Poland. Monica is in my class, wearing my clothes and treating me as if I don't exist. Although I try, there is no way I can capture her attention. I try shaming her by asking if she likes wearing my clothes. She looks at me and tosses her head away. I try being nice by offering her some of the books that Papa sent me. She doesn't even bother to refuse but totally ignores me.

Our lessons take place in the morning. After lunch, when the classroom is used by the older children, we are free to do as we please. I love going to school. The work is simple for me and I am eager to learn. I feel successful. I am a good student, receiving praise from Sister Leticia who often scolds the other children. She is a tough taskmaster and her praise makes me feel smart and competent. I learn to read and am quickly captivated by the heroes and heroines I meet in books. Books lead me to places I have only dreamed of. They fill me with hope and glimpses into other worlds. Oh, to live in Sherwood Forest, among Robin Hood and his men, or to be Heidi, living in the Alps with her beloved grandfather. I identify with my heroes, weep when they're saddened and rejoice when they succeed. These fictional people are so different from the characters who inhabit my world and the witches and ogres that live in my fairy tales.

No matter how often I heard the stories of the Grimm Brothers I was never convinced that the endings would come out happy. With each retelling I feared for the main characters. My experiences prepared me for the worst scenarios: Cinderella might not be rescued by Prince Charming; the seven dwarfs do not have to appear in Snow White's forest and what would have happened if the Prince never came to Sleeping Beauty's rescue? In my life, wishes didn't come true even though my mother kept our own fairy tale alive by telling us how happy we were all to be when we came to America.

The heroes in my new books are real. They don't depend on the whims of magical beings, frightening ogres or evil witches. The things that happen to them can happen to anyone, even to me. It is in this little classroom where I learn to read, that I come as close as possible to having wishes granted. Reading allows me to enjoy trips to safer lives and escape from the everyday dangers of my life. I will become a life- long reader.

CHAPTER 22

———— ✄ ————

IRONICALLY, NOW THAT it is safe to be Jewish, I desperately want to be Catholic, go to Mass with other children, take communion and line up for confession. One Sunday morning I stand at the heavy, ancient wooden door to the chapel where mass is taking place. I inhale the aroma of the incense and am transported to the cathedral in Krakow. I feel familiarity and comfort of the Catholic Church. I hear beautiful singing coming out of the chapel. It sounds like angels. I close my eyes and imagine what heaven must be like. Suddenly, a door swings open and the old priest comes out into the vestibule.

"What are you doing here, child?" he asks gently, smiling at me, his face broad as the shining sun, his blue eyes sparkling, twin ponds on a sunny morning.

"Oh, I don't know," I reply. "I wish I had a nice place to pray in."

"But you do," he holds his palms up to me in welcome. "Come right in and join us. Here, follow me," he offers me his warm, soft hand.

I recall the anti-Semitic girls in Poland who tormented me for being Jewish. I am certain that the priest wouldn't want me in his church if he knew I was Jewish.

"I can't," I protest. "I'm Jewish and your God doesn't want me in your church."

"Nonsense," he replies gently, "There is only one God and He loves all children. He loves you too. Come, come in with me."

Father Yosef –Kristus has been the priest here in Liebenau for over twenty-five years, long before it became a prisoner of war camp. He came as a young pastor and stayed on ministering to the souls of the mentally ill residents. He loves them: their innocence, their child-like wonder and the pleasure they take in the mass: true believers, simple, accepting, never questioning God's ways. Unfortunately their minds are often invaded by hidden demons and vicious spirits who take possession of their souls and make them perform ghastly deeds. Often it is only Father Josef-Kristus who can reach them, talk them though the nightmares that parade through their wakeful states. This was his calling and he feels blessed to be here, to accept it. Of course all that changed when Liebenau became a prisoner of war camp. First of all, many of his most difficult parishioners were taken away by the Nazi officers who now have charge of the camp, and have taken the very sick to gas chambers where they were executed in order to make room for the prisoners of war. He prays for these lost souls, both those cursed by illness and for the Gestapo as well who destroy people not for what they do but for who they are.

The British and Americans who now came to mass regularly are an entirely different population. They want more stimulating homilies, longer times in the confessional and discussions about the presence of God in such a Godless world. These demands are challenging, keeping him sharp and alert. The new inmates argue with him, ask unanswerable questions but everyone admires and respects his humility and dedication.

"Come in my child," he opens the door to the chapel

I feel warmly welcomed, but I must think it over. I have a strong urge to enter a house of prayer, especially a church, where I am familiar with the rituals I miss. The priest is an honorable, credible person and he is urging me to go into the chapel. I know that I want to go there but I am confused. On some level I feel it would be wrong for me to participate in a Catholic service. But I really want to enter, be part of that mystical ceremony. How could something that feels so right be wrong? I think my mother would be upset if she thought that I was entertaining such actions. But do I have to tell my mother? How would she ever find out? She, herself would never go into a church voluntarily. So, I could keep it a secret and not tell anyone. Wait a minute, I tell myself. How could she disapprove when she was the very person who took us into the church in the first place? Wasn't she the one to tell us to kneel at the cemetery?

The argument in my head isn't over. She only did that because it was dangerous to be Jewish. We had no choice before we went to the ghetto. It was, "Be Catholic or be taken away on one of those awful trucks." I struggle. I want so very much to do something I think is wrong. After lots of arguments with my conscience, I arrive at a compromise. I will attend, but only for the choir. The music coming from the church is overwhelmingly enticing. The voices of the children are so clear and pure, that I feel I have to go in.

I join the choir, am assigned to the soprano section and begin rehearsing for midnight Mass on Christmas Eve. Most of the carols are sung in German and English, with a few in Latin. I feel important. I want to shine, and I try to sing louder than all the other sopranos, hoping for a solo. But it doesn't happen. Little Peter Schoeffler, son of an important Nazi officer, captures all the solos. Peter is a boy soprano, probably my brother's age. His blond hair is parted on the side and carefully combed back. He is serious and never smiles. His attention is riveted on the conductor and the singing of the carols. His blue eyes never stray from the baton. He is called Bubbi, just like my own little brother. I marvel at his pure voice straining towards where the angels live.

The Schoeffler family consists of three children, Little Peter, his two older sisters, Uta and Hannelore, and their mother. Herr Schoeffler, or rather Officer Schoeffler is a high ranking general in the Nazi party. He rarely comes to visit his family. The Schoefflers are offered the protection of the POW camp because of his high status. The camp, of course, protected by the Geneva Convention and by international agreement is not subject to air raids or bombings by the allies. Uta, Hannelore and Peter don't play with the rest of the children. Whether they are instructed by their parents not to mix with the children of the prisoners or it is their own choice is not clear. Nevertheless, they never join us in our games, do not eat with us and do not go to school. Pete, however, had been encouraged to join the children's choir, and join he did!

He is so small that a special robe has to be made for him and he has a platform to stand on in order to be able to see the conductor. He is beyond envy, in a realm of his own. When little Peter sings the rest of us are breathless, waiting for a miracle to occur. I love him, his voice and modest demeanor. Sometimes he closes his eyes and sways gently to the music, completely enveloped by it. His voice rises right up to the arched ceilings of the church where a slight echo brings it back to us. For the rest of my life, every time I hear Gloria in Excelsis carol I see little Peter standing in the choir loft, looking up to the heavens, his blond bangs in his eyes, singing his heart out. Years later, when we are in America, I remind mother of Peter. "Did he become famous, is he an opera star?"

Mutti knows and doesn't hesitate to tell me. He, his two sisters and his Nazi parents were executed right in the gardens of Liebenau by the allies, as soon as the war was over.

I gasp in horror, "Why? Why was little Peter shot? What did he ever do to anyone but bring joy and pleasure?" I start crying, forlorn and outraged by what by what my mother has just told me. I question God outright, "is this world a better place without Peter?

My kind and sympathetic mother, becomes uncharacteristically cold and skeptical. "The Nazis shot many, many innocent children. The only difference between the Russians and the Nazis is that the Russians just shot everyone while the Nazis only killed the helpless, the innocent and the Jews. Don't waste your pity, don't waste tears on Peter. His father was a murderer. All your cousins were killed by people just like him for no reason other than being Jewish. Innocent people die during a war." She indicates that the discussion is over, that there will be no more said about little Peter and the deaths of his sisters and parents.

I can't believe what happened to my sweet, gentle mother. I will never bring the topic up again but I realize that the death of Peter brought home all the atrocities of the war. Peter personalized the war for me. Of course I knew all about the deaths and the concentration camps that gassed people, my people. But all of that didn't seem real to me. Peter was real. I stood next to him, heard his angelic voice, I watched him take a breath before reaching for the high notes. Now, he is gone, wiped off the planet, because he had the bad luck of being born to a Nazi officer and his German wife. His death made the war real for me.

CHAPTER 23

IT IS THE evening of December 24th. Outside the snow is deep and soft, reflecting the moonlight and the stars. Large evergreens stand like dignified giant sculptures of brave heroes. The branches, acting as multiple arms extended toward heaven are adorned with heavy sleeves of snow. It is Christmas Eve. The church is warm and smells of pine incense. Everyone is seated in the pews. The "loonies" and the prisoners are dressed in their best attire. *Mutti* does not comment on my participation. She can't bear to deprive me of this pleasure when so much has already been taken from my childhood. The air is still with anticipation. Everyone is waiting for something special. We children wearing the white gowns we were given stand straight and proud in the loft, out of sight, but certainly not out of earshot.

Hundreds of soft candles flicker, their long shadows hover like monks swaying in the sacred place. The conductor lifts her arms and we raise our voices in response. "*Stille Nacht, Heilige Nacht,* Silent Night." Gentle harmonies, shimmering candlelight and peaceful spirits send goose-bumps up and down my arms and spine. Little Peter's voice soars above our voices, suspended in the air like a silk cloud, rising and falling, gently. Everyone in the church inhales deeply. Some even close their eyes and travel to their own corridors of tranquility enjoying this moment of respite from the war that rages outside our camp. When we get to the last carol, "Hark the Herald Angels Sing," we hear ominous buzzing overhead and the sad wail of sirens warning all of us of an impending air raid. We continue singing, determined to ignore the whining alarm. Surely, we are convinced, nothing can happen to us here, in church, on Christmas Eve. The bombers don't hear our voices and the reverberations of the first bomb shake the church. It is an echo that is not merely heard but felt by each one of us.

As if by previous agreement we all stay put and continue singing, "God and sinner reconciled." It is a moment of peace that everyone wants to prolong. We linger over the last "amen," finish the carol, look at each other and quickly follow the route to the cellar of the cloister, while the bombs outside the camp shake the ground for miles around.

We sit on the whitewashed floor our backs leaning against the walls for support. We cover our ears trying to block out the thundering echoes of the shattering bombs, as the patriotic British applaud enthusiastically, hopeful that every blast will bring the Allies that much closer to a complete victory over Germany.

"Hip, hip hooray! Our boys are getting further and further into Germany," Mrs. Furman exclaims happily, her white hair like an angel's halo around her radiant face. It must be after two a.m., when the all-clear siren wails. In spite of the hour, the kids run outside and claim pieces of shrapnel still hot to the touch. Strands of thin aluminum streamers are scattered all over the snow covered fields. We are told that the streamers are used to confuse the enemy anti air craft. At night the Germans can't distinguish between planes and the silvery strips of paper used to confuse them. They waste their ammunition bombing their own country, shooting at mere metallic ribbons of foil. We stand in awe, gazing at the red horizon of the nearby munitions factory lighting up the pre-dawn sky.

We get up early on Christmas day to await the arrival of Father Christmas. I don't know what to expect, but I am excited. We are all gathered in the large reception room of the *Schloss,* drinking cider and eating ginger cookies when we hear a bell announcing his arrival. He is regal in his scarlet suit, red-cheeked, white bearded, his shoulders covered with melting snow. He is huffing and puffing.

"Merry Christmas boys and girls, merry Christmas," he call out in a familiar high-pitched voice, with a distinct British accent.

"Line up, line up children, presents for all the good little boys and girls. There is something here for every good child." We are breathless; fearful that perhaps we haven't been as good as we should have and therefore will not receive the coveted present. All the packages are brightly wrapped and tagged with names.

"Were you a good little girl?" Father Christmas asks me smiling behind his crooked beard that has been dislodged by nodding his head too often and too vigorously.

"I think so," I reply earnestly. He hands me a box.

No one is left out. Apparently we have all been good enough to be rewarded with a gift. Mine is a beautiful imitation leather sewing kit, complete with needles, a thimble and many colorful spools of thread. I am thrilled and plan a sewing project, perhaps a shirt for my brother. As we are admiring and comparing our gifts, the wail of sirens announces yet another air raid nearby. Once again, we all run down to the shelter in the cellar, clutching our gifts and feeling happy.

CHAPTER 24

—— ✿ ——

MY BROTHER IS now called "Michael." We are told that no one in Great Britain or the US has ever heard of a name like "Moschel". I dearly love my brother whether he is Michael, Bubbi or Moschel. When we were in Wieliczka, I practiced being his boss. He was my closest friend, companion, doll and favorite "toy." When we were at home I dressed him up and gave him directions on the roles he was to play. He was very agreeable, and I loved him for it. Once we began to run for our lives my feelings for him intensified. I felt protective towards him, responsible, always making sure that my mother or I was holding his hand. I feared that he might make a mistake and give away our religion so I tried to answer all the questions asked by others before he had a chance to respond.

Since coming to Liebenau, and being around other children, he attempts to pull away from me. He resists my interfering and prefers the company of boys his own age. This is hard on me. At first I am hurt and later angry with him. I don't stop looking out for him, especially because our mother has been ill since we arrived here and is in the infirmary much of the time. She tells me to make sure he wears a jacket in cold weather, takes baths, does his schoolwork and is getting enough to eat. I am in charge of him, but Michael doesn't listen to me and is hard to control. I'm only eight years old and already feel like a mother who can't get her child to obey. Moreover, when he does something mischievous, like grabbing an extra helping of dessert, or running into someone because he is not looking, some of the foolish grown- ups actually come up to complain to me, as if I could really discipline him.

"Michael is being terribly rude," Mrs. Knightbridge tattles. She is a short, fat woman with wire rimmed eyeglasses that look as though they are permanently imbedded in her fleshy nose. "He has terrible manners. I stopped him from running in the halls, and pointed out to him that not only was it dangerous to run indoors, but his shoelaces were untied, and he might trip," she continues with her diatribe, oblivious that she is talking to an eight year old. "Instead of thanking me, he ignored me and ran away. Imagine! He just ran off!" She is appalled by his rudeness. She peers at me, waiting for me to soothe her, to tell her that indeed, Michael is not only rude and disrespectful but to assure her that he will be properly disciplined. I don't know what I'm supposed to do. I listen carefully, not wanting to appear as rude as Michael, and then I promise to speak to him.

"Speak to him? Humph! He needs to be punished, not spoken to." She trudges off heavily. Now she is not only angry at Michael, but I feel she is angry at me also. I scold Michael as soon as I find him but he looks at me and laughs. "Mrs. Knightbridge is a busybody," he tells me. "Next time she comes crying to you about me tell her to mind her own business."

He runs away laughing with his friends and I feel guilty, responsible for his bad behavior.

He and the other boys are taken to the nearby town for haircuts. They come home with their heads shaved, laughing and pointing to each other is glee. My heart is broken for my little brother who now looks like the village idiot. I run to my mother crying that my little brother looks like one of the "loonies." But she assures me that Michael's hair will grow back, and besides he likes looking like all the other boys.

Because poor Michael can never get a pair of shoes that fit his wide foot he wears some old shoes, cast offs from some lady. The shoes are much too big for him and they constantly fall off his feet causing him to trip. He also lost the belt to his trousers. He shuffles around trying to keep the shoes on while holding on to his trousers to keep them from falling off. Some of the grown-ups tease him calling him Charlie

Chaplin. It breaks my heart, but he doesn't seem to mind. I take the teasing personally and end up with a lump in my throat trying to suppress my tears. I love my little brother and feel hurt when he is being teased.

Sometimes, Michael and the other boys and girls sneak out of the camp to a nearby farm. They climb over a fence to large a field and steal fruits and vegetables. They never invite me to come along even though I would love to join them. I know I would feel silly tagging along after my younger brother. When Michael and his friends return from their escapades, their pockets bulge with little carrots and juicy peaches. They are excited, eager to share their bounty with the others. He reminds me of Robin Hood and I wish I could be more like him: brave and daring. None of the grown-ups question him or the other children as to where the fruit is coming from and all enjoy eating it.

Eventually Michael and the others are caught. Wanda, one of the pirates has filled her pockets and her shirt with peaches and she drops some on her way back to the camp. The irate farmer has been on the lookout for the scavengers. He climbs over the fence and charges into the commandant's office. "Some of your ruffians have been stealing my fruit. What are we going to do about them? First they bomb us then they steal our food! The little thieves." He is furious.

By now it has become a police matter. While I am terrified that Michael will be taken to prison for his crime, I am relieved that I wasn't among the culprits. All the children in the camp are rounded up and forced to turn their pockets inside out. Whoever is found with peaches is remanded to stay indoors for two weeks and of course, must return the prized booty to the farmer. I never eat another peach until we arrive in the US, and somehow they never taste as sweet and delicious as the peaches in Liebenau.

CHAPTER 25

WE ARE PLAYING hide and seek, and I have found the perfect hiding place. No one will find me here at the bottom of a stairwell. I am holding my breath, waiting to hear, "come out, come out, wherever you are." But I don't hear it. What I do hear is the slap-slapping of sandals on the bare concrete floor. Only one person in the entire camp wears sandals during the winter, and that's one of the loonies, a man all the kids call *"Glatz Kopf,"* baldy. He is also the only one of the loonies I've dared to tease—always from a safe distance and surrounded by other kids. He never seems to pay attention to us so I join in the chorus: *"Glatz Kopf, glatz kopf* do you wax your head?"

Now he is coming down the stairs toward me, and I am alone and terrified. He approaches me slowly, treading softly, looking over his shoulder as if expecting someone to be following. He is whistling tunelessly between his teeth. I look behind me and to my sides. There is nothing between us, just a flat wall. I am trapped. I look up at the stairs and see the sandals, brown socks, striped trouser legs of *Glatz Kopf* steadfastly make their way down toward me. I try to flatten myself against the wall, become invisible. There is nowhere to run. I am trembling. I feel certain that he's going to hurt me. I know how these loonies get when they are angry. What do I do now? I think that perhaps, if treat him like a normal person, am polite and act friendly he will leave me alone.

"Gruss Gott," I address him, curtsying.

He looks at me through lash-less, unblinking eyelids with the lightest of blue eyes, scrutinizing the wall behind me, his thick hands hanging

113

limply at his sides. He shakes his head, looks dazed, before he focusses on me.

Abruptly, without warning he grabs me, holds me tightly and starts kissing me, first on my cheeks, then searching for my mouth. His rough, stubbled, beard scratches my face. My cheeks burn, I am mortified. The only people who have ever kissed me are people who love me or at least like me. Why is *Glatz Kopf* kissing me? How could he possibly love me? Why would he even like me after all the joking and teasing? I struggle against him, kick his stomach, but he only increases his grip on me. I am desperate to break free. Instinctively I know that what he's doing is wrong, that his kisses and embrace are not coming from a place of love. I'm afraid to scream, scared that if I scream, I will antagonize him. So I continue struggling. I dig my elbows into his chest, push him away as hard as I can but nothing will dislodge his grip and to my horror tries to pry my mouth open with his tongue. I start gagging, pounding on his chest, shoving him away with my knees. I clench my fists, hit him hard, and kick him in the shins. But he holds on tightly.

"*Ich liebe dich, liebchen*" he rasps into my ear. "I will never hurt you. Just let me kiss you and stop crying."

I can't get away from him. He is stronger than anyone I've ever met, and he will not let go. No matter how hard I try I can't get away from his sweaty grip.

"Oh please let me go," I plead. "I beg you. My mother is surely looking for me and so is everyone else. It's time for dinner. They'll punish me for being late." I start crying. "I'm sure everyone is looking for you as well," I tell him, "All the loonies eat before we do, and I know I'm late for my dinner."

He ignores my pleas and I continue struggling. He smells like cow manure and his beard is scraping my face raw. "Please, please, let me go. I must go to the bathroom," I try another ploy; "If you don't let me go I'm going to pee all over you."

He doesn't seem to care. "*Ya*, go ahead and pee, I don't mind."

I struggle, uselessly against him. I make good on my threat and feel the warm liquid streaming down my legs and onto his trousers. That doesn't seem to deter him. He is licking my face, my neck, I am nauseous. I start gagging. "I'm going to throw up, vomit. You will get your whole shirt messed up."

"*Ya, ya liebchen*, soon I let you go, just one more kiss." he drools all over my face. I start gagging and choking. "You first must promise me you'll come back later, after dinner, and then I let you go now."

"Yes, yes," I assure him. "I'll be here again right after dinner. Only, please let me go. I told my mother I'd be in her room and now I'm already late."

Suddenly, he releases me, backs up toward the stair, turns and starts climbing, slowly, heavily. Again he whistles tunelessly, hissing through his teeth. He looks back over his shoulder. I do not move. I wait for him to disappear. I feel the prickly burn of his whiskers on my face and his smell ingrained in my clothes and hair. I spit on the floor and try to erase him off me. I am frightened and confused. I can't believe all this happened to me and try desperately to wipe it out of my memory.

I let a few more minutes go by until I no longer hear his tread, and then I run for my life. I burst through the door into my mother's room. "*Glatz Kopf* kissed me all over my face and neck," I cry out to my mother while gasping for breath. I hate myself. I'm not the same. "Please," I beg, "Please, please, help me wash his smell off. I've got to get his smell off me. I'm scared he'll catch me again." I can't stop sobbing and trembling. "He kissed me and he tried to get my mouth open with his tongue! Oooh, I'm forever different, smelly, ugly, disgusting!" I cry hopelessly.

My mother looks at me in disbelief. She shakes her head, "no, that is not possible. Don't be silly. It's not true. *Glatz Kopf* never kissed you. You're imagining things again, always making things up. She tries to change the subject. "Such an imagination can be good for writing a book but it can also get you into trouble. If you make up stories, they are called lies, and it is wrong to lie."

I don't know how to respond, not sure I am hearing her correctly. Is she saying that I'm lying, that I made up such an awful story? What can she mean? "*Mutti*," I shout, "look at me! *Glatz Kopf* kissed me." I grab her shoulders and peer into her face. "I'm not the same anymore. Do you understand? *Glatz Kopf* spit all over me. I'm disgusting. I hate myself." I scream at her thinking that if I am loud enough I will convince her, make her believe me, make her respond to me, reassure me, tell me that I'm still who I always was. But she won't take me seriously and keeps insisting that it never happened. "You mustn't tell lies. You shouldn't pass your stories off as truth. *Glatz Kopf* did not kiss you. He couldn't have caught you. Why would you make up such stories about someone? Forget all this. It is nonsense, none of this happened. You're acting as if it's the end of the world."

She doesn't realize. It *is* the end of my world. "I can show you where it happened," I plead with her. It is so important that she believe me, trust me, and know me. I am desperate and quite suddenly realize that I am almost as outraged by my mother's disbelief as by *Glatz Kopf's* assault. "Why would I make up such a horrible story? Do you really think that I'm a liar? Please, *mutti*, don't you believe me at all?" She persists in her denial. She is convincing, adamantly refusing to accept what I am telling her. So confident is she in her denial that I start to doubt myself. Did it really happen? Could I possibly have made it up? It is unthinkable for me to question her convictions. I always pretend to believe her stories about my father, America and my happy life to come.

I try to force myself to forget it. I begin to put it out of my mind. It is safer accepting her version of denial than my own truth. I can't risk losing her love and I'm scared that if I keep pushing the truth she will pull away from me. She hands me a piece of cotton soaked in disinfectant. She looks upset and I feel like she is angry at me. She must think I'm lying. She takes my hand in hers and speaks softly, "let's not talk about this anymore. Nothing happened and no one needs to hear your stories."

But part of me can't let go of the *Glatz Kopf* episode. I know that it occurred but my mother won't accept that. It's not as if I made up a lie to get something or keep me out of trouble. I begin to wonder about my own worth. Am I not worthy of being comforted after such a harrowing experience? Am I not important enough to be believed? What does my mother think my imagination is like, that I would make up a story about *Glatz Kopf* kissing me? Doesn't she realize how awful I feel? Surely this is not a story I can invent and yet she keeps insisting that I have a lively imagination and that it never happened. In years to come the *Glatz Kopf* episode will haunt me, etched as it is in my feelings but fuzzy in the details. However, it became unforgettable because my mother refused to believe it; a hard pebble embedded itself in that secret place between my head and my heart. Her denial will cause me to always doubt myself, my observations and most of all, my feelings. It was my entrance into the state of denial, a place I will return to over and over again.

Years later, when I myself am a mother to a daughter, I ask her what her thinking was. Why did she refuse to acknowledge my pain? She looks at me, "It never happened," she replies shaking her head. "It never happened."

CHAPTER 26

———— ✥ ————

BLUE SMOKE IS rising out of the rear of the open truck standing at the gate. A crowd is gathered looking on expectantly at the three British Army nurses in their khaki uniforms with matching hats. We've all come to wave good-bye. The nurses look stunning, happy, excited, smiling and waving. They will be leaving the camp. Among them is Miss Elliot, the most beautiful person in the entire camp and my mother's nurse when she was in the "sick room." Everyone is pleased for them but we hate to see them leave. They are old friends and hard to part with. Many women are crying and not out of envy. We will miss them, especially Miss Elliot. Once, in March, an American Army airplane swooped down to the ground and dropped two dozen red roses for her birthday. There are rumors that her secret admirer is none other than Clark Gable. She never tells anyone who sent the roses. She simply smiles when questioned, her dimpled cheek like a twinkling star.

A short time later, I walk into the grown up quarters looking for my mother. The women are all talking at once, excited and not listening to each other. Some of them are waving typewritten letters.

Hela Gehorsam, a young woman in her twenties, with a head of wild, curly, red hair and a face sprinkled with freckles that look like raisins strewn across a white tablecloth is gesticulating, a letter in one hand and a piece of bread and butter in the other.

"I have to eat when I'm excited. I have to eat," she explains to the rest of the group. Her cheeks are flushed as she gobbles up her slice of bread and goes for another.

"What happened?"

"We're leaving. We're leaving and going to France to our husbands," she answers breathlessly.

"How come?" I ask.

"I don't ask questions, I just follow directions," she answers, giggling, "especially directions that are going to get me together with my husband."

Several others are going too. Exhilaration spreads like dandelion fluff among the lucky women. They are now part of a unique sisterhood, "the luckies." We watch them pack their belongings, as they trade warm woolen sweaters for delicate, silky finery in anticipation of their happy reunions.

When I ask my mother why we aren't joining them, she explains that they will be reunited at another camp in Vittel which is in occupied France; that their husbands are in a camp for men, just like Liebenau is for women. Since our papa is in America, we are not going to leave yet. I am sad and envious and feel deprived. I hear all kinds of wonderful things about Vittel.

"We are going to be living in a hotel in Vittel," says Celina Rozenweiss, a young woman with shiny red cheeks and dark curly hair. "It has tennis courts and a swimming pool. You can leave the camp any time you like as long as you're back at night. You can go to stores, theaters, even eat in a restaurant. They don't care what you do, as long as you're home by nine o'clock."

"In Vittel, the married couples share villas. You don't have to share a room with anyone but your husband. Sounds like heaven to me," Johanna Stillman, her nostrils flaring like an excited horse, adds in a hysterical high pitched voice. My mother pretends to be happy for them. She forces a smiles but I can see her biting her trembling lower lip. She wipes a tear from a corner of her eye with her sleeve. "I wish you so much happiness," she gushes. "You are going to be together with your husbands and I can't tell you how happy I am for you." I know she is lying to them. Since the *Glatz Kopf* incident I often catch her telling a lie. Why would she be happy that someone else is getting what she so desperately wants? I don't blame her for being envious, feeling left out, that is exactly how I amd feeling. She is trying hard to make them think she is happy for them.

"Why not us?" I whine. My mother wants to show by example that nice people act happy when others have good luck. But I'm not happy and I'm not going to act happy. It isn't fair, I tell myself. Why can't we be with our Papa? I ask myself watching the excited preparations with a heavy heart.

Two days later the "luckies" board a truck that will take them to their husbands and away from here. I stand at the gate waving an unenthusiastic farewell. I feel like Cinderella watching her mean stepsisters go off to the ball. They wave and blow kisses to us from behind the gate, while I wonder if our turn will ever come.

CHAPTER 27

WEEKS LATER I venture into the common sitting room. "Look at this," Mrs. Ducket says to a group of women who are sitting in chairs and around a table. They call themselves the "News Club." She is reading from a copy of the London Times. "'Leslie Hore-Belisha, former secretary of state for war, marries Cynthia Sophie Elliot, a decorated army nurse.' That's our Miss Elliot," she exclaims enthusiastically taking a long puff of her cigarette.

By now I have come to know most of the women who congregate in the room to listen to Mrs. Ducket, an authoritative, take- charge British woman who wears warm pullovers and tweed skirts year round. About once a week, one of the guards swaps an English newspaper for a pack of cigarettes. When that happens all the women rush in to hear her read the latest news.

"How could she have married such an old man?" Angela Raynor a tall, attractive, woman who wears incredibly short skirt asks. "He must be at least twenty years older than she is."

"Well," Mrs.Ducket says defensively, "he's not some bum off the street you know. He's been a member of Parliament, Minister of Transport to say nothing of being Secretary of State for War."

"But he's Jewish, isn't he?" says Mrs. Webster, scratching her practically bald head with her bony index finger. She sniffs the air several times as if smelling some strange odor.

"What does that have to do with it?" snaps Mrs. Korn. She is irate, her thin body is rigid with fury and her black eyes are on fire. I can't take my eyes off her. She is formidable when outraged. Two bright pink splotches darken pale, white cheeks. Her voice rises to a hysterical pitch, "He's good enough for the beautiful Cynthia Elliott, but to you he's just a Jew. Like all Jews are the same to you Cora Webster; slimy, undesirable creatures with a penchant for money. Tell me, Cora, is being Jewish a crime in England also, or just in continental Europe?" She raises her head, stares menacingly at Mrs. Webster and glides out of the room. The silence in the room is awe inspiring. I can hear each woman breathe. I cannot believe what I just witnessed.

"My Goodness!" pipes up Mrs. Webster to the disbelieving group. "Aren't we being a wee bit oversensitive?"

A week or two later, I walk into the common room in time to see Mrs. Ducket throw a newspaper on the floor in dismay, only to quickly retrieve it.

She sighs, inhales deeply and frowns. "Listen everyone, oh my God, listen to this headline," she whispers in her hoarse voice. 'Jewish Internees Reunited with Their Families in Vittel Are Rounded up by the Nazis.'" She clears her throat and continues in a trembling voice. "The Vichy Government of German occupied France has sent a transport of Jewish American and British citizens to Auschwitz and Birkenau." The women gasp in horror. The friends they had so envied, sent to extermination camps? It can't be true!

"That can't be true, not under the Geneva Convention," Isabella Swartz whispers. She is a fat, quivering woman who hardly ever expresses an opinion. Mrs. Ducket continues reading, looking at the familiar names, "Jacob and Hela Gehorsam, Theodore and Celina Rozenzweig, Chaim and Johanna Stillman." She shakes her head sadly, "I guess they weren't the lucky ones after all." Tears glide smoothly down her weathered cheeks.

Disbelief and gloom settle over the room as Mrs. Ducket continues reading: "The Germans occupying Vittel only keep a limited number of Jews incarcerated. When there is a surplus they are disposed of with as much thought as one gives to trash. Let us not forget ladies," she adds hastily, this is all done with the cooperation of the Vichy government in France, of course,"

"You can always count on the French traitors to do the expedient thing, self-serving bastards that they are," Mrs. Manchester a children's writer spits out uncharacteristically harsh. "As if human beings are goods or commodities, to be disposed of when deemed as surplus." The women cry as they remember their friends.

I turn the word "surplus" around on my tongue. "Surplus, surplus?" I don't like the feel of the word. It has a harsh sound, just like the word "orphans." I think that I've heard it before but I just can't remember where. I see Sister Margret Emanuel in the hall. She has always been kind to me. I know she'll he give me a definition of any word I ask her to. She is an English teacher and before the war taught in a prestigious Catholic *Gymnasium,* secondary school in Berlin. "What is surplus?" I ask her.

She has no idea why I'm asking her. "Surplus, dear, is when there is too much of something, more than enough."

"What do they do with the surplus?"

"Well, sometimes surplus goods are saved and distributed to people in need, at other times, when there is more than can be used, or if the goods are worthless they are destroyed."

I shudder at the prospect. "Could there be a surplus of people, children or their mothers?"

She has not yet heard about the news article but it doesn't take her long to grasp that there is a reason for my questions. "Why do you ask? Of course, people cannot be surplus. We are all God's children not one of whom is considered surplus."

"Our friends in Vittel are surplus," I tell her. "They've been shipped away to concentration camps in Auschwitz, Dachau and Birkenau. I just heard that about our friends in Vittel." She recoils at the news, tells me she is certain that it is a rumor. She bends over me and hugs me.

"You're all right. Your father is in America, not Vittel. Nothing bad is going to happen to you." I don't feel safe. If Hela Gehorsam, with her lively head of hair and raisin- like freckles can be sent to a death camp, so can I, and Michael and my mother and everyone else I love and care about.

In the coming weeks, there is no further news from Vittel. I have no idea of the world outside the camp. I am trying to forget what I saw in the ghetto and what I experienced on the outside while hiding as a Catholic girl. There is such a long list of things I must not remember, things that I could swear are true but am told by my mother that they only live in my imagination.

It is late autumn of 1944. Rumors circulate among the women. Most of the tales are kept from the children. But one day, I walk into the common room when the News Club has gathered. Mrs. Ducket has again managed to obtain newspaper and she is reading out loud to the rest of the women.

"The Germans are retreating," she announces joyfully. "The Red Army liberated Kovno, Lithuania, and trainloads of prisoners are liberated. The Nazis have been driven out of Russia." The women listen attentively as she comes to the end of the article. "Germany's allies in Italy and the Balkan nations are defeated and, ladies," she adds before going on, "the Americans captured the German city of Aachen; the first German city to be captured by the Allies. Hip, hip hooray. We're making progress. France was liberated in June, the Allies brought Italy to its knees; we'll be going home soon!" The room is noisy, filled with applause.

She turns the page and goes on to another section of the Times. Suddenly, before reading one more word to us, she gasps and coughs uncontrollably. She clears her throat but can't seem to find her voice. "Here Maxine, you read it," she whispers, handing the newspaper to Mrs. Manchester. One of the women quickly brings her a glass of water, but she motions with her head to take it away. "I'm alright," she gasps, "Maxine, you read."

Mrs. Manchester puts down her knitting, and cleans her glasses. She has a pleasant round face, frizzy blond hair and is always attentive in spite of the fact that she never stops knitting. She glances at the paper, "Oh my word," she exclaims and then looks at the women, not sure if she should continue. "Oh my Goodness," Mrs.Manchester exclaims again. "What evil are human beings capable of inflicting on other human beings?" She clears her throat and reads softly, "Hungary, after being liberated from Nazi occupation, is cooperating with the defeated Nazis, rounding up the Jews, killing many of them and forcing the remainder to march to the death camps; starving, shoeless, weak and freezing through the harsh, icy countryside. What monsters !" She sighs deeply and lays the paper across her lap unable to continue.

Impatiently, Mrs. Mills grabs the paper from her and begins in a confident, husky voice. "Even though Hitler's armies have been defeated his plan for the Final Solution is not yet over," she pauses to take a drink of water, "the commanders in the camps are still killing the Jews. The starving and sick prisoners forced to march from Auschwitz to Dachau, Bergen-Belsen and Sachenhausen." She pauses as she reaches for more water and blows her nose. "Those prisoners that did not die during this long and treacherous march were gassed when they reached their destination. Meanwhile, the Germans and Poles are dismantling the crematoria and dynamiting mass graves in Auschwitz in an attempt to hide the magnitude of the atrocities." Mrs. Mills sighs deeply, puts down the paper and shakes her head, "Well," she adds, "no one ever accused the Germans of being human."

"Can it be true?" Mrs. Roth, a Jewish woman with a splotchy complexion and beige teeth sighs.. "How can men, women and children be taken to concentration camps to be burned while the rest of world stands by and does nothing?"

"Of course it's true, Rosa," Mrs. Oberstein exclaims impatiently—her dark skin is shiny, covered by a thin layer of sweat. Her shiny black hair is pulled back severely in a bun causing her eyes to appear slanted. "Didn't we see it with our own eyes? The trucks, the train stations, the cattle cars full of miserable people, stacked together like bales of straw? Where did you think they were going- to a resort?" She becomes agitated and little balls of spit gather in the corners of her mouth. "What do you think Hitler meant when he said he is going to make Europe *Juden rein*.?" She takes a handkerchief and wipes her forehead.

"Shhh, quiet," Mrs. Mills catches sight of me and interrupts the agitated women. She compresses her lips and points to me, saying kindly, "Rita, be a dear and go out to another room. Go outside play with the children."

I leave the room but position myself outside the door to eavesdrop. I know that grown-ups' conversation always becomes interesting when they ask me to leave. I don't know what concentration camps are. I've heard of them, of course, but no one ever told me why they exist and if they have anything to do with the war or being Jewish. I have a pretty good idea that they are awful places, where people are burned. I just don't understand why.

"No need to frighten the children, Rosa," through the door I hear Mrs. Mills tell the other women. "They have enough to contend with in here without having to worry about what's going on outside. Where is the Geneva Convention? Aren't they supposed to protect these people? "

I heard of the Geneva Convention, but don't know what it means. Later on my mother will explain to me that the Geneva Convention is an agreement among all the civilized nations of the world. It clearly spelled out the rules of war and how prisoners of war are to be treated. They are to be fed, sheltered, clothed and not harmed during their incarceration. That's the reason why the Swiss inspectors come to our camp once a month to ensure that we are getting enough food, clothing and even medical care.

For weeks the camp has quieted down. The women go about their business silent with no friendly bantering or even noisy arguing. The children are affected also. We keep our games quiet and have given up teasing each other. We strain to listen to adult conversation. We go to school, do our homework and read or draw. It's as if something dark and scary, maybe a ghost or a skeleton is hovering above us. We are all grieving but do not know what for.

CHAPTER 28

I COME INTO the room my mother shares with four other women. It is unusually quiet, my mother sits like a grief stricken statue while the other women are busy performing tasks in silence; some are knitting, one is playing solitaire while others play cards. My mother looks like a sculptures of the Virgin Mary that I have seen in churches, hugging her elbows, bent over in grief, like she's made of stone. I sense that something terrible has happened to my mother, and hesitate before approaching her. I do not get the usual greeting, a smile, hug and kiss. She turns away from me, shaking her head. She can't talk.

I try to cheer her up. *"Mutti,"* I start to say, "Maurice promised to make a picture of the seven dwarfs for me." I am sure she'll be pleased with this bit of news. Maurice is a wonderful artist and a picture from him is a prized possession. But my mother stares at me, shakes her head and then in a voice I've never heard before, she moans, rocking back and forth.

"My sisters, my brothers, the children, all of them gone, perished, burned, shot," she sobs, her shoulders convulse. What happened? I've never seen anyone so dejected let alone my always optimistic, encouraging *Mutti*. She clutches a letter she received that morning from my older cousin Iziek, but it is written in Polish, which I can't read. One of her roommates tells me that our entire family has been killed in Poland. Most of my aunts and uncles, countless cousins, and my little cousin Halinka; little Halinka, whom my mother thought she might be able to save by having her picture on our papers. Three year old Halinka was in Wieliczka where she was hiding with the rest of the family in the bunker underneath the factory. She had a painful sinus infection, and cried too much. In order to protect the others from being discovered by the soldiers upstairs, her mother put the child on her chest and covered her head with a pillow to muffle her cries. In the morning Halinka was dead: smothered. Some, like my Aunt Matilda, got away, but most were discovered by the Gestapo, rounded up, sent to concentration camps, or shot in the forest close to Wieliczka. I start to cry. I know something awful has happened, but it is impossible for me to grasp the magnitude of our loss.

I try to conjure up my dead family whom I haven't seen in a long time. I remember them all, my aunt Angie, the funny one who made us laugh by disguising her voice and speaking in silly accents, Aunt Paula, who unlike *mutti* had dark hair, was serious and unsmiling, Aunt Fela, fat and generous, never without something sweet in her apron pocket to hand out to the children. Uncle Motek, was the only unmarried member of the family. He had a gorgeous voice and had wanted to become an opera singer. It was my Uncle Yaakov, a serious newspaper reader who gathered us together every evening to read the latest news, just like Mrs. Ducket. I recalled my cousin Isaac, fifteen, tall and thin with dark curly hairy, blue eyes and a rosy complexion. He played the violin like no one I have ever heard since. My cousin Giselle, who, though only seven years old, seemed like a grown up because she could read and write and towered over me. Her older sister, Rita (Ruthie), who at sixteen was already considered a beauty with her long blond braids and dark brooding eyes. Rita played the piano and was my mother's first piano student. She was never seen without a book unless she was eating or playing the piano.

I can't believe they're dead. Gone, killed, tortured, gassed, shot; by those handsome marching boys in their smart uniforms. I am eight years old. I can't imagine what being dead really means. I feel as though a cold wind has inserted itself into my heart.

I try to console my mother. I put my arms around her and hold her close to my little body.

"No, no," I say to her. "That is not true. It's only your imagination." I use the same words of reassurance I've heard so often from her when she wants to make me feel safe or help me forget. She is too devastated to hear me. I want to comfort her but don't know how. I am helpless by the magnitude of her grief.

"You'll see," I reassure her. Squelching my fears and sounding, I hoped, more grown up than I felt. "We'll pray and it will be all right. It's a bad dream, just a bad dream." I try to soothe her as a dark gray fear washes over me. So many things are going on that I don't understand, but I sense the danger. It is the first time in my life that I feel encumbered by a deep, abiding sadness that will rarely leave my heart. When difficult times occur, as they do in everyone's lifetime, a feeling of familiar terror and helplessness will cover me like a heavy iron blanket. I will never stop running, even when I am safe.

CHAPTER 29

A LARGE CROWD of American women are standing in front of the dining room wall. There are shouts of triumph, much pushing and shoving. I, too push my way to the front of the crowd. The object of fascination is a short, typewritten list of names. scrutinizing a typewritten list of names. I ask "What's going on here?" and am told this is the list of women who are to be sent out of Liebenow to join family in the US. I scrounge over to look. I scan the list and notice that it is alphabetical order. At the bottom of the list I see our names in print. I feel as though I have found a treasure, joyful, hopeful; a dream has just come true. I look for my brother to show him what I feel is my personal triumph. "Look, look Bubbi. There are our names, Fraida Schmelkes *sic*, Moschel Schmelkes and Rita Schmelkes."

My brother glances at the list, I do not know if it is because he cannot read or if he is too young to understand. He is clearly not impressed. I bend close to his ear trying to convince him. "Bubbi look. It says you are on the list. Here," I point my finger to his name, "look, right here it says Moschel Schmelkes."

He looks at my finger, glances at the list and shrugs his shoulders. "My name is not Moschel. It's Michael. No one has such a stupid name like Moschel." He tosses his head in defiance of the old useless name and cannot bring himself to celebrate what this implies. Our names are finally posted on the exchange list. Monica and her mother are on the list as well.

My mother, who is so good at striking a bargain, exchanges cartons of Camels, Lucky Strikes and Old Gold cigarettes for woolen coats, sweaters and a huge brown leather suitcase. She trades a can of Spam for a brown leather purse that hangs from the shoulder, a container of cocoa and some playing cards and four packs of Camel cigarettes for a pair of fur lined boots, a heavy woolen sweater and inexplicably Tyrolean *lederhosen*, leather shorts, too large for Bubbi. They are the epitome of the German/Austrian folk costume. It is winter again and she knows we'll probably be cold. She lays the suitcase open on the floor, its lid up, a yawning hungry giant waiting to be fed. We are ready long before the transport truck arrives to take us to the train station.

My father who has been notified by the State Department of our release but for security reasons not been informed of the exact date and place of our arrival, writes to my mother telling her to destroy all the "coats and cover ups" that he had sent her when we were in Poland. "They are out of fashion in the U.S.," he explains, "and will make you look like foolish foreigners. Throw them into the ocean when you get far out to sea." My mother understands that "coats and cover ups" are code words for the counterfeit documents (covers for her identity) that he has sent her and that they could get us into trouble with the American immigration department. If he were to write to her directly, not using the code, the message could fall into the wrong hands, the German censors or even the American immigration and cause us to look like the frauds we really are. If they discover that my mother's papers are worthless we could possibly end up in one of the concentration camps. My mother understands all this and writes back telling him she certainly plans to look stylish when she come to America.

It feels like years later that we find ourselves sitting in an unheated train that is going nowhere. The train remains stationery, unmoving like a cow reclining in the meadow on a hot summer day, only it is freezing cold and the train is unheated. It lurches every now and then, shuddering and clanging, raising hopes before sighing loudly and giving up. I'm almost nine years old, cold, hungry and hopeful. This time, I tell myself we are really on our way to America.

The only time I'm allowed to leave my hard wooden seat is to go to the bathroom. "*Entschuldigen uns bitte*, excuse us, please," my mother disturbs the people who are sitting on the floor in the aisles while she accompanies me to the toilet, which is filthy and reeks. My mother lifts me up so that my body does not come into contact with any part of the seat. "There are so many germs and diseases that you can get off the toilet seat," she warns me. I shudder. I know. I do my business quickly in order to get out of there, remembering the loathesome can in Montelupi.

We return to our seats and suddenly, and with no warning the train emits a loud groan, shudders like a volcanic eruption and slowly starts to move. If I had still been in the toilet I would surely have ended up in the filthy excrement. We sit, tightly packed one against another. I feel the breath of the old man next to me, he snores quietly. His head falls on my shoulder and I try not to stir for fear of waking him. It is nighttime and we move past darkened cities, with the sound of the train churning "to America, to America, to America…."

The scenery changes when dawn ascends. Bombed out cities blackened tree stumps, parts of buildings, shards of broken glass, and toppled lampposts slump all around looking like toothless ogres grinning hideously standing in front of burned out forests, trunks and disjointed branches leaning against piles of debris. The train comes to a stop when the sun rises. It only moves at night, my mother tells me. The reason for that is because a moving train is an easy target to spot from the air, and the Germans don't want their trains being bombed by the aircraft overhead. We are out of the protected zone of Liebenau. We sit in a station all day long and travel for short periods of time when it is dark, coming to a halt before dawn lights up the horizon.

Since yesterday we have been sitting for hours on this frigid, still train, not moving, going nowhere. German soldiers in their warm, woolen green uniforms and knee- high boots come through the cars shouting orders in menacing voices. Every now and then different officers swagger onto the train. With red cheeks, shining noses, and cold blue eyes like the icicles hanging from the eaves of the stations. The soldiers descend onto the halted train. They look well fed and healthy though not jovial like they did Krakow. They sweep through each car, demanding to see identity papers. Each inspection presents a new threat. Our survival, for this day is up to the whim of the inspecting officers. If the next officer does not approve of our papers, we will be ejected from the train and left on a strange platform with nothing. We smile ingratiatingly, are polite and pleasant. My mother distracts one of them. She speaks in German.

"Where are we now?"

"Nowhere special, *gnadige frau,* gracious lady," he answers her politely taking in her obvious Aryan persona. "This is just a small village on the way to Switzerland. It's not even an express stop, only halts once a day, on good days," he adds. He nods at her and walks down the aisle. I watch him stop at one of the seats demanding papers from an elderly couple.

My fear intensifies as I watch some people crying or begging for their lives while others are being dragged from the train, pulled by their arms, pushed and kicked as they try to resist. I shudder. "Are we next?" I wonder.

'"Move over," an officer orders us after one such intrusion, shoving the man at the end of my bench toward me. "You are being joined by new passengers." Obediently, we huddle closer together. A woman and a child squeeze onto our bench and we are so close together I can't even catch a glimpse of them to see if the child is a boy or a girl.

While the train moves at night I sleep in an upright position, never more than one hour at a time. Each time I am jolted awake I wonder where I am. I have to remind myself that we are on our way to America. In the meantime, the January wind blows relentlessly through the draughty cars. I wonder if there will ever be a time when I don't feel the cold. Somewhere a child is crying, a man is coughing and someone is moaning. I try to differentiate the people around me as the winter sun sends its cool rays through the shaded windows and the train lurches to a stop.

I hear a man explaining to his teenage son that since we are out of the confines of the camp and traveling through German cities we are no longer protected by the Geneva Convention. There it is again, "Geneva Convention." Now that I know what it means I know it's not going to offer us any safety. The man whispers to his son. He tells his him to avoid the officers' eyes.

"Look down, Leo, don't attract any attention to yourself. The best thing that the soldiers can do to us is to ignore us."

Too often, I am back in the world of the fairy tales, where witches punish young girls for not inviting them to their weddings, where a princess is forced to marry a frog and a stepmother can cast her stepdaughter out of the palace, from royalty to slavery. I relive all the dreadful things that can happen to children. I know the endings are happy, but I am not there yet. I am stuck in the middle of the frightening ordeal and I'm not at all sure if the ending to my story will be happy. My fears perpetuate themselves, feeding on each other like crows devouring carcasses. I am unable to let go of the terror; afraid to question my mother, afraid that if I give a voice to my anxieties they might become a reality. I also know that she might once again tell me it is all in my imagination. I am no longer comforted by her lies.

I make a mental list of "what ifs:" "What if we get separated and can't find each other? What if one of us gets sick? What if one of us is pulled off the train and left on the platform alone? What if my mother dies? What if the train gets bombed?" The list is endless and frightening. I shift my mind to magical thinking, protective thinking: "If we only make three stops today, then nothing bad will happen. If five more people come on the train, then we will be safe. If one of the Nazi officers coughs before he speaks, we will speed off and make no more stops along the way." I play these mind games constantly, hoping to gain some sort of control. They serve to distract me from the present.

When I am able to chase the demons out of my mind, Michael and I entertain each other playing a long noisy game called "refugee." The game involves lots of loud pleading, begging, shouting and tears by my brother who acts the part of Moishe Mogen Dovid, the poor Jew pleading for justice. I play the part of the officious secretary gesticulating and arguing, determined to keep him from seeing the commandant.

"Please, oh please," begs Moishe M. Dovid, "I have to see the commandant. I've been waiting here all day."

"What is the nature of your business?" I inquire in a self-important voice, my arms crossed authoritatively in front of my flat bosom.

"I have some papers," he replies. His hand is shaking with fear as he extends them to me. "They have to be signed by the commandant."

I wave the papers away without so much as glancing at them. "I'm sorry, but the commandant is very busy. He can't possibly see everyone who comes in here off the street."

"But listen," he folds his hands as if in prayer and places them under his chin. "I have an appointment to see him today."

"Hmmph," I sniff, "Lots of people have appointments. The commandant is very busy today. Come back tomorrow. Maybe tomorrow will not be so hectic."

"Tomorrow? Oh, all right," Moishe responds meekly, "Shall I come tomorrow in the morning, or perhaps in the afternoon? Can we make an appointment?" He asks meekly.

"What are you crazy?" Now I am shouting at the cowering figure of my brother. "Do you think you can have an appointment with the commandant? If you want to see him you take your chances. There are no appointments in this office unless the commandant schedules them!"

"But I did have an appointment for today."

"Let me see your papers." I demand in a loud, officious voice. Moishe hands me a piece of paper. I pretend to read it.

"This paper is no good," I say sternly. "This paper is of no use. You need new papers." I tear the paper to shreds while Moishe looks on helplessly.

By now my poor brother is really sobbing. He has really gotten into the spirit of this game and seems unable to distinguish it from fact. "I had a good paper. It was good, it was real, and now I have nothing! What was the matter with it? What kind of people are you?"

"Sir," I say with disdain. "You'll have to leave the office. You are causing a commotion. We cannot have that in this office. This is not one of your little Jewish places where it is alright to scream. This is a dignified office. Now get out!"

"My goodness," a tall woman, wearing a heavy navy blue coat turns to my mother, "aren't children wonderful? They manage to turn everything into a game."

My mother agrees with her: "I just wish they weren't so noisy. Some of the others are trying to sleep through this journey."

CHAPTER 30

After sitting on the train for two weeks, we arrive in Switzerland. Everyone gets off the train, stretches and looks around. Rolling white fields meet puffy, gray clouds. It is difficult to discern where the land ends and the heavens begin. I am awe struck. I don't even mind the frost. There is no wind, just the fresh pristine world, untouched, unblemished, a scene from a fairy tale set. Stark silent mountains mostly gray but painted with bold white streaks look down on us. We are midgets, dwarves in their presence. My mother holds my hand tightly. "We are free," she whispers. "Switzerland is a neutral country."

The Swiss might be neutral, but they certainly are not friends to the Jews. They make this eminently clear by separating the Jews from their fellow travelers and assigning all the Jews to quarters in an empty, unheated barn filled with dirty straw that smells like the animals it once housed. The other refugees are assigned to a heated building.

We sleep with our clothes on, our hands clasped between our thighs and feet curled up under our bodies. Michael is not well. He has developed shiny red cysts on his neck and legs. He writhes in agony and is running a high fever. There is no thermometer to take his temperature but a mother knows when her child is sick. My mother kisses his forehead and realizes he is burning up with fever. The cysts have developed into swollen, shiny red boils. One boil on the back of his neck is so large and infected that he cannot move his head or swallow. Michael has become sicker in the middle of the night. He has stopped crying, he whimpers softly, and has stopped fidgeting under my mother's coat. The only sign of life is his occasional cry and his labored breathing.

My mother is panic- stricken. Had we come all this way for her to lose her little boy to this horrifying infection? Pride and arrogance are gone as she approaches one of the Swiss guards. "Could we please get some help for my little boy?" She asks him. Her blond hair, good looks and command of the German language serve no purpose here. She is just a mother begging for someone to save her child's life. The guard looks at her. Unlike some of the Nazis he has no fear of humanizing his charges. They're all the same to him. He has seen them all; the sick, the ignorant, the educated, the young, the old, the ugly and the beautiful. He does not bother to distinguish one from the other. He treats them all alike. Many transports have come this way and he cannot be expected to deal with the diseases and illnesses of these refugees.

"We have no doctors here, we have no health facilities either," he informs her indifferently in Pidgin German. His domed forehead is shiny and his eyes betray not a trace of humanity.

She acts as though she has not heard him and again repeats her plea for help.

"Madam, our job here is to facilitate the transfer of refugees; that is all. We are not responsible for their health. I have seen people die here from nothing more than a common cold that turned into pneumonia; healthy one moment, coughing another and then poof," he snaps his fingers loudly," dead. The fact of the matter is that you are fortunate to be here at all. If it were up to the Nazis you would have been dead long ago," he adds as nonchalantly as if he were telling her the population of birds up here in the mountains. My mother swallows hard and looks into his eyes.

"You are telling me that there are no doctors in Switzerland, that you cannot find someone to help an ailing child?" She holds Bubbi close to her. "The Swiss protected us through the Geneva Convention while we were under Nazi supervision. They came to our camp once a month to ensure that we were properly fed, well cared for in the infirmary, had warm clothes and here, in Switzerland itself there is no one to take care of a sick little boy? How much must we endure to satisfy your appetite for Jewish blood?" She is clutching Michael to her breast and her voice rises above his head. She would never speak this way to an authority but the panic for her child's life is such that she will risk everything to protect it.

"Don't make a scene, madam," the Swiss guard warns her menacingly. "It won't do you any good. We are doing the best we can. We have been assigned an impossible task and instructed not to get involved in any business with the inmates. My job, no I mean our job, is to stand guard, feed you and make sure that no one runs away." With this he nods his head and moves away.

Frantically she carries Bubbi from one person to another hoping that perhaps one of the prisoners is a doctor, or that someone will come up with a remedy. Finally, one of the men in our transport takes pity on her and offers to lance the angriest boil on Michael's neck with a penknife. Although he is not a doctor, and the conditions are far from sterile, my mother gratefully agrees. She has no other options. The man presses the sharp knife against Michael's neck and a spurt of putrid, green pus squirts out. Michael howls as the thick, green venom oozes out slowly. When red blood has started to flow from the wound, the man presses a handkerchief against the lanced infection hoping to hasten the process of healing and slow down the infection. Suddenly Michael passes out. When he regains consciousness, he is dazed, but a few days later the temperature abates and he regains his energy.

We might be out of harm's way here in Switzerland, out of the jurisdiction of the Gestapo but we certainly do not feel free. Swiss hospitality has not made itself known in this part of the country. The guards are menacing and arrogant, far more intimidating than the guards in Liebenau. We are all impatient, eager to get out of this miserable, unforgiving country.

The train to take us away finally arrives and we board, grateful to be leaving. Michael has recovered and we resume our game of refugee:

noisy and disruptive as it always is. We are traveling through the neutral zones of Switzerland and occupied France. New people get on board every time we stop. The train moves quickly, stopping only to take on more passengers. Bombed out cities are a rarity here and we haven't heard the ominous wail of air raid sirens since we boarded in Basel, Switzerland.

Finally, in late January, we pull into Marseilles, the French seaport where three ships sit in the harbor. The biggest and most beautiful is the Swedish luxury liner, the Gripsholm. It is as tall as a three story building and just as wide. I crane my neck to see its majestic smoke stacks with their yellow and blue stripes. Lively music is blaring from loudspeakers. The Gripsholm sits in the harbor like a proud and haughty princess reigning over her territory. Two inferior sister ships hover nearby. One is a large white ship with a red cross on its smoke stack; the other is the ugly stepsister with no promise of redemption. Small, dark and gray with rusting railings running around the deck, it cowers in the background.

I plead to God that we will be sailing on the big beautiful ship; sailing to the Promised Land. Two hours later we are standing on the deck of the Victoria, a dark, ugly ship, the smallest of the threesome. It is gray, dirty and smells of mold.

The cabins below deck are dark and cold. Rows of bunk beds covered with straw mats are lined up against the walls. We lie down sharing the quarters with many other passengers. In the middle of the night, I awaken to a brushstroke of fur along my arm and the sound of tiny footfalls overhead. Later in the morning I see what was tap dancing overhead. Rats the size of kittens scurrying in and out of holes in the wall. I shiver, I have never shared a bed with a rat.

CHAPTER 31

———— ✢ ————

`Dr. Osiek, a young Jewish pediatrician is on our ship. We first met him on the train going to Marseilles. Victor, a little boy is with him. My mother tells us that Victor is not his son.

"He is an orphan boy Dr. Osiek found wandering the streets of Vilna, alone. When he realized that Victor had no living relatives and no hope for a future he took him along and now treats him like the little son he never had."

I love the story. A little boy is lost and alone, not in the woods, but in an equally dangerous place. He is found by a big, strong man who becomes his father, and, I add, they live happily ever after. It's like a fairy tale, but Victor does not act like a hero in a fairy tale. He is strange and seems to live in a faraway place, always staring off into the distance, not talking to anyone, never smiling or crying, and most disturbing of all, he is constantly chewing on his tongue. He is fair skinned, blue eyed with blond curly hair and a porcelain pink complexion. I am determined to get through to him.

"Victor," I nudge him, pulling on a thread of his unraveling sweater, "do you believe in Father Christmas? He came to our camp and he gave me a gift." I produce my precious sewing box with all the colorful threads intact. Victor ignores me. He doesn't even look at the box. "Want to see some pieces of real bombs?" I take out my stash of shrapnel collected after air raids. Again, he does not react. He just sits on a rickety deck chair, chewing furiously on his tongue and staring at the horizon as if waiting for something to appear. I don't give up easily. I offer him some chocolate. He doesn't even look at it.

I am obsessed with Victor. I ignore all the other children on the boat and devote my time to eliciting a response from him. How can I make him answer my questions or acknowledge my friendly overtures? I am not one to ignore a challenge. I must get Victor to at least look at me. I resort to my last trick. My right hand creeps up slowly behind Victor's back. I tickle his neck hoping for the reaction I always get when I tickle someone. He doesn't even blink his eyes. "Victor! Are you dead or alive?" I scream into his ear. He continues chewing his tongue, more rapidly than before. What can I do to make him notice me, to bring him out of wherever he is, to rescue him? None of my ploys meet with success. I am terribly frustrated and suddenly burst out crying.

"What's wrong with him?" I ask Dr. Osiek. "He acts as if he's dead. Does he hate everyone? Does he ever talk to you? "

Dr. Osiek tells my mother the story of Victor's rescue. He wants her to tell me to stop trying to make Victor happy. He is concerned for my well-being and dealing with the constant rejection of my offers of friendship to Victor. My mother tells him that he has a better chance convincing me than she does.

Dr. Osiek invites me for a walk on the deck. "Victor is a very, very sad boy," he explains to me. "He saw his mommy, his daddy and his two younger brothers, twin babies actually, killed by the Gestapo. He was hiding under the bed or he would have been killed as well. Victor saw a lot of blood and heard a lot of screaming." I listen as Dr. Osiek tries to explain Victor's silence. "It is very kind of you to try to make Victor happy, but it will take a long time," Dr. Osiek shakes his head sadly. "Victor is so sad that he is living in a strange world of his own making where no one can enter and nothing can hurt him again."

"But we're going to America," I insist. "It's going to be a happy place for Victor."

"Rita, you are a sweet little girl, and kind in trying to help. But neither you nor I, nor anyone else can make Victor forget what he's seen and heard. Only time will help him." I tear up with this sad news. Dr. Osiek pats me on the head. "But there's no reason for us to stop having fun." And with that he tells me a joke that I never forget, about two idiots caught in the rain. In spite of Victor, I have to laugh at the punch line where one of them goes home in the pouring rain to fetch his pajamas after having been invited to stay at the other's house in order not to get soaked on his way home.

I try coaxing a response from Victor a few more times, but it's no use. Dr, Osiek is right. He is not going to be distracted or brought out of his world by anyone right now. The ship sits in the harbor for days, going nowhere. Eventually, I join the other children running up and down the deck, making lots of noise, trading treasures and waiting for something to happen.

Someone has heard a rumor that our ship is bound for Africa. What has become of our voyage to America? For me, Africa is a place full of wild animals and naked cannibals. I have read about the Belgian Congo in Liebenau. I'm not going. When I ask my mother about it, she shrugs her shoulders and tells me to be grateful that at least we are out of Germany and out of danger.

"Why do I always have to be grateful when something goes wrong?" I ask my mother.

"Look," she says, "there are no airplanes flying overhead, no sirens forecasting bombing missions. We are not in any danger of being killed," she doesn't even address my question. "There aren't even any shelters on the boat. We are safe. That's something to be grateful for."

"But we're standing still, and we might be going to Africa instead of the beautiful life in America, with my Papa." I am bewildered and saddened. I make a compromise with God. If we could just get to America I won't complain about sharing my bunk with rats.

None of the ships have sailed. Several days later, with no explanation, we are taken off the ugly ship and moved to the Red Cross hospital ship. What a relief. The wounded soldiers have not yet arrived and the hospital ship is full of beautiful, young American nurses wearing pink striped uniforms and sporting long red nails. They are kind and generous to us and they talk to Michael and me in serious tones. "So, when is your birthday?" one of them asks me. I tell her it's on February second.

"Why that's today," she exclaims, "We'll have to celebrate."

I have no idea what *celebrate* means.

"We'll meet in the cafeteria in an hour and we'll have a birthday party for you." What is a birthday party? I had never had a birthday party in my entire life. I know that there are parties for Christmas, for Easter, for Independence Day. But who ever heard of a party for my birthday?

I am about to find out. Michael, my mother and I are invited to the nurses' cafeteria. I am awed when I see it has been decorated with a colorful paper tablecloth and matching napkins. Several other nurses have joined us and they all sing "Happy Birthday." My guardian angel scoops out huge portions of vanilla ice cream, pours hot chocolate sauce over it and brings each of us a large saucer full of ice cream.

"All for me?" I feel overwhelmed, and embarrassed. We sit down to eat and I can't believe what I'm eating. I have never tasted anything like this before. The unexpected surge of soothing, cold, smooth, velvety texture slides down my throat without my even swallowing. My ninth birthday is the most memorable one in my entire life. The nurses play with us and treat us as the families they left at home. Grown-ups have never been so attentive and kind to us before.

CHAPTER 32

Again, and with no explanation, we are told that we will have to leave the hospital ship. By a strange unaccountable twist of fate we are taken to The Gripsholm. It is hard to say good-bye to the warm and generous friends we made on the hospital ship. They hug us and wish us good luck.

This new ship is an entire floating city. The decks are long and filled with cushioned deck chairs. Downstairs, beneath the deck many small boutiques sell silk dresses, lingerie, high heeled shoes, perfumes, scarves, purses and belts. The sitting rooms or salons, as they are called, are furnished with purple and green velvet sofas. Huge gilt mirrors hang on the walls and soft carpeting lies on every floor. I listen to jazz music with its new unfamiliar sounds and strong rhythms. A tall, smiling American soldier stops us on our way up the stairs. He smiles at us, puts his hand into the pocket of his navy blue jacket and takes out two Hershey bars. "This is for you kids," he tells us as he hands Michael and me a Hershey bar. I thank him and curtsy as I've been taught to do.

"You can stop curtsying now," he tells me smiling. "In the United States, no one curtsies."

"Really?" I say, in my British accent, "But all well-mannered girls curtsy."

"No," he laughs at me, "pretty girls like you only have to say 'thank you' when they are given something." Soon after that, a tall African-American soldier, a chef actually, extends his arm and hands us two oranges accompanied by a smile that spreads across his face like a silk fan. This is the first black man I have seen up close. His size, ebony skin and jovial manner make him unforgettable. I remember not to curtsy, but I thank him and run to show my mother. I had seen pictures of oranges, but this is the first time I taste the sour juicy fruit.

Our stateroom is small and crammed with essentials: a petite porcelain sink with hot and cold running water, two sets of bunk beds, clean linens, plenty of blankets and towels. Moreover, the room is warm, cozy and clean. For the first time in ages I stop being cold.

The dining room with its crystal chandeliers, soft green carpeting, tables draped with long graceful cloths, quiet music and embossed menus look like what I imagine a palace must be like. We are seated at one of the many elegant round tables on velvet upholstered chairs, with linen napkins, silverware, china plates and, as if that isn't enough, Swedish cooking, with as much food as we want. I am in heaven.

I meet many children that I have never seen before. One in particular is unforgettable because of his air of arrogance. His name is Marek, and he is older than we are, about eleven. His long blond hair, un-parted is slicked off his forehead to the back of his head. He is wearing a black cowboy hat that hangs between his skinny shoulder blades fastened by a shiny leather string. He is dressed up like he is going to a costume party: a black shirt, and a jewel studded belt with leather holsters on each side and most impressive of all are the two shining toy pistols he is twirling on his index fingers. This, he tells us, is a cowboy suit. "There are many cowboys in America. They carry guns and shoot people," he informs us. He acts smart, confident and with a brazen sense of bravado, clearly enjoying our admiration and envy.

"*Doolers*. You can get everything for *doolers*," he tells us in Polish, though only a few of us speak or understand Polish. He swaggers and pretends to take aim at some object with his shiny pistol. The other kids are all impressed whether they understand him or not. "My mother's got plenty of *doolers*. We got them before we even started on our trip. We're rich," he brags unaware or not caring that only a handful of us understand what he is saying. He comes from Warsaw and was never in a camp. His grandfather lives in "*Tzchicao*" and now he's going to live there with his family.

"What's *Tzchicago*?" I ask.

"The biggest city in America," he tells me.

"The only American cities I've heard of are New York, Philadelphia and Hollywood, where Shirley Temple lives."

"Well, little girl," he sneers at me in Polish, shaking his head from side to side, "You don't know everything. *Tzchicago* is a very big city in America, bigger than New York and Philadelphia combined." I try to act nonchalant and respond with a clever comeback when I realize that he doesn't speak any English. That fills me with a good deal of confidence.

"How are you going to get around *Tzchicago* if you don't speak English?" I ask in perfect Polish.

"Don't worry about me," he says disdainfully. "In *Tzchicago*, everybody speaks Polish. They even have Polish schools."

He swaggers away with a bunch of stupid boys, including my very own brother. What can they be thinking? That he's going to give them one of his precious guns? Boys are so dumb, I tell myself.

Suddenly the smokestacks emit several loud blasts and we are inching away from the pier. We are finally going to America. We stand on the deck, watching the land getting smaller and further away. When we wake up the next morning all we can see on every side of us is the ocean expanding to infinity. I feel a burden lifting from my heart. We are really going to America; this is definitely not my imagination. It's true; my mother was telling the truth.

The trip is long: three weeks. We have to travel slowly, I am told by one of the soldiers on the boat. We have to keep a sharp lookout for mines hidden under the water. "Mines can make the whole boat explode and the captain certainly doesn't want that to happen." By the second week of the journey a fierce north Atlantic winter storm roars, accompanied by a howling wind, and waves as tall as mountains. Our huge ship is battered from wave to wave like the paper boats we made and sailed in the bathtub. The raging storm comes crashing down washing the decks with salt water that leaves the floors glazed and sparkling. Long ropes are suspended above our heads in the hall ways for passengers to hold onto as they navigate from one section of the ship to the other. The dining room is half full. Many people are too sea sick to come out of their cabins and I can hear them moaning when I pass their rooms. I don't feel sorry for them. I'm not sea sick, why should they be? Then, one day, just as suddenly as it appeared, the storm is gone. The sun is shining and the decks are covered with a salty sheen that reflects the sun's rays.

There is always something going on aboard. Often in the evening we watch movie, and it is here that I am introduced to the famous Charlie Chaplin. Indeed, my brother did look like a small version of him, shuffling around in shoes too big and baggy trousers. All that's missing is Charlie Chaplin's trademark moustache. There is something pathetic and familiar in the actor's eyes that only I seem to notice. Michael had that forlorn appearance before my father's generous packages started arriving, when he was holding onto clothes that were never meant not fit him.

At night, after my mother tucks us in as she goes out of our cabin to be with other adults. She knows we are safe on the ship without her. She turns out the lights, kisses us and tells us to be good, go to sleep and keep quiet. That's when we pick up our game of "refugee." We start out quietly, whispering our parts. Before long the game gains momentum and our voices rise, we are shouting and crying. Somehow, when we are together we always return to the game of "refugee." It is an old friend, always available, always there for us to pick up and played with. We continue playing it for many years, even after we are living in the U.S. and own a Monopoly game.

The ship's primary mission is to transport wounded American soldiers and other soldiers whose tours of duty are over. They make up the majority of the of the ship's population. The wounded soldiers haunt me for many years. They are handsome, wear beautiful uniforms, and they are kind and friendly to everyone. They don't seem to notice the difference between the Jewish kids and the Christian kids. In spite of their youth and good looks, most of them are maimed, missing parts of their bodies; an arm, a leg. Many are amputees, some on crutches, some in wheel chairs; a set of identical twin, who now can easily be identified, since one has lost his right leg and the other his left; a handsome blond soldier walking behind his buddy, holding onto his shoulder because he is blind and needs his friend to take him everywhere. I am so sad when I see them coming. I feel like I am going to cry, there is still so much sadness around me. "Is there ever a place where everything is all right?" I ask myself. The most disturbing injury is to a soldier whose face has been entirely burned and scarred. His skin is red and yellow, with little peaks and valleys, some of them oozing a clear liquid. A black opening remains in his face where his nose had been, he has no lips, but his teeth and smile are intact, and although his eyelids are badly burned, his blue eyes have miraculously survived his ordeal and he can see. He frightens and fascinates me at the same time. He has the body of a man and the face of a monster. I hide every time I see him coming, only to stare at him from some invisible corner of the room, from behind closed drapes, crouching behind a sofa.

Underneath that frightening horror mask is an active, friendly human being. He jokes around with his buddies, greets everyone he meets with a loud "hello," plays ping-pong and seems to be unaware of his appearance. Slowly, I begin to lose my fear of him and stop avoiding him.

"Hey Blondie," he says to me, rumpling my hair. "Want a candy bar?"

Nothing is as it appears. The beautiful Nazi soldiers are mean and ugly on the inside. This scarred, disfigured man approaches me with a candy bar and an attempt at a grin.

"I've got a little girl just like you waiting for me at home." I thank him and smile up at him. I know his little girl will not recognize her father. I shudder inside. What does my own father look like, I wonder? I haven't seen him in such a long time that I've forgotten everything about him.

Part Two
Immigrant Girl

CHAPTER 1

— ⚬ —

MY MOTHER PULLS our blankets off. "Come on. Get up." It is 5 A.M. and she sounds cheerful and excited, "we'll be passing the Statue of Liberty this morning and I don't want you to miss it. It is a sight you will remember for the rest of your lives. You never forget some events in your lives and the first glimpse of the Statue of Liberty is going to be one of those things."

I glance at the clock on the edge of the sink. It is 5:00 in the morning. I shiver, yawn and stretch. "What *liverty*? What's *liverty?*" I mumble half asleep.

My mother laughs, "Liberty, not *liverty*; a statue that welcomes all immigrants to America. You'll tell your grandchildren how thrilling that day was for you."

"What's 'liberty?'" I ask through a long yawn.

She is excited and happy. Michael resists a bit, complaining of being tired. I, who don't know what she's talking about and am dying to go back to sleep too. We rush up to the deck to see what all the fuss is about. It is crowded with noisy spectators. "There, over there. Look, you'll see it as soon as it comes into view," a soldier says to his buddy. He is pointing towards the horizon which is surrounded by a dense foggy mist. I look to where he is pointing but can hardly see my hand in front of my face. What are all these people doing here I wonder? I see nothing in front of me and nothing above or below me. Yet the deck is full of people straining their eyes into the misty horizon, trying to see something that does not appear. We are entering New York harbor and the woman next to me tells me to keep my eyes open for "the green lady with the torch." I scan the horizon carefully, hoping to see a green lady, but we miss her. Whether it's due to the fog or perhaps that the captain has taken a route that avoids her, no one claims to have caught a glimpse of her. We look in the distance and see land.

A sprawling three-story building looms ahead of us. Constructed of red bricks with white accents it supports two ornate towers on each end and large, arched windows. It dominates the entire vista. Ellis Island has its own history. Established in 1892 as an immigration processing center, island's size has been extended by earth salvaged from the construction site of the New York subway system. It served as an immigration processing center until 1934 when its use became restricted to the special cases. Apparently, we belonged to that category of people with special problems or questionable paperwork or serious illness, or suspected of being spies. Because my mother possesses no official papers and no identification her status is questionable. She will be interrogated extensively with the grim possibility of being sent back to Germany. Fortunately, I do not know this. She admonishes us to tell only the truth and only when we are questioned. Under no circumstances are we to volunteer any information.

"And if you're not sure what to answer, just say, 'I don't know.'"

We are taken into a small private room overseen by two immigration officers.

My mother explains her plight to the officers behind the desk at the immigration bureau on Ellis Island. She tells them how we happened to land in a POW camp even though we are not American citizens yet. They listen patiently writing the information she gives them into a notebook. They are nothing like the uniformed officers I'm used to seeing. They are wearing white shirts and black trousers, with only a small badge on their shoulders identifying them as having official status.

They confer in private and in English. I strain to hear what they are saying to one another, and although they turn their backs to us, I can hear and understand enough to make sense out of their conversation. They agree that she does not have the bearing of a poor Jewish woman who suffered in Europe. Moreover, her English has a strong German accent. The officers ask Michael and me a few questions; how old we are and why do we want to come to the US. We answer truthfully, in the upper- crust British accents we have acquired in Liebenau, we want to be with our Papa in America. The immigration officials look puzzled. Again they hold a private discussion, thinking that I can't hear them. They are not aware of my well-developed art of eavesdropping. They whisper to each other.

"What do you think?" one of them asks.

"I don't know," the other one answers. "She looks like a Brunhilde to me."

"The kids sound like Brits. You think they're legit?"

"She hasn't got a single piece of identification in her possession and she claims that her husband is living in the US?"

"She could she a German spy." They talk some more with much throat clearing and shoulder shrugging. They have come to a conclusion. "You are going to be detained on Ellis Island while the immigration bureau investigates your case. After that, if we do not find anything suspicious you will be sent to a judge before the immigration bureau who will determine the status of your immigration request and rule on the disposition." I listen, breathless and suddenly start to tear up. So many new words and so scary sounding: "disposition, status, immigration."

The immigration officer realizes he has frightened a child for no good reason. "Don't you worry little girl," he tries to reassure me. "If what your mother and you said is true you will soon be seeing your Papa."

Michael and I hear everything but understand very little. We are ushered into a tremendous hall called the "great hall" with high ceilings and a long balcony encircling the upstairs. There are many doors on both sides of the hallway behind the iron railing. Benches are lined up against the walls and a huge clock hangs above one of the entrances. It rings out the hours reminding everyone that time is passing. We are led up the stairs by a short, stout woman who is introduced to us as a "matron." She is assigned to show us around and answer any questions we might have. She is matter of fact, all business. In spite of that she seems kind. She opens one of the doors with a large key that hangs from a larger key ring and leads us into a small dormitory -like room containing triple decker bunk beds with mesh wire instead of mattresses. We are given blankets and towels, and told that this is where we are to sleep.

"Breakfast, lunch and dinner are served at eight, twelve noon and six p.m., respectively. And," she adds, a food cart that will come around several times a day where we can get a snack: cake, fruit and candy. "You are to remain downstairs during the day and only use this as a bedroom. Do you have any questions?" She is reserved but pleasant enough. "Now, please follow me." She leads us to a large room where doctors in white coats check our throats, ears, eyes, hair, skin and nails. It is dark when we return to our little room and we are exhausted. It has been a very long day. My mother sits down on one of the cots, her elbows on her knees her face in her palms. She cries silently. When Michael sees this, he immediately bursts into tears himself. Only I am dry-eyed.

"*Mutti, mutti* why are you crying?" I ask trying to soothe her. "We are in America. Papa will be here soon and he will take us home to our mansion."

"I know, I know," she says, "I am crying for joy." But I don't believe her. I know that there is no joy for her in a room with barred windows and hard wire beds. We remain on the island for about two weeks oblivious to the fact that our fate is being determined somewhere on the mainland. Some people are taken off the island and board ships that will take them back to Germany. When I ask why this is happening, I am told that they are spies for the Germans. I don't know what spies are but I assume it's nothing very good because why are they being sent back to Germany.

We attend a school that has been established on the island for children who stay for extended periods of time. A real classroom with desks firmly bolted to the floor and inkwells in the upper right hand corner. A blackboard with alphabet cards above it hangs on one of the walls and a large map, like a window shade of what we will later on learn is the United States hangs on another wall. An American flag with 48 stars hangs at an angle from a pole that is fastened to the side of the blackboard. We each receive a generous allotment of school supplies: black and white marbled notebooks, pens, sharpened pencils erasers, crayons and small bottles of Waterman's blue-black ink.

I know we will not stay on this island for long and our lives feel unpredictable. In spite of this I like Ellis Island. I feel comfortable and safe. The routine is not demanding. There are no angry Nazis, no sudden air raid sirens no one in charge of us except our own mother. A teacher comes into our classroom for two or three hours a day to instruct us in English. She holds up pictures of a window, chair, table, door, book, dog and many other everyday objects. She tells us to repeat the names of the pictures on the cards and then copy them into our notebooks from the blackboard where she has neatly written them. Michael and I already know how to speak English and blurt out all the answers before anyone else has a chance to respond. The classroom is like a revolving door. New children come in and old ones leave. We are the only ones who have been here more than a week.

The lessons are easy and when the school day is over we get our lunches. After lunch we play games and run around on the tiny piece of turf that is designated as the playground. There are four swings, and nothing more. It is a damp and chilly March and we look forward to 4 p.m. when the food cart arrives in the great hall. Michael and I, who have been introduced to Drake's devil dogs, sink our teeth into the two soft chocolate cake slices separated by a layer of luscious, sweet white cream. It's the best food under the sun, and I will eat these whenever I can.

Several times during our stay a ferry comes to the island and people leave. "Where are they going?" I ask. No one knows, but the matron overhears my question and answers me, "Some are going to be reunited with their families in America. Some are being taken to the immigration

157

office in Manhattan for hearings as you will be soon, and others are being investigated. They might be spies."

I shudder. I remember that the immigration officials said we might be spies. Now that I know what spies are I am sure that we are not them but I worry incessantly. Suppose they think we are? I heard what they said, and I understood what the matron said about spies. What's going to become of us? No wonder *mutti* was crying. I re-enter my own world of worrying, waiting and ruminating.

One afternoon we are told that on the following morning we will be taking a trip to New York City itself. Our destination is the immigration bureau on Columbus Circle and 59th Street in Manhattan. My father who has been notified of our arrival is catching the first train from Philadelphia, where he lives and works to meet us in New York, to attend the scheduled hearing. My mother is overjoyed.

"Can it really be?" she asks me, once again assuming that I'm a grown up. "Will we finally be seeing your father?"

To my great surprise and horror, I realize that I don't want to see my father. Coming to America and being with our father is a dream I have nurtured over most of my young life. It is embellished and invested in daily, but it only fits comfortably in the confines of my mind and not in the real world. I feel apprehensive and scared. Suppose he has a scarred face like the poor soldier on the Gripsholm? I don't know what awaits me. This place, Ellis Island, is safe. I know what to expect and I don't want to face the prospect of yet another change let alone a disappointment. Suppose my father is nothing like the father I have created? Suppose he is ugly, hairy and mean? What if I don't like him? Or worse, what if he doesn't like me? I don't want to see him. I don't know what I want, but one thing I am sure of; I want to remain on Ellis Island. I cannot admit these fears to anyone. What am I going to do? I don't want to see my Papa, and I don't want to leave Ellis Island, and this foreboding sense of apprehension and doom is definitely not part of my imagination.

It's raining the next morning. "How can we go on a ferry in the rain?" I ask my mother, hoping she'll tell the people in charge that we will have to postpone our trip. "We'll all get soaking wet and the ferry is small ship. This could turn into a bad storm like the one we had when we were on the big ship. We might all drown in this awful rain. Let's wait until a sunny day."

"Don't be ridiculous," my mother answers impatiently. She hasn't a clue why I'm suddenly so concerned about the weather. "Weren't we safe in the middle of the ocean when it was storming? Nothing will happen with the ferry. It's used all the time."

"Aren't we supposed to be going to school today?" I ask the matron, hopefully. Maybe she can squeeze one more day of safety on Ellis Island for me.

"Not today, dearie," she answers, "today, you will be seeing your father. And won't that be wonderful?" She has a strange accent. Much later on, when I hear an Irish brogue I recognize it and always associate it with her.

I realize that I have left all my precious school supplies on the island. I am ready to get off the ferry. "I'm going back for my school supplies," I announce to my mother before we are to board the ferry.

"No, you're not. You're being silly," my mother tells me. She pulls me by my arm. "Don't you think you will have everything you need? Your Papa will take care of everything." The ferry starts to move slowly away from my latest home and as I watch the island recede I feel a pang of regret. I don't want to leave this place I've become comfortable in. I have to abandon every place I've come to feel safe and protected in: Vienna, Wieliczka, Montelupi, Liebenau, the Gripsholm and now Ellis Island. I remember leaving Wieliczka, the running in Krakow, the ghetto, the horrible train rides, the unwelcoming stay in Switzerland. I know too well that not all change is for the better.

When we land in New York we take a taxi to our hearing. It is March. I am nine years old and overwhelmed by the sights of this city. It is pouring and I can't believe how many people are walking through the streets. All are rushing; some are carrying umbrellas, while others protect themselves by placing newspapers on their heads. No one seems to be looking where they are going, but they all seem to know how to get there.

When we arrive in the hearing office, the matron who accompanies us explains that she has to leave and go back to the island. "Now be patient dearies," she tells Michael and me in her melodic voice. "T'will be a long day for you. The judge is a busy man and has many people to see."

We are led to a row of chairs and told to sit there until the clerk calls our names. My mother warns us to behave. We sit silently for about half an hour, and then we start a "quiet" game of refugee.

I turn my chair around so that I can face Michael and appear like a proper secretary. He sits, hunched over in his seat, looking at his shoes.

"Yes?" I demand, sour- pussed as possible. "What do you want?"

"Oh please, please, I have come to see the commandant," he implorers.

"That is completely out of the question," I say crisply.

"Why not? I have an appointment and I have papers."

"What? You have papers. Let me see them!"

Before long, the game escalates into a shouting, crying match and my mother, who is embarrassed, has to separate us. She seats each of us on either side of her. We look at each other, trying hard to suppress the giggles that are erupting from our clenched lips. Our fates are to be sealed in this office today, and it is impossible for us to act dignified and serious.

CHAPTER 2

— ෯ —

WE SIT IN the waiting room of the Immigration Office, for what seems like hours. There is nothing to divert us: no picture on the walls, no books, just chairs and a few benches. We are the only people in the big room, with only an occasional clerk who slides by soundlessly. We try to behave, not make noise and to be as good as our mother has told us to be. The boredom is suffocating. We look at each other and start laughing. This is the perfect time for Michael and me to play our game of "refugee" and we have been strictly forbidden. After all, we are in an office that deals with refugees every day, all day long. Why is my mother being so strict with us? We look at each other over my mother's lap and around the back of her chair, trying to make each other laugh. Michael, pleading with his folded hands and I am shaking my head "no." We are engaged in a silent game of refugee.

Suddenly I am distracted. "Look *mutti*," I cry. Are all American ladies so beautiful?" A dark haired woman wearing lots of make-up, very high heels and a wrap- around purple shawl has entered the hall. My mother looks at her, and a shock of recognition registers on her face. It is her sister-in-law, Sari, my father's younger sister. I never knew we had an aunt in America.

My mother rushes towards Sari. The two women greet each other, hugging across a low wooden barrier and bursting into tears. Sari, who lives in New York, has received a telegram from my father informing her of our imminent arrival. She rushes over to Columbus Circle as soon as the telegram arrives. Telegrams are the only means of rapid communication. It is 1945, and telephones are an unaffordable luxury. A guard in the immigration tells my mother to please return to her seat and instruct Aunt Sari to sit behind the wooden barrier. Communication between the immigrants and unauthorized persons is strictly prohibited.

Sometime later, a dark, unshaven man comes rushing in. He is wearing a brown fedora hat and a black coat and he looks around, somewhat dazed as though not sure of where he is. I make a silent wish, "please, God, please let that man not be my father." The wish is not granted. He recognizes my mother and runs up to us. He hugs her and then us. I feel the sharp scrape of his whiskers on my cheek. Oh no! I am back in the empty stairwell embraced by *Glatz Kopf.* (a man who molested me in the POW camp)

"I left the factory in such a hurry that I didn't have a chance to wash up and shave," he apologizes for his appearance. "Can anyone imagine my joy and shock when I was telegraphed that you were here?" My father wipes tears from his face while my mother is sobbing.

I stare at my feet as though afraid they might take off on their own. He looks nothing like the image I had created in my fantasy. I retreat behind a wall of shyness and fear, mute, while Michael, eager to have a father, any father opens up like a gushing fountain.

Michael is impatient. He has waited for this moment all of his life. "*Mutti, mutti* is this Papa?" he looks up at her with imploring eyes, begging her to say "yes it is." We are all ushered into a room where an American judge, sitting in front of an American flag hears our case. He is a friendly, pleasant man who wears a US army uniform. He smiles at all of us. "Believe it or not," he tells us, "I am the father of two children who are the exact age of," he glances at the paper on his desk, "Rita and Moschel." For once my brother does not correct someone mispronounces his name. The judge is nothing like the surly, barking officials in Poland, Germany and Switzerland. He goes on, "I can only imagine how difficult life must have been for the four of you to be separated for so many years. I am going to make this as easy for all of us as I can while staying on the right side of the law."

He asks Michael and me why we want to come to America.

"To be with our father, of course!" Michael replies in a loud voice, while I nod in mute assent.

The judge asks my parents some other questions and I notice tears in my father's eyes. It is the second and last time I will ever see my father cry. The judge talks to my parents. I am not listening and if I were, I probably wouldn't understand anything. I hear strange words like "citizenship" and "naturalization." What they mean when they are finally translated to me is that the judge rules in our favor. We are permitted to leave with my father and live in America, provided that we go to Canada for several days and enter the US as Canadians. We don't have to return to Ellis Island where I want to go in order to collect my precious school supplies and meager possessions.

"Today is Purim," my father tells us. I have a vague recollection of Purim in Wieliczka when young men came to our house dressed in funny costumes, hoping to collect a few *groschen*, pennies.

"Purim," my father reminds us is a Jewish holiday celebrating the miraculous redemption of the Jews who were supposed to be hung in Persia by the tyrant Haman."

My mother thinks he's joking, that he's making up the fact that today is Purim. She thinks he does that for personal reasons, that it is Purim for us because we have been freed, just like the Jews in ancient Persia were so many years ago. She tells him so. "No, no, he assures her. Today is really Purim, March 14, 1945. Our redemption takes place on Purim day in 1945. Like the Jews of Shushan in Persia, we too are rescued.

CHAPTER 3

━━━━━━━━ ❧ ━━━━━━━━

WE GO TO a kosher restaurant, Schreiber's, on the upper West Side, where I am not impressed with the lovely surroundings. After all, I have just spent three weeks on a luxury liner eating Swedish food in an opulent dining room. Schreiber's is considered the best kosher restaurant in New York City but it does not compare to the *Gripsholm*. The restaurant is full of well- dressed, prosperous looking diners, but to my mother's amazement they are eating chicken with their fingers. "That's how Americans eat chicken," Sari explains. As she herself picks up a drumstick and brings it toward her mouth. "We get right down to the meat and who can blame us? It is so much more efficient to eat chicken with your fingers than to attempt to debone it, daintily, with a knife and fork." My mother is shocked. That could never happen in the cultured Europe she was raised in. "Such bad mannered people would be asked to leave the restaurant," she replies.

By the time we finish dinner the sky outside is totally black and New York City is ablaze with lights. To me, it is a fairy tale city: red and green traffic lights blinking on and off automatically, yellow street lamps, reflected in the wet pavement, neon signs flashing in brightly lit store windows. The world we have just left was dark, illuminated only by the moon and stars.

"Won't the enemy planes able to find us with so many lights on?" I ask Aunt Sari. "What happens when there is an air raid?"

"We've never had an air raid," she replies.

"But what if there *is* an air raid?" I persist.

She tries to assuage my fears, "America is too far away for the Germans to get here," she declares. "We're safe. We don't even think about an air raid. We've never had one and we never will." I doubt her certainty. I know that Germany is just as close to America as America is to Germany and I remember the bombs, the air raid sirens, the loud uniformed soldiers and the warm shrapnel.

I love the lights of New York, indifferent to the war, like a wealthy princess flaunting her jewels. But I worry. I am convinced we are in danger and the bright lights are disclosing our location to the enemy.

My father has found an apartment for us in the Washington Heights section of Manhattan, a German-Jewish neighborhood, full of refugees from German speaking countries. We aren't ready to move in yet. So Michael sleeps with my parents at a small hotel, The Endicott, on the West Side, and I stay with Aunt Sari in a room she shares with her good friend Thea. In the mornings, my parents bring Michael over to my aunt's apartment and we spend the day exploring the sights of New York, while they go out and get our new home ready.

My aunt is taking a week off from work so she can show Michael and me a good time. We leave her house early, well before noon. The streets of Manhattan are full of people in a hurry to get somewhere. We go to the underground, through a turnstile that requires a coin to let us pass, stand on a noisy platform and wait for a train to come. Once on the train we are jostled from side to side heading at what feels like breakneck speed inside a black tunnel. We are thrown about and the noise is deafening, but no one seems concerned. Some passengers try to shout above the din to make their voices heard by their companions while others are engrossed in their newspapers, magazines and books. Everyone seems fine, not aware of the disaster that only I seem to be aware of. Even Michael looks comfortable. Am I the only one who feels the impending danger?

When the ride is over we get out of the train into the bright sunlight. I question my aunt, "What is wrong with that train? Why is it so noisy and shaky? Are all of them like this? I feel like I'm going down into the very bottom of the earth and hearing the roaring of giants."

She laughs at my concerns. "Welcome to the New York Subway system, and yes, it is noisy and lurching, but it is safe and it gets people quickly to where they have to go. You'll get used to it." Then she adds, "and now that we are where we want to be let's have some fun."

What excitement awaits us! I get to eat my first banana from one of the sidewalk fruit displays. I have only seen pictures of bananas, but I never tasted one. It is surprisingly smooth and bland and it certainly does not meet my expectations.

After the banana comes the best part. Aunt Sari takes us to the Radio City to see a movie. We pass under a brightly lit marquee, through thickly carpeted, luxurious lobbies and past uniformed ushers wearing lots of brass and satin trim who help us find our seats. The theater is very dark, and the screen is huge. A pleasant smell that I will associate with movie theaters for the rest of my life permeates the auditorium. We sit in soft, comfortable seats and the music comes at us from every direction as we are transported to the delightful world of Disney's animated film "The Three Caballeros," featuring Donald Duck, lots of other cartoon characters and many real singers and dancers. Every color is sharper, every sound is clearer and every costume is more outrageous than anything in the world outside. It is enchanting and I never want it to end.

From the movies, we head to the Automat for lunch, where another miracle takes place. We put nickels into a slot in the wall and a magic window opens and presents us with the food of our choice.

CHAPTER 4

WHEN THE WEEK is over, it is time to enter the real world. Aunt Sari has to return to work and we have to start our new lives. My father has decided to move from Philadelphia to New York where he thinks we will have more opportunities to learn and practice Judaism.

My parents arrive to take us to the apartment in Washington Heights, which is on the upper west side of Manhattan, near the George Washington Bridge. German is spoken on the streets, at the grocery store, in the fruit stands and the bakery. People stop each other on the street and inquire, in German, where they are from, how they spent the war years, do they have any relatives in Europe. I hate the language, guttural and dissonant and reminiscent of the times and places I want to forget. That won't be possible in Washington Heights.

We climb up five stories to get to our apartment. "Are we there yet?" I ask my father at every landing. "Not yet," he answers, trying to catch his breath. Finally, on the fifth floor he takes out a key and inserts it into the lock of one of the three doors opening onto the hallway, number 53. He throws open the door and stands back, proud of his find. I have no idea of what to expect, but what I see is exciting and full of promise. Two doors are located on the left side of the dark corridor, one leading to a narrow bathroom and the other to the equally narrow kitchen, where we will spend most of our time doing homework, listening to the radio and of course, eating. A big bright room, with windows that face out "across the alley" has an open view of our neighbors' apartments. We can peer into their lives just as they can into ours and right in front of the window a rusty, iron fire escape clings to the outer wall.

"*Mutti*, look," I say excitedly, "we have a balcony!"

"No, no, no," my father runs over to explain. "That is not a balcony. That is called a fire escape. If there's a fire in our apartment we have to run down all these steps to get out of the house."

"But can't we use it as a balcony until we have a fire?" I ask hopefully.

"Well," he explains, "it can be a bit dangerous. No," he thinks it over. "Well, if you're very careful you can sit on the window sill and let your feet rest on the fire escape's floor. That way you can pretend that you are sitting on a balcony."

I open the window and climb out on the fire escape. Once I step onto it I freeze. Looking past the railing I see what my father means by dangerous. Its steep and narrow steps appear treacherous. One tiny misstep and I will plunge between the two buildings where I would shatter like a porcelain doll. I can see myself lying, broken on the ground. I grab hold of the rail and carefully back myself inside our new living room. This is not a balcony I will ever use.

The two other rooms are going to be bedrooms. The larger of the two belongs to my parents and the smaller one to Michael and me. Beds on opposite sides of the room are already made up for us and one large dresser that we will share is next to the closet. There is only one window in a corner of the room and it is much darker than the rest of the apartment. I like it. It's cozy, it's clean and it's ours. Michael and I try out the new beds. First we lie down on them, pretending to sleep, and then we jump up and down. We make lots of excited sounding noise, laughing and screaming.

My father comes into the room. "Stop that," he shouts at us. It is the first time I hear him raise his voice. It shocks and frightens me. "You're going to break the springs on the beds. Beds are made for sleeping on and nothing else." I stop, carefully step off the bed and back against the corner of the dresser. His voice, when angry, reminds me of the male voices I heard in Poland when the menacing police officers shouted at the cowering Jews. This is not the gentle voice of the Papa I had dreamed of all my life.

"Alex, please," my mother says to him, "these children have had so few things of their own. What harm will it do for them to jump up and down on a bed?"

My father turns to her and I can see he is shocked by her response to his scolding us. "Fredel," he says to her quietly, "did you forget that parents should never disagree in front of their children?"

My mother remembers what she learned in the *mutter schule* so long ago when she was pregnant in Vienna. She sighs, her shoulders sag and she gives in. "It's been such a long time since we were able to be two parents to our children. I forgot." At night, when Michael falls asleep, I listen to my father speaking to my mother in German. "You cannot imagine how hard it was to find this apartment," he tells her. "With the war still on, no new buildings are going up. Apartments are impossible to find."

"How did you manage to find this one?" she asks, curious.

He explains that he had literally gone from one building to another asking the superintendents if they had a vacancy. By chance, he met an Austrian woman, Mrs. Flesch in the lobby of this one. She told him of this vacancy on the fifth floor. "A miracle," he adds.

He goes on to tell her what life had been for him in the United States. "You have no idea how it was. I came here with nothing: no family, no money, no job. Nothing. I tell you. No one to even talk to. The minute I left Vienna I was overcome with loneliness for you and the children, for my parents and, believe it or not, the city of Vienna itself. After all, I had lived there all my life, and although I hated what had happened I loved the city itself. Music seemed to come from every corner, beautiful people, beautiful clothes, wonderful smells coming from the *cafe-hauses*. Love it or hate it, it was familiar. I knew where every street was located, where to shop and where to *daven* (pray). By the time I got to Philadelphia I thought I would go out of my mind." I can hear my mother whispering but can't make out all of her responses. He continues, his voice taking on an urgency and intensity. "I stayed with Sari in New York so that was a help. Of course she went to work every day and came home from her factory job too tired to even talk. One *Shabbes* I went to *Shul* and someone told me about a job in Philadelphia, a cutter in a leather factory. I took the train went to the factory and took the job." He sounds pleased with himself, his resourcefulness and independence. "Of course Philadelphia is not a place to raise the children," he goes on. "New York will give them much better opportunities."

My mother is impressed. "It's wonderful that you were able to go from an office job in Vienna to a factory, working at anything that would bring you some money." She is filled with admiration for the man she married: who saved our lives, was willing to accept any kind of work and walked the streets of New York to find a suitable apartment for us. He tells her that he chose New York because he knew it would be easier to bring up Jewish children in New York than any other place on earth.

"Here, in this neighborhood, we are not a despised minority," he assures her. She tells him what a wonderful choice he made. "I know that this is a splendid apartment for us. It's a good place for the children to grow up in, lots of sunshine, fresh air and a good place learn about their new country and old religion."

Now that my father has assured her of the appropriateness of the neighborhood he goes on to explain his having to accept a menial job. "Believe me, there were no jobs in the insurance business for refugees. Metropolitan Life, John Hancock; they would rather hire an ignorant American *Goy* than a well-educated, smart refugee, especially a Jewish one. As soon as they found out I was Jewish they dismissed me. Some never interviewed me even though I appeared in response to their want ads. It wasn't easy going from a nice clean office, with my own desk to a dirty, noisy factory. But the money was good and I had no choice. Anyway, I have no cause to complain. Having you and the children with me? I never dreamed that we would be together again." There are a few moments of silence and then I hear him go on.

"Sometimes I felt lost in this big country. All I wanted was to see you and the children. Now that you're all here I see that there is so much to do in order to give them opportunities, help them understand that they're Jewish, and get them a proper education. How can I ever make up to them what they have lost?"

"Be patient, Alex," I hear my mother say soothingly. "It takes time to get used to a new life."

"I know, I know. But here, in America? I am nothing. I have no position and no chance of becoming anything other than a factory worker. At least in Vienna our family was respected, we had relatives and friends. Here, we have no one except for Sari: no family, no real friends." The contented tone of voice of only a moment ago is gone. He sounds sad and resentful.

"I hate the factory. You can't imagine what kind of people I work with, the lowest of the lowest." He continues and I listen.

"How I miss my old life in Vienna: the coffee houses, the music, the *intelligensia*. Look at how many great Jewish minds started out in Vienna: Freud, Herzl, Mahler, Buber, Kafka. You could hear Strauss in the sound of the tram cars. And the Jewish life! How much freedom we enjoyed, there was no anti-Semitism in my Vienna. The Jews had the same rights as any citizen, or so it seemed. I was the assistant to one of the vice presidents at the insurance company. Unfortunately, the Austrians did not need much persuasion from Hitler and his henchmen to change all that."

CHAPTER 5

———— ❦ ————

MY MOTHER DOES the best she can to make the apartment cheerful and comfortable. She goes to the Woolworth store and buys two potted plants and places them on the window sill. She buys an inexpensive mirror at the second hand furniture store, lugs it up the five flights of stairs and hangs it on the wall opposite the window. She is delighted with her decorating skills. "Look," she says to my father, "You see how the mirror reflects the windows? Now it's like we have four windows in the room instead of two."

We unpack the new dishes, pots and pans. My mother washes them in the kitchen sink, I dry them and my father puts them up on a shelf. It is an assembly line, and I enjoy the status conferred upon me by making me be part of it. The table, my father tells everyone, is made of a new product called "Formica."

"It's the latest material available. You can put hot stuff on it and it won't burn the top. You can spill things on it and it won't warp. It is totally impermeable; a miracle." He demonstrates its attributes by putting a lit cigarette on the table to show us that heat will not harm the new product. The top layer of Formica slowly starts to melt. A blue flame is reaching upwards and the smell is awful. Quickly *mutti* throws a glass of water on it and douses the flame. My father looks shocked and embarrassed. After my initial fear I laugh at the mishap, "so much for the miracle of the new Formica table."

My father becomes angry at me. "You're being disrespectful," he scolds me. "You never, ever should laugh at your parents." I don't know what to say. I'm frightened. He raises his voice and I see he's angry;

and it's me he's angry with. I don't know what to do to make his anger disappear. I feel ashamed and look down at the floor, but he goes on, "I obeyed and honored my parents and I expect the same from my children. I would never dream of laughing at my father or mother."

I still don't understand what it was that I did to make him so angry. No one had ever told me that laughing at something I found amusing was bad. I feel uncomfortable and squirm at his outburst. Now I've not only made him sad but angry as well. The more he talks the angrier he becomes. How could my stupid giggle have provoked so much emotion?

"I was a good son," he begins reminiscing. His voice turns from rage to sadness. "I did everything they asked of me. I sacrificed a secular education in order to respect my father's wishes and with it a chance to have a profession."

I feel guilty and sad thinking that I somehow am responsible for the disappearance of my *oma* and *opa*. I try to think of what I did and how to change the somber mood since I was the one who made my father angry. I use my mother's cheerful voice and try to distract him, admire the table.

"Look," I exclaim, my heart full of pain while my demeanor brims with excitement. "Look at the two extension pieces at either end of the table that slide out and have to be lifted. "They're almost like a piano." I turn on the radio and pretend to be playing along with the music being broadcasted..

My mother chides him later that night. I listen in on their conversation. "Alex. Why did you get so angry at Maidi when she laughed at your cigarette experiment? She didn't do anything disrespectful. She thought it was funny and so did I."

"She was belittling me and laughing at me," he tells her earnestly, "and that is not the kind of behavior I expect from my child. I want love and respect from my children, not ridicule. I may be nothing on the outside world, but here, from my children, I expect appreciation and love, not ridicule."

"She wasn't laughing at you, Alex," she tells him, "she was laughing at the situation." I feel relieved that my mother is sticking up for me.

CHAPTER 6

⸎

I AM WEARING my mother's blue bathrobe tied at the waist, a beret tilted on the side of my head, and am standing next to the wall, leaning against it. My left arm is bent at the elbow, resting on my hip, my mother's purse hanging casually from it. I am putting on a show for Michael. A pencil is dangling from my lips, a make believe cigarette, my eyes are half closed and I'm, trying to get the soprano pitch of my voice as deep down as it will go."*Unter der laterne,*" I croon. I am being Marlene Dietrich singing *Lili Marlene*.

The door opens and my father looks in. Instinctively I stop singing. I'm surprised and embarrassed. He hasn't said a word and yet I'm ready to crawl under the bed. I feel as though I've been caught doing something I shouldn't be doing. He sees that I have stopped, seems about to say something, halts and backs out of the room. I feel weird. I don't know how to act. I'm not sure I know who I am. I feel strange because my instinct is to shrink away from him, not let him see me this way. I feel that I don't know right from wrong. I am terribly uncomfortable in his presence.

I take great pains to dress in the bathroom, where there is no chance of his walking in on me naked and I make sure to be extra quiet when he is home. I try to keep away from him as much as possible. This is the first time in my memory that I've had to share quarters with a man and I am uneasy and embarrassed. I never expected to feel this way about my father and I wish it was different. Not only is he nothing like the man I envisioned, but he is moody and unpredictable. And, I am nothing like I thought I would be when I finally got to be with my father again. I never know what to expect of him or of myself.

My father who has had virtually nothing to do with our upbringing and hasn't seen us for six years is determined to take charge. Among his concerns is the fact that Michael and I know nothing about Judaism. I overhear him telling our neighbor Mrs. Flesch, that we don't know an *aleph* from a *bet*. "They're like *goyim*," he tells her lamenting his predicament.

"Mr.Schmelkes," she interrupts him patiently, "where were they supposed to learn Hebrew? At the ghetto? or at the camp in Germany?" He doesn't answer.

He promptly enrolls us in the Yeshiva, an ultra -Orthodox day school. Girls are expected to wear long sleeves and longish skirts and boys, *tzitzis*, ritual fringes that hang outside their shirts. Nothing is explained to me and I don't know any reasons for what is happening. The school is housed in an old synagogue that has one large sanctuary and a warren of makeshift classrooms haphazardly separated by partitions and room dividers. A moveable blackboard is wheeled from one room to another and shared by many classes.

My school day is noisy, chaotic and completely undisciplined, nothing like the regimented classroom in Liebenau or the public school, P.S. 189, across the street from our apartment. P.S. 189, is an imposing brick building taking up an entire city block. A large school yard surrounded by a chain linked fence runs along its perimeters. On the Jewish holidays, when I don't go to school, I watch the children running around having fun before school starts and during lunch recess. They scurry into line when the whistle blows and quietly enter the building in two straight, silent lines. The shortest kids line up in the front, with girls on one line and boys on the other. Everyone seems to know exactly where they ae going even though there are so many students. I watch them enviously. I long for the disciplined atmosphere with its rules and standards which is lacking in my school. All the children that live on our street attend P.S.189 and they all seem to be having fun.

Since I am new at the Yeshiva and have recently come from Germany, the faculty assumes that I can't read or do math. Even though I am nine years old I am assigned to the first grade with six- year olds. I am hurt, disappointed and outraged. I object loudly. I bristle at the unfairness of it all. No one has ever established what I am capable of and they presume that I know nothing. "What am I doing there with all these babies?" I ask my parents. My mother understands. She too is upset by my being placed with first graders, but she is at a loss. She is unfamiliar with the way things are done in the US and tells me to be patient.

Later on, I complain to my teacher, who also tells me to be patient. I have been patient all my life; waiting to meet my father, waiting to come to the US, waiting to go to a real school. I am not going to be patient for one more minute. Without asking permission to leave the room, I march right over to the principal's office, burst in, without knocking on the door. He looks up from a book he is scrutinizing, surprised to see me. Before he can utter one word I start talking.

"I can read, I can write and I can do arithmetic. Why do I have to learn the sounds of the letters when I have already read many books?" Gone is my shyness. I speak with the upper class British accent I learned in Liebenau, which some Americans mistake for arrogance. I am demanding and not the least bit concerned with being polite. When it comes to school I know who I am and what I am capable of. "I'm not a baby and I will not go to a school that can only teach me what I already know."

The principal is taken aback by my outburst. He acts as if he has never heard such a demanding request before. "Well," he answers me slowly, astonished at my boldness, "we just want to make sure you are comfortable and not in over your head. We want you to be happy here and not frustrated by the difficulty of a new language."

My words spill out forcefully. "This is not a new language for me. I think I speak it rather well. As for being frustrated by the difficulties, I am finding the work totally boring. I'm not in over my head. I'm drowning in boredom. I want to be with children my own age, in a class where I can learn something new. I already know how to read. I don't need to be taught that C-A-T spells cat." The years in Liebenau, when I was responsible myself as well as for Michael, have taught me how to fend myself.

"Ohh," He nods, "Mmmm, I had no idea. I see what you mean. Let's give it a little more time and see how you do in the first grade, and then if you do well, we'll move you up."

"Not good enough," I tell him, staunchly, crossing my arms in front of my bosom. "I'm not going to be in first grade one minute longer."

"Look," he says to me, "go back for the time being. I promise you that I will take care of things and have you placed in you correct grade."

Reluctantly I go back into the classroom. The class work is ridiculously easy. A week passes and he comes into the classroom. He has a quiet chat with the teacher. I see them looking at me while she nods her head. He announces to the class that I am to be moved to second grade. This announcement is met by a loud protest. "No fair," the other children shout. "Why is she going to second grade?"

Unfortunately, second grade is just as boring as first and I am once again in a situation I can't control and feel I can't live in. I become disruptive in class, humming, tapping my fingers on the desk, calling out wrong answers. When the teacher speaks to me I explain that I want to be in a higher grade. "No, not want to be, should be. I can already read all the books the rest of the class is struggling with and I can do the arithmetic in my sleep. I hate being here with these little seven year olds. Do you know that I am nine years old?"

The teacher, a young woman with curly black hair, round eyes looks at me from behind thick eyeglasses. She is sympathetic. She seems to understand my disappointment. "I am going to help you go to a higher grade," she tells me. "Give me a chance to speak to the principal."

My tactics work. I am placed into the third grade, still a year older than my classmates, but I give in. I know when I am beaten. I also learn how to fight for a just cause and how get my way when I am incensed at injustice. The school justifies their actions by assigning Tovah, a pudgy third grader to help me "catch up." I don't realize this at first, but Tovah is an unpopular girl who has no friends. Tovah, they figure, will be provided with a new friend and a dose of self- esteem by becoming my mentor.

It is not going to work. Tovah is a little Gestapo maiden. "Dress not frock, potsy not hopscotch, store not shop, cayn't not cahn't." Tovah's nasal voice drones on and on. When I do things my way, she calls me "dumb." My way of writing is wrong; my way of doing subtraction and addition is ridiculous. Everything I do is criticized by Tovah. During recess she walks around the schoolyard with me while all the other girls are having fun jumping rope and playing hopscotch. She is forever correcting my pronunciation and language usage, making fun of my foreign ways, my lunch, my book bag, the braids my mother painstakingly plaits early every morning before I go to school.

I resent her and it is clear that she does not like me either, but relishes her role as my boss. I understand that feeling. I have been in charge of my brother for a long time, so I know how good it feels to be boss. But I am not about to take directions from some fat girl who is younger than I am and has no friends. I hate her and I hate the grown-ups at the school who are allowing this.

"Quiet," she hisses at me when I raise my hand to answer a question. "You don't know the answer to that question, so put your hand down." I do so know what the capital of Portugal is and no one else in the class has their hand up, including Tovah. I ignore her, and wait to be called on. "Lisbon," I reply, gloating at Tovah.

For a nine- year old, school is life and my life is letting me down. I looked forward to school since I was four years old and watched my older cousins go off to school in Wieliczka. I enjoyed the school in Liebenau, where even though we did not have enough supplies, I felt that I was learning and the atmosphere was disciplined. Even the little classroom in Ellis Island provided a room with a blackboard, lots of school supplies and a structured environment. This school in America with its haphazard classrooms, young inexperienced teachers and a principal who walks around the school pushing his refrigerator sized belly, while nodding and smiling at everyone but not even knowing my name. This is nothing like what I had experienced, read about or expected.

I soon realize that I am losing parts of myself. I am not the same person I was before I came here. I feel like the stranger walking around in my body has taken over my identity. I no longer know who I am. Before coming to America I had a pretty strong idea of who I was. In Liebenau, I was a seven and eight year old girl. I went to school, played with other children, participated in performances, took care of my little brother, had tasks and responsibilities I could I could master. As difficult as things were for us in Liebenau no one tried to take me away from myself. I was listened to, given sensible answers to my questions. On the Gripsholm all I had to do was to play and eat. In Ellis Island I was once again a student in a classroom. For the most part I was an obedient, compliant child, aware of what was expected of me and willing to meet those expectations.

Since coming to America, all my expectations have been invalidated. My father is a moody unpredictable man whom I am forever disappointing. My mother, who was my staunchest supporter, friend and protector has allied herself with my father and is no longer reachable. The children in my school mock my accent, laugh at my last name, and exclude me from their games. I am placed in a grade that not only doesn't challenge me but is far below my level and to make matters worse charges a younger bully girl to be my mentor. When I make my needs known, I am ignored or lied to. It is truly too much for me to accept. My personality is being stripped away from me at an alarming pace.

I complain to my mother about the school. "We don't have enough of anything we need: textbooks, blackboards, maps, dictionaries. Everything has to be passed from one classroom to another. My helper Tovah makes me re-write all my compositions. She checks my spelling, scribbles comments on my papers in red pencil and makes me do everything over again crossing out lots of my details. The teachers don't even correct my work. That task is left to Tovah, who hates me and whom I hate."

I can't articulate how dreadful I feel. How does a nine year old explain the disappointment of being thrown into this chaotic environment, of having her dreams and hopes cast aside? Nothing is as it was promised. My father is not the loving Papa I had hoped for. I am afraid to speak to him for fear that I will say something that will anger him. My school is a hodge- podge of disorganized adults supervising rowdy, undisciplined children. I don't know how to tell my mother how I'm feeling. I don't have the language or the awareness to express my frustration. The kids at school call me Nazi because I have an unfamiliar accent. I hate my school, I hate my life. I feel more prejudice in this little Jewish school than I have ever experienced personally.

At least in the ghetto everyone was treated the same. In the camp, the nuns and teachers judged everyone fairly and by the quality of their work. Here, in this little school I am being discriminated against: and why? because I am totally ignorant of my religion, because my English is different from theirs, because the teachers can't take the time to pronounce my last name correctly and call me 'smelkase' or some other ridiculous sounding name. Every child in my class has parents who speak with an accent; German, Russia, Polish, yet I am being discriminated against because of mine. My father encourages me to hold on to it. "It sounds so much more refined than the New York accent," he tells me.

One day I hand in an assignment the teacher has given the class. Tovah has not done hers and when the teacher questions her, she complains she is unable to do her own schoolwork and supervise mine as well. I am taking up too much of her time and she wants an extension. I am ready to explode. Now she is blaming me for her uncompleted work. The teacher never looks at my completed assignments. She hands them over to Tovah and tells her to check it. In return Tovah gets the extension she asked for and my homework is marked up in Tovah's red handwriting.

I give up. I make up my mind that I am never going to return to this school. The next morning I don't get out of bed. "This is not going to be a 'sick' sore throat day," I tell my mother. "This is going to be the day when I never go back to that school again." I am lying in bed, rigid and inflexible. "Michael will have to go to school without me because nothing is going to make me change my mind. There is a perfectly good public school across the street and if you want me to go to school, any school, it will be that one." I fight a hard battle. Without my father in the room, I can still stand up for what I consider my rights.

My mother sends Michael off alone. She sits down on the edge of my bed. "Tell me," my mother says gently, stroking my shoulder lovingly, "You were looking forward to school all your life. What happened in school yesterday that is making you so unhappy?"

"It wasn't just yesterday. I have no friends, certainly not Tovah. No adults recognize anything that I am doing. I get no praise, I get no directions. This school simply does not feel right." I burst into tears. "I hate that place. Everyone pokes fun of accent; they even call me a Nazi. Me a Nazi I who am the only girl in the school who felt the power and the terror of a Nazi! I have to be insulted by being called a Nazi? The teacher never even looks at my work. I have no one in that school; no one to talk to, no one to play with. I hate Tovah and her bossiness.

I'm not going to a school where a stupid kid who doesn't like me and whom I hate is my teacher!" I cry and hold fast to the sides of the bed. No one is going to be able to force me out. My mother lets me stay home while she goes to the school administration to tell them about my feelings. I must have convinced her because she is gone for over an hour. When she comes home she reasons with me.

"I talked to the teacher and the principal. Tovah will no longer be your helper," My mother pleads with me. "Try the school again and I promise you that if things do not get better, you will go to public school."

I agree and return to school the next day. Tovah is relieved of her exalted position. She is reduced to just another kid. She must be missing my companionship because she tries to win me over by showing me some of her jewelry, and offering to share a snack with me at lunchtime.

CHAPTER 7

———— ❧ ————

With Tovah out of the picture I finally find a real friend, Yetta. She is my age and a grade ahead of me in school. We enjoy being together. School gets better for me after I have Yetta. She is an only child, lives near the school and has a job walking two little girls home from kindergarten during lunch time. She offers to share her job and salary with me. It is a wonderful opportunity for me. We each get fifty cents a week, a veritable fortune for a nine year old in 1945. We love the job, pretending that we are mothers walking our children home from school. It provides us with money, companionship and a sense of responsibility.

To get the kindergartners home, we have to cross many streets, some of them quite busy. But we are careful and conscientious and with money in our pockets, we feel rich. Every day on our walk with the two children, Yetta and I engage in "grown up" conversations. We make plans for our futures. We will be beautiful and marry handsome boys. We will live next door to each other and our children will play together. We will visit every day and have lunch at each other's houses and then rush home to prepare dinner for our husbands.

"So, Yetta," I say, "what are you making for dinner tonight?"

"Oh," she answers, "I'm fixing up some leftovers from *Shabbes*. Sam loves the meat loaf I made, and I made enough for a couple of days."

"I'm just going to warm up the *cholent* and make meatballs with potato kugel."

We talk in grown up voices trying to sound like important, responsible housewives.

I try to tell Yetta about my life before coming to America. She knows I have an accent, but she doesn't care. Her parents also have accents. "You know, I've have been in a real Ghetto, a prison and a camp," I tell her.

She has no idea what I'm talking about. No one has told her about the war and what has happened to the Jews of Europe. The only thing she knows about is that her parents both come from Europe, Germany, as a matter of fact. She quickly changes the subject. "Let's talk about something else," she says. "Do you know that Fanny Rabinowitz is getting a bike? Imagine, a girl riding on a bicycle!" It is 1945 and orthodox girls are not encouraged to do anything that might compromise their hymen, be it a bike ride or a split in a gymnastics class.

Yetta is full of information. She gives me my first lessons about sex. She tells me how important it is never to let a boy kiss you because that could make you do other things that would ruin my life. I don't understand what she means, but not wanting to appear ignorant I agree with everything she says. Why would I ever let a boy kiss me anyway? I ask myself. Boys are disgusting. The very thought of getting close to one is repulsive. They sweat, they smell.

I go over to Yetta's house after school. It's raining and since Yetta lives close to the school she suggests that I stay at her house until it stops. Her parents are much older than mine and seem like relatives to me. Her mother is short, stocky and kind. She hugs me when I come into the house. "Come in girls," she invites us into the kitchen. "Good you decided not walk home in this rain," she tells me welcomingly. She takes the milk out of refrigerator. "Drink, drink, it's good for your teeth," she tells us as she opens a box from the bakery and serves us chocolate éclairs. Her father comes home. He is gray and wears glasses. Like my parents, they speak German to each other and their home is warm and welcoming. I call them "*tante* and *oncle*," and feel like I am their niece. "You'll stay for dinner, ya?" her mother asks. I would love to but I must get home. My mother is surely worrying about me.

Their family comes from Berlin where her father was a physician. They emigrated to the U.S. before 1935 and Yetta was born in New York City two weeks after they arrived. Her father does not have a license to practice medicine in America but he works a pharmacy not far from their house. My mother often consults him when any one of us is ill. He is a generous, kind man and gives freely of his knowledge. If the condition requires a prescription, he tells us to go to another doctor who is licensed to write prescriptions. But doctors are expensive for our struggling family and he often saves us money as well as looking after our health.

They invite me to go places with them; museums, parks and the zoo. Yetta and I pretend we are sisters. In school, we tell everyone that we're cousins, that my mother is her father's sister. Her parents are better off financially than we are and pay for me to do things with her that I could never ask my parents for. I come home and tell them of our wonderful adventures and the things we did. My mother is happy that I am getting opportunities to go to educational places. When my father acts upset at my having to accept favors I can't return she tells him that since Yetta is an only child, her parents are happy to provide her with the companionship of another child. My father knows that the Levys spend money on me and he is not comfortable with that. He tries to justify their generosity.

"They brought money with them from Berlin and invested it," my father tells my mother. "They can afford things that are unthinkable for us. Remember, I had to leave under very bad conditions. I had to leave everything: my family, my job, my friends and my beloved parents. If I had had the luxury of taking my time I would have been able to bring more than simply money out of Vienna. Besides," he goes on, "Dr. Levy has a profession and could always get a job here if he weren't so rich and lazy. He could get a medical license too." For some reason he appears to be angry at Dr. Levy. "If I had disobeyed my father, and gone to the *Gymnasium* and to the University, I would also be able to provide my children with luxuries." He sounds bitter. "I don't want to encourage Rita to take things from people. It's like accepting charity."

"But Alex, they are so kind to Rita," my mother says to my father. "They worked for their money; got it out of Germany and now they can spend it as they wish. They deserve everything they have. And if they want to give their child the pleasure of a companion, who are we to judge them for it?"

"There you go again," he tells her, "always arguing with me."

She tries to appease him, "No, no, I'm not disagreeing with you. Of course you would have brought money out of Austria, if you had the chance. But look, you did save us and bring us to America. How many people did that?" She tries to soothe him without damaging the image of the Levys. My mother is happy that I found a friend whose parents can offer me some advantages that she can't.

My father doesn't hear her, can't let go of his anger, "Do you think I like being poor?" he asks. "In Vienna I made a good living, dressed well and worked at a respectable job. I know what you went through during the war, but don't think, for one moment, that it was easy for me." I feel badly, that somehow I cause my father to be unhappy because of my friendship with Yetta.

"In Vienna, at the Phoenix Company, everyone called me Mr. Schmelkes. Here, every *pischer* calls me 'Alex.' You think that's easy for me?"

Later on I ask my mother what I've done to make my father so angry at the Levys and so sad and poor. She assures me that I've done nothing bad.

"Don't worry maidi," she says to me, using my old nickname, "these problems are no concern of yours. You go on and have a good time with Yetta and her parents." She sends me off.

"Now," Dr. Levy says, "what do you girls want to do? Do you want a pony ride or a camel ride?" We are at the Bronx Zoo, standing in front of the ticket booth where kids are lined up to ride a domestic animal. All the children in line are holding a grown-up's hand and jumping up and down with excitement and anticipation. The ponies and the camels smell awful, but I am not about to give up an opportunity of a lifetime.

It is a hard choice but I opt for the pony, figuring it is shorter and if I fall I will be closer to the ground. Yetta's father takes my picture. They are enthusiastic and compliment me, "You looked like a real cowgirl," they say when the ride is over. I am thrilled.

School improves. I am ambitious, driven and determined to succeed. I study for tests, read books and write reports without Tova's messing them up with her ridiculous red pencil. I receive praise from my teachers and feel rewarded. I work hard to get their approval. My test grades are high and I'm feeling successful. Just as I tried in Wieliczka to improve my Polish accent, I now practice speaking like an American. It isn't hard at all. "Cain't instead of cahn't, wadeh, instead of water, claiss instead of clahs, exaimple instead of example, dayncing instead of dahncing." When the spring semester comes to an end, I organize the girls to put on a play. I have had plenty of experience with that sort of thing in Liebenau where we put on shows for all sorts of occasions.

We write the show. It has dancing and singing and all the girls participate. We rehearse during recess and by the time we put it on, we feel ready for Hollywood. The boys say we are a bunch of show offs, but we don't care. The teachers and the administration love our performance and we certainly love the attention and recognition we get.

Summer is coming and I overhear my parents talking about sending us to camp. I'm not supposed to be listening to their conversation, but I can't help pricking up my ears. I barge into their bedroom where they are quietly discussing my fate.

"Camp? What camp?" I interrupt. "We're not going back to the camp, are we?" The only camp I know about is Liebenau and I certainly don't want to go back there.

"No, no," my father tells me. "We are thinking of a summer camp, a nice place where children go on vacation and to be with other children."

"I don't want to go. I want to stay where I am. I don't want a summer vacation, whatever that is. Not having to go to school every day is all the vacation I want, and believe it or not, I know what I want."

My father listens to me but does not appear swayed by my determination. "We love you maidi," he tells me gently, "and we want you to have many, many opportunities that you cannot possibly have just by staying at home. Trust us. We know what is best for you. Now go to bed and stop worrying. We will never do anything to make you unhappy, maidi."

CHAPTER 8

———— ❦ ————

I WAKE UP sweating. My hair is damp, my pajama top is wet. I am out of breath and panting. I realize I've had a nightmare and I try to reconstruct it before I forget.

I am alone in a train with no other people. Large, shiny black birds are pecking at the windows, breaking the glass and flying into the train. I run from one seat to another but cannot find my mother or Bubbi. The gigantic birds encircle me, close ranks and make it impossible for me to move. I try to shield my eyes as they peck at my hands. I wake up, panting and out of breath. I look around not sure of where I am. In my mind I am still in the bad dream. I cannot shake the feeling of great fear.

Where is my mother and where is my bed? I look around. Nothing looks familiar. I am not on a train. I am not on a ship, not on Ellis Island. I realize I am lost. Where, oh where am I? The room is full of cots, full of other girls sleeping, but I am lost. This is not the nursery in Liebenau. I shake my head to as if to clear it of flying bugs and creepy spiders. I realize that though I am awake my physical reactions and my feelings are still in the middle of the nightmare. I suddenly realize I am in camp.

Why am I here? I sit up and let my eyes adjust to the darkness. I taste dust in my mouth and a cold empty cave opens up where my stomach used to be. I recognize the feeling as the same panic I had when waiting in Wieliczka and the Ghetto for my mother to come home from a dangerous errand, a return to my dreadful past. I am so frightened. I can't crawl into my mother's bed. I can't wake up the counselor and I certainly can't go back to sleep. How did I get here?

I reconstruct the process that got me into this situation. My parent, my father really, wants me to become acclimated to America, and most important of all, to become more familiar with being Jewish. He is convinced that the most efficient way of doing this is to send me to a Jewish summer camp. I remember their conversation. My summer is settled without a word of input from me.

"I don't know if it's such a good idea to send the children away," my mother says quietly to him one night when they think I am sleeping. "We've only been together for three months. Don't you think they should become acclimated to us as a family before they are thrown into a foreign environment? They can get used to being Jews and Americans next year."

He tries to convince her, "Fredel, you have no idea how hot, stuffy and humid New York is in the summer. There'll be nothing for them to do here. Let them go out of the city, where the fresh country air will do them good. If the Jewish community thinks it's important enough to give them a camp scholarship who am I to argue? They've had lots of experience helping Jewish families adjust and besides they don't like to throw money out." He continues attempting to win her over. "They have to learn how to live in as Jews in America. Think of what we've had to give up in order to remain Jewish. Surely giving up a summer of New York City heat and humidity to be in the fresh country air and at the same time learn about their religion is not a bad thing," he adds a bit of sarcasm. "They'll enjoy being with other children and getting used to their lives in a free country. They have all their lives to get used to us."

She resists. "Maybe we could all go to the mountains together and not have to send the children away the first summer we are a family again."

"Fredel," he tells her, "I don't know how to say this, but the children are too close to you. They have to get away from you for a short time. It isn't good for them, it isn't natural to be so tied to their mother. Beside I couldn't go away for more than one week, and that would still keep them in the hot humid city for most of the summer." He urges her, trying to get her to agree to the idea of camp. "Believe me, when the summer comes and they have no place to go, you'll realize that I was right. Only by then, it will be too late to do anything about it. The country air will give them what they can never get here in the city." They discuss it some more, while I stand frozen, horrified, listening to them making plans for my summer.

The "country air" sells her on the idea. The country is good for growing children, she agrees. "I just hope that they won't be unhappy away from us," she is not completely convinced or willing to give up the children whom she saved at such great effort.

"They'll have a good time in camp. All the other children there have parents in the city, and they won't be alone. Besides, they get to play and swim. This is important," he addresses her concerns.

I can't bear the idea of a separation from my mother. Everything was possible as long as we had her. She made us believe in a happy tomorrow, she made everything seem better than it was. Now she's agreeing to send me away? I feel abandoned and betrayed. She promised us that we would be with our father, a real family. How can she send me away? "Please don't make me go away," I beg my parents after having been told that I will spend six "wonderful" weeks away from them. "I don't want to go to a camp. Besides, I can go to the country with Yetta. Her parents said I could come along." Yetta and her parents feel like family and I know I would be happy with them.

"No, you can't go away with the Levys. I can't be taking so much from them without being able to give anything back. Besides you'll love camp. " My father speaks authoritatively although he's never been to any kind of camp. "You'll see. You'll be happy there," he tells me. "There are lots of other girls your age. You'll go swimming every day, play games and put on shows. Believe me, I wish I had had such an opportunity when I was a boy." I pray the he doesn't go into how much he gave up to please his parents and honor their desire to make sure he remains an observant Jew. Before he has the chance to bemoan his fate I jump in with my response.

"No, no. I'm not interested. I can have a wonderful summer right here in New York City. I don't want to leave my home. I just got here. Why do I have to keep leaving places as soon as I get to know them? First Vienna, then Wieliczka, then Liebenau, then Ellis Island. You don't understand, I can't leave any place again." I am determined not to give in. Suddenly I have found my old voice, the me who knows what she wants, the one who fought on Michael's behalf and was able to get rid of Tovah. "I'm not going. I don't want to go away from here." I am determined to stay in New York for the summer, even if it means grabbing a bed post and refusing to be pulled away from it. My mother knows of my ability to stand firm. They call in all the troops.

First, my Aunt Sari tells me that summer camp is nothing like Liebenau.

"You will love it there. Only lucky girls get to go. Imagine, you'll be living with friends, swimming, playing ball, and you'll be in the country." I don't know what she means by the "country." New York, USA is the country I'm in now and I don't want to leave my country. "Give it a try." She encourages me, "Camp is a wonderful experience and a great opportunity for you." Easy for her to say, she's never been to any kind of camp. She tries hard but I am not moved. I am not going to camp. They'll have to tie me up and throw me on the train.

My cousin Elsie is called in next. It was her idea to send me to camp in the first place. She talks to me about the fun I will have in camp. She's a doctor, single, glamorous, and, moreover, she herself has been to camp as a camp doctor. She knows all about it.

I protest. "I also know about camp, I spent a long time in a camp and believe me, it was not the best fun I'd ever had."

"Camp in America is nothing like Liebenau," she assures me, even though she'd never heard of Liebenau until she met us a few months ago. "You'll have fun, you'll have friends, you'll be happy."

"I don't want to go," I protest, beg and cajole. "Please, please, mutti, let me stay here with you. I'll be good," I promise. On some level, I think that if I say I'll be good, I'll get anything I want. It's no use. My mother sews name tags on all of my clothes and the trunk is packed

CHAPTER 9

———— ✿ ————

ONCE AGAIN I am on a train, headed for an unknown destination, surrounded by strangers. Only this time, my mother is not with me to reassure me and tell me all unpleasant things are products of my imagination. It is the beginning of a nightmare but this time I am awake. At least, when we traveled to Switzerland and Marseilles, I thought that we were on our way to America to see my father. Now, all I am aware of is that what I am leaving is my mother, father and little brother.

I find myself in an ultra- Orthodox girl's camp called *Beis Yaakov*, while, Michael who unlike me wants to go, is at an equally Orthodox boys' camp called Camp *Mesifta*. One thing my father, aunt and cousin were completely right about is that: *Beis Yaakov* is nothing like Liebenau. It is much, much worse. At Liebenau I had my mother and brother nearby. I was among other people in similar situations, children and their mothers going to be with their fathers and husbands. Here I am desperately alone, a refugee with no friends, no familiar faces, participating in activities I had never even heard of, praying three times a day in a foreign language I can neither understand nor pronounce.

The unbearable attack of loss and loneliness take up residence in my heart as soon as I say good-bye to my mother at the train station. It lodges deeper than any injury I've sustained. I actually feel real pain in my right shoulder and it extends to the middle of my chest, between my two unformed breasts. My ribs crumble collapsing against where I think my heart is. The ache attacks my throat, joining forces with the pain that originates from my shoulder. I can't get the clump in my throat to move aside and permit me to cry. I feel like I swallowed a rock. The waves of grief tower over me just like the ocean loomed above the Gripsholm in the middle of the frightening storm. Instead of washing the decks with salty spray it washes over me making all my prior fears worries and calamities a reality. Loss of my mother; the worst has caught up with me. I look around at my fellow campers. They are oblivious to my pain. They talk, laugh and make plans, while I am treading water, trying desperately to keep afloat and survive this ocean of panic.

I have not seen my mother for five long days. I have never been separated from her, not even for one single day. Why did she permit me to be taken away from her when she held on so tightly to me before? The questions go around in my head all day and all night long. I am convinced that I will never see my parents or brother again. My fear takes on a life of its own. It is no longer a feeling I possess. It is a fear that possesses me, all of me. It resides in me, owns me and dictates every breath I take. It is like an uncontrolled fire spraying sparks into an old lumber yard igniting one dry piece of wood after another. My fears are like random sparks flying from one wild fire to another. The demon of my "wonderful" imagination tells me I will never see my mother again. My parents will never come back for me. What if I lose my brother and end up back in Liebenau with the loonies? For me separation equals permanent loss, I clam up and suddenly understand why Victor can't talk. Not only am I unable to talk, I can't eat or sleep. I have lost interest in everything around me. I swallow and the lump sends arrows of pain into my throat.

The dining room is filled with the chattering and laughter of girls. I have a mouthful of cheese and noodles and cannot get them past the lump in my throat. I don't swallow and I carry the chewed up mouthful with me hoping to find a place to spit it out. Finally when I get to the swimming pool, I go to the toilet and get rid of the mushy noodles. I don't speak. I haven't heard my own voice for days, and finally am forced to face what I have feared the most. My parents have disappeared and I do not know where to look for them.

I feel like Hansel and Gretel when they wake up in the woods; lost, alone with no one to turn to. Of all the fairy tales I've heard, I identify most closely with Hansel and Gretel. But my own version stops at the point where the woodchopper sends his children away and they realize they have been abandoned. My own story is worse. My brother is not nearby to take my hand the way Hansel was took Gretel's. I have no one.

The other girls get mail daily. I am the only one who hasn't received a single letter or post-card. I am forgotten. This is further proof that something terrible has happened. I will later understand that my parents, who have no experience with camp, do not know that they are expected to write to me every day. In the meantime, when I don't hear from them I tell myself that my mourning is justified. Days go by, and it gets worse and worse. I can do nothing to comfort myself, escape the reality of my despair. I am unable to tell anyone what is hurting me. "Oh God," I pray, "please, take me away from all of this. I really don't want to live any longer. I can't go on from here. If You can't bring me my mother, then let me die." I would run away from camp, search for my parents, but I have no idea in which direction to go.

The camp staff is aware of my anguish, my inability to let go of what is hurting me. My parents have no telephone and can only be reached by mail or by direct contact. The people in charge of the camp feel that they can't wait a day or two for a letter to reach my parents. They need to do something immediately to alleviate their camper's suffering. The head counselor, a mother herself, decides she will stop in at my parent's apartment when she goes into New York to buy kosher meat for the camp. She drives a station wagon to the city every week to buy kosher supplies and she feels she must communicate her concerns to my parents. She doesn't know exactly what is troubling me because I haven't told anyone, but she sees that something is wrong and knows she has to speak to my parents immediately. She tells me nothing of her plan so I am surprised when I hear my name called over the loudspeaker a few days later. I am standing in the ball field battling with a mouthful of cornflakes which I can't swallow. I am summoned to come to the office immediately. I hurry, trying not to think of the bad news that might be awaiting me.

Rushing over to the office door I see my parent, waiting to greet me. My mother is wearing a new pink sundress with a bolero. Her blond hair is pulled tightly off her face into a bun, her widow's peak outlining her heart shaped face. She looks more beautiful than ever. My father is wearing an open necked, short sleeved sport shirt. They smile happy to see me. "How did you find me?" I ask certain that I was somehow lost to them just as they were to me.

"We took a bus to Monticello in the Catskills, and a cab to Ferndale where the camp is and here we are." They hug me in a three way hug. They have made the trip to at the behest of the rabbi's wife who told them they had to come to camp directly to see me. An incredible stone has just dropped from my heart. I am elated. I take my first full breath of air since getting to camp. It is as though they have returned from the land of the dead. All the tears that have solidified behind my eyes come pouring out. My mother takes out a hairbrush from her bag.

"Maidi, maidi," she croons, not addressing my tears, "your hair needs to be brushed and combed." She untangles my braids and brushes my hair lovingly. I feel as though I've just been saved from drowning. She tells me that she and my father are close by, at the Empire Hotel in the Catskills. They will come to visit me again in a few days. The very next day a postcard arrives from the hotel they are staying in. After that, I receive at least one piece of mail a day. I save all my letters under my pillow and reread them several times a day.

Slowly, I begin to participate in the activities, many of which are centered on religious ritual. I learn the long grace after meals said after every meal, morning, afternoon and evening prayers. I learn many Hebrew songs and dances. And about a country that existed in ancient times, "*Éretz Yisroel*,." a country that has yet to be established but to which every Jew yearns to return to. I gain a great deal of knowledge about my Jewish roots. I have always loved religion. I loved it when I was Catholic and went to church, and I now that I am beginning to learn about Jewish ceremonies, I start to enjoy the new rites and rituals associated with Judaism.

Camp is a quick but total immersion into the religious pool. In addition to all the laws associated with the Sabbath, and keeping kosher, there are other holidays having their own rituals. *Tisha b'av"* is a fast day which commemorates the destruction of the first and second temples in Jerusalem, as well as many other tragedies that befell the Jewish people. It takes place in the middle of July. We are not supposed to buy or wear new clothing and are not permitted to eat meat on the nine days preceding it. Most of the girls in my bunk, who like me, are nine or ten years old observe it like the grown- ups do. Even though they are not required to fast until their twelfth birthday, which marks the age of adult responsibility, these girls fast until one hour past sunset. We try to be serious, not joke around. We sit on the ground (a sign of mourning,) do not wear anything made of leather (which was considered a luxury in ancient times), and we read from the ancient text the Book of Lamentations. We do all this for events that took place more than two thousand years ago.

I love the spiritual aura that settles on the camp on Friday afternoons. We make preparations for the Sabbath "Queen." Everyone takes long showers, washes her hair and dons party dresses. "*Riva* (my Hebrew name), you look beautiful in that dress," my friend Malka says, and then generously offers me her new white belt. "It will look so good with the pink flowers on the dress." The Sabbath is referred to as the 'Sabbath Queen, the bride.' We are encouraged to act like bridesmaids getting ready for a wedding.

The welcoming for Sabbath service is held outdoors in the sweet smelling clover fields during sunset. We sing *L'cho dodi,* inviting the Sabbath Queen into our midst. I envision the beautiful princess in her long, white gown floating into our camp with her train gliding gracefully behind her.

Our innocent, high-pitched young voices chant a haunting melody that surely drifts all the way to the heavens. The service ends as the sky darkens and we walk holding hands, through the sweet smelling uncut clover, under starlit night into the bright dining room.

When not reciting extended prayers the Sabbath is spent resting, reading, singing songs and playing games like Ghost, a spelling game and 20 questions. Evening comes slowly to the summer sky and we start looking for the three stars that signify the end of Sabbath. When they are spotted we gather in a large group and *Havdallah* is chanted. The rabbi holds a large braided candle with many wicks which send their rays across the dark field. The girls hold their open palms up to its glow at the end of the service. And the candle is doused in a cup of wine.

CHAPTER 10

— ✿ —

I MAKE IT through the six weeks of camp and came home a changed person. If my father wanted me to become interested in Judaism he was successful beyond his wildest dreams. I become an expert on religion: "this is not kosher, this is a sin, this is not permitted on the Sabbath," I proclaim with authority while parading around the apartment. "Prayers are to be said three times facing east, six hour must elapse after eating meat before dairy may be eaten, water must be poured on each hand three times before the *motzi* (blessing recited before taking the first bite of bread)." I check on the level of my family's observance, declaring with great assurance what is permissible and what is forbidden. "This is *moochseh*," I point to a pencil lying on the kitchen table. Not permitted to be touched on the Sabbath; a pencil along with an umbrella, a pair of scissors, a needle, money; a plethora of other objects not to be touched on the Sabbath. My parents are not sure they like the way I have taken on the religion. They themselves, although observant Jews, never went to the extremes I have gone to and now am inflicting on others.

"What's this?" my mother asks. Even she is not familiar with the long grace after meals called *"benching."* In her family, grace was recited quietly not sung at the top of one's lungs.

"She's *benching*," my father tells her. "It's the Jewish-American way of saying grace."

"For ten minutes?" my mother asks, her blond eyebrows rising towards her hairline. She laughs, "It takes ten minutes of singing to thank God for one potato and one hamburger?"

"It is too late for me to change my ways," I inform them, my newly acquired fervor has made me a bit arrogant. I have been indoctrinated at camp and am hooked on Judaism. I pray three times a day, "*Shacharit, Mincha and Maariv*," the traditional morning, afternoon and evening prayers, rocking back and forth like the girls at camp did. When someone interrupts my, prayers I turn to them angrily, hissing, "Shhh! Can't you see I'm *davening*?

By my religious standards, my parents are "*Goyim.*" My mother does not wear the traditional head covering and my father does not wear always cover his head, even when he leaves the house. I am deeply concerned about this. If I am caught walking with my father and his head is uncovered my school friends will surely ostracize me. In school I try to give the impression that my family is very religious. I want to really belong to this ultra- orthodox circle but the truth is that my father is slowly moving away from some of its stringent practices.

He takes us to the library on the Sabbath and carries books home, ignoring my loud protest y that "you are not allowed to carry on Sabbath." My parents also go to the small grocery store on the corner and pick up a quart of milk and some eggs. They don't pay for their purchases because they do not carry money on the Sabbath. Mrs. Nussbaum, the owner of the grocery writes our purchases down in a notebook and we pay up on Mondays. By carrying books and grocery bags, my parents have the potential of exposing me to my schoolmates who might be out on the street taking a walk. If they see me with my parents who are clearly desecrating the Sabbath I will become open to the harsh scrutiny of my religious peers. I want appear observant and I'm scared of being "caught" with parents who act like *Goyim*.

My mother is an elegant woman. She usually wears a hat when she goes out. But my father is another story. "Please," I implore him, "can't you please wear a hat or yarmulke when you leave the house? I want everyone to see that we are a religious family."

"No," my father tells me, lightly, "I gave that up while you were in camp. I don't really believe that covering my head is going to make me a better Jew. I carry my Judaism in my heart, not my hat." I feel resentful. Why do I have to obey all of his religious edicts while he is not willing to do one single thing to meet mine? For a while I consider not going to the library with them, staying home and asking them to bring me a book.

But I love the library, the long wooden tables and comfortable chairs, the long, shelves full of all kinds of books. They beckon to me, daring me to try and read them. I love the smell of books, the crinkly bindings, the promises of things unknown and places unheard of. All of this is free and available to me for the mere possession of a library card. I can spend hours removing books from shelves, inspecting them, consider their worth and rejecting them or taking them home. It is always a hardship for me to limit myself to three books per week.

The children's librarian enjoys helping when I ask her for a good book for a girl my age. She introduces me to the "Honey Bunch" and "The Nancy Drew" series as well as "A Tree Grows in Brooklyn," Laura Ingalls Wilder's "Little House" series and "Little Women." All are stories about girls my age who do courageous things. I especially identify with Francie in "A Tree Grows in Brooklyn." Like me, she lives in New York City, in an ethnic neighborhood. She has a younger brother, just as I do whom she protects fiercely. Her family, as ours, is poor but does not feel deprived. We are both avid readers and achievers and it is almost as though I am reading about myself. Her adventures are my adventures.

As soon as I am introduced to "Little Men" like a fickle lover I shift my allegiance from Francie to Jo. Jo is one of the sisters in "Little Women" and the main character in its sequel "Little Men." She marries a professor with a foreign accent together they start a home for orphan boys. I love what she is doing. I want to be just like her when I grow up. I tuck her away in my memory, hoping someday to be able to have a home for children who have lost their parents. What I admire most about her is the way she does things her own way. She is tomboy at a time when girls are required to act like little ladies, she is brave, kind, warm and nurturing. The best part about Jo is her love for "lost" boys: boys like Victor and my own little brother. For all her unladylike behavior, she nurtures them and gives them a home. That is what I want to do when I grow up; give motherless children a home.

I love the Saturday outings to the library, but I know we are committing a sin by carrying on the Sabbath. I am torn between orthodoxy, my allegiance to my parents and my passion for books and the library. All the things I love are in conflict with each other. This feels just like the day the priest in Liebenau invited me into his church. Carrying on the Sabbath, I am certain a very big sin.

It is unavoidable. The neighborhood is small, all the Jews live near each other, everyone goes out for a walk on the long Sabbath afternoons. I get caught one Saturday as we are returning from the library. My heart sinks. I know what the consequences will be. I have been caught not only committing a grave sin but also caught in a lie. I don't know what is most upsetting. Losing face and being caught as a liar seems like the worst thing that could happen to me. I have just made friends with the girls in school and now will surely lose them as well as having to endure their scorn for me.

I dread the thought of returning to school on Monday morning. I know that the "religious committee" set up by my friends will confront me. My fears are justified. Hannah, the ringleader, and her friends accost me in the schoolyard. With her arms crossed in front of her flat bosoms Hannah loses no time to charge at me. "We saw you on *Shabbes*. You were carrying books and your mother was carrying a pocket book, probably filled with money." Her contingency of friends stands behind her in a semi-circle, disapproving, judging me, witnesses to my shame.

The hot dagger of humiliation has inserted itself deep into my heart. It radiates to the other parts of my body causing a burst of paralysis and a blush that feels red hot spreads across my upper body. I feel the dreadful prospect of tears threatening to spill on my flushed cheeks. Gone is my resolution to be strong and brave like my idol Jo. It is the moment I have been dreading. I feel worthless. Oh God, how could I have been so stupid. The pulse throbbing at my temple is surely obvious to the girls staring at me.

Hannah does not let go. "How could you lie to us like that?" She interrogates me with assurance much like kind the gestapo used on my mother. "You probably don't keep kosher and I'll bet you ride on the Sabbath." The girls standing around her do not utter a single word, but I feel their scorn and disapproval.

This is too much for me to handle. I am shame, deeply hurt, dissolved by her accusing me of not eating kosher and riding on the Sabbath. In spite of my resolve not to show weakness or cry in front of them, I feel the hot tears of humiliation cascading down my burning cheeks. "You know what you are Hannah Werthheimer" I ask her? "You are worse than the Gestapo. You have set yourself up as a policeman for God, deciding who is worthy of you and who is not. You have made yourself the police of the Jews, you have turned all my friends against me and there you stand accusing me of being a liar. You are nothing but,....but a…" I search for words strong enough to express my feelings. "You are a hypocrite and a rat with your red hair and splotchy red freckles." I am crying, frustrated, humiliated and shamed. Hannah ignores my pain. It gives her strength. She tosses her red hair walks away and tells the others to leave me there crying on the sidewalk.

The other girls stare at me. I can see that some of them are not comfortable with the confrontation. Hannah's tirade has forced them to choose sides. Even though they squirm through this encounter, not one has come to my defense. Eva becomes preoccupied with a pebble that she is trying to dislodge from the hard packed earth, Claire inspects a hangnail on her index finger while the other girls stare at the ground. I desperately hope that one of them will come up to me and tell me she still wants to be my friend. But they can't chance it. Hannah is a strong leader and no one will defy her. Finally, they walk away holding hands while I stand on my little island of humiliation. I am an outcast, banned by my village of peers.

Hannah has gotten to Yetta. Yetta, who has always been a bit of an outsider herself is invited to join ranks with the popular girls. It is difficult to resist. At first she avoids looking at me and when that is not possible, she actually turns her back and walks away when I go near her. I am afraid to start a conversation with her because I can't afford to take the chance of being openly rejected. I can't believe I have lost Yetta, my best friend and ally. She made room for me, gave me a place, made me feel like I belonged. I not only lost Yetta but her parents as well. I felt that her family was my family. I love her parents and their generosity, acceptance of me and their warm, welcoming home. Now she is gone from my life. I feel bereft. Somehow I sense that Yetta feels badly about the way she is behaving. She has not given my job to another girl and she walks the kindergarten children by herself now. I know she misses me and that walking alone must be lonely for her. I feel a small jolt of triumph that she has to miss lunch recess and walk with two young children and then all by herself back to school. At least no one else has taken my place.

My God, I think, experience has taught me that there is so much hatred in this world, and so much of it is unjustified. The Catholics hate the Jews, the Jews hate the Catholics, but now I see that there are some Jews who hate other Jews. I am afraid that I'll never find another friend. Gone are the wonderful days we spent together, dreaming of the future. I begin to feel alone again. "I'm the only one of my kind," I tell myself, and I hate the way that feels. A nasty worm is boring its way into my heart. I can't explain it, and all I know is that it is with me when I wake up and when I go to sleep. I can't seem to shake the feeling of doom and sadness. I stop singing and dancing, and only answer questions when I'm addressed. School is again becoming a burden for me. I stay indoors during recess, unable to face the girls who were once my friends.

My mother doesn't notice this, and when I tell her that I am feeling sad because of Yetta, she doesn't understand. "I know Yetta will come back to the friendship," she tries to console me just the way she did when she told me all unpleasant things were due to my imagination. This loss of my friend is not due to any imagination on my part. I watch through the window before school starts and see Yetta jumping rope with the other girls. I feel as though my heart will break. My mother tries to comfort me, "you can make other friends, you know. Yetta is not the only child at the school."

"No, no," I say, "there will never be another Yetta. I hate America where Jews hate other Jews. At least in the camp we were all nice to each other." My mother looks at me with pity and distress. She doesn't know what to say and in trying to make me feel better she denies my rage. She scolds me and says that I am being ungrateful.

I can't even talk to my sweet, gentle mother. When I tell her how badly I feel about losing a friend, she answers by telling me that I am one of the lucky few who lost nothing I can't replace. She turns things around so that I'm always feeling guilty. "Look what happened to your cousins, your aunts and uncles. You should be grateful, count your blessings living here in America with your mother, father and brother alive." Once again, I am being told to be grateful when I'm feeling sad and alone.

CHAPTER 11

MY FATHER IS disgruntled. He hates working in a factory, making other people rich and answering to an ignorant foreman. He has decided to go into business for himself. He has worked in the leather industry for a long time and he is an expert in manufacturing leather coats and jackets. He has several contacts and including a connection with a leather wholesaler. Now that the war is over and the manufacture of parachutes no longer in demand, nylon has become cheap and available. Nylon has become all the rage for hosiery, lingerie and worst of all outer clothing wear. My father convinces himself that leather will never go out of style.

"You know what?" he asks my mother, "Leather has class, it's a luxury. People with money would much rather wear a leather coat than one of those slippery, shiny nylon jackets. There is no comparison. Nylon is a passing fancy, a poor man's choice. One little rip and the whole jacket falls apart. It can't even be repaired. Leather lasts for years. It is a living, breathing material. Leather protects people from rain, wind and cold. You can polish it and restore its luster. It will never go out of style. I may be the only one who sees a future in leather, but I am going to give it a try. You watch and see. We are going to be rich."

He contacts a distant cousin and gets a loan to start his business. He is an honest man. Everyone knows this and when he says he'll pay it back, he is trusted. He convinces another leather cutter to join him in his venture and become his partner. They rent space in a dark little shop in North Philadelphia and together they work from Sunday afternoon until Friday. He is proud, he is a business man. He would much rather have been a professional person but without the proper education that is not an option.

When he comes home from Philadelphia on Friday afternoons we walk on eggshells. We cater to his every wish and try to make him happy. My mother prepares all his favorite foods and serves them. Standing over him and urging him to eat. My father is wearing one of his leather jackets and brings another home to give to the generous cousin who made the loan. He knew he was taking a risk investing in my father's business and my father is not going to let him down. Papa is in a good mood. He owns a business. He is proud of his achievement. My mother is happy too. She is married to a manufacturer and she's proud. Several months go by with my father leaving New York every Sunday afternoon and returning early on Friday afternoon to spend *Shabbes* with us. He is optimistic. Leather is bound to make a comeback from the popular post war nylon.

Despite his dreams and plans nylon is a tenacious product. It has grabbed onto the garment industry and it seems to be used in every manufactured product, from underwear, to men's socks, coats and jackets. Nylon has surpassed cotton in the manufacturing of all clothing. It has many advantages over cotton. It dries quickly and does not require the tedious task of ironing to look presentable, moreover it is stronger than any natural product. Nylon is cheap, it is easy to work with and inexperienced, unskilled workers can assemble items in minutes. People love the light weight, variety and pliability of the new fiber. It is worn by men, women and children alike.

In the coming weeks, my father comes home less enthusiastic. "It's not so easy," he tells us, "I have to hire a salesman to go to the department stores to try and sell the jackets. I have to pay him a salary plus a commission, extra for every jacket he sells. It is almost impossible to compete with nylon." One Friday afternoon, he comes home lugging a heavy suitcase up to the fifth floor. When he opens it, leather coats and jackets tumble out. His face is ashen and I notice for the first time the deep lines imbedded in his cheeks.

One look at him and my mother's face turns white.

"What happened?"

He sighs and looks upset. "I can't sell a leather jacket for a dime. I can't even give one away. Everyone is wearing nylon. It's stronger, it's lighter and it's warmer. This was a bad time to get into the leather jacket business." I feel so badly for him. He looks utterly defeated.

My mother refuses to grasp the situation. "Does that mean that business is bad?" she asks naively.

"Business is not bad," he responds sarcastically. "Business is gone. There is no business."

My mother slumps. She looks like a balloon that all the air has escaped from. "What are we going to do?" she asks, looking at him and then up at the ceiling.

He has to find a job in anywhere he can. His experience with leather is of no advantage and the salary for nylon workers is lower than it was for experienced leather cutters. He will have to take a cut in his previous salary and he is forced to do so. My mother tells us that we have to start being careful with money. Since when were we ever careless with it I want to know? She buys day old bread and bruised produce. We eat a lot of potatoes. We never go hungry again but there is no variety in our diet and the gloomy atmosphere invades every corner of our lives. She alters my dresses. She cuts them at the waist line turns the bottom of the dress into a skirt and the top into a bolero. It is sad to be poor and I have learned not to ask for anything.

Now begins the long period of unemployment filled pain with anguish, especially for my father. He leaves the house every morning, carrying his brown grocery bag containing his lunch, a cheese sandwich and an apple, and returns every evening, the bag is empty and so is he. At night when I'm supposed to be sleeping I listen in on their conversations. I know I shouldn't. Just listening brings fear, uncertainty and sadness to me and I feel guilty for eavesdropping. Yet I can't keep myself away from it. Like the proverbial moth drawn to a flame, I lie in bed and listen to their painful discussions knowing that when I finally fall asleep it will be like death to the moth.

My father reminisces sadly. "I can't help missing all that I gave up. I loved Vienna. To me it was more than a city. It was a way of life. It held my hopes, my dreams. I used to sit with my friends in the *café house* talking about everything: politics, religion, poetry, philosophy, nature, music, art, the endeavors of gigantic minds like Freud, Herzl, Brecht, Marx, even the futility of Communism. I was always part of a lively discussion. For the price of a cup of coffee I was a welcomed member of an *intelligesia*. I loved my life. I had no idea of what I was giving up by coming to America. I didn't dream that we would never see Vienna again. I feel as if I have lost all that. No, not lost, it was all taken away from me: along with my parents, my relatives, my friends, my *shul,* my community, my life. Coming to America robbed me of all that was my life."

My mother listens to him. She doesn't interrupt. She's heard all this before and doesn't know what to say or do to make him feel better. He goes on, "here a person is not measured by what he has achieved or whom he has inspired. The only thing that counts here is how much money you have. And the worst thing of all for me is that I can't even make a living here."

I am so sorry. Listening to him makes my heart feel like it's being turned inside out. Opening up like this does nothing to relieve his anguish. On the contrary, it only serves to increase its intensity. "I am nothing here. I have no relatives except for Sari. I have no real friends. I leave the house every single morning, go from one part of the city to another and there simply is no job for me. Every idiot and moron can get a job, but not I. This may be the land of the brave, but believe me, it is not the land of the free. Everything costs money, and I haven't got any. All I need is job that will pay sixty dollars a week, enough for our rent and the food, and I can't get it. There is nothing in this country for me."

My mother sighs and takes a few moments before she answers, "Alex, you can't only think of your troubles. Remember, we are together. We have each other, we have two wonderful children. Think of all the others who really lost everything, their children, their lives. We still have so much to be grateful for."

"You just don't understand what it feels like for a man not being able to provide for his family, to have no profession, no hope. You don't know how humiliating it is to be turned away from one potential employer to another. Don't talk to me about lucky. I certainly don't feel lucky!"

I feel pity for my sweet, brave mother who never lost hope during those awful years; who turned every loss, every trial into an adventure; "part of coming to America," she would tell us bravely, trying to keep us from being frightened. Now even she herself is losing hope.

I tear up silently. I too am afraid. What will happen to us if my father never earns enough to take care of us? Will Michael and I have to go to an orphanage? Will we be sent to live with strangers? There is no one I can turn to for answers, certainly not my mother. No one must know that I eavesdrop on their discussions. I put the pillow over my head attempting to fall asleep. It takes a long time and I am plunged into a dreamless nightmare. When I awaken I feel like a heavy yoke has been placed on my shoulders.

The next day my mother is brisk, distracted and efficient. My father leaves the house carrying the brown bag with his cheese sandwich and an apple for dessert. Michael and I leave for school. My mother says very little that whole day. She is still silent when we sit down at the dinner table. While we're all still mashing our potatoes with left over gravy my mother comes to life. She has eaten nothing but I notice the resolve in her eyes. The same resolve she had when she faced the Gestapo officer in Montelupi Prison so many years ago. She remembers the dream about her mother, my grandmother, coming to her and telling her: "remember, you are beautiful, smart and rich. She draws strength from it. "Alex, and you children also, listen and listen carefully. We may be poor but we are not without hope." She turns the rest of her speech towards my father. She has had the whole day to think about what she wants to say and no one will detract her from her message. "I know,

Alex, how much you had to give up coming to America. I, too, feel pain and frustration at having to leave our comfortable lives in Vienna, and can only imagine how hard life was for you, constantly worrying about us while you were in America alone. Perhaps, on some level it was easier for me and the children. All we had to do was to survive the day and live to face the next one. You, on the other hand, had to worry about our safety. The imagination can do far more harm than the reality. I understand that. But you cannot rob us of our joy today. We have to choose whether we are going to bemoan the past with sorrow or live the present in reality and joy. You, Alex will get a job, maybe not today, maybe not even next week, but eventually you will work again. In the meantime we have to be grateful for what we have, the fact that we are together, that we will never go hungry and that our lives will never again be threatened or endangered by a corrupt, anti- Semitic government. This government, and this country, will always ensure that no one is murdered because of what he or she believes. And for this we must be grateful." She ends the speech by picking up the dirty plates and noisily stacking them in the sink before turning the faucet on, full force.

"Wow," Michael says. "Good speech *Mutti.*"

That night when I get into bed I close the door. I don't want to eavesdrop on my parents anymore.

CHAPTER 12

───── ❧ ─────

My FATHER COMES back from *Shul* one Saturday and I can see he is in a black mood. "Some people are so lucky," he tells my mother at the table ignoring Michael and me. "They have children they can be proud of, sons who go to *Shul* with their fathers and who *daven* with *kavoneh* (respect). Oh, what I would do to have such children." A stab from the long, sharp sword of guilt punctures my heart. Something is wrong. We have done something that displeases my father and makes him angry. I just don't k now what it is.

My mother becomes protective while trying not to irritate him. "Whatever can be wrong that you come home so agitated? I made a nice lunch for us and the children have been home with me all morning."

He looks at her as if seeing her for the first time. "You just don't understand," he tells her, and out of nowhere he starts complaining. "Yes I managed to save your lives, and I got us through the war but for what? There is nothing is here for me in America. I never even get an *aliyah* (the honor of being called up to the Torah). In America they are sold, to the highest bidder." He laughs bitterly. "How can I ever justify spending $ 5.00 on an *aliyah* when I have to watch every penny so that my family doesn't starve? Everything in America costs money, even getting an *aliyah*. In Europe the *ballabatim* (synagogue members) showed respect and were honored to have me take an *aliyah*, here I have to buy it like a bag of potatoes." In spite of my mother's words of encouragement he returns to his old theme of bemoaning his luck.

"My children? My children aren't all that they could be. Other people have sons they are able to take to shul who make them proud. But not me. My son doesn't know a *brocha* (blessing) from a brush stroke. Other people's children make their parents proud. Mine can barely get by." My mother shakes her head. She is unable to penetrate his armor of resentment and self-pity. She doesn't say a word, and clears the dishes from the table.

I want to be "like other people's children," but I don't really know how to do that. I think about my friends and realize that they are other people's children but cannot seem to grasp what they are doing that my father wishes we could do. How can I make my father proud of me, make me like other people's children? I want so much for my father to love me and be proud of me. But I am scared of him. I never know how he will react to me. I wish for the days when he was gone all week in Philadelphia; when I could be myself and not have to worry about upsetting him. Immediately I feel guilty for my selfish thoughts and chastise myself. I remember my mother's words. I should love and respect him. After all he did to get us out of Europe. He is trying to provide for us. Am I being an ungrateful, unloving daughter? I am feeling unworthy and unappreciative. Much later on, when I look back on this period of my life, I will realize how much these early feelings have contributed to my battles with depression and learned helplessness.

Michael and I do not plan to be disrespectful, but every time we do something my father disapproves of we are accused of being disobedient and ungrateful. My mother tells us that our father wants what he knows is best for us, and that we should honor him instead of trying to get our way. Even the Ten Commandments state that we should "Honor" our father and mother. My dreams and expectations of a perfect family, seated happily on a sofa in front of a warm, crackling fire while a beautiful mother plays the piano and a handsome father reads to his rapt children will never come to fruition. The mother I had known and loved all those years disappears. She changes, slowly and gradually becoming quiet and acquiescent. She is committed to the idea of presenting a united front, and is convinced that in order to do that she has to take sides; she either continues defending and protecting her children or gives in. It is safer to obey him. She does not hear my silent pleas and yearning for acceptance and love.

"Be grateful that you have a father who cares about you," she tells me when I complain to her about not being able to play with one of my friends. With or without meaning to she has the capacity for inflicting guilt. Over and over again she brings up my poor cousin Miriam whose father died and left her an orphan. "Not everybody is so lucky," she intones. "Look at your cousin Miriam. She doesn't have a father anymore." I don't know what to think, how can remembering that Miriam's father died make my father feel that I respect him?

Just as I have my dreams of the perfect father I invented over the years, he has dreams of perfect children. He wasn't there for our formative years and has now undertaken the task of molding us. During the long years of separation he dreamed about his little family and what we would become: Michael a scholar, obedient and open to Jewish studies: me, a little lady, polite, quiet and dainty.

Our dreams and hopes are a recipe for disappointment. We are powerless and he is stubborn, unwilling to cut us any slack. He cannot accept the fact that his children have dreams, desires and wills of their own; that even he, with his strong dedication and commitment cannot change the way we are.

I am ten years old and I want to get my long braids cut. I have had them all my life and I want to look like a grown up. There is a post-war fashion trend, called the "new look." Dresses, skirts and coats are long and hair is short. I can't have a new dress right now, but I think can get a haircut like all the girls I know.

"No, I like the braids," he tells me, when I say I want to look like my friends. "You don't have to look like all the other girls who are trying to look older than they are. The braids are nice; they make you look different, unique." Different and unique is exactly the last thing I want to be. I want to be just like every other girl in my school.

Walking home from school one afternoon I find a purse containing two shiny quarters. My heart leaps with this discovery and I consider all the things that I could buy with such a windfall, but my nagging conscience worms its way into my plans and reminds me that the money is not mine and I must return it to its rightful owner. There is no identification in the purse and it is impossible to find out who in Washington Heights lost fifty cents. I am resourceful and take the purse with its contents to the police station on 181st Street. The red-faced police officer sitting at a tall desk tells me come back in about two weeks and that if no one claims the purse I get to keep it. Fortune has finally smiled upon me. Two weeks later, with my newly acquired asset I make my way into the toy store on St. Nicholas Avenue.

"Do you have something for a ten year old girl? I've got for fifty cents."

The elderly shopkeeper looks at me and tries to size up my interests. "Hmm…" he muses "How about a book?"

A book is exactly the right thing. A book of my own to read, cherish and read again, a book that does not have to be returned to the library in two weeks. It is a perfect suggestion.

We go over to the book section and select "Little Women" by Louisa May Alcott. "You'll like it," the salesman tells me, "It is about a family of old-fashioned girls like you," he says, taking note of my long braids.

"I know. I've already read it, but I think I want to own it." My very own book, the first book I select and pay for by myself, with my own money. I skip home, happy as I haven't been in a long time. I tell the storekeeper not to wrap it and clutch it close to my bosom.

"What a ridiculous way to spend your money," my father tells me. "Go and return it. Get your money back. You can get any book that you want in the library and it's free. I don't want you to throw your money out on something you can get for nothing."

"But the money is mine," I protest. I am so close to tears that my eyes actually hurt. Unable to explain my desire to own a book, a book I can read over and over again at my leisure. I feel frustrated and to my shame the tears slide down my cheeks So much was promised to me before I came to America and now I am not allowed to keep this book which I purchased with my own money.

"It may be your money, but you are my responsibility," he counters," and it is my responsibility to teach you about money; not waste it or spend it on items you don't need. You can buy yourself some socks and save your family the expense."

My mother pauses, trying to decide what to say, "Look, Rita," she says kindly, "what daddy says is true. You know you can take 'Little Women' out of the library. And if you want to read it again, you can always renew it. Maybe you could buy a game with the money?" She adds gently. "A game you can play with Michael. You can play a game over and over again and it always comes out different." I know she doesn't care about a game or a book. She wants me to obey my father and return the book and bring peace into the household. At this point, the battle becomes larger than the book. It is just the first of a long series of battles that my father and I will wage; my desire to be allowed some leeway in my life against his strong need to control me. The purchase of the book was not an unreasonable purchase but more than that I wanted my mother to defend me and my father to give some freedom. I stop caring about the book. Just once, I want to win a battle and get my way.

I confront my mother privately, "Why can't I spend the money I found the way I want to?"

"Listen to your father," she tells me, "he knows what's best for you. We want *shalom bais,* (a peaceful house)." I shake my head in disbelief. The autonomy and freedom I enjoyed while a prisoner of war, is being replaced with new rules and expectations imposed on me by my peers, teachers and most of all my parents. I refuse to return the book. I keep it and hide it under my pillow. I will read this book again and again, always surprised by how exciting it is each time I read it.

Now that Yetta is out of my life, I play with the neighborhood kids after school. We play outdoors, on the sidewalk on most days: jump rope, hopscotch and bouncing ball games where we recite a singsong chant while doing tricks with the pink rubber ball we call a "spaldine." My new friend Suzanne comes to my house after school. After she leaves my father tells me that he doesn't want me playing with her. He doesn't want me to have non-Jewish friends. Jews have to stick together with other Jews. He tells me that all *goyim* hate Jews. Is he telling me that Suzanne hates me because I am Jewish? I can't accept his logic. I decide not to argue with him but sneak over to her house. Her mother is nothing like Yetta's mother, who feels like my aunt, offering me food and love, but she is very nice to me. How could she hate me when she invites me into her house and is friendly towards me? Once again I get caught committing a sin. I lie to my parents. I tell them I will be playing in the park but instead I sneak into Suzanne's house. When I come home, my parents question me. Where have I been? What did I do? I tell them that I was in the park but they assure me that they had scoured the park and could not find me. "Now tell me, where you have been?" my father insists. "You weren't in the park, of that I'm sure. Why are you lying to us? Why can't you just tell us the truth? **Where were you?**" I blurt out the truth, trembling, not sure what the consequences will be. My father beckons me into their bedroom.

"Sit down," he tells me pointing to a spot on the bed. He goes to the closet, takes a box from the shelf and produces two photographs of his parents, my *oma* and *opa*. They look just as I remember them. I study the photos and wonder why my father has taken this moment to show them to me. He tells me that he has not been notified of their death and is still hoping that they are alive and that by some miracle they survived the Holocaust. He hopes to hear of their whereabouts any day now. They were in their fifties when Hitler came to Austria and he has been unable to acknowledge their fate. He searches for them fruitlessly consulting with various agencies and refuses to say *Yiskor*, the memorial prayer that children say for their deceased parents in the Synagogue. He does not light the memorial candle in his home on Yom Kippur eve. He feels that to do so would be tantamount to sentencing them to death. During the war, he was preoccupied with trying to save us. Now he realizes that while he was able to get us out of the fires of Europe, his beloved parents probably went to their death when Hitler came to Austria. He will most likely never see his parents again.

He speaks gently to me. "These good people are my parents and I am becoming convinced that they were murdered by the *Goyim*. I don't want you to be friends with them. They hate us and they hate you too." He is very serious, "Suzanne is not a friend for you. If her family was in Vienna during the war, they would have turned you over to the Nazis." I feel overcome with guilt. I almost wish I could agree with him, but I can't relate to what he is saying. Is he telling me that Suzanne is one of the people who had his parents killed? He tries very hard to convince me to give up my neighborhood friends and I want to respect his wishes, but what am I to do? The girls at school shun me because they say my family is not religious, and there are no Jewish girls my age to play with, plan and dream with. The only options I have are to be by myself all day long or disobey my father.

I look at the photographs and my heart fills with sadness. My grandparents look just as I remember them. My *oma*, with her ill-fitting *sheytl*, tilted slightly on her head, smiling as if especially for me and my *opa*, a thin, half smile above his white beard, with eyes piercing and sad. I'm torn up. My father tells me that by playing with Suzanne I am betraying my beloved grandparents. I can't sustain the guilt. I give in to my father's orders. Once more I am friendless.

CHAPTER 13

AFTER MONTHS OF leaving each morning, searching for employment, my father has finally gotten a job. He leaves every morning to work in a factory that makes ladies' handbags and wallets. I am ecstatic. No longer frightened of losing our apartment and fearing hunger we give up the steady potato diet. My mother quickly brings us back to reality. Any thoughts of prosperity I might have been harboring are quickly dispelled as she tells me that although my father now has a job we are to be very careful. His salary is very low and then, there's always the possibility of future unemployment. We are far from being financially secure, she tells me. If plastic or nylon takes over the pocket book industry, he will be out of a job and we will be out of luck." I wish she did not say this to me. How can I be careful of spending money when I've never any? Her admonishments make me feel poor, helpless, as though I will never have security. My outlook is changing. I feel burdened, overwhelmed. I start to obsess and worry, what will happen to us when he loses this job? I feel helpless. Is there nothing I can do to improve our lives.

I am also beginning to question the whole concept of God and religion. If religion is so wonderful, why are so many religious people unhappy, dissatisfied and fearful? Why are the religious kids in my school so mean and unaccepting? After all, my parents lack of religious fervor are responsible for my loss of Yetta"s friendship and caused my other friends abandon me? Religion is losing some of its luster for me. So many people hold so many views. What is sanctioned by my parents is viewed as sinful by my school friends. I am confused; I loved being Catholic when we were in Poland, felt comfortable being Orthodox in camp and school, I love my parents, I like my gentile friends, I love the Saturday trips to the library. All the things I love are in conflict with one another, and I am not sure of what I am or what I believe. I try to adhere to my parents' principles, but realize that religion is not buying me peace, happiness or the friendships that I yearn for. When I question my father he tells me to stop asking so many questions. "Of course religion can't buy you happiness," he tells me cynically. "If it did, everyone would be religious. You just do it because you believe in it." I am afraid to tell him that I don't believe the way he does, He is so unpredictable, he might react in a violent manner or refuse to talk to me for heaven knows how long.

Some of the laws of orthodoxy make no sense to me at all. For instance, why can't we turn a light on the Sabbath, why are the men and women separated when they pray in the Synagogue, why are men required to put on the Tallith and wind phylacteries around their arms and women are on prohibited, why are only men counted into a quorum of ten in order to worship and women don't count at all? These and many other questions bother me but I dare not ask for fear of displaying my ignorance at school or causing my father to tell me that a truly religious person accepts without questioning.

CHAPTER 14

———— ♋ ————

"ONE, TWO, THREE, four," Miss Ricky claps her hands, the pianist stops playing and we stop dancing. "Girls, girls, stop, please. Listen to the music, and for heaven's sake try to keep in time with the beat." Nine girls of varying sizes in tights and pink ballet slippers are reflected in the mirror that occupies one entire wall in the room.. I am part of a dance class that my parents have agreed to let me participate in. They hope that it will cheer me up and make me feel special after the awful loss of Yetta's friendship. Moreover, they reason, the lesson will help me appear graceful and improve my posture. The YMHA offers dance classes. They cost ten dollars for a semester of twelve weeks. This is like a dream come true, I have something wonderful to look forward to every single week.

The ballet teacher, Miss Ricky, in her pink tights and black leotard, smiles encouragingly at my efforts. She is thin, has long arms and legs, and her hair is styled short, a stiff, black helmet on her head. I want her approval more than anything in the world. I strain to get the difficult positions and receive the nod of encouragement from Miss Ricky. "Good work, Rita," she tells me so the whole class can hear. A compliment from Miss Ricky is a sought after reward. The backs of my legs feel like poison has been injected into them but I feel compelled to be the best one in the class, try everything and get it right as quickly as possible. I want to become an American girl, make my parents proud of me, maybe I can even to get my father to talk about me in the Synagogue and have others refer to me "as other people's children."

My Aunt Sari, who ever since she married a rabbi frowns on the dancing lessons. "It isn't fitting for a Jewish girl to wear tight leotards and show her body off like that," she tells my father. He doesn't respond and I don't care what she thinks of me. I have already been excommunicated by the Orthodox kids anyway and I look forward to Thursday afternoons, where I become part of a group of the more serious dance students, who sling their pink satin toe shoes over their shoulders on their way through the halls of the Y. It is a gratifying arena for me to compete in and be rewarded for my efforts. Miss Ricky tells my mother that I'm the best pupil she has all week. She wants me to come for lessons twice a week. "At no extra charge," she quickly adds. "This is strictly a well- earned scholarship." My heart is bursting with happiness. Like the book I bought with my own money, I earned a scholarship on my own.

My father is quiet. He seems to take little pleasure in my dancing success. He nods his head and tells my mother that he will pick me up at the Y after my lessons. He does everything methodically, seriously, there is no room for joy, light heartedness or humor in his life. I try to engage him in dialogue and tell him that I saw a robbery on the street. This really is a figment of my imagination. "You're lying," he says. Of course he's right, but I did hope he would play along with me. I want to spark his interest: to question me, to ask me if I was scared, what the robber looked like, and what was he stealing. I want to make up a fantastic story for him, to get him to listen to me and respond. He is silent.

He is having another "black mood," that comes upon him when least expected. He tells me I am not behaving like the daughter he thinks I should be. I don't help my mother around the house, do not do things spontaneously and have to be told to do the obvious: like pick up objects that are out of place, wash dirty ash trays, put away books and fold laundry. He complains that Michael is stupid and lazy, preferring playing ball to studying and doing his homework. His outbursts are unexpected and can be triggered by nothing more than an innocent remark. His moods affect the whole family and make me feel not good enough or worthy. I wish I could be a better daughter, more like other people's children. My dancing scholarship does nothing to raise his opinion of me and I am finding myself brooding along with him.

CHAPTER 15

───── ∞ ─────

I<small>T IS</small> J<small>ULY</small> of 1946, I'm ten years old, standing behind Rena, waiting my turn at the jump rope. I'm next. Two girls are holding the rope on each end and three girls are standing on the sidewalk behind me, waiting for their turns to jump in. We sing our jingle jump in line and run away from the rope without stepping on it. "Rinny- tin-tin, swallowed a pin," I sing out as I always do but suddenly I feel self-conscious and uncomfortable. I become aware that my body feels weird. It has changed. My here flat chest has acquired a new roundness and it jiggles up and down with every jump I take and I feel ridiculous. I cross my arms in front of me and try to scrunch down a bit. I can't stand the way I look. None of the other girls have developed breasts and I feel gross. I step on the rope on purpose. I will miss my turn, but that's alright. I am not going to jump any more. I take hold of the end of the rope turning it so the others can jump. I become, what is called "a steady ender," someone who always turns the rope, a job usually reserved for clumsy girls.

I stand in front of the mirror. What is going on with my body? I have stabbing pains in my breasts, and now they are getting bigger. I touch them and they feel springy and soft, not like the flat, bony chest that I had a few months ago. No one has told me about the changes that take place in a girl's body before she becomes a woman. I wonder if I'm getting fat and need to go on a diet and lose some weight. I am taller than all my classmates and my new body is getting in the way of all the games I play, not only jump rope, but hopscotch, tag and hide and seek, even roller skating makes me feel clumsy.

I need new clothes, ones that will not stretch so tightly across my bosoms. I want to get my braids cut off so I don't have to look like a little girl with big breasts. I want to look like everyone else and at the same time, I want to be noticed. I do not want to be me. I am sad much of the time. These moods are unanticipated and come for no apparent reason. They start as a slow sense of foreboding and soon take over my conscious thinking. I feel guilty, frightened and helpless. I have no idea why I'm feeling the way I do.

I come home from the outdoors flushed and soaked in sweat. It is early July and I run up the five stories to our apartment to go to the bathroom and get a drink. My mother has just returned from a shopping trip to the Bronx, to a bargain store called Alexander's. I see two beautiful dresses laid out on her bed. One is a butter yellow piquet, with puffy sleeves and a sailor collar, the other is navy blue linen with large white buttons that go all the way down the front and a red and white belt around the waistline. I am overjoyed.

"Oh thank you mommy, I am so happy." It's been such a long time since I've gotten a new dress. And now I have two of them! I shed my sweat soaked dress and stand in my underwear, put my arms into the yellow dress ready to try it on. My mother stops me.

"No, don't. These are not for you." she tells me. I feel as though someone has slapped my face. "I'm sending these to Palestine, to Aunt Matilda and Miriam. They are so poor. They have nothing. We have to share what we can." This is not the first time my mother has done this. Only last summer a neighbor gave me a pink satin evening gown, splattered with sequins and rhinestone and covered with layers of tulle. She wore it to her sister's wedding and knew that she would never wear it again. She wanted me to have it for dress up games. "I've always wanted a dress like this when I was your age," she tells me. "At least I can make my dream come true for another little girl." I am overjoyed!

One day, I look in the closet and realize that the dress has disappeared. "Where's my evening gown?"

"I sent it Palestine, to Miriam and Matilda," she explains, not sounding the least bit apologetic for having sent it without even telling me. "They will have opportunity to wear it, and you would only use it to play dress-up."

"But it was my dress. It was given to me," I whine.

"And whom do you belong to? You're mine," she says affectionately, patting my head and kissing me.

I'm not buying into her whimsy. "I want that dress. I need it for a special occasion that will surely come along soon. Why would you give my things away without even telling me? Taking things away from your own child?" I cry tears of outrage and hurt.

"Don't be selfish," she reprimands me for wanting what is mine. "You have much more than Miriam, and if we can make her life a bit more pleasant, we should feel privileged to do so."

If she thinks I'm ashamed of my feelings, my greed, my unwillingness to share, my unhappiness about having my things given away, she is mistaken "Share?" I scream at her. "What do I have that I can share? I haven't had a new dress since Aunt Sari's wedding a year ago. I am bursting out of my own clothes. I'm too embarrassed to jump rope because I look so awful!"

She is stunned by my reaction. It was not her intention to hurt me. She just never gave my needs a thought. She reminds me as always that I still have my father and we are living in comparative luxury in the United States, while Aunt Matilda and Miriam have to share a bed in a small room.

I don't listen to her. I put on my sweaty, damp dress and slam out of the apartment to hold the rope for my friends.

CHAPTER 16

⸕

THIS IS THE summer when I have made arrangements with my teacher Mr. Serkin. I will study all summer long, write essays, read books and write reports on them do math problems and send everything to Mr. Serkin every Friday for the entire summer. I want to skip a year of school. I feel the stigma of being the oldest child in the class. I will be eleven in February and am only in the fourth grade. I realize that I am a year and a half a year behind my classmates, and to me that's a big deal. I am taller and more developed than any of the girls in my class. I very much want to make that year and a half up, and be placed with students who are my age. I broach the topic with my teacher who promises me that he will help me accelerate by letting me take home textbooks and do lots of work which I will mail to him on a weekly basis during the summer.

I live up to my part of the bargain spending long, hot mornings studying geography books, doing math problems, reading and answering questions about history that are in the back of each chapter. I read fiction and write book reports, and dutifully make the trip to the post office and send my work to him each Friday afternoon. I am committed to achieving the goal of going into sixth grade in September.

When I enter the school, I tell my old classmates that I will be going into the fifth grade. It is not going to happen. When I return to school in the autumn, I find myself placed the fourth grade. My new teacher knows nothing about my arrangement with Mr. Serkin and moreover Mr. Serkin is no longer at our school. He has taken a job teaching public school. I can't believe what she tells me. I made a bargain with Mr.

Serkin, I kept up my end of the agreement. How can the school let me down because he quit? I feel humiliated, betrayed and outraged. My classmates make fun of me.

"So," the other kids taunt me, as they did when they discovered me coming back from the library with books in arms, and my mother carrying a purse, on the Sabbath, "you were bragging and lying, just as you were when you lied to us and told us you were religious. You were so sure of yourself. You were going to go into the fifth grade by September? Well September is here and you're still in fourth grade. TS, tough situation." I am infuriated by the injustice.

I approach the new teacher; she is young with very pale skin, rosy cheeks and she wears glasses. Her name is Miss Abromowitz and she looks kind and gentle. I tell her about my deal with Mr. Serkin. She tilts her head to one side, sympathetically.

"Nobody told me about that. I only know that you are on my class list and that this is the fourth grade. I am so sorry about the misunderstanding. Let me see if there's anything I can do."

I feel myself getting sick, choking with humiliating tears stinging the core of my eyes, ready to spill onto my cheeks. I can't accept my helplessness. "I made an agreement with Mr. Serkin last June. I've worked all summer long, and sent him all my assignments. This is just too unfair."

"I will do the best I can. I can see how hurt you must feel." She tries to calm me for a second time. She is the first kind person I have met in this school, the first one who seems to be taking me seriously. "In the meantime, stay put and do the work with all the other children in the class. I'll have an answer for you by Monday when we have our staff meeting."

I swallow hard, holding back the tears. Today is Wednesday; Monday is five long days away, interrupted by a week-end. The wait seems to go on for ages. It is unbearable. I endure the teasing of all the kids in the class, not only being left out of games but being called a bragging liar. I remain silent, refuse to defend myself. I am scared that when Monday comes, I will still be in the fourth grade.

On Monday morning I get to school before anyone else. I wait in front of the locked building for my teacher and there is only one thing on my mind.

"Well," I greet her expectantly at the door, my hands on my hips, "What was the decision?"

"Oh, we're not meeting until lunchtime, Rita. I'll let you know as soon as I have the answer, after recess." It is an agonizing morning. I don't go to recess. Instead, I remain in our classroom waiting for Miss Abramowitz to return.

"What is going to happen?" I demand as soon as she gets into the room.

She looks sympathetic and bends down to my eye level. "Rita, I know how much this means to you, but none of the other people in the school knew about your arrangement with Mr. Serkin. Apparently he and his family moved and no one knows how to get in touch with him. The administration can't just let you go on to fifth grade on your word alone. I'm afraid you're just going to have to spend the year in the fourth grade and then next summer I'll see to it that a proper arrangement is reached." I am deflated. This is more than I can bear. I've worked hard all summer long, did as I was told and now I'm being punished for something I had no control over. I have no friends or allies in this school, only taunting peers and unsympathetic staff.

I pack up my brand new notebooks, pencils, erasers, ruler and pencil case and stomp out of the classroom, out of the school and onto the hot, sunny September afternoon. It is 2 PM when I get home.

For a second time, I announced, "I am never going back to that school again. This time I mean it," I sob. "This is not a real school. You make agreements and work hard and they don't care. I told everyone in school that I would be in fifth grade and now they're all making fun of me. I hate that school! You don't learn anything there anyway. I'm going to a real school. I want to be smart."

My mother is appalled. Her eyes actually fill up with pain and sympathy for my plight. She watched me work all summer long, plod off to the post office and send my thick envelopes to Mr. Serkin. To her ever- lasting credit, she becomes my "old" loving mother. She does not argue or try to talk me into going back. Without even consulting my father, she takes me across the street to P.S.189, to the principal's office, where I am warmly welcomed and enrolled in the sixth grade! This school began a week before the Yeshiva and things are already in full swing. A teacher gives me an achievement test and the next day, I am placed into the S.P., Special Progress class, what today is called an enrichment class.

CHAPTER 17

———— ✂ ————

"BOYS AND GIRLS," Miss Weinstein tells the class, "this is Rita Schmelkes." She pronounces my last name correctly and I am grateful for that. Fifty eyes stare at me as though I am an alien, and indeed I feel like one. One glance at the other girls in the rooms assures me that I am wearing the wrong clothes. Everyone in the room is dressed casually, while I'm wearing one of those outfits my mother created by cutting an old outgrown dress in half and making a bolero from the top half of the dress and a skirt from the bottom half. The blouse I'm wearing under the bolero is tight. I'm hot, sweating and am having difficulty breathing. My outfit cries out "refugee girl" and my long braids make me feel as homemade as yesterday's mashed potatoes, and about just as attractive. I want to disappear, be sucked up into the air. Here I am the new kid dressed like some foreign refugee. I just got here and already I feel I don't belong. Indeed, do I belong anywhere?

Miss Weinstein leads me to a desk in the middle of the room, between two girls. I look at them hoping they will like me. She returns to her stool and continues with the math lessons as though nothing has happened, oblivious to the fact that I'm burning up with embarrassment. I take a peek at her. She is tiny, bony like a small bird, perched on her tall stool. Her legs are crossed and I can see the tops of her garters.

It is Tuesday afternoon and time for Social Studies. "Oh, oh," I think, "what *is* Social Studies?"

"Come up front Ellen," Miss Weinstein says, "let's hear your report. Quebec, Right?"

Ellen, a short, pudgy girl wearing a black jumper, glasses, and short pig tails, stands up in front of the class and gives a report on Quebec. She speaks slowly and pronounces each word with thought and precision. A large map hangs on the board behind her, like a blue, green and brown window shade. I try to listen carefully to see if I can figure out what social studies are without calling attention to myself. I am totally distracted by the room. There are about thirty desks bolted to the floor, with tops that lifts up where books and school supplies are stored. A small round hole covered with a metal lid in the upper right hand corner is called the "inkwell." The windows are tall and occupy an entire wall; afternoon sun streams in, warming the left side of my desk. Ellen walks up to the map several times during her report to point out important facts. After she finishes, she asks for comments and criticism. The rest of the class sits up, and a few kids raise their hands.

Barry Berk, a skinny blond boy with a crew cut is next. His report is on Victoria, British Columbia. It is not nearly as detailed as Ellen's, but I am getting the idea. At the same time, I hear a lot of unfamiliar words like "bibliography, research, and population."

"John Reilly, you're next," Miss Weinstein says after Barry's report. "Um, your report is on Winnipeg, is that right?"

"I couldn't do it, Miss Weinstein," he tells her. "My mother was sick and I had to take care of the baby."

Miss Weinstein sighs, shrugs her shoulders. She looks up from her grading book. "Really?" she says. It's clear that she doesn't believe him. "Last week you didn't do your homework, used the same excuse, and now you are unprepared for your report. This is not fair to your classmates who are doing their share. I'm not going to give you extra time. You're going to have to take a zero. Rita," she turns to me, "why don't you do the report on Winnipeg and have it ready by Thursday. We need to finish up with our neighbors to the north and get started on our next project."

My face is aflame. I've been in this room for less than an hour and already am given an assignment that will put me in front of the whole class? I've never heard of Winnipeg, I don't even know that it's in Canada. I haven't the first clue about how to write a report, let alone get information. We never had reports in the Yeshiva. We never even had kids standing in the front of the room talking to the whole class. I am so scared. The rest of the afternoon is spent ruminating. I badly want Miss Weinstein to like me, to think I'm smart, that she can count on me. How can I do that, when I have no idea how to gather the information and write and present a report? I'm scared of standing in front of the whole class and giving a talk, especially since I don't know how to find the information.

I must succeed in this school. It was my decision, my choice and I have to prove to my parents that I am worth listening to. But what if I fail? I ask myself. It doesn't take a minute for me to visit "Catastrophia" the country that exists in my head. My mind goes right from fear of doing the report to being kicked out of the school. I start obsessing immediately; if I get kicked out of this school there will not be another chance. I'll have to stay at home with my mother and do nothing all day long. I won't be able to play outside because then everyone will know that I don't go to school. How am I going to find out how to do a report?

At the end of the day, I gather all the courage available, it isn't much, and I go up to Miss Weinstein. "Excuse me," I mumble, staring at my new brown, oxford school shoes, "but I don't know how to write a report."

She smiles at me, "it's not as hard as it seems," she says. "Go to the library and ask the librarian to help you find books about Canada. Then look in the index, and find as much information as you can about Winnipeg. Don't worry," she continues, "you are a smart girl you can do it." She is not going to coddle me or give me a break. She is friendly but she means business. "Alright," I say," but what is an index?"

It is Tuesday, not a library day, but my mother lets me walk the ten blocks to the library by myself. The librarian, who is already my friend, is very helpful. When I tell her I have to write a report about Winnepeg, she takes me over to a shelf and hands me five or six heavy volumes.

"These should to the trick," she says. "Now," she instructs me, "the things we want, is to find out some important facts about Winnipeg, like the population, industry, climate, history and any famous people who come from Winnipeg." She shows me how to organize my report, how to keep it short and focused on just the important items. I sit at the library table until it is dark copying information about all the areas I will touch on.

I spend the next two days rehearsing the report in front of the bathroom mirror, and have all the information memorized. But when Thursday comes, all I can think of is 2 o'clock and how am I going to be able to stand in front of the whole class with everyone looking at me.

Standing in front of the large map of Canada, I take a deep breath, swallow several times, and then, from somewhere inside my throat, I hear a voice that I don't recognize. "Winnipeg is the capital of Manitoba, on the Red River, in Canada. It is one of the coldest cities in the world and its main product is wheat." I walk over to the map hanging behind me and locate Winnipeg as well as the Red River. Somehow, I get through my report. My cheeks are so hot that I touch my temples to see if my whole head is on fire. Ellen is the first to raise her hand when I am finished. It is time or "criticism."

"What I learned from Rita's report is that Winnipeg is very cold in the winter, like some our own mid-western cities."

Rhoda comments that I gave a very good report with only a few days to prepare. "I learned that wheat is the main industry in Winnipeg."

The comments from my classmates are complimentary. Miss Weinstein congratulates me, "You've done well, Rita," she says "especially since you had so little time to prepare." She gives me an "A" on the report and I traipse to my seat, relieved and elated.

We are ready to tackle our next project in Social Studies; Minority Groups and their Contributions to Our Country. Miss Weinstein's sixth grade classroom is where I am first introduce to the injustices that are heaped upon the "Negroes" as they are called in 1946. The only place I have seen them was on the Gripsholm and on the subway subways.

There are none in our class and very few in our neighborhood. We open our social studies book and read about how the Negroes lived in the South; persecuted and enslaved. I perk up, suddenly becoming aware of something I can identify with. I hear the word "prejudice" for the first time in my life. Miss Weinstein defines it, "it's when one group of people hates another group because they look or act different. They try to take things away from them, won't give them a job, or rent an apartment to them. It is caused by ignorance and intolerance (two more words I don't know the meaning of.)" But I do know all about prejudice. I've experienced prejudice in Austria, Poland and Germany. I even experienced it in my last school, where some of the kids shunned me because I was not as religious as they.

Miss Weinstein hits a familiar nerve within me. "The Negroes in the United States are scapegoats, just like the Jews were in Germany, Austria and Poland. We **must** take their plight seriously and help erase bigotry." I wonder whether she is Jewish and if she knows about my life in Europe? It feels as though she is speaking directly to me when she tells us about the prejudice towards the Negroes. She uses words I have to look up in the dictionary, "bias, discrimination, deprivation, ignorance, intolerance, bigotry and racism." I feel at home in this classroom, with so many Gentile children. Miss Weinstein is not embarrassed to use the word "Jewish." I have never been able to say it among Gentiles without feeling self-conscious. If the good citizens of Germany, Austria and Poland would have understood what Miss Weinstein is saying, then all the slaughter of the Jews would never have taken place. I adopt her outrage and sense of fair play. I promise myself that I will never sit by and watch an injustice committed against someone for reasons beyond their control.

"You count," she tells the class, "every one of you can make a difference in someone's life by treating them as fairly as you want to be treated."

I'm important I tell myself. Miss Weinstein says that we can all make a difference in the world. I can't wait to start. I join a group of young people who stand in front of the subway stations with tin cans, asking for contributions to help the Negroes in the South. We are collecting money to send school books to the children in the segregated schools in Georgia, North and South Carolina, Alabama, Mississippi and Louisiana.

"Marion Anderson, the great Negro singer is not permitted to sing in the Metropolitan Opera House in New York," Miss Weinstein tells the class. "Paul Robeson cannot use the same bathrooms as the white citizens of Georgia, Lena Horne can entertain high society, but she is not permitted to eat dinner with them in the restaurant if she is performing in the South. What did the American soldiers fight for in Europe when some Americans citizens are not allowed to have the same rights as others?" She is sounding angry, outraged and accusatory. "I thought we fought for freedom, yet there is no freedom for certain people right here in our very own country." She pounds the table with her fist emphasizing the last three words she has just uttered. "We need to share our freedom among each other and not forget about our brothers." She encourages us to take a stand, talk to our parents, and ask them write letters to our Senators demanding that all Americans be treated justly.

I run home, brimming with the enthusiasm. "Did you know, Daddy that America is not truly a free country? There are all kinds of injustices heaped upon the Negroes."

"What?" he says. "Where did you hear that?" He is not crazy about the fact that I attend public school, is not sure he approves of Miss Weinstein's filling my head with all sorts of propaganda. He certainly does not approve my new concerns. He agrees that the world is not fair to many people, "Yes," he concedes. "The Negroes in America are not always treated fairly, but they're much better off than the Jews of Europe," he quickly reminds me. "They never have to fear for their lives, nor are they in any danger of being sent to concentration camps. Yes, I feel sorry for some them but I do not want you to take part in any collections or demonstrations on their behalf. It smacks of Communism. In fact," he says, "Miss Weinstein had better be careful what she tells her students. She has some radical ideas. She is sounding like a Communist herself." He is cautious. The threat of Communism is turning all sorts of people into cowards with no opinions. "We can't afford to be different, to stand out. It wasn't so long ago that we were without a country."

I do not listen to him. I don't even hear him. "What's this concern with Communism? Isn't this a free country? Did you forget it was just this kind of indifference that made the Jews scapegoats?" I ask filled with all the indignity of an 11 year-old can muster.

"No, I did not forget about the Jews in Europe. It is exactly for this reason that I don't want to take any chances here in America." I don't know how we even got to the topic of Communism let alone the plight of the Jews. I am talking about the Negroes and their lack of freedom and civil rights. Why does he always manage to turn every discussion, every conversation into a Jewish concern? Aren't there any other people in the world? I want to do what Miss Weinstein charges us with: to stand up for the rights of others, but my father only knows how to stand up for the Jews.

Sometime in May of that same year I come home from school and my mother is sitting in front of the radio. Tears are streaming down her face and she can hardly talk. I fear for the worst, thinking that she just got some dreadful news of another person in our family who was killed.

"*Mutti*, what happened?" I ask, alarmed. She looks up at me, blows her nose and tells me to remember this day. "It is the most important day of our lives, in the lives of Jews all over the world. A Jewish state, a homeland has been declared. The new country of Israel will accept Jews from all over the world. No longer are we strangers living in the diaspora. We have options! We have a country! The world has seen the outrage perpetrated against the Jews and has decided to establish the state of Israel, the Jewish homeland." She is ecstatic. She hugs me and sobs into my neck. "We have a country. Oh, that my brothers and sisters had lived to see the day when our dreams would come true. I remember the parlor in Wieliczka where a large, sepia portrait of a man with a long beard, not wearing the traditional kippah of orthodox men was hanging on a wall. When I asked who he was I was told that it was the picture of Theodore Herzl, the founder of modern Zionism, a man my family revered. He had a dream of a Jewish state, located where Palestine now existed. Now, that dream has become a reality.

The relatively new organization called the United Nations held a meeting and voted to recognize the State of Israel as an independent country. I had been learning about the UN in school. They are going to solve all of the world's problems around a conference table; talk about problems instead of fight wars. Miss Weinstein told us that with the UN there would never be a need for war. In her class we have Current Events where we bring in articles from the newspaper to be discussed in class. The UN is a frequent topic and Miss Weinstein never fails to remind us that war is not the answer to anyone's problems.

At this time, the radio becomes a major source of entertainment and information. It is one Wednesday in early November that I find out that Harry Truman defeated Thomas Dewey for the presidency of the United States. The country was so certain of Dewey's victory that the New Your Daily Mirror was forced to revise its headlines, *Dewey Wins,* printed late the night before. A whole new edition must be printed.

I run home from school at lunchtime, up the five flights of stairs, out of breath, in time to listen to my favorite soap operas. "Our Gal Sunday," the story of an orphan girl from Silver Creek Colorado who marries England's richest, most handsome, titled lord. The announcer asks the same question of the audience every day: "Can a girl from a small mining town in Colorado find happiness as the wife of a rich, titled nobleman?"

This soap is immediately followed by "The Romance of Helen Trent," which sets out to prove that a "woman of thirty-five or older can find romance." I ask myself why such an old woman would be interested in romance. I am faithful to these shows and eager to discuss them with my friends when I return to school.

The minute I come home at 3:15 it is time for Superman.

"It's a bird! It's a plane! It's Superman!" The excited voice of the announcer shouts out gleefully.

Fifteen minutes later it is time for the "Lone Ranger" who sails onto the air waves shouting, "Hi -ho Silver" followed up by Tonto's subdued response, "Giddyup Scott." If there is time I tune into "Tom Mix," the all American cowboy. His show is sponsored by Kellogg's Pep a popular cereal which is making a remarkable offer to its consumers by enclosing a button of a favorite comic book hero. We eat the Pep as quickly as we can, accumulating and trading doubles in order to complete our collections. For mailing in one box top from the Kellogs' Corn Flakes, the Kelloggs' company will send a magical weather ring that not only will tell when it is raining, but will predict the weather as well. This is something I must have. I nag my mother into buying the cereal, rip off the box top and send it away. The ring does not arrive and I am told by Simon Marks, Michael's friend that I was supposed to include ten cents for shipping and handling. I give up on the ring and am thrilled when suddenly it appears in a brown envelope, addressed to Rita Schmelkes.

The shows these cereals advertise have a huge impact on my thinking. I learn that people who perform good deeds are rewarded with super human strength and evil-doers are punished. It is easy to identify with the characters and on a very subtle level I become conscious of the how much lower the status of women is. The women in my soaps are not autonomous, cannot make the changes in society that men are able to. This is 1948 and the message to girls is clear: marry a strong man who can give you what you want and can protect you from harm.

CHAPTER 18

THE FOLLOWING SEPTEMBER, when school opens, Miss Weinstein is not there. It is the height of the McCarthy era and the fear of Communism is as rampant as the fear of terrorism becomes in 2001. I hear whispers in the schoolyard. The kids are saying that she has been "blacklisted." She, along with Arthur Miller, Ring Lardner, Elia Kazan, Leonard Bernstein, Charlie Chaplin, Orson Welles and many, many others are being investigated by the HUAC. Careers are destroyed and lives are ruined, all because of the fear of a philosophy which is being espoused by a country very far away from us.

"She's a Jew and a Commie," John Reilly says disdainfully. He's still mad because she saw right through him, saw him for the lazy, uncooperative boy he was and still is.

"No, no," some of the other kids say. "She was a great teacher!"

"Yeah, right. She is a Jew and a Communist. My dad told me. There ain't room for people like her in our country."

I can't stand this name calling. I start to cry, not the tears of shame or fear. They are the tears of outrage. Suddenly I feel my power, remember what Miss Weinstein said. Never let an opportunity to stand up for others get lost. Miss Weinstein made all of us better than we would have been without her. I remember "my voice," and I use it now.

"You, John Reilly are a stupid, ignorant slob. You didn't deserve a teacher like Miss Weinstein!" The other kids cheer me on.

"Atta girl, Rita! You tell him!"

I do manage to tell him but I still miss my old teacher. She, as all the others I have lost creates a vacuum, a hole in my heart. She taught me about prejudice and my personal responsibility to speak out against injustice. She made me feel important by insisting that every single one of us, yes, even I, could make a difference in other people's lives. She certainly made a difference in my life. I will never forget her.

CHAPTER 19

IN SEVENTH GRADE everything changes. We have "departmental," which means we go from one classroom to another for various subjects. We are also assigned special privileges. I get the one I want the most, being a crossing monitor. This very responsible position is allotted to only ten students in the seventh grade, and I am one of the lucky few. I get to wear a big blue button that says "J.C.G." which stands for junior crossing guard.

"Get back up on the sidewalk," I shout, "I didn't say you could step off yet." The little kids in the lower grades are scared of me. I might report them to their teachers. I love being bossy, telling children when to get back on the sidewalk, holding the hands of the kindergartners and walking them across the street, being kind or mean, whenever I want to.

My grades are excellent and my parents tell me to help Michael. He is in the Yeshiva and is struggling with all his subjects. My parents have been called in to the school and told that Michael is not a serious student, that he is playful and immature. I really don't want to help. I want to do my own work and go out to play. Michael does not want my help, he is uncooperative. Whenever I try to correct him, he tells me to "fix it up" for him. I know I'm being bossy and officious. It's almost like playing refugee, but this time it's for real, not a game. I shout at him, "Why can't you do this easy arithmetic problem?" He shouts back at me. We get nothing done other than re-establishing the old pecking order. He fools around and tries to distract me from my "responsibility." I demand the respect due a higher authority.

"You're so stupid," I tell him. "Why can't you follow a simple direction like watching your plus and minus signs?"

"You know, you're not my boss anymore," he answers me. "If you really want to help me, just do my homework for me. Nobody does homework at the Yeshiva and no one checks it either." I happen to know this is true.

"That's cheating," I say self-righteously, "I'm not going to do that. And what are you going to do when you get tested?"

"Cheat," he says matter- of –factly, like a little psychopath.

I am appalled and attempt teach him a lesson on morality and ethics. We argue some more. Our voices escalate and my mother comes into the kitchen. "Why can't you help your little brother without causing such a fight?" my mother asks me. "When I was young my sisters were kind to me. They fought over who would help me."

"He doesn't listen to me, and he won't do his work," I whine.

"Just show him what to do and be kind instead of mean and bossy."

"Now I'm mean and bossy?" I shout at my mother, "I want him to learn something, and you accuse me of being mean and bossy."

"It's no use," I say to myself. I take his homework from him and do it. This goes on for the rest of the year. Michael graciously accepts the homework done for him and turns it in as his own. The end of the semester comes and with it report cards arrive. I run up the five flights, out of breath and excited. "Look mommy and daddy, I got all A's." I'm thrilled with my achievements.

Michael is in the corner of the living room, slumped on the floor. He looks defeated. My father turns on me raging, "If you weren't such a selfish sister, you could have helped your brother. What kind of a girl is happy getting good grades when her brother has to come home with such bad marks?" Michael has already gotten his beating, now I have to be punished for only thinking of myself and my grades. "Go into your room," he tells me, angrily. I feel awful. All he cares about are Michael's bad grades. How about my good ones? Even though he hits Michael, I am convinced he cares more about him than about me.

"He's lazy. He's stupid. He doesn't know how lucky he is to be able to go to school. I never had those opportunities. If he puts his mind to his studies like he does to his playing, he could go to the university someday. What in heaven's name is going to become of him?" He is complaining to my mother about Michael, as if Michael were out of earshot. My mother listens, but says nothing. I am feeling weird, self-righteous, happy that I'm not being yelled at, and also guilty for being glad that it is Michael who is being punished and not me. Yet at the same time I'm jealous that he gets all the attention for being bad, while I'm ignored for being good.

My mother takes a deep breath. I hear her sigh, "Please, Alex," she pleads, "don't aggravate yourself so much. This is not the end of the world. He's just a little boy. He'll do better next time."

My father turns on her, pushing away her ideas. "Are you telling me he tries hard enough, or are you saying that he is incompetent, a stupid child? Do you really think our son is a dummy?' he is irate. "It's your coddling and babying him that makes him so lazy."

"I have a selfish daughter and a stupid son," he tells my mother, "and much of it is your fault. I don't know what I did to earn such a reward. I want him to be successful, and he doesn't care. I want her to be generous and helpful and all she cares about is herself."

My heart has a hole in it and it's leaking sadness. We are a source of shame for my father. My jealousy fades. I suddenly feel overwhelming sorrow for Michael and myself. My little brother, whom I had protected during our imprisonment, who was teased for looking like Charlie Chaplin, who was afflicted with painful red boils, who I love with all my heart, is being bullied and beat up because he is not smart enough. I am angry and in pain.

Why can't my father love us the way we are and not the way he wishes we were? Why must he be ashamed of us? Gone is the happy, self-righteous gloat I was sporting only a few moments ago. I should have tried to protect Michael. Instead I was feeling superior and happy. I think of what Miss Weinstein would have done had she seen someone helpless being bullied and beaten.

I make up my mind. I will go out and tell my father not to touch my brother. I am ready to defend Michael, stand up for him as I had done in Liebenau but when I open the door and see my father I shrink and my resolve blows away like smoke on a windy day. His fury is so great that I am afraid of further enraging him and getting beaten up myself. Fear robs me of the drive and quest for justice inspired by Miss Weinstein, to defend those who can't defend themselves.

I have to be on guard lest I arouse his anger. I try to be "good" and do everything I can to please him, but I feel it's never the right thing and it's never enough. I can no longer wear Miss Weinstein's mantle of outrage at injustice, and I begin to lose some of the resolve she implanted in me. I can't do anything right. I can't protect Michael from the bullying rage of our father and I can no longer tell myself I am a fair, just person. I berate myself relentlessly for being an unprincipled coward. The bad feeling is back, and this time I invited it by and doing nothing as I watched my brother being humiliated. "When I grow up," I promise myself, "I will never witness an injustice without standing up for the victim."

CHAPTER 20

⌀

MY MOTHER AND I are climbing up the steps to our apartment after an afternoon of dancing lessons. I see a tiny dwarf woman standing in front of our door. She is much shorter than I, has the blackest hair I have ever seen and eyes like sparkling sapphires. I am about a flight of stairs ahead of my mother, when the woman runs over to me. She hugs me, and says in Polish,

"Freda, Freda, You haven't changed at all!" She looks astonished and chuckles in delight. I don't know who she is and why she is hugging me and calling me by my mother's name. I have no idea why she thinks I am my mother. My mother, stops in her tracks, reaches for the railing and gasps. It's as if she's seen a ghost. She stares at her, speechless and slack-jawed.

"Mirka, Mirka Fisch," my mother finally whispers. She is pale and quivering. "Can it really be you?" My mother sits down on the steps and I watch them hug and weep. After a few minutes, when we are in our apartment, my mother turns to me. "Mirka is a dear, dear neighbor from Wieliczka. I was your age the last time I saw her in Wieliczka." This explains why Mirka thought I was my mother. The last time they had seen each other *Mutti* was twelve years old, my age.

Mirka, along with her parents and brother had left for America long before Hitler came into power. Mirka's father, who was a carpenter in Wieliczka had no trouble finding employment in the US. Good carpenters were sought after in America where new buildings were erected every day. He is and was a master craftsman.

There were no opportunities for a Jewish carpenter and his dwarf daughter in Wieliczka, so the Fisches along with Mirka and their son

Alec came to America before anyone had ever heard of Hitler. Now, when Mirka sees me, she sees the spitting image of my mother with two long blond braids and freckles across the bridge of her nose, exactly as she remembers her.

"Freda, my dear Freda," she speaks, this time to my mother, "I looked all over for survivors of our family, your family and anyone who might have made it out of Wieliczka and Krakow. As soon as the war ended, I went to the Hebrew Immigration Aid Society (HIAS) office in Manhattan. Can you imagine what it felt like for me to see your names? It was like seeing someone emerge from a grave. At first, I didn't believe my eyes, so I asked one of the clerks to read the name to me. When she confirmed what I was seeing and not just wishing, I cried so much that they had to show me to a seat and give me a glass of water." She continues after pausing to catch her breath, "You made it through a cyclone, an earthquake and a volcano eruption. I knew I had to see you immediately. I couldn't take the time it takes to mail a letter and await your response. So, here I am. I waited an hour in front of your apartment. I knew you'd have to get home sometime." The reunion is tearful as my mother tells her of all our relatives who have not survived. Mirka sobs out loud.

"How can such splendid people disappear: such a beautiful family, so generous, so smart, and so talented?" Mirka and my mother both weep for a long time while I sit in the living room still wearing my coat. "Oh my God," both my mother and Mirka are now sobbing together, "how can such a family be killed so brutally? Wiped off the earth, like a cloud in the windy sky?" Even though Mirka is tiny, her emotions are big, her tears flow down her face and her feelings are overwhelming.

She tells us that her parents are still alive. They live on Division Avenue in Brooklyn, among other Chassidic families. Mirka married an American housepainter, Jack, and they live with her parents, whom she takes care of. Her parents are old and need help managing their lives.

My father comes into the house. He has never seen Mirka; she left Wieliczka before he met my mother. He is surprised to find us in the apartment, sitting with our coats on, laughing and crying at the same time. "Alex," my mother says, "this is my old friend Mirka Fisch from Wieliczka." My father does not understand.

"What?" he says in surprise, addressing Mirka. He thinks she has just arrived from Wieliczka. "You mean you just came to America now, after the war?" He is excited. It takes no time for his mind to race ahead hopefully. Maybe there are some survivors left in Poland, maybe some in Austria. He immediately thinks of his parents. Dare he think that they might be alive somewhere? He was never notified of their death.

"When did you arrive? Do you have a place to stay? How did you manage to survive?" he is full of questions.

"No, no," my mother explains to him trying to clear up his confusion. She tells him that the Fisches left Poland many years ago, before they met. "They have been here for over twenty-five years. They are citizens."

Mirka stays for dinner, until late at night, reminiscing with my mother. They stop often to touch each not believing that they are awake and not dreaming. A visit is planned for the following Sunday. Alec, her brother will pick us up in his car, and take us to Williamsburg to visit Mr. and Mrs. Fisch.

Later on that evening, my mother tells me that Mirka is several years older than she is, even though she is not taller than a seven year old. Her family was very poor. They lived in a small hut, in the middle of Wieliczka. My mother and my aunts loved running down the hill to Mrs. Fisch's house where Mirka would read stories to them and play games. Her small size had nothing to do with her brains. She was and is very smart my mother tells me.

The following Sunday, after a much enjoyed ride in a car, we climb up a flight of rickety steps that lean precariously against a wall. They remind me of the stairs in the building my *oma* and *opa* lived in. The hallway is dark, the banister is shaky and unstable. I cannot believe that such an old building is still standing. It doesn't look anything like the tall brick buildings in the rest of New York. And there, at the top of the stairs, are two elderly people waiting for our arrival, looking just like my *oma* and *opa* did so long ago in Vienna. Old Mrs. Fisch is wearing her *sheytl* and old Mr. Fisch, his velvet yarmulka. The little apartment is crammed full of furniture: wooden cabinets, shelves, china closets all hand made by Mr. Fisch in his spare time. The cabinets are filled with wooden carvings, miniature trees, cows, horses, a detailed chess set, all crafted by this artist- carpenter. Mrs. Fisch has roasted a large turkey. It is the first time I've seen anything like it.

"What a huge chicken," I exclaim.

"*Dus is not uh cheeken, honey, dus is uh toiky.*" Mrs. Fisch laughs as she points out my mistake. He ill -fitting dentures become dislodged and she quickly cups her hand over her mouth. The turkey looks like a pol- ished wooden bird, something Mr. Fisch carved in his spare time: brown and shiny. Alec has us all pose for pictures, while he stands, draped behind a tripod. He is an amateur photographer and he wants to pre- serve this moment. They talk in Polish, Yiddish and English, reminding each other of Wieliczka and the times they had spent together, pausing to cry and shake their heads in disbelief. How much has happened since they said good-bye to each other so long ago! I feel at home with them, they remind me so much of the beloved grandparents I left so long ago. I feel happy here, wanted, welcomed and at home with people I can love.

Mr. Fisch carves the turkey and after dinner, they catch up on the past, while Michael and I play cards. It is dark outside when we return to Alec's car. He still has a long trip, from Brooklyn to Washington Heights and then to Riverdale where he lives. Alec married an American woman and is very successful. Before we part, he invites us to his home for the following Sunday. He is honored by my mother's presence. He remembers her from Wieliczka, when she was the youngest daughter of the wealthiest resident in town. He wouldn't dream of having such esteemed guests take the subway, and so he again picks us up the fol- lowing Sunday in his new, green Packard.

He tells us that he is in the air conditioning business which is a brand new field and only becomes available after the war. We have never heard of air conditioners, but they must be something everyone wants judging by the private house he and his family live in. There is a large front yard that is covered with snow and the inside looks like my idea of a palace. It is carpeted everywhere, wall to wall in dark green velvety looking fabric, so thick that my shoes sink into the pile. The furniture is upholstered in heavy brocade and ornate fabric drapes the windows. There are paintings hanging everywhere, and a carpeted indoor staircase that leads to the bedrooms. I have never seen such opulence. Maybe someday, I think, I too will be able to live in such a house. I am eleven years old and have spent too much time living in a fantasy world to give up my hopes and wishes.

A tall, massive, shiny, black piano stands against a wall in the living room. I practically salivate when I see it. A piano! I go over to it and gently stroke some of the keys with reverence. I hold my breath. I have not touched a piano since we had fled from Poland. It feels like it's been waiting for me all my life. I stroke it gently and quietly play the only thing I can, the first six notes of *La Donna Mobile.* While the grown -ups go on talking, eating and making up for lost time, I spin on the piano stool, staring at the shiny dark giant, not daring to play anymore on it. Ida, Alec's wife comes into the living room with my mother and Mirka. The men stay in the dining room, smoking and chatting.

"I would love to get rid of this old piano," she mentions casually. "My girls don't play anymore and all it does is sit here and collect dust." Is this my overactive imagination hearing what it wants to hear?

"Yes," she goes on what I'd really like to put in its place is a television set, a console. If I could find someone to take it, they can have it. All they have to do is get a mover to get it out of here."

I glance at my mother imploringly. The possibility of owning a piano is something I dare not dream about. I wonder if we have enough money to pay a mover. My mother shares my excitement. Somehow she will find the money to pay a moving company. She has already moved mountains.

"Really?" she asks. "We would love to have it, that is, if you're sure you don't want it anymore." We leave late at night, and I fall asleep in the back of the car dreaming about music and pianos.

CHAPTER 21

—— ✤ ——

AN EXCITED CROWD of men, women and children is standing in front of our building, craning their necks upward to watch the swinging black giant. My piano is dangling from a crane like a yo-yo suspended from the roof of our building. The piano is held by two ropes attached to pulleys. Onlookers are gazing up at it, pointing, excited, and shouting advice to the men on the roof who don't hear them. Suddenly the massive giant slides to one side. Every onlooker runs away screaming, scared that the black piano will slip from its restraints and crush them.

"Oh my God," I say as the shrieking crowd runs in every direction, fleeing the menacing ogre. Someone screams, "It's King Kong!" I don't move. I am mesmerized, certain that if I run away, the piano will somehow be lost to me. "Please don't let it fall and shatter into millions of splinters." I pray, gazing upward, my hands folded in silent supplication.

I look up at the dangling instrument. "Why are they hoisting it up through the roof and the front of the building when our windows face the back?" I ask my mother who alternates between watching from the outside to running upstairs to check on the indoor progress.

"They have no room in the alley for the large truck," she explains. "They have to get it on the roof, move it across and over to our side of the building, and then through a window into the living room." I remain downstairs, my eyes fixes on the swinging piano. My mouth is open. I pray that it can be squeezed into our house like sardines into a flat can.

"How in heavens name are they going to get that big piano through our little window?"

"They will ease it in through." She answers while gazing upwards.

I run upstairs to watch the progress from the living room. The window, the one with no fire escape, is removed as well as the window frame, and the piano is gently coaxed, on its side, with the keyboard facing down, through the empty frame and into our living room.

The shiny dark ebony instrument is in place. It occupies an entire wall: a regal, exotic African queen, glowing and resplendent. She dominates the room with haughty grandeur. She is majestic and she is ours! I am going to take real piano lessons at last. America is getting better! My mother is going to be my teacher and we are both excited.

She goes to a music store on Broadway and 49th Street, Tin Pan Alley, as it is called. "I'm going to start my little girl on piano lessons," she tells the clerk. "What would you recommend for a beginner?" He doesn't hesitate for a minute before handing her a copy of John Thompson's piano book, "Teaching Little Fingers to Play." The book is easy since all the notes are numbered with corresponding fingering. I learn all the pieces in it simply by following the numbers. I become acquainted with the keyboard: the importance of middle C, the time value attributed to all the little eggs, black, white and dotted scattered on the five lines and four spaces. The two duets at the end of the book are my favorites, "She'll be Comin' Round the Mountain" and "Home on the Range." My mother plays the bass line and I play the melody. Any visitor who happens to come by is forced into a seat and stay for a "concert." The wild galloping rhythm of "She'll be Comin' Round the Mountain and the lazy, slow pace of, "Home on the Range" are real music with rich harmonies.

I am eager to play for anyone who comes to visit us. After a bit of chatting, my mother tells everyone that I am learning to play the piano and would they like to hear me play? No one has the nerve to turn down such an offer when they are sitting in our living room eating her cookies and drinking her tea. They applaud and marvel at my progress, while envying us for having a piano.

My mother decides to consult an expert piano teacher who happens to be a cousin of hers: Poldi Zeitlin, who in addition to being our cousin, is also a niece and student of the world famous pianist Artur

Schnabel. She invites Poldi over for a Sunday afternoon visit. Poldi and her husband Marc come puffing up the stairs.

She bursts into the apartment. "Goodness," she exclaims, "Freda, how do you manage these stairs? No wonder you are so thin." Poldi is a beautiful, tall imposing woman. She has short black hair, dark plucked eyebrows, pink cheeks, olive skin and the whitest, brightest smile I have ever seen off the movie screen. She is talkative, dramatic, using her hands to make every point. My mother invites everyone to the table for tea and Viennese pastries. Poldi talks with her mouth full, gesticulating expressively, with pastry crumbs flying all over the front of her dress. She asks questions about our escape, and tells us about her career as a music teacher and editor. The powdered sugar collects on her chin; she talks quickly as if afraid of running out of time. After they have finished, my mother asks Poldi if she would mind listening to me play the piano.

"Mind? My dear, I wouldn't dream of leaving your house without hearing Rita play." By this time I have already graduated from "Comin' Round the Mountain" to a Sonatina by Clementi. I am very anxious to make a good impression. My mother has warned me that Poldi's opinion is vital. I have practiced hard for this moment and sit down at the piano stool. I am eleven, not yet aware of the paralyzing power of stage fright. I feel secure in executing all those running passages and trills that make me think of tiny brooks in a German forest. I put my soul into this performance and feel good about it.

Poldi goes into raptures. "*Sei ist fablehaft.* (She is enchanting, fantastic). She has only been playing for three months? *Unglaublich,* (unbelievable)!" She uses words I never heard before: "gifted, talented." I don't know what those words mean, but I know I like them because she is so very enthusiastic and extravagant in her praise.

"She must take lessons with me," Poldi exclaims and adds generously, "of course I would never charge relative for lessons, especially one so talented,"

It is decided that I will to go Forest Hills, for a lesson in Poldi's studio every other week. My mother will continue teaching me on the off week and supervise my practicing. I am eager and filled with hope. I practice every morning, before school starts, while my mother brushes and braids my hair. She strokes my head lovingly. One hundred brush strokes for each braid. Then she plaits each braid, tying the ends with ribbons she ironed the night before. I love this morning ritual when I have my mother's undivided attention and love. She is my old, sweet *Mutti* for a half an hour each morning.

We take the train to Forest Hills, to a "rich" neighborhood. Trees surrounded by small gardens with colorful flowers cast shade on the sidewalk. Poldi's building is two short blocks from the subway. It is impressive. A uniformed doorman opens the door for us and asks us where we are going.

"Mrs. Zeitlin," my mother responds.

"Ah, yes," he nods in recognition, the piano teacher."

We enter and Poldi asks us to sit in a small hallway, the waiting room, while she finishes her lesson with another student. I listen to him play. I am envious, he is playing difficult music. When he leaves, she ushers us into the living room, her studio, which has two baby grand pianos facing each other. I am overwhelmed. She motions me to sit down at one of the pianos and she sits down next to me on the piano bench.

"Well," she says to me, straightening her back, and looking directly into my eyes, "what would you like to play?"

"I can play the Clementi Sonatina."

"No, no. I've already heard that. What new piece would you like learn?" I don't know what to say.

"You mean to learn to play now?"

She demonstrates, playing a few selections for me and tells me to choose the one I like best. I opt for the Mozart Rondo in D major. It is a lovely, light piece of music, with lots of room for dynamics and complicated passages that will require a lot of practice.

She approves my choice. "Good," she agrees, "You will play it for the November recital." Oh, oh, it feels like the social studies report all over again.

"What is a recital?"

"It's a small concert, where all my students perform for each other and their parents. We have them twice a year, one in the winter and the other in the spring." She is casual, making it sound routine.

We start with scales, move on to exercises, and then go to the Mozart. I feel my excitement mounting. This is what I've been waiting for all my life. The Mozart is challenging, more difficult than anything I've tackled before and I concentrate, trying to sight read such a demanding piece.

"I don't know if I'll be able to play this for a recital," I tell Poldi.

"Don't worry," she says, "you'll learn it. Once you've played it through a few times, it will "fall" into your fingers." I go home and practice, a few bars at a time. By the time my next lesson with Poldi rolls around, two weeks later, I've memorized much of it.

CHAPTER 22

—— ✣ ——

THE GRAY NOVEMBER sky is promising to deliver either a chilling rain or a wet snow before it turns black. In Poldi's apartment chairs are lined up in neat rows where an excited audience of parents and grandparents and anxious performers sit and wait to hear or perform what has been practiced for the past several months. My father is at work, my aunt Sari is busy with her new baby, but Mirka sits next to my mother awaiting my "debut." Little Mirka, whose tenacity to find lost Jews from Wieliczka is the person who managed to connect me with my precious piano. She is carrying a large package, wrapped in brown wrapping paper tied with string which she places on her tiny lap. She looks at me expectantly, nodding her head. I perform making two terrible mistakes which only I am aware of. After the recital, when we are ready to go home, Mirka thrusts the package at me.

"Open it when you get home," she tells me. "This is a gift from Harry and me, to celebrate your first concert."

I can't wait to open my present and see what is inside. I rip the paper off as soon as we get home, impatient to see what it is. A wooden box with two brass hinges opens to reveal the most opulent set of paints I have ever seen. Tubes of every imaginable color of oil paint nest on three trays, stacked up onto each other. Four shades of everything in gleaming pretty colors. I step back in awe. I have never owned a paint set, let alone one so full and dazzling. My mother marvels over it too.

"I will share it with Michael," I tell her generously. I don't want to be greedy and I can't use it now because we don't have any drawing paper. I can't be wasting paints like these on plain paper. Reluctantly, I slide the beautiful box under my bed and start saving for a pad of good paper from the art supply store.

Every day, after school, I check under my bed and take out the paints, admire them, count all thirty-six of tubes, regroup them and rearrange them before sliding the box carefully back under my bed. They fill me with incredible joy. I must save up to be able to afford the special paper that such a set demands. Money is hard to come by and I sacrifice my daily ice-cream cone money until I have saved enough to break open the paint.

The day finally arrives and although I haven't examined the paint set in days I rush home with the paper from the art supply store. Finally, I will be able to use what I have waited for so long. I slide my hand under the bed, feeling around for the familiar square box. I feel nothing. I look under the bed thinking that perhaps it was moved, slid to another spot. I do not see it. I can't believe it. How did my paints get away from the safe spot under my bed?

"Where's my paint box?" I ask my mother who is in the kitchen chopping onions.

She stops to wipe onion tears from her cheeks. "Rita," she sighs deeply and sits down. I can sense something awful has happened to my paints. Before she goes on, I think that maybe Michael took them to school and lost them, or we had a robbery and someone came and stole them. Or maybe Mirka wanted them back for her nieces because I hadn't gotten around to using them yet. I was prepared for the worst.

"Be a big girl and try to understand," she starts by way of explanation. "I got a letter from Aunt Matilda, and Miriam got into a wonderful art school in Tel-Aviv." I don't bother listening to the rest of the story. I already know what happened to my paints. Just as my aunt and cousin got the dresses I thought belonged to me, the paints that I know are mine are now on their way to Tel-Aviv, to Miriam. I run to the bathroom. I can't let my mother see my tears, how upset I am. I know what she'll tell me: that I'm ungrateful, that I'm the lucky one to be living in America and still have my father alive, that I should be happy to be able to share, that I shouldn't be greedy. I am not in the mood to hear about my good luck. Right now, I just want to feel sorry for myself. How come I'm always made to feel as if I'm expecting too much? Why am I supposed to feel lucky when things are taken away from me? I feel awful, undeserving, unworthy and unentitled as well as greedy, ungrateful, and mean.

CHAPTER 23

MY FATHER COMES home from work in the evening and tells my mother he has bad news. She has not looked this distraught since we left the Ghetto. My father has lost his job. The familiar feeling of terror does not take a second to spread its awful tentacles across my chest. I look at them, afraid of the answer I will get if I ask what is going to happen to us. He tries to reassure us and says that he will start searching first thing tomorrow morning.

I am thirteen years old and this is not the first time my father has been out of work. But this time it's worse. Again he leaves the house early each morning and returns depressed each night. The gloom that settles over our house is deeper, more penetrating than it has ever been before. He is out of work again and the whole family feels like we are wrapped in a dark, sad fog. I don't want to imagine what will happen to us if he doesn't get work soon, but the dread comes over me without my conscious provocation.

I find myself feeling sorry for him, he looks so sad and lonely. Again he leaves the house, carrying the thin cheese sandwich my mother made the night before, wrapped in wax paper. And every evening he returns with the empty bag neatly folded and pressed into his pocket. He is dejected, defeated and depressed.

I wait for him on the stairs, listening for his footsteps. I do "active waiting" again, a familiar activity, only this time I'm not waiting for my mother to return from one of her dangerous trips. I can tell by the sound of his footsteps that he hasn't found anything. His tread is slow and heavy. I run into the apartment not wanting him to be aware that

I'm waiting and worrying about him. That would be too embarrassing. Instinctively I know that he would feel humiliated by my concern. I bury my head in a book and pretend that ever I am reading. I hide behind the swinging door in the kitchen. I want to hear what he tells my mother. One desperate night, after weeks of searching, he sits down at the kitchen table, holding his head in his hands.

"I don't know what we're going to do," he whispers, "I go from shop to shop and there is nothing out there for me. I can't seem to earn a living in this country. First it's the leather jackets and then the bosses want me to come in to work on Saturdays; on *Shabbes*. I can't work on *Shabbes*. No one in my family ever desecrated the Sabbath. I'm going to start now? Now that I'm in a free country where supposedly there's no anti-Semitism?" He shakes his head in disbelief.

"The long and the short of it is that every foreman of every factory I go to tells me that if I can't work on Saturdays I obviously don't need the work. And these," he adds bitterly "are Jewish bosses. The non-observant Jews are the worst. They think that if they don't observe a holy day no one else needs to. I'm mad. I'm mad, but I'm also scared," he tells her, "what will we do when the unemployment insurance money runs out?"

I peek through the crack in swinging door that leads to the kitchen. My mother grips his hand as tightly as fear grips my heart. He looks so sad. My heart is breaking for him. The old familiar enemy is creeping back into our lives. Will we go hungry? Will we lose our apartment? Will we have to move to another neighborhood? I go to sleep every night praying that he gets a job tomorrow, scared that we will have to go into an orphanage for poor children.

Maybe he can ask Aunt Sari for a loan, he confides in my mother. He hates to borrow from her but he has to buy food. What else can he do? We have no other relatives close to us, and he certainly cannot ask a friend. He is too proud to do that. For a long time we eat nothing but potatoes. They cost twenty-five cents for five pounds and they keep us from being hungry. My creative mother doctors them up and serves them in many different ways, baked, boiled, fried, mashed, painted red with paprika, with a bit of dill on top. They're only potatoes, but they are delicious food for hungry people.

"I never had a chance to go to the University and have a profession," my father bemoans his fate. "If I had, then we would never be in all this trouble now." He shakes his head, in disbelief. "If I even had a trade, like a plumber or a carpenter I would be able to support my family. I didn't want to learn how to work with my hands. I used to think that having a trade was beneath me," he laughs mirthlessly. "How foolish I was! I used to think that smart people used their brains and stupid people used their hands." We all watch helplessly as he laments his fate. "Now I know better. Smart people work and make a living, the others, like me feel sorry for themselves. I was able to save your lives, in Hitler's Europe, but now I can't keep you alive in America. How ironic is that?"

It is July; he has not worked since March, before Passover. School is out for the summer and Michael and I spend entire days on the street in front of our house, escaping the sadness of our house. We fear the worst when we are at home: outdoors we are free. I play with the girls. Because of my shame at my changing body, I have retained the unwanted job of "steady ender," permanent rope turner. In return for this task, I get to pick the jingle and to arbitrate unfair moves. It's the prize I get for holding the rope all day long.

"My mother, your mother live across the way,

Nine-sixteen East Broadway…..

"Change it, change it. Let's move on," I call out,

"We're changing to 'Down the Mississippi Where the Boats Go Push." At least I can still be a boss over something. I manage to distract myself from some of the awful realities in my home by practicing piano in the morning and spending the rest of the day playing on the streets.

CHAPTER 24

"LET'S TAKE A walk, just around the neighborhood," my mother suggests one summer day. I would like nothing better. It's so seldom that I get her all to myself. When she is away from my father she often acts like her old loving self, making mundane things exciting.

"Where are we going?" I ask.

"Oh, nowhere special, it's a lovely day so let's enjoy it."

We amble along, window shopping and exclaiming over the displays: furniture shops with living rooms and bedrooms all laid out, dress shops with dummies posed as if caught in the middle of a party, toy stores with roller skates, dollhouses, chemistry sets; everything I want is in every window we pass. We are talking and laughing, just like in the old days. On a side street, she notices a shop window, with darkened shades and a sign that reads "Help Wanted."

"Let's go in and see what kind of help they want?" she says.

The shop is dark and cool. It takes a few seconds for our eyes to adjust to the dimness indoors. Fans are spinning in the corners of the room blowing dust and particles of fabric around. The room smells like nail polish and several women are sitting at a long table, sewing pastel leather slippers. They are hand stitching Omphies house shoes. I realize that my mother planned this trip before we left our house. I don't know if she's looking for a job for herself, for my father or maybe even for me. What I do know, is that she's desperate to bring home some money.

"I see you have a 'Help Wanted' sign outside," she tells the fore-lady, a heavy woman in a housedress with a shower cap protecting her hair. "I can probably do this kind of work." She is uncomfortable. She has never asked anyone for a job before and she's not sure of how one does it. Yes, the forelady tells her, pleasantly they do need help on the week-ends, Saturdays and Sundays, when the big boss is there. She is told that she can start on the coming Saturday.

"Could I just work on Sundays?" she inquires hesitating, knowing that there is no way she could work on the Sabbath.

"No, I'm sorry," she tells her, "We can't train somebody for just one day a week." I notice she has a heavy accent. We leave the shop. Her cheerful mood is replaced by the now familiar sense of quiet desperation.

She confides in Poldi. She tells her of the dreadful financial plight she is in and how it is becoming impossible for my father to find any type of work. Poldi, in her kind, generous and impulsive way comes up with an immediate solution.

"I can help you," she offers quickly.

"No, no, please," my mother tells her. "I could never take money from you. That would be awful for me."

"Who's talking about taking money?" Poldi asks. "I have more students than I can handle. In fact I have to turn some of them away. You can become my assistant teacher."

My mother feels that she is not equal to the task. She demurs, saying that she has an accent and no experience.

"Nonsense," cries Poldi. "An accent is an asset to a music teacher. Everyone assumes you were trained by some famous European concert pianist. People want teachers with an accent. And as for experience, my dear, you are doing a magnificent job with Rita. I would love you to be my assistant."

Poldi has a way of turning everything around to an advantage. My mother's career as a music teacher is launched! A student in Forest Hills is referred to her and she is getting three dollars an hour for a weekly lesson. She takes the long subway ride penniless and returns with money in her pocket. This is the first time in her life that my mother is earning money on her own! What a sense of liberation it produces. She comes home from every lesson and places her earnings on the table. It is not much, but it buys us food to add to our potato diet. Having saved Michael and me, protected and fed us during the war seems insignificant when compared to the power of earning money.

My father is not thrilled. "First thing you know," he warns her, "is that you'll feel that now that you are earning your own money, you are free to do as you want."

"No, no," my mother assures him, handing him her earnings, "It will always be our money." This is three dollars a week they are talking about.

In addition to traveling to Forest Hills once a week to give a lesson to her student, with Poldi's encouragement, my mother gives weekly pre-instrumental lessons to children in our neighborhood hoping she might drum up some piano lesson business closer to home. She gets rhythm band instruments, tambourines, triangles, drums, bells and several music books with directions for giving young children a musical experience. She puts signs up in the grocery store, the library, and next to the mailboxes in all the buildings in the neighborhood.

It works! Her class is very successful and soon she has ten little girls coming up to our apartment for their lessons. While my mother teaches the songs and the rhythms, I accompany them on the piano. I am thirteen years old and helping my mother to earn a living. She charges 75 cents per hour for each student. That is $7.50 a week, $10.50, when you include the money she gets from her private lesson. This is more than she had in ages. She pours her soul into those lessons. I, in the meantime, am pounding on the piano, sorry to give my free time but proud contributing to the family's welfare. I would love to ask my mother for a cut of the $7.50, but I don't dare. I know I wouldn't get it but I would get a lecture on how I should feel privileged to ……blah, blah, blah.

Unfortunately none of the girls in the pre-instrumental class come back to take piano lessons after the course is over. Seventy-five cents a week for the parents of these kids is one thing, but buying a piano is another. Pianos are expensive, and moreover piano lessons will cost more than seventy-five cents. But my mother attracts another group of children and gives the same course again. Seven dollars and fifty cents an hour is a lot of money in 1949.

Even though, her plans for giving individual lessons in our neighborhood don't materialize, my mother does start teaching more and more in Forest Hills, where people are affluent and can afford the three dollars per hour that she charges them. Word of mouth spreads. She is a good teacher, kind and encouraging and one student recommends another. Within one year she has enough students to make a significant contribution to the family's finances.

My father finally gets a job as a cutter in a ladies sweater factory, and we feel more secure. But his temper does not abate and the terrible rages go on, directed at Michael, myself, and sometimes at my mother, who takes pity on us and indulges us in small treats. She buys gifts for everyone. One day, I come home from school, and there, lying on my bed is a beautiful green woolen skirt with a matching sweater. I am careful lest I appear selfish. I don't even touch them before asking my mother whom they are for. She tells me they are mine. "Are they really for me?" I ask. "I thought they might be for someone special."

"They are," she answers, smiling at me, "they are for you!"

CHAPTER 25

WE CALL IT cooking class, but the school calls it "Home Economics." The class is for girls only; the boys go to "shop," where they make a wooden stool or book-ends. Our "classroom" is divided into four section pleasingly furnished with a living room, kitchen, bedroom and bathroom where we practice the art of homemaking. Mrs. Davis is our teacher and she sends three or four of us at a time into each of the rooms to practice being housewives. In the kitchen we are given horrible recipes from an ancient cook book and told to make the worst tasting mush in the history of cooking; milk toast. We are required to eat what we cook. We set the table, placing the fork on the left, on top of the napkin, and sit down to eat what we have prepared. The milk toast is inedible, it taste like warmed over white bugs. When Mrs. Davis goes to check on girls who are ironing, we rush to the window and drop the milk toast from the fifth floor. It drops onto the sidewalk below, where it lands like a solid lump of clay. Another group is assigned to the bedroom to make beds with hospital corners, or to the living room to dust the furniture. When left alone, we gather in one corner of a room, whispering, and exchanging every bit of information and misinformation gathered about sex. We talk softly, reminding each other to keep our voices down.

"Did you hear that Elaine Bolkowski's sister is pregnant?" Anna asks.

"No!" we answer in a chorus, outraged. "You've got to be kidding. She's only sixteen."

"Yup," the knowledgeable Anna nods, her head going up and down. "She 'went all the way,' with Jerry O'Brien. She's easy. She's had lots of boyfriends. Anna shrugs her shoulders. "Well, that's what happens when you do French kissing. Now she has to drop out of high school." We have a vague idea of what 'all the way' means, we're not sure about what French kissing is.

"What's French kissing?" Joyce inquires. Anna tells us.

"Yuk, who would ever do that?" We groan with disgust. We hear the heavy footsteps of Mrs. Davis, coming down the hall.

"Oh, Oh, chickie the cops." We stop talking and pick up the dust rag as she comes into the room to inspect our progress.

I get my period before my eleventh birthday and I have been developing steadily, but no one has explained what puberty and adolescence is like. I am not totally ignorant about "the facts of life," as we call sex education in the 50's, but there are definite gaps in my understanding. Most of information I receive on this encroaching part of my own life, is what I am able to garner from my girlfriends during cooking class: never kiss on the first date, petting is necking below the neck and should be indulged in only when you're engaged and above all, virginity must be preserved for the "wedding night."

Even though I know I am not the only girl in my class whose body is changing, my development seems to come at an earlier age, and coupled with the fact that I am older than my classmates I again feel different: an American living inside a refugee's body. I look at myself carefully. What is going on with me? I seem to have no control over my growth. I wonder if my newly formed curves and size 34 C bra are caused by becoming fat. Every time I ask my mother, she brushes me off, saying that what's happening is "natural." It's not just my breasts that stretch my blouses and sweaters, my skirts are too tight across my hips, my skin is seems to be breaking out in ugly zits, and my feelings are constantly bruised.

I cry when I see an old man in a wheelchair, a child with a limp, a blind person with a cane, a dog run over in the street, a lifeless bird. I think about them all day long feeling sad. What is happening to me, I wonder? Only a year ago I think I felt like everyone else. Now I feel like a freak, a spectator looking down at my life.

My father catches me inspecting myself in the mirror.

"Stop admiring yourself," he says caustically. "You are more inter-ested in your face than your fat behind which is ten time bigger than your face."

I feel the hot current of shame course through me. I am trying to diet and lose weight but it takes forever and in the meantime I feel gross. My parents are no help. My mother tries to reassure me and tell me I am growing like a normal girl. I can almost hear her telling me that it's all in my imagination, and that I am perfectly fine, while my father points out my every defect. Every forward step I take he tries to make me take a step back. He says it's in the interest of turning me into a "decent" girl. My parents want me to be mature, but they won't let me grow up. I resist, I rebel but in the end I return, helpless and forlorn. My ego is not strong enough to support my will. I believe them when they tell me I am fat. I go on diets, but my body has a mind of its own, and it is filling out and developing in spite of the restraints I put on it.

Other girls in school envy me. They wish they had something to put into a bra. This is the era of Marilyn Monroe, when being sexy and desirable means having big breasts. I envy their slim bodies, they envy my curves. I have a feeling that my parents wish I looked more like a girl and less like a woman. I have the same wish but I can't control what is happening to my body.

It is after lunch but recess is not over. I am carrying a heavy card-board panel decorated with sketches of a seed turning into a plant. "From Seed to Plant" is printed in bold letters across the top. This is my science project and I don't want to be pushed while standing in line. I carry this cumbersome, heavy piece of oak tag. I have a "pass," permission, to come up early and bring the panel upstairs before the afternoon classes start. Two boys from my class follow me up the stairs.

"What are you doing here?" I ask them. "You're not supposed to be here."

They approach giggling. Paul, the taller of the two, sprouting a few black hairs on his upper lip looks at me uneasily. He takes a deep breath and walks over to me, holding his head to one side. He appears to be very uncomfortable. Suddenly his hand shoots away from his side. He reaches over, touching my breast, intent on groping me. Burton, his friends comes up from behind and snaps my bra strap through my blouse. This is no *Glatz Kopf* experience and I am not in the least bit scared.

"Get away from me, you parasites," I snap. "Parasite" is a new word I just learned in science. I love the staccato way it bounces off my tongue and I try to use it as much as possible. "You're not gonna get a cheap feel off of me." I know all about getting felt up. All the girls in my class have been talking about it and I had been wondering when it was going to happen to me. I pretend to be outraged, but secretly, I am glad that someone finally tries it with me.

CHAPTER 26

I COME HOME from school with a blue application form for the High School of Music and Art. My father looks at it and asks "what's this? An application to high school? What's Music and Art?" It seems as though there are some things I know more about than he does.

"Every year the eighth grade students in the public and private schools in New York City try out for the 'special' high schools in New York," I explain, playing the role of the patient teacher, "Bronx High School of Science and Stuyvesant High School for gifted math and science students, Hunter High School for smart girls, Performing Arts for dance, music and drama, Washington Irving for fashion design and Music and Art for those interested in music or in art." He looks interested, so I go on, "I want to try out for Music and Art. You have to sign the application form that says I can take the test. And then, if I pass, I can go to Music and Art." He looks at the form, studies it, nods his head, and runs his tongue over his lips before taking out his fountain pen. He reads it carefully, sighs and nods.

He smiles and I look at him critically for the first time in my life. He is not a bad looking man, I think. When he smiles, deep dimples on each side of his face imbed themselves into his cheeks. His thick eyebrows frame his dark eyes and when he looks happy he glows with pleasure. I'm pleased. I've done something to make my father smile and I don't get to do this often.

"This sounds almost too good to be true," he is enthusiastic, "only in America is there an opportunity for such an education." He strokes his chin. "Just one word of warning," he cautions me. "This looks like a hard school to get into. Don't be disappointed if you don't get in."

"Don't be disappointed?" I ask incredulously, "I won't be disappointed. I'll just quietly commit suicide by jumping off the roof." He's smiling and I can afford a bit of humor.

"Why must you always be so dramatic?"

My best friend, Alice, applies to Bronx Science and Hunter High School. Before she takes the entrance exams she urges me to apply to both schools as well as to Music and Art. That way, she tells me, I will have more choices, and we'll have fun being in the same high school. I know I have no other talents. I love school and am a good student, but I really am not good in math or science, nor am I interested in anything as much as music. It will have to be Music and Art or George Washington High School.

CHAPTER 27

I AM WEARING my new dress, with multi colored polka dots. My mother
made it using a Simplicity pattern and fabric that she bought at a remnant store for twenty five cents a yard. My parents have finally given in
and let me get my hair cut. It is gathered in a tight pony tail that swings
between my shoulders. I clutch my music folder against my chest and
walk slowly. I'm early for my test. It is a bright spring afternoon and
I have just gotten off the IRT subway, at 125th Street. I walk through
Harlem up to135th Street and Convent Avenue. As I get to the corner,
I stop to listen to a soprano voice coming through one of the open
windows. Ten steps further on, I hear string instruments. The music is
coming from everywhere. I close my eyes and stand on the sidewalk,
listening. There is no traffic, there are no other sound, only the gentle
breeze stroking my face. "God," I say quietly to myself, "please, please
let me become a part of this."

The test consists of three parts, pitch discrimination, rhythm, and
performance. The first two parts are easy. Pitch discrimination is taken
in a large classroom by all the applicants. All we have to do is write "S"
or "D" to designate whether the first and last note of a series of tones
are the same or different. The rhythm part is taken individually, one
examiner per applicant. We have to tap back a rhythmic sequence that
has been presented. The rhythms become longer and more complicated, but I know I got them all right.

The performance portion of the exam is going to be hard. I wait
outside of the room I have been assigned to. There are four other can-
didates, prospective students, waiting to take the performance portion

of the exam. We listen to the hopeful applicants behind the closed door, trying to ascertain if they are better or worse than we are. We sit in the hallway and the rumors start flying.

"Someone told me that if you're very good, they stop you at the beginning," one of the girls says, "they don't need to listen to the whole piece if they can see right away that you're good."

"Now isn't that stupid?" I hear someone else say, "Why would they have to listen to a bad performance in its entirety? Why would they only spend time listening to bad music, and stop you if you're good?"

"Didn't you ever hear of giving someone the benefit of the doubt?" The first person answers, "how can they tell if you're really bad without listening to the whole piece?"

We distract ourselves from our anxiety by trying to understand the process of acceptance or rejection.

When it is my turn, I enter the room to take the scariest part of the test. This is the part I am most anxious about. A baby grand piano sits in one corner of the room, facing the windows, on the opposite side, seated at a long table are three judges. I am nervous as I hand my music over to one of the three examiners who will rate the performance. I take out a handkerchief and dry my sweating palms. Poldi has told me that this is what all professionals do and it is bound to impress the examiners. I play two preludes by Bach. I play the entire pieces without being interrupted. Is this is a good sign, or a bad sign? I try to read their expressions but they don't give me a clue. "Thank you for trying out for Music and Art," they tell me as they hand my music over to me. I've been in the United States for five years. I'm still not sure how to respond to certain statements.

What do I answer? "You're welcome?" Somehow that doesn't sound right to me. So I smile and say "Thank you!" Before I leave the room, I turn around and ask them. "How did I do?" I'm dying to find out, get a clue at least.

"You'll be notified in a few weeks," one of them answers not betraying any emotion.

On my way back to the subway, I start praying, making a deal with God. "Please God; I am willing to sacrifice ten years of my old age in order to get into M&A. I will make charitable contributions to the poor beggars that sit in front of the subway stations. I will never throw away any morsel of food while there are children starving all over the world. Anything You want. Just let me get into Music and Art. I will never ask You for any other favors as long as I live." I implore every Deity I can think of. It is going to be Music and Art or George Washington, the area high school. George Washington, I am told, is not a particularly "good" high school, but if I don't get into Music and Art I will not have any other option. I feel cautiously optimistic and very scared at the same time.

I go back to P.S. 189 and wait for the result. Time creeps by slowly. I have no idea of how I will be notified. Fear of humiliation and rejection lodge themselves deep in my heart, refusing to be shoved aside for even just a moment. I remember how embarrassed I was when I told all my classmates in the Jewish school that I was going to be put ahead one grade and what a let-down it was when they told me it wasn't going to happen. I must prepare for every eventuality. Will I have to be embarrassed in an assembly and told in front of the entire school that I have not been accepted, or will it be by mail? I have told everyone that I was applying. Big mistake. What if I don't get in? Will I have to tell everyone that I failed? How embarrassing is that? Am I jinxing myself? Suddenly, I picture myself being rejected. I am so humiliated. Will I go to George Washington High School for one year and then apply again? Students are accepted up to tenth grade and after that, if they fail to get in, they are banished forever. Do I have chance to pass the test the second time around if I have failed it the first time? How am I going to make the days go by faster? My mind can't seem to slow down.

Finally, well into the month of June, Mr. Gross, the principal calls all of the applicants into his office. I stop breathing and concentrate only on praying. I have one last chance to convince God that I deserve a break. I feel that God still has time to intercede on my behalf. Until I hear it from the principal's own mouth there is the chance that prayer might be helpful. I close my eyes, cross my fingers and stop breathing. Mr. Gross, informs us that of the ten who had applied, three of us got in; "Marilyn Basmajian," big deal, I knew she'd get in, "Roy Hill," hmm, I didn't even know he plays an instrument and "Rita Schmelkes." Hey that's me!! He congratulates us and sends us back to our classroom and tells the others that they shouldn't be discouraged. They can always try again for tenth grade.

I can't believe my luck. Not long ago I was at the Yeshiva being bossed around by Tova and now I'm going to Music and Art! Oh Glory, Hallelujah, I'm going to live happily ever after! I run home with the good news. Both my parents are thrilled but they warn me not to tell anyone about it.

"We don't want you to brag, it isn't nice" they tell me, "everyone will find out on their own, and then we can act as if there was never a question of getting in. Think of how surprised they will be." I love the idea of surprising everyone, especially Monica, who I know has applied as well. I wonder if she got in. Monica's family and my family have been in contact with each other ever since we arrived in New York. I can tell from what I hear at home that my father does not like Monica's father at all, has little respect for him and his snobby ways. Behind his back he calls him *rzhygac,* which means "vomit" in Polish, instead of by his real name "Ziggy." Her parents have sacrificed everything for Monica's education. They live in a rooming house, sharing one room and using a bathroom at the end of the hall that they have to share with all the people on their floor. They have a tiny kitchen inside a closet, where Monica's mother cooks all their meals. But in spite of this, they did purchase a spinet piano so that Monica could practice. They enrolled her at the Julliard prep school. Our parents are very competitive with regard to their daughters and my mother is afraid for me to lose ground.

"Why can't you write neatly, the way Monica writes?" my mother is looking at a composition I have just finished writing. She reads it. The content is good but the handwriting is atrocious.

"I was in a hurry to get my thoughts down and didn't have time to be neat," I reply.

Monica, unlike me, is careful and neat. Her piano playing is precise. She observes every rest, lifting her hands off the keyboard dramatically to make sure everyone can see how true she is to the composer; every dotted eighth note is held for accurate duration. I don't like her playing, it is dry. Mine is emotional, although not perfect. Our mothers make us play for them and for each other every time we get together, and for days I hear about how clean and exact Monica's playing is.

I know that the main reason my mother doesn't want to brag about me is because she wants to astound, shock Monica's mother. I too, feel that it would be great if I could surpass her, if I got into Music and Art and she didn't. I haven't forgotten Montelupi and Monica's greed. My parents steer away from the topic during subsequent visits, but I can't contain myself any longer.

"I'm going to Music and Art in September," I blurt out. "How about you?"

"Well," Monica answers, "I go to such a wonderful Junior High School that my parents decided it would be better for me to stay there until the end of ninth grade."

"Yeah, right!" I say to myself, certain that she did not get in.

Graduation from P.S. 189 is a few weeks away and then I will become a student at Music and Art. In the meantime, the eighth grade girls are required to make their own graduation dresses in homemaking class. Boys are still working at the shop. They're making little boxes with tight fitting lids. Boys are required to wear dress shirts with ties. They're lucky. They don't have to wear their mistakes in public. Only the girls have to wear homemade dresses. Everyone goes shopping for white fabric and Simplicity, McCall's and Butterick's patterns. Most of us get Simplicity patterns or McCalls; they cost twenty-five cents. Some of the rich girls splurge and buy the expensive Vogue patterns. They cost as much as one dollar each. And the very rich girls have their dresses made by a dressmaker. Organdy, dotted Swiss, and starched pique are the standard fabrics.

We sit at the old fashioned Singer treadle sewing machines during sewing class. There are about fifteen machines in the room and all of us are busy basting, threading and pumping the machines. Even the girls who are having dresses made by professionals are sewing. They are required to wear the dresses they made, but who's going to kick them out of the graduation assembly if they show up in a dress made by a professional dress maker? It is a tedious task.

"Miss Dratty," I call, "my fabric is getting bunched up under the needle." Miss Dratty comes over. She resembles a salty brown pretzel, skinny, with a face that looks like it's made of crepe paper. She has a tiny white bun on top of her head resembling a sugar donut. "Let me see," she says in a shaky quivering voice. "Oh dear," you've got thread caught in the bobbin." She makes a few adjustments to the fabric and the machine. "Let's try it now and see how we make out."

I have little patience for sewing class. Graduation from elementary school is definitely not something to worry about. Everyone graduates from grade school, I know, but how many get to go to Music and Art? I am feeling superior and blasé about the idea of graduating. I sew as best I can, taking many short cuts and achieving a misshapen dress with a waistline that fluctuates from above my rib cage to below my stomach. The hemline dips to my ankles on one side and rises above my knees on the other. But what the heck? I've only got to wear this dress once, on graduation day.

I try the dress on as soon as it's finished. There is a big problem. I can see that it is never going to make it over my hips, let alone to graduation. I panic, and then quickly recover. I am going to be calm in the face of a crisis. This is a problem I am sure I can solve. I take the dress apart and attempt to try again. I leave more room at the seams and baste the top to the bottom. Basting stitches are the quick running ones that permit the seams come apart with one tiny pull of the thread. After securing the top of the dress to the bottom, I take a batch of safety pins and pin the dress to my slip to make sure it doesn't fall off my body. I work on it all Sunday, taking great pains to make sure it looks alright. I try the dress on struggling not to loosen one stitch lest the whole dress becomes undone. I stand in front of the mirror on the closet door and scrutinize the results. Well, it certainly is not perfect, and no one could possibly mistake it for having been made by a professional dress maker, but if I keep my arms crossed in front of my waist no one will notice how uneven it is. Besides, we're all going to be wearing white, standing close to each other. Until I walk up to receive my diploma I will be invisible. I plan to hold my arms crossed at my waistline, hiding the worst imperfections while ensuring that the bottom doesn't detach from the top. I have cheated fate. "If I don't cough or laugh too hard, or take a very deep breath, I'll be fine. Besides," I tell myself, I'll never have to wear this dress again, so who cares if it stands up to wear and tear?"

We are lined up: Girls on one side, boys on the other. The piano starts out with Sir Edward Elgar's Pomp and Circumstance March and we follow each other to the front of the auditorium. After the Pledge to the Flag we sing The Star Spangled Banner and sit down. The principal, assistant principal, and our eighth grade teacher make long speeches telling us that we're on our way towards our futures, that we are obligated to become responsible citizens, blah, blah, blah,...... I'm not listening. I'm dreaming and planning. We line up alphabetically to receive our diplomas and stand up to sing our school song to the melody of "Auld Lang Syne."

> *Enthroned between two rivers bright,*
> *Our schoolhouse nobly lies.*
> *And love and honor to us all*
> *She humbly implies.*
> *She stands for all that's good and true,*
> *So therefore let us be,*
> *As true to all of her ideals*
> *As she would have us be.*

We are serious and happy. We are going into a hopeful world. The Second World War is over, there is a United Nations Organization that will resolve all conflicts through debates, we are at peace and I will be going to Music and Art. My mother and Aunt Sari sit with all the parents. My father has to go to work but I am too happy to feel sorry for myself for not having him present. Everyone is proud of their child, but my mother is the proudest. Her daughter has been accepted to one of the most prestigious high schools in the city, perhaps in the United States. I graduate with a gold seal on my diploma.

CHAPTER 28

For graduation I get exactly what I ask for: a brown leather loose-leaf book, with a zipper that goes all the way around, and my initials RBS stamped in gold on the front. It is a beautiful gift and I know that it cost a lot of money. My parents had to save up for it and I feel rich and privileged, and above all worthy. Inside there are pockets for stray papers and a zippered case for pens and pencils that fits into the binder. I have filled it with three holed paper and have even put in subject dividers. I stroke it, smell the familiar odor of leather, and hold it against my cheek. I plan for my first day of school, what I will wear, how I will act, and how I will wear my hair.

"How does it look better?" I ask Michael holding onto my leather loose-leaf, "in front of my chest, held with both arms? That's how the girls in George Washington carry their books, or held in one hand against my body, looking more casual?"

I hope I'll be popular, have girlfriends and boyfriends, be smart and fit in. I'm wondering. Should I take the beautiful leather binder to school on the first day? I really want to, it has been waiting for this day all summer long and I am eager to show it off. But something tells me not to bring it on the first day. It is a bit too much. I feel I should make myself as inconspicuous as possible, to go to school with nothing but an assignment pad to write down what sorts of school supplies I'll need. My inner battle rages and I've made a decision I've waited too long for this treasure to leave it at home for one day longer than necessary. Most of my classmates in P.S. 189 had such a binder when they entered a seventh grade, departmental class. I assure myself that no one will make a big deal out of it, and against my better judgment I decide to take it.

Horror of horrors! Not only am I the only student in the entire school to be carrying such an obvious, huge loose leaf book, but as I look around I am also the only girl not wearing lipstick. I feel so wrong, like I'm at the bakery wanting to buy shoes. I look around, my face is on fire. I am sure that everyone is staring at me, laughing, and saying to each other, "did you ever see such a refugee in your life? Doesn't she know better than to bring a loose-leaf on the first day of school? " That old, familiar terror surges and once again I feel like the outsider. I am unable to take notes, pay attention to the teachers, or get my bearings. All I am able to think of is how everyone must be whispering about me about me behind my back. I slide the binder under my seat. I wish could disappear with it.

After school, instead of getting off at my bus stop, I get off at 181st Street and head directly for the Woolworth, Five and Dime Store. I know exactly what I want; a Pond's lipstick, the shade called "honey." It is bright, bloody red, comes in a small aqua tube, and it costs ten cents. My mother gave me fifty cents to take to school for an emergency. Well, I consider this an emergency! I buy it, put it on and smile at my reflection in the small mirror provided at the cosmetic counter. I feel much better. My teeth are sparkling, my lips are red, shining, and I am feeling glamorous. All the girls I know are wearing that shade of red. Some of them even used it while at P.S.189, carefully wiping it off before entering the school building, but leaving a telling residue on their lips. The teachers all knew which girls used lipstick. "Fresh as paint," Miss Meehan said, her arms crossed tightly across her bosom, her thick ankles bulging above sensible oxfords. I, however, obeyed my parents and resisted buying the lipstick while in elementary school.

All the girls in high school are wearing bright shades of lipstick and after this humiliating first day, I am determined to look as much like everyone else as possible. I apply the lipstick carefully and then wipe it off before my father comes home from work. I will tackle the lipstick dilemma on the Sabbath, when my father might be in a good mood.

We sit down to Friday night dinner and I debate as to whether or not to come clean about the lipstick. Then, before I know it my announcement pops out of my mouth. "From now on," I start bravely, "I am going to be wearing lipstick to school. Every day," I add for emphasis.

My father is indignant at my announcement, "No you're not," he declares, "that's not at all what we have in mind for you."

I persist. "Every other girl in school wears it. I will not look different from everyone else."

"We want you to look like a decent girl from a good family. Teachers will like you much better if they see that you don't paint your face. You need to make a good impression."

"What are you talking about?" I interrupt, hysterically. "This is America. The teachers here don't judge you by whether or not you're wearing lipstick. Besides, if they think badly of me then they'll have to think badly of all the girls in the school, because they all wear lipstick."

We go back and forth. I keep insisting that I will wear whatever I please, and my father insisting I won't. My mother says nothing, as always, determined to present a united front. The front that keeps reminding me my mother is not the *Mutti* who loved and cared for me before we arrived in America. Neither one of us is going to budge. "We know how grown -ups think. Only cheap, trampy girls wear lipstick and paint their young faces."

With this declaration, my father turns his back and makes for the door. He has said his piece and his word is final. I run after him, trying to get him to at least hear me out. He turns around to face me, "I know. I know, I'm only the father in this house," he looks at me pointedly, raising his hands shoulder level, palms out, in a mock pose of surrender, "I only love you more than anyone else. I saved your life, and I support you. So why should you listen to me?" he says sarcastically grabbing the doorknob in his hand. He turns away and then changes his mind facing me, "you are not going to wear lipstick to school while you're living in my house," and he closes the door.

I wish my mother would intercede on my behalf as she had done in Liebenau, but by now I know that she won't. She stays silent, perhaps because she is afraid to contradict him, or maybe she really believes in the "united front" conspiracy against children. It is not the lipstick I am fighting for. The issue for me has little to do with lipstick. If I want to, I can put it on every time I leave the house and wipe it off when I return. It is more important for me to prove a point and get them to hear me than it is to wear the lipstick. I am trying to assert my independence and still gain their approval. It is not going to happen. "Let me grow up," I scream inside my head, "and accept my ideas once in a while. Or, at least hear my argument before closing the door on further discussion

CHAPTER 29

⚭

Now, THAT MY mother is teaching piano every day, the house is empty until 5:30. Michael, who attends the Yeshiva University Prep School, brings his friends over to the house. Their school is around the corner from my house and this is a very convenient place for them to congregate. His friends are good looking, funny and "regular guys," which means that they are athletic and prone to mischief. I love it when they come over. Today they are all cutting 8th period and playing cards and smoking. I run back and forth from the kitchen to the living room, providing the boys with drinks. One of them, Wally, pays a lot of attention to me. I find him staring at me and he manages to brush up against me whenever he gets the opportunity. He runs his hand down my bare arm and I shiver, feel myself turning red; painted with a brush dipped in blood. I run to the bathroom to catch my breath and look in the mirror. Wally follows me and closes the door.

"Hey, Rita," he says, leaning against the wall, hands in his pockets and a cigarette dangling casually from his mouth, "how would you like to go to Fort Tryon Park with me on Saturday?" Fort Tryon Park is an easy fifteen minute walk from my house. I don't want to appear too eager, but on the other hand I don't want to discourage him either.

"Well," I hesitate. I'm dying to go with him but I'm also scared, unsure of myself. I don't know how I'm feeling. I wonder, is he asking me out on a date, is he just being friendly, or is he setting me up, just testing me to see if I'll show up? I don't trust boys and I certainly don't trust myself. I have to make a quick decision. It will just be a walk in the park on a Sabbath afternoon. I don't say "yes" or "no."

"Why don't we meet at the front gate of the park on Fort Washington Avenue at three o'clock, weather permitting, of course?"

Wally is very tall, has long arms and legs, a slow sexy smile that reveals perfect white teeth, and wavy black hair with dark sideburns. His friends call him the *shlang,* the snake. He looks so handsome, I would love to carry his picture in my wallet and tell my friends in school that we are going steady. But I'm scared to meet him in the park. I'm not sure if he's asking me for a real date or just suggesting that we meet. If I'm there and he doesn't show up I will die of humiliation. My dilemma is solved by Mother Nature. It pours on Saturday so there is an opportunity to buy time. I wish he'd ask me out on a real date.

Whenever he comes over we escape into the bathroom where we neck and grope each other. We practice French kissing, something I had found so repulsive only a short time ago and now can't get enough of. It is Wednesday evening, the night before Thanksgiving. I am so excited. I have made wonderful plans for the week-end. Tomorrow we will be having Thanksgiving dinner with my Aunt Sari and Uncle Avrom. Friday will be spent doing homework that I normally do on Sunday and on Sunday Michael and I will go out on a double date. I have been carrying my brother's picture around in my wallet and showing it to all my friends.

"Oh, he is gorgeous, adorable, sexy," my friends all agree. And indeed he is. He is six feet tall, has black hair, well defined eyebrows, long black lashes that brush his cheekbones, sideburns and a fuzzy black moustache. He is "tall, dark and handsome." All my girlfriends want to get fixed up with him even though he is a year younger than they are. I fix Mike up with Sylvia Hanly, a good friend of mine. I will be going with Wally. We will all go to the movies on Sunday afternoon and then get a soda afterwards. Michael and I are both happy. We are discussing our plans for Sunday, when my father overhears us.

"What's that you're planning?" he asks

Innocently, I tell him that Mike, Wally, Sylvia and I are going to the movies. "On a double date, so Mike and I can look out for one another," I add to reassure him that I won't be alone with Wally.

"What date?" he asks. "Who said you had permission to go on a date, and make one for your brother?" Unexpectedly I have unleashed his fury and provoked an uncontrollable fire.. "You know you still live here, and it would be nice if you consulted with your mother and me before you make plans not only for yourself, but for Michael." I'm still waiting to hear what I did or said to cause such an outburst.

"What's the big deal?" I ask, my voice quaking with fear. "We're all going to the movies together, Michael and his friend, me and my friend. We're paying for ourselves."

"And who gave you permission to arrange this so-called date?"

"I don't know," I reply, "it just sort of came about."

"Well, Michael is not going to the movies with any of your girlfriends and you are certainly not going with any of Michael's friends."

"Tell me, what's wrong with going to the movies?" My fear is quickly turning to anger.

"Plenty's wrong with that. You are not going to decide when, where and whom your brother is going out with. He's a poor enough student and doesn't need to be thinking about girls."

I feel a hot spark of defiance shoot through my upper body. I take a deep breath, "we made plans and we are going." I don't know where I get the courage, but I am determined not to give in, not to disappoint Sylvia, not to lose out on an opportunity to be a real teenager on a double date, just like Archie, Betty, Veronica and Reggie. "We're going," I shout, "and that's final."

"Watch your mouth," he warns me. "It is not your place to decide what Michael is going to do. I'm saying he is not going and that's final!"

I stamp my foot, and shout at him. "You're always keeping me from doing what I want to do. When I'm religious, you're a *goy*. When I want to do something like go to the library on Shabbat, you suddenly pull it away from me and become religious. You think you own me and that I have to be forever grateful to you for saving us. Well I'm not grateful." I stop just short of telling him I hate him. But he gets the message.

His hand flies away from his wrist. Suddenly, I feel a sharp blast across my cheek. It sends me sprawling onto the bed behind me. I shake my head, trying to catch my breath. He can beat me to death, but I'm determined to get my own way. Something in me refuses to budge. "You can kill me, but I'm not going to listen to you."

Michael and my mother cower behind the doorway in the hall. My father grabs me by my blouse and slaps me again and again, holding onto my upper arm so that I cannot fall back onto the soft bed. "You are not going to win a fight with me, young lady" he shouts, "I might not count for much out in the world, but in this house, I am the boss." He lets go of me, leaves me to fall back on the bed. "This is one Thanksgiving you will never forget." Time will prove him right. I have underestimated his power.

I sob. I hate my father, for what he's done to me, Michael and my mother; for what he wants me to be, for not caring about my feelings. I'm supposed to be an obedient puppet, with no rights to my opinions, not worthy of being heard. I cry on my bed until I fall asleep, exhausted. When I wake up, my father tells me that I will not be going with the rest of the family to my aunt on Thursday. I am being punished for my fresh mouth and bad behavior. I'm glad. I don't want to go anywhere with my parents. My mother only cares about my father and Michael. She never stands up for me. I look in the mirror and I see bruised cheekbones and two black eyes. My arms are black and blue from my elbows to my armpits. When everyone leaves the house, I pick up the phone and call Sylvia. She's disappointed but says she understands.

On Monday I return to school, my bruises have turned green and yellow, a hideous map across my face. I tell my curious friends that I tripped over a wire at night and fell against a table.

CHAPTER 30

"LET'S GO TO Lord and Taylor on Saturday," my friend Sandy suggests. "They're having a sale on sweaters. Cashmere," she adds. I can't tell her that there is nothing in that store that I could ever afford. So I tell her the other truth about myself.

"I can't, I'm religious."

"Oh yeah, I know, kosher."

Music and Art opens a glimpse into a world I can't belong to, but am dying to enter. As long as I was attending P.S. 189, I was in a homogenous environment. None of the kids there had much more than the others. We never felt poor, because most of the families were just like ours, struggling immigrants, trying to make ends meet, battling unemployment and acclimating to the American dream. Only a few were comfortable enough to have dresses made by a dressmaker or shop at Lord and Taylor and in eighth grade, they were the outsiders.

Music and Art is totally different and although I feel completely accepted and have many friends, I know that I am different. The special high school draws students from all over New York City and offers them what no public or private school can. I am the only immigrant in Music and Art, at least the only one I know of. Most of the other kids come from middle class families, many of them wealthy, living on Park Avenue and Central Park West. Their fathers are doctors, engineers, business men and lawyers. A few, as I, come from less affluent families, living in working class neighborhoods, but they are tough on the outside, noisy, and wild. They run into the bathrooms between and during class and smoke cigarettes. They play drums and saxophones, while we play piano and violin. I feel more comfortable with the rich kids, the ones that use expressions such as, "my mother will kill me for not wearing a sweater," or "I've got to be home right after school, my family rule." Those are the values that my own parents espouse. Norman, one of my friends, comes over to our lunch table. He is carrying a tray which holds a steaming red frankfurter, cuddled in a soft white role and topped with a mountain of sauerkraut. I look at it and suddenly I am in Krakow, starving while soldiers are coming out of the delicatessen laughing and eating. I stare at Norman's lunch, salivating. I know I can't have a frankfurter, for one thing, it isn't kosher, besides, it costs a quarter, which I don't have. But I want it badly. I don't ever tell anyone in school about my background. I am not willing to appear any more different than I already am. I want so badly to fit in and be like everyone else, almost as badly as I want that frankfurter. Most of us bring a lunch bag to school. We buy a snack, milk, coco and ice cream for dessert. A few buy hot lunches every day, most are able to afford them and everyone can eat them. Not me. I cannot afford it and I cannot eat it.

When my friends go shopping or to the movies on Saturdays, I stay home and go to synagogue. They are considerate and invite me to join all their activities. I, of course, cannot participate in anything that would violate the Sabbath. I can only attend Saturday night parties after the Sabbath is over. In the springtime, during daylight savings time, I can't leave the house until as late as 8:30 P.M. after dark. Music and Art students live all over the city and I often have to travel over an hour to get to a party. I have a mid-night curfew. My mother waits for me to return by 12. She is sitting in the living room holding a hot water bottle against her nightgown to ease to pain of her ulcer. The condition is aggravated by anxiety and my being out late at night certainly contributes to her worry. I know only too well what waiting for a loved one to return feels like, I don't want to make her wait and I don't want to be punished for breaking curfew.

Sometimes I don't get to the party until 10:00 P.M., only to put in a quick appearance and leave alone at 11:00 P.M. Sometimes, a boy who lives in my neighborhood offers to take me home but I refuse. I don't want to appear dependent and more than that, I don't want anyone to feel sorry for me. I am determined to be independent and self-reliant.

I wait on deserted subway platforms, in the middle of the night. Then, when I get to my stop, I have to walk from the subway to my house, on empty streets, through a neighborhood that is not all that safe. My parents feel that a "nice, decent," girl has to be home by mid-night. They do not seem to be aware of the fact that the subways and the streets could be dangerous for a young girl traveling by herself in the middle of the night. Without meaning to they put my decency above my safety thereby exposing me to danger. There is no way to reason with them. The united front is solid and once my father announces his proclamation he is finished. There is no discussion, no appeal. My father says what he has to say and leaves the room.

The reality of who I am and who I want to be widens. It is not just my parents' restrictions that set me apart from my peers. I come from another world. I was born across the ocean and though I live in New York, my home life is different from theirs. While they are enjoying free-dom and independence, having choices, encouraged to grow up, I am kept in a strict protective environment where I am not even permitted to choose my wardrobe. My friends joke around with their parents, are encouraged to express their feelings and are given spending money while I have to keep a careful lid on my emotions, stay respectful and "decent." At times it appears as though I am still a continent away from where I want to be. In many ways Music and Art is my salvation, but it also defines me as an outsider.

My own family, although goal oriented toward success and achieve-ment is economically disadvantaged when compared to my friends. I often envy the girls with cashmere sweaters and matching skirts, new loafers and haircuts at Best & Co. My best friend's father is a lady's clothing manufacturer. She wears a new outfit to school every day, while I make do with hand-me-downs from Mirka's nieces.

I don't know one other Orthodox girl in the school whom I can be friends with. If there is one, I have never met her. I am the only girl in my group of friends who lives by a different set of rules. I am embarrassed to talk about being Orthodox. I'm forever hiding from the real me, unable to accept who I am. I want to fit in everywhere and sense that I fit in nowhere. I am ashamed to be the daughter of a factory worker who is often unemployed. Since my father is now working in a sweater factory, I tell everyone at school that he is a sweater designer. I try to be part of the middle class group.

CHAPTER 31

⚭

LOCATED ON 135ᵗʰ Street and Convent Avenue in Manhattan's upper west side, Music and Art is right in the middle of Harlem, next to City College. The students call it the "Castle" and indeed it looks just like one. It is seven stories high, the top floor being a tower, with tiered seating, where the junior choir meets every morning at 7:30, before school starts. It is a beautiful room with a high ceiling, flawless acoustics, and a stage with a piano

I join the choir even though I am not a voice major. I am assigned to the first soprano section. We are singing Haydn's "Creation." It is written in four part harmony, rousing and inspiring. I am not used to singing with baritones and basses. In the Glee Club at P.S. 189 we only had sopranos and altos. I am immersed in the harmonies when, suddenly, I hear the purest, crystal clear, soprano voice coming from the rear of the room, little Peter's voice from Liebenau. I turn around, as do all the others to see, Thomas Young, a big, muscular, black he-man, singing with the voice of a heavenly angel. He has decided to join the choir. He is the last person, I think, who would be interested in doing anything he isn't required to do, but his voice is magnificent. Usually, in all our other classes he sits in the back of the classroom, cracking jokes under his breath and making the rest of laugh. I try to sit close to him in our classes, and catch all his hilarious mutterings.

He explains that the only reason he has joined the choir is because he has nothing else to do early in the morning before classes start. His father, a biology professor teaches at City College, which is next to our school, and he drops him off early at school. I don't know if my ears or my eyes are deceiving me. How can such a high, pure voice be coming from such a big man? No one dares to tease him, he is too big and strong and we respect him for his gorgeous voice. He refuses to take solos. "That belongs to the girls," he tells our director, grinning.

Every piano student is required to take an orchestral instrument. I am assigned to the french horn, because I am one of the few ninth graders who is not wearing braces on my teeth. I don't want to play the french horn. It looks like brass intestines, rolled up and held on the lap. I have my heart set on the cello.

There are four of us in the french horn room, two boys and two girls. I am lucky. Thomas Young is in all my classes including instrumental music. In addition to having the most beautiful voice in the choir, Tommy is assigned to the horn, and he never stops making us laugh. We hold the horns to our mouths, giggling hysterically each time the teacher leaves the room. There is no way to play the horn while laughing. And since our teacher is out of the room part of the time, instructing other brass sections, Tommy has free reign. The individual rooms are soundproofed and Mr. Lawson, our teacher does not suspect that we are fooling around instead of practicing.

In spite of all this fun, some of us do manage to make progress. Instruments can be rented from the school for the week ends for five dollars a month. I don't ask my parents for such a sum. I know they cannot afford that, and I have learned never to ask for what I can't get. So, between all the fooling around during practice time and no opportunity to work more seriously at home, I do not become a very proficient player. Nevertheless, at the end of our freshman year, we are all assigned to an orchestra or a band. The difference between the two is that there is no string section in the band. There is no fooling around either. I am assigned to Junior Orchestra where I play with three other horns. Goose bumps crawl over my arms when the string section floats over to the back of the orchestra where I sit with the other members of the brass section. I am engulfed by the music and enjoy listening to it so much that at the first few rehearsals I miss every cue.

In addition to daily practice and orchestra periods, music majors are required to take theory, harmony, keyboard harmony, counterpoint, and dictation. Not all of these courses are offered in the same year, but we all have at least three periods of music per day, in addition to all the academic courses we are required to take. Our school days are longer than the average high school, and all of us have to travel to get there. But no one ever complains

CHAPTER 32

EVEN THOUGH I know I am different from my peers, the school gives a strong sense of belonging. The shared interests, struggles with difficult musical passages the passions and un-verbalized communication helps me enter this unifying community. Music and Art has a profound impact on my life. It shapes and defines me, helps me set my goals and opens a world that I could never have entered through any other passageway. I am changing and I will never be the same again: playing and listening to music with my friends, discussing the merits of the figured bass in block chords as compared to the flowing *continuo,* happy to argue the merits of Bach over Handel: whose music is on a higher level? Bach's B minor Mass or Handel's *Messiah?* We share a joint "sameness" while being uniquely different from each other. This is the first time in my life that I found a place of my own.

During lunch, we sit at one table listening to two clarinetists playing Bach's Two Part Inventions, while at another table folk songs accompanied by a guitar are sung in harmony. I float from table to table. I love listening to the Inventions and singing the folk songs. My friends and I communicate non-verbally. As we play or sing, we make eye contact, nod our heads imperceptibly and a message has been sent or received with only a gesture, a smile or raised eyebrow, an acknowledged agreement. Making music together is making profound connections. I go to school with kids from every socio-economic and ethnic background. In this school it is only talent that counts. We feel that we are part of an elite group. We are snobs and look down on kids from the neighborhood schools.

The teachers are the best that the city has. My voice, my opinions and ideas are listened to in my classes. No one puts me down for asking a question or saying what I think. Here I win some respect which is so lacking in my "other" life." Mr. Gross, my algebra teacher is kind and patient with me, even though I am an idiot in math. Dr. Sayers, the ninth grade English teacher makes the Iliad and the Odyssey as real as today's headlines. Dr. Patterson opens my eyes to Renaissance, Roman, Romanesque, and Gothic architecture; and there are examples of it all over the city. The Medieval French architecture of the Cloisters in Fort Tryon Park, housing an incredible ninth century art collection built around serene gardens, and the perfect gothic example of St. Patrick's Cathedral on Fifth Avenue.

We meet and go to free radio broadcasts on Sunday afternoons at the Frick Art Gallery, and on Tuesday evenings, the NBC Orchestra, and "The Firestone Hour," where I listen to Fritz Kriesler play the violin, Richard Tucker, Jan Pierce and Bjorling sing and Arturo Toscanini, Bruno Walter and Guido Cantelli conduct. Thirty-five cents buys us seats at the Lewissohn Stadium to hear young Leonard Bernstein play the piano as he conducts Mozart's 17th Piano Concerto, and in Carnegie Hall, we watch and listen to Erica Morini play Brahms violin concerto. In the middle of the performance, she pops a string, turns to the concert master, exchanges violins with him and continues without missing a beat. We see "Porgy and Bess," at the City Center, and on a Saturday night in October, I meet up with classmates to listen to Artur Schnabel play four Beethoven piano sonatas at Hunter College. While I am too young to appreciate the extent of my education and the unusual opportunities afforded me by the generosity of New York City's cultural events, I will never forget them.

We aren't serious all the time. We make lots of room for fun. Once, on April Fools' Day, the entire orchestra decides to play a trick on the teacher who conducts the orchestra. We are rehearsing Aaron Copland's "Fanfare for the Common Man," a piece of music that starts out with an ear splitting clash of the cymbals and roll of the bass drum.

The conductor raises his arms, poised to cue in the percussion section. His baton comes down swiftly, the percussionists stand mute. Dr. Richter, the conductor shakes his head, raises his arms and once again gives the signal. Nothing happens, utter silence.

He raps his baton, "O.K., people. What's going on here?" The cymbal player stands with the cymbal poised against his chest making direct eye contact with the conductor who again signals for the clash and roll of the percussion section: stunning silence. "What the heck is going on?" he blurts out. "Can't you follow a simple cue?"

"April Fool," we scream in unison.

Another time, the senior orchestra conductor is absent and a substitute teacher comes in to take his place. He is a capable musician and looks forward to substituting at our school. It is time for another trick. All the kids exchange instruments. Violinists take the oboes, the horns take the cellos. No one is holding their own instrument when the teacher ascends the podium. I don't remember what we are playing, but it must have been a classical selection. He picks up his baton and raises his arms. A cacophony of noise, in unison assaults him.

"What's going on?" he asks, stunned. "Isn't this senior orchestra? You're supposed to be the best of the best. You sound like you can't even play your own instruments." We shrug our shoulders, desperately trying to suppress the laughter that is threatening to explode.

CHAPTER 33

AT HOME I behave like a "decent," religious girl who doesn't wear lipstick or slacks. But as soon as I leave the house, I become someone else. I remove the skirt under which I've rolled up my trousers, put on lipstick and get on the subway. I try to act like what I think regular teenagers act like. Archie, Betty, Veronica and Jughead are my models. Of course, no one I know acts like them, but I talk the way my peers do. I say "cool, dig, hip," a "cool cat" is a slick guy who knows how to act, a "hip chick" is the female version of the cool cat. These are phrases my parents would never understand. I interject the word "like" into every sentence; "'like' I was going to 'like' the subway, when I 'like' met this weird character. 'Like' he was smoking on the train." I sneak on the forbidden lipstick every time I leave the house and even try smoking outside the building before school starts. I have memorized the words to the latest songs on the Hit Parade and sing along with my friends during lunch or on the subway. I love Tony Bennett, Dinah Shore, and Les Paul with Mary Ford and Nat King Cole. I also love Artur Rubenstein, Rudolf Serkin, Isaac Stern, and Roberta Peters.

I get a pair of white bucks; the white buckskin tie shoes that everyone, boys as well as girls are wearing, a felt skirt with a poodle painted on it. I earn the money for these luxuries by babysitting on the Saturday nights that I don't go to a party. I am working hard to fit in and on some levels I think I may be succeeding when one summer day, I hear my father's voice.

"You can't wear that bathing suit," his voice and manner remind me that I am not like everyone else. It suggests that only he knows what is best for me. Under the guise of constructive criticism, he is insulting and humiliating me.

"Why not? I like it, I think it looks great, my friend Myra thinks it looks good on me and I paid for it with my own money."

"Don't you see how you look?" He asks me, "Compliments from your girl friends? Do you really think they want you to look good? The worse you look the better it makes them look," he continues with his crazy logic. "That suit is not for you. It makes you look fat and it's indecent."

"Indecent?" I ask, "How is it indecent? It's one piece. Nothing is showing that shouldn't be."

"First of all it's strapless and cut low and second of all it makes you look fat." He walks out of the room, leaving me to contemplate my dilemma. I bought bathing suit, with my own money. I have just spent $10.99 earned by babysitting and, bathing suits cannot be returned. All my friends are going swimming in the pool in St, George's Hotel on Sunday. I look at myself in the mirror. I know that I'm not perfect, but I like the suit, it fits and I think it looks good on me. I want to obey but I want to go swimming with my friends even more. I rationalize: "If I could return the suit, I would probably do it, but at fifty cents an hour, which is what I'm paid, eleven dollars represents twenty one hours of baby- sitting. It is an awful lot of money to lose on a bathing suit that looks fine.

He returns to the room to remind me, "You look fat in that bathing suit and I'm only telling you this for your own good. If I didn't love you and have your best interest at heart, I wouldn't be telling this."

I'm supposed to feel grateful to be the recipient of so much love. I start crying.

"Stop your stupid sniveling," he shouts. "I hate to see you cry like a baby because you're hearing the truth." He is relentless and I am inconsolable. "Your girlfriends will always say you look good when you don't. They are happy when you look fat, it makes them feel beautiful. Only I will tell you the truth." I continue sobbing. Even my father thinks I'm ugly.

I wear the suit. I put it on under my dress, take a towel and go to the pool. I've made a decision to do what I want, wear what I like, not ask for permission and not worry about the approval I might or might not get.

Everyone in the family is enlisted to help me lose weight and become a more attractive person. My cousin, Elsie, who is the doctor, puts me on a diet, and prescribes appetite curbing pills. I wonder why I can't sleep at night. I am, as it turns out, on speed, the reducing drug of choice during the early 50's. I gobble the appetite suppressing pills and look in the mirror to see if I've made any progress.

CHAPTER 34

I CARRY THE heavy books up the five flights of stairs to our apartment, drop them at the door and take the key out of my pocket book. I hate coming home, leaving the "castle" for the dungeon. The apartment is always cold. Ever since we have come to live here the superintendent of the building has been skimping on the heat.

"Go down and ask the super for some heat," my father tells me. I hate these trips to the dark basement. The damp smell of the cellar brings me right back to Liebenau, the bottom of the steps and *Glatz Kopf's* slobbery kisses. I knock on the super's door. One eye peers out of the open crack.

"Yeah, whaddaya want?"

"Could we please have some more heat? We are freezing upstairs."

"Yeah, Okay." He slams the door in my face. When I get up to the fifth floor I tell my parents that he said okay. We wait for the heat to come hissing through the radiators. We are all wearing our winter coats waiting for the welcoming sound of sputtering, a sign that we will soon be warm. We hear nothing. My father starts banging on the pipes, sending a message to all the tenants. Everyone below us joins in, banging, trying in vain to get a response from the super. We go to sleep wearing our coats over our pajamas. Will I always be cold, like I was in the furniture factory in Krakow, on the journey to Liebenau, on our trip to America, and as cold as we were in Switzerland? I feel like I'll never get warm in the winter.

A note in my mother's European handwriting is lying on the kitchen table; "Dear Rita, peel four or five potatoes, boil them, then you can mash them with some oleo. The meat is already sliced, so you only have to warm it up. Cut up an onion and fry it, then add the meat. Please, also, prepare the string beans that are in the fridge. I'll see all of you around 8 o'clock." Sometimes there is a laundry basket full of clean clothes that my mother leaves for me to fold and put away. I hate these additional tasks and I hate coming into this cold, empty apartment.

The house feels desolate and lonely without her. First of all it is dark. In spite of the fact that our apartment is on the top floor of the building all the windows face the building behind us. There is no room for one sliver of light to beam into our winter windows, and by 4:30 when I get home it is already dark outside. The silence of the rooms is palpable. Second of all, the apartment smells empty. If there is such a smell as "empty" then this apartment smells deserted: no cooking aromas, none of that dishwater detergent, no smell of my mother's cologne. Before my mother started working I used to come home to the sound of the radio, the smell of something cooking and the heat from the stove. Now that my mother has so many piano students she has to leave the house before 2 o'clock in order to get to Forest Hills by 3. I am in charge of getting dinner on the table. I'm feeling overburdened, overwhelmed and unappreciated. Between 4:30, when I get home from school and 10 P.M., when I go to sleep, I have to get my house chores done, do my homework and at spend at least two hours practicing. Dinner has to be ready by 5:30 when my father comes home, and I'm to clean up the kitchen. The rest of the evening is devoted to homework and practicing. I know my mother is keeping us afloat financially as she goes from house to house giving piano lessons, but I miss her warm companionship and I resent the new tasks that are heaped on me. I'm sixteen and I'm not ready to give up my mother's companionship and take on her responsibilities.

During this time, my father is becoming more and more religiously observant. New edicts are issued every week. Gone are the anticipated Saturday afternoon trips to the library, he wears a hat every time he walks out of the door. "It is a sin to carry on Sabbath," my father tells us, as if I didn't pay dearly for that bit of knowledge. "It is a sin to turn on the lights, listen to the radio, write, answer the phone and tear on the Sabbath." We tear toilet paper squares on Friday afternoon and stash them in the bathroom window sill, thereby avoiding the sin of tearing. We get a Sabbath clock which is plugged into a lamp. It turns the lights off on Friday night, whether I've finished what I was doing or not. When the lights go out, there is nothing to do other than to go to bed. I long to read, but it is too dark. The robot clock turns the lights on again on Saturday afternoon, at 5 P.M. whether it gets dark by mid -afternoon or not.

It is Saturday afternoon; we are sitting at the Sabbath table finishing lunch. The table is made festive by a white table cloth protected by a plastic sheet, tall shining silver candle sticks that used to belong to my grandmother, a square bottle of purple Manischewitz kosher concord wine, and crumbs from the challah. My father and brother are wearing embroidered yarmulkes, long white sleeved shirts and ties. They have returned from the synagogue and we have finished eating. We are all relaxed and looking forward to the week end. We are chanting the *Birchat ha Mazon*, (grace after meals). The mood is suddenly shattered by my father's angry outburst.

"Lechem, not lehem," he spits out at me, emphasizing the guttural Hebrew "ch" sound. "Can't you learn to say it right?" His outburst is explosive, sudden and unprovoked. It shocks my whole body. I feel so dumb. I start to cry.

"Leave the table," he bellows, pointing his finger accusingly at me. "You're pissing through your eyeballs at my *Shabbes* table. You're disturbing my *Shabbes*."

I run into the bathroom, hot with shame. How clumsy and stupid I am. I hate myself. I resolve that I shall never cry again. I press my frozen tears into icicles and store them somewhere between my ribs and my stomach. I shall never cry again, I promise myself.

My father comes home between 5:00 and 5:30. He is unsmiling and uncommunicative at the dinner table. He berates Michael. He was late coming home from school and apparently left his jacket in school, or lost it. This is not the first time Michael has lost an article of clothing.

Last October he left his baseball jacket in the park and when he went back to retrieve it, it was gone. "What kind of a person are you that you can't get anything right. You're lazy and you're forgetful, and unappreciative. You think money grows on trees? That jacket cost $25.00, and I only hope that it will be there tomorrow when you go back to school. All you think of is having fun. It's like fun will make you a success. When I was your age I was a serious student, only I wasn't lucky like you are. I wasn't allowed to go to high school. Everything I learned I taught to myself. You've got all the advantages and you're going to grow up to be nothing." My father makes a face and blows his nose. "I'm only telling you all this for your own good. If you don't buckle down soon you'll find yourself in a factory making buttonholes for men's shirts."

Michael appears unfazed by these assaults on his character. He acts as though he is actually listening to my father, at times even nodding his head as if in agreement. My brother is reacting as if my father were talking about some stranger else, someone he doesn't even care about. He appears to be enjoying his dinner, chewing slowly and thoughtfully.

I, on the other hand, feel desperate at these bullying sessions. Does my father really think that what he is saying is going to help Michael become a more serious student? I get angry at Michael. Why can't he do what he is supposed to do? Why doesn't he at least defend himself.? Why does the atmosphere at the table always reek of anger?

I don't know if I am sad or angry. I'm angry at my father for being so mean, sad that he is so disappointed. At the same time I am sad for my brother for being the target of this anger but also angry for not being more compliant and doing what he is supposed to be doing. Most of all I am sad and victimized for myself for never getting recognition or attention for the good things I do, the good grades, the preparation of the daily dinners, for cleaning up. Why does he get all the attention for being bad, while I don't even get a "thank you?" I'm jealous of Michael for many reasons that I cannot understand. Surely I don't crave this negative flare-up of my father's anger, nor this verbal barrage aimed at him.

I do envy Michael's popularity with the opposite sex and his popularity among his own friends. All my high school girl friends like Mike and often I think that they only befriend me to gain access to my brother. He is literally the most popular kid in two high schools, while I feel no one cares about me. I envy his thinness, his unblemished complexion and his relaxed acceptance of everything that comes his way, even my father's anger. I'm absorbing the brunt of my father's fury, while Michael, at whom the rage is directed is nonchalant and has entirely removed himself from it.

I'm angry at everyone in my family, my mother for leaving us with my hostile father, my father for being so mean to us and especially with Michael, who in spite of my father's wrath seems to be carefree, happy and most of all popular. He's got everything I want, while I carry the guilt for his behavior strapped to my heart. One Saturday afternoon I decide to rat on him. I tell my parents that he has gone to a friend's dormitory room at Yeshiva University Prep School where several of his friends meet to smoke cigarettes and listen to the baseball game on the radio; all on Sabbath. My father never questions my sources or my honesty but reacts exactly as I had expected him to. He is furious. The cinders of his rage swirl about my head and shoulders.

"My son brings me nothing but shame!" he shouts at my mother and me. "He not only desecrates the Sabbath, but he does it in a religious school. Listening to the radio on *Shabbes* is not enough for him. He has to smoke as well." My father is out of control. "Whose room is he in that he feels comfortable smoking and listening to the radio?" I don't want to tell. At first I say I don't know. He persists, I must tell him or else, he threatens, he will go to the dormitory and bang on all the doors in order to find Michael and the rest of his hoodlum friends. If I didn't know him better, I might take this as an idle threat. But I'm familiar with his rage. When he's this angry nothing can restrain him. When he is angry and shouting like this, I inadvertently feel myself back in Monteloupi Prison, with the angry Nazi guards threatening me. Now I have lost complete control of the situation and will have to deal with the demons that will pop out of the Pandora's Box; demons of my own creation which I have invited into my mind. I tell, I reveal Michael's accomplice.

"Really!" He exclaims, smiling, suddenly pleased, "Sammy Ehrnfeld? What a hypocrite his father is. He goes around the *Shul* telling everyone how *frum* (religious) his little Sammy is. My father rubs his hands in glee. His sense of vindication far outweighs his rage. "After *Shabbes* I'll give him a call and tell him what a "wonderful" son he has." My father can't wait for sundown. He derives visible satisfaction at being told about someone else's "bad" son. His anger at Michael subsides perceptibly.

Now I have not only ratted on Michael but on his friend as well. Michael comes home at sundown and is immediately dispatched to his room. "So, you were listening to the radio and smoking in Sammy's room today," my father accuses him, slapping his face. Michael doesn't wince. He's gotten big and strong, he doesn't cry anymore. "Get out of my sight. I'll deal with you later. First I'm going to make a phone call to that bragging hypocrite." My brother glares at me. There is only one person who could have betrayed him to my father and gotten his best friend into trouble at the same time.

I hear shouting from the hallway where the telephone stands on a little table.

My father comes into the living room. He is livid. "Imagine the nerve," he splutters to my mother. "Instead of being grateful that someone is looking out for his son's welfare, he tells me to mind my own business. He actually hung up on me. No wonder his son smokes on *Shabbes*. Ehrenfeld has no manners, he's not only unappreciative, he's rude. Imagine, hanging up on me, the nerve!" His angry mood is restored. Michael is forbidden to ever talk to Sammy again. "He's a bad influence on you," my father tells him. "His parents can't even take care of their own son. He lives in the dormitory because his parents are divorced and he has much too much freedom for his own good. Be happy you've got parents who care about you." Michael nods his head. He willingly agrees to sever his friendship with Sammy as though it doesn't mean a thing to him, while I do not collect my reward for tattling. I am left with an empty feeling of betraying my brother, friend and ally.

The one time I gain positive attention from my father is when I play the piano. He loves classical music and he enjoys listening to me. Although he never tells me directly, I believe that he thinks I am talented and I am thrilled by his silent praise.

"Play that passage again?" he asks me. I do as I am told.

"I would play it softly, *pianissimo,*" he advises, showing great interest and sensitivity to the music.

"Yes, that's much better. Each time you repeat a passage, play it softer than the time before. That way the music has more meaning, it goes from a shout to a whisper." He sits back, reading the paper, listening carefully. He interrupts me every now and then with a comment or suggestion. I try to do as he says. I am finally being heard albeit through Mozart or Schubert. He is actually listening and sharing his opinions with me without dictating or forcing his will on me. He often tells me that he would surely have played an instrument if given the opportunity. I love playing for him. I feel as though this is the one common bond we have; a silent language around the music that I am struggling with. It has nothing to do with Michael, this is all about me. His praise is hard to earn, and I am thrilled when he says "wonderful," after one of the pieces I play. I know that he looks forward to his evenings listening to me. I do my practicing after the dinner dishes are done so that I can bask in my father's appreciation.

CHAPTER 35

─────────── ⌘ ───────────

MY PARENTS ARE arguing in the kitchen. "The rents in Forest Hills are very high. It is out of the question," I hear my father tell my mother when she broaches the topic of possibly moving. "Besides, I have my *shul* here, Sari lives nearby. We will not discuss it anymore." He makes his pronouncement and leaves the room.

Life continues at a predictable pace. Mike is being Mike, while I am being "good," but not good enough to be rewarded. My mother's schedule is becoming more and more hectic. She wants desperately to move to Forest Hills, where she could eliminate her travel time of two hours a day. My father won't hear of it. He's made his proclamation and as far as he's concerned the case is closed. Even though she contributes more money to our financial welfare than he does, he will not help ease her burden if it interferes with his desires. He does not treat her as an equal. He is satisfied in Washington Heights, and Washington Heights is where he says he's staying.

My mother, who has been meek as a mouse with my father has developed a feeling of emancipation. Earning money gives her new self-esteem and confidence. Without his knowledge, she has been investigating apartments in Forest Hills. She comes home one night and tells him excitedly that she has founds an apartment in Forest Hills. "The rent is affordable and I could probably take on three or four more piano lessons a week to make up for the difference. I left a small deposit with the superintendent, and told him I'd be back to see it with my husband." She begs and cajoles my father into at least looking at it. He resists.

"I told you weeks ago that the case is closed. I will not move to Forest Hills. If you love it so much there, then you go and move by yourself. Nobody cares about my needs," he adds. "Now that you're earning money you think you are completely independent. Go ahead. Try it on your own." She has no intention of leaving him but the power of earning money has given her the gumption to stand up to him.

"All right Alex," she counters. "I understand how you feel, but I'll have to cut back on some of my lessons. I can't continue to teach four hours a day and spend two and a half hours on the subway. If you can't at least look at that apartment with me on Sunday, I will cut my teaching schedule even though I know how much we've come to rely on the money. You know that I'll never move away from you, but I will take better care of myself."

I listen to her, astounded. "Atta girl!" I cheer silently. Even though I don't want to move it's great to hear her old spirit take him on. This is the first time I've heard her challenge him and I realize that he's afraid she means what she says. She sounds strong, not the timid little person she's become since coming to America. Reluctantly, he agrees to go see the apartment in Forest Hills. "It is only to take a look, to please you," he tells her. "Don't think I'm planning to move."

On the following Sunday, they look at the apartment, explore the Forest Hills neighborhood as my mother points out several synagogues, kosher butchers and bakeries. He spots two men walking on the street wearing skull caps, deeply engaged in conversation. This doesn't look as bad as he thought it would. He becomes less resistant to the idea of moving. Without having been consulted, I am told that we will be moving on March 31st.

I am not happy. I have finally found a group of observant Jewish teenagers, girls and boys, who congregate in the neighborhood park on Saturday afternoons. I hate the idea of moving away from Washington Heights and giving up this bit of socializing, especially since my father has warned me that I could only date Orthodox boys. The Saturday afternoon meetings are informal, but they give me something to do on the long Sabbath afternoons in the spring. I look forward to them eagerly. The boys are dormitory students at the Yeshiva Michael has been expelled from. He still has many good friends there and I tag along, happy to hang out with them and flirt with religiously acceptable boys. For the first time I appreciate the long Saturday afternoons. A lot of good looking boys hang around in the park and I sense that they enjoy my company as much as I do theirs.

I get my first glimpse of the new apartment on moving day, a balmy day in April, when I take a day off from school to help. In no way does it compare to my expectation. I thought we'd be moving into a Forest Hills apartment building like Poldi's, with a uniformed doorman guarding an opulent lobby. Instead we move into a dark, ground floor apartment that doesn't have a lobby or carpeted hallways. The windows are level with the sidewalk and look out onto street. When I peer outside, the view is one of shoes attached to legs, but no torsos or heads. The kitchen is too small to accommodate our Formica table from Washington Heights and it can only fit two chairs and a small square card table.

"Gosh it's small," I tell my parents. "What are we going to do? Where are we going to put the piano? Are we going to take turns eating in the kitchen? We can't all fit inside at one time if we put a table in." My parents ignore my comment. They are busy directing the movers. There are two bedrooms; the smaller one can only accommodate a small bed and an unpainted dresser which doubles as a desk. Since Michael and I are much too old to share a room, we will take turns sleeping in this tiny space. For one week he will sleep in the living room on the sofa while I sleep in the little bedroom and then we will switch. The week-ends in the living room are hard on us. The sofa has to be made up early, and we will not be able to catch up on our sleep for two weeks every month. Privacy is not even taken into consideration. The one sleeping on the sofa has to take clothing to the bathroom in order to get dressed. With one bathroom which doubles as a dressing room, and four people in the apartment, everyone is clamoring for its space every morning.

"Hurry up, you've been in there for an hour," I bang on the door to get Michael out. I have to get ready for school and there is no way I'll be on time if he hogs the bathroom all morning long. He takes his time. He is in no hurry. He's shaving and his school starts later than mine.

Getting to Music and Art from Forest Hills involves four train changes, and a one hour ride to and from school. However, it has its up-side. I get to ride with all my friends who live in Queens. We shout to each other to make ourselves heard above the roar of the train, scramble madly for empty seats, and sing the latest hits oblivious to the deafening noise and the amused or annoyed glances from our fellow passengers.

Michael and I have made several friends in the new neighborhood. They attend the same synagogue as we do and are our age. We join a youth group that meets on Friday evenings after dinner at each other's houses. We hang out in front of the synagogue on Saturday mornings and when the weather is good we meet at the local park in the afternoon. I still miss the Saturday afternoon get-togethers with the Yeshiva University students, but I'm managing.

The move marks a significant change in the way my parents start to regard me. I hear talk about finding a suitable *shidduch* (match). Are they serious? I ask myself. I'm only seventeen, still in high school. What sparks this sudden interest in my marriage-ability is the engagement of one of my new friends, Naomi. She has just gotten engaged and she's only seventeen.

My Forest Hills girl-friends and I are standing outside the synagogue one Saturday when Naomi flounces down the street, holding her hand in front of her face, admiring it so attentively that she trips over a crack in the sidewalk.

"Hello ladies," she chirps. "Wanna see something gorgeous?" She holds her left hand up for inspection.

"Wow, what a rock!" Regina exclaims, squealing, grabbing Naomi's hand and holding it up to the sun. "Tell all!"

We crowd around her. Naomi is a pretty girl, tall thin, with long blond hair which she wears in a page boy. She goes to Forest Hills High School and I know she is a member of ARISTA, the honor society.

"It was a blind date, which I happen to know is the Americanized term for *shiddach*. He is just what I've been dreaming about all my life."

"What does he look like? How old is he? What does he do?" We clamor for answers. We need to know everything about him.

Naomi savors her celebrity status. "Well," she hesitates before going on, "he's much older than I am; well, he's actually, twenty-two, but he's very smart."

"Yeah, what is he? What does he do? Is he still in school? Does he go to college? What's he studying?" The questions come at her so quickly, she can't respond rapidly enough to satisfy our curiosity.

"He's in the diamond business. This stone is two and a half carats and perfect, blue-white." Naomi smiles, holds up her left hand, admiring her ring.

"Um, no. Well… yes, and no." Naomi is not sure how to answer. "He takes courses at City College in the evening and works during the day." she pauses, "He's studying Business."

"When do we get to meet him?" Malky asks.

"When are you getting married?"

"What does he look like?"

Our curiosity is only overshadowed by our envy. Me? I am slowly turning the color of lettuce. What I wouldn't give to be engaged!

My father comes home from Shul that afternoon. "Such a wonderful *shidduch*," he says. "She managed to get the richest boy in the diamond club." I can see that I am not the only one who is envious. Marriage is the ultimate goal for every girl in the 50's, especially within the Orthodox community. Being an old maid is a fear that is harbored in my breast as well as in all my girlfriends' breasts. I am hardly eligible for old maid status, but already minds are spinning. I love the idea of getting married young, being desirable and pursued. I haven't had a serious boyfriend yet, but that doesn't keep me from dreaming. I believe in love at first sight and hope I meet him soon.

And then I meet Richard, Naomi's fiancé. He comes to spend *Shabbes* with her family and she brings him to *Shul*. He is a pudgy, round, little man, with a pot belly, receding hair line, thick, coca-cola bottle eyeglasses and is perspiring visibly under his gray fedora. He stares at the ground as she introduces him. I don't believe my eyes. How could she settle for someone is so dull, so homely? He is about four inches shorter than she is and looks like an old man: thirty, at least. He is wearing a navy blue suit that stretches across his middle. I look at his feet, his shiny black oxfords, tiny, like a little kid's. I can't imagine going to bed with someone who must have such small feet. How is Naomi going to spend one night with him, let alone a lifetime?

I feel such disappointment in her choice. How could she "cop out" like this, settle for the this man? Was it just for the ring? Can she really be in love with him? I feel as though she betrayed her desires, her hope for passion and romance. She "copped" out, took herself off the marriage market. Is she so afraid of being an old maid that she needs to settle for him at this point in her life? She has violated some private ethic that I am harboring. She has done what I swore I would never do: marry someone I wasn't in love with. I cross her off my list. I have lost all respect for her.

I look around at my other friends. No one seems as disapproving as I.

"Are you getting married after graduation, next year?" Randy asks her.

"I'm not going back to school in September," she tells us. "I don't need any diplomas or degrees now," she says confidently. "I'm getting my MRS. and that's good enough for me: my own apartment, my own dishes, a big bedroom with beautiful furniture, a living room set with a sectional sofa. What else do I need?"

I am annoyed with myself. Why am I taking this so personally? Am I scared that I too might feel pressured into marrying an ugly, old man? Everyone else is taking it in their stride, while I'm overly upset with his appearance. I imagine giving up romance and love for the sake of safety: cooking, shopping and cleaning for this little man for rest of my life. Is this what it's all about, I ask myself? The ring is beautiful and Naomi appears to be happy. Well, I console myself at least Naomi did not get the best man possible. There's still a chance for me.

In Music and Art being popular with the opposite sex is a valued asset. Many of the popular girls are pinned to college men. On

Mondays the girls talk about their dates on the weekend. I talk also, but most of my dates are all the result of imagination and wishful thinking. In my generation, having a date on Saturday night is a critical symbol of desirability and status. Rules of dating are clear. This is before a girl would dream of phoning a boy. No self- respecting girl would ever phone a guy. Some of the boys in school call me and ask me out, but they are the ones who are unappealing. I couldn't think of kissing them good-night. Most Saturday nights, I choose to baby-sit or stay home and dream about my ideal boyfriend; tall, thin, curly dark haired, funny and smart and with preferably blue eyes. So far, I have never met such a man, let alone dated one. I would love some attention from one of these boys, but since Wally, I haven't gotten any.

I am attracted to several boys in school, but they are not interested in me and I can't bring myself to go out with someone I don't feel attracted to, who might want to kiss me good night. I suddenly miss Wally and our bathroom encounters in Washington Heights.

"Please Mike," I beg, "call Wally and ask him how he's doing." I'm hoping that hearing from my brother would rekindle some spark of interest in Wally and tempt him to call me. I bribe Michael, promising him the use of the bedroom for three weeks in a row. Mike makes the call.

"May I speak to Wally?" he says into the mouthpiece. He holds onto the receiver for a few moments before hanging up and laughing.

"What happened? Whom did you speak to?

He looks at me shaking his head in disbelief. "His father answered." Mike laughs. "You know what his dad said to me? He said, 'my son's name is *Valter* not *Vally*.' And he is not going to talk on the telephone to you Michael Schmelkes! Then the old man hangs up." Michael is hysterical. He repeats "*Valter not Vally.*"

CHAPTER 36

I HAVE JUST turned eighteen but am still in high school because I am half a year behind. My mother suggests that on Friday afternoon, we go shopping for a nice new dress for me. "In fact, "she says, "we'll go to Ruth's Dresses."

There's got to be a reason for this, I think. It's not my birthday; I'm not going to anyone's wedding and I'm not even near to graduation.

"How come?" I ask suspiciously.

"You've stopped growing so you'll be able to keep it for a few years. You're already eighteen and I think it will be nice for you to have a good dress, something special."

Ruth's, the "expensive" store is a small shop, nestled between several boutiques on a pretty side street in Forest Hills.

"May I help you?" The saleslady has a French accent, I'm sure it's fake. She's wearing a smart black dress with a light blue silk scarf draped over one shoulder. She wants to make a statement about herself and the store: appear sophisticated and elegant. When my mother tells her why we are there, she looks at us appraisingly. "How much are you interested in spending?" My mother who knows that Ruth's Dresses are expensive doesn't want to appear out of her element.

"It doesn't matter," she tells her indifferently. She remembers shopping at expensive stores before the war and never having to ask the price of anything. She squares her shoulders, stretches her neck and looks around the store disdainfully. She too knows how to appear rich and sophisticated. "We don't care about the price. Just show us what you've got in a size ten."

The saleslady is not impressed. She hesitates, assessing us. She puts me off. I'm feeling poor. I'm much more comfortable shopping at Lerner's or Alexander's where no one cares what I want to try on. She purses her lips moving her head to one side. "Is this a dress for a formal occasion? Do you want something for the evening? Or do you want something tailored?"

We know exactly what we want. I want something that will make me look thin and my mother wants something that is cheap. That probably narrows the choice to just about nothing in that store. Of course, we don't share this information with her.

"We're not sure," my mother says, unwilling to close off any options.

The woman persists, trying to appear patient with us. "Do you want wool, silk, knit, linen?" When she sees us hesitate, she goes on arrogantly, "you have to tell me. We have many dresses in the back and I can't possibly bring out everything we have in a size ten."

Why not? I say to myself. You have no other customers in the store and you don't seem to have anything else to do. I watch them, the saleslady and my mother. They are sizing each other up, having a silent confrontation, as if marking their territory. I wonder, can the saleslady see through us and realize we are poor, and that we probably will not be able to afford anything in her store anyway?

My mother regains her footing. She remembers what it was like being rich. She places her hand on one hip, tilts her chin and addresses her in an imperious tone, "show us something in wool, preferably a bright color."

She brings out several dresses. I try them on. My only criteria is "do they make me look fat?"

"How do I look?" I ask my mother.

"Hmm, maybe a little bit fat," she says looking at the price tag and realizing that this it is more than she is willing to spend.

"Take it away, I don't want it!" I peel it off and discard it, just as if it were a layer of unwanted fat.

After a half hour of trying on everything she brings out, we finally find the perfect dress. It is pink wool, fitted at the waistline with a full skirt, affordable and, most important of all does not make me look fat. I love it. I inspect myself from every angle and decide that I am beautiful. I never give another thought to what it was that spurred this project although the plan has been germinating in my father's brain ever since Naomi came to Shul with her big diamond.

CHAPTER 37

—— ✠ ——

MY FATHER SPEAKS to my Uncle Avrom, who speaks to a friend of his, and word is out. They are looking to make *shidduch* for me. I am the subject of discussion between my father and my uncle. I wonder how they're going to go about it, but do not ask. I continue my senior year in high school, making plans of my own. I know that I want to go to college and that it will most likely be Queens College, which is close to my house and is free to students who qualify academically. Moreover, Queens has an excellent music department so I will be able to continue with my studies.

"Alex, you have a telephone call," my mother calls to my father. "It's Avrom."

My father so rarely receives a phone call that the whole family stops what we're doing and listens intently. We hover around him, catching only his side of the conversation, spoken in Yiddish. He nods his head in agreement with my uncle, not in the least bit mindful of the fact that the only ones who see him agreeing are my mother and I. When he gets off, his face is shiny with excitement. He beckons my mother to go into the bedroom. I put my ear up against the door, but I can't make sense of their whispered conversation.

"Uncle Avrom met a very nice young man in Shul," he tells me when he comes out. "He told him about you and now he wants to meet you. Do you want to go out with him on Sunday?"

Ohhhhh, I say to myself. Now I understand the reason for the expensive dress from Ruth's. It's not a reward for my growing up, or my good behavior; its gift wrap for my body to package me for the marriage market. If it's someone like Richard, Naomi's fiancé, I will die. But on the other hand, I say to myself, he might be more like Wally.

"Who is this 'young man'? What does he look like and what does he do, and how old is he?" My father has never seen him or spoken to him but he knows that he is a professor of French literature in one of the city colleges and that he's a little bit older than I am. "A little bit older?" I ask, skeptically. I think of Richard who was only twenty-two and already looked like an old man.

I put on my new dress and sit in the living room waiting for Joseph Winetraub: Professor Joseph Winetraub, to come to pick me up. He is thirty-three, shorter than I am, and I am only 5'2." He is very polite, shakes hands with my father and bows his head in a continental manner to my mother. I look at him and inhale sharply. He is carrying an umbrella! No one I know carries an umbrella. Well, that's not true, my mother carries one when she has to go out in the rain. Once, when caught in a downpour, I wished I had an umbrella. But today it is only drizzling. How am I going to get through this day, I wonder. And what will I do if we meet someone I know?

We go to a vegetarian restaurant on 47th Street in Manhattan, a restaurant endorsed by the Orthodox community in New York. We talk quietly, but I just can't get over how disappointed I am. Poor guy, I say to myself. His looks are not his fault. I try to assuage my guilty conscience for placing such importance on looks alone. He starts eating and I notice that his hands are smaller than mine, petite, pretty.

"Are you taking French in high school?" he asks me, trying to make conversation.

"No," I answer politely, "I'm taking Spanish. I like it, but I think French is a nicer sounding language. Anyway, Spanish might be more useful to me, given the fact that there are so many Spanish speaking people in New York."

"True, true," he agrees taking a bite of his potato *latke* (pancake). I look around the restaurant and notice other religious couples talking earnestly. To me all of them appear to be mismatched. The girls are young, well dressed, nice looking, with smooth, shiny hair. The men are much older, wearing suits and ties and haven't got a trace of their boyhood left. They are "men" with "girls." I wonder, how many of them are arranged "matches" like mine and what the girls are thinking. Joseph is a nice enough man and sensitive enough to realize that we are not going to be a couple. I try to be pleasant and attentive, but I can't wait to get home and do my homework.

My parents are waiting, expectantly in the living room for me. "Well?" they inquire, "how was it?"

I answer with a Polish quotation I've heard my mother use, "*ste monki chleba niebencze,* (from this flour there will be no bread)." My father shrugs his shoulders. Much to my surprise, he doesn't seem disappointed at all, in fact, if I didn't know better, I would say he looks relieved. Maybe he realizes the folly of attempting such a match. "There will be others," he tells me, thinking I need to be reassured. "Besides," he admits, "you really have to finish high school and hopefully go to college."

My father appears to be as conflicted as I am. On one level, I feel that I must go to college, become more educated. I am not ready to give up my youth. On the other hand, I desperately want to get married, get out of this house and be on my own. I know that my father loves me more than anyone in this world. He has often told me that his way of expressing this love is by constantly trying to keep me safe, make me into being the best that I can be; his version of the perfect young girl. It becomes apparent to me much later, that he is terribly frightened of losing me to someone who will not be able to provide for me, who will force me to live the same insecure life that he is living. He tells me that he realizes that I am growing up and closer to womanhood than girlhood.

In a rare moment of intimacy, he calls me into the bedroom and closes the door. We sit on the bed and I look in the mirror at our reflections. He looks small, strangely vulnerable, not the angry father I am used to. It is more uncomfortable for me to be with this strange, gentle father that the shouting man I've gotten to know. He takes my hand and looks into my eyes. I can see that he is struggling with some inner demons.

"I want you to go to college, become independent, be able to support yourself and never have to rely on anyone else," he tells me. "Women need a profession just as much as men do. Look at your cousin Elsie. Being a doctor did not stop her from getting married." I wonder, is he talking to me or trying to convince himself of the need for me to get an education? "The only difference between her and most women her age is that she can afford to buy a big, beautiful house, hire a housekeeper to clean for her and take care of her children while pursuing a highly respected profession." I agree with him. Elsie does, indeed, have a rewarding life.

He reminds me. "If I had a profession I would never have had to worry about paying for food and rent." He continues, not sure of what he will say next, "but on the other hand, there comes a time when it is important for a girl to get married. You go beyond a certain age and you close off your choices. I know how men feel," he adds, "They want a pure, young pretty wife. And once you get into your mid-twenties there are fewer choices. " I realize that he's in turmoil, sending me two messages. Get an education and get married, and that somehow he is sure that the two are mutually exclusive. I suddenly feel sorry for him. He really thinks that he can make choices for me, as if they were his for the making, or even mine for that matter?

My uncle has not given up his in his pursuit of the ideal suitor.

"Max," my father tells me several days after my date with Joseph, "is younger and not as serious as Joseph. Uncle Avrom assures me that Max is a fun loving, intelligent young man. He is very successful in the jewelry business, actually very rich. Would you be willing to go out with him?"

I feel sympathy for my father. I can see that he is not anxious to marry me off, especially not to a business man, but now that Uncle Avrom has been recruited and is trying so hard to find me a husband, my father does not want to take his efforts for granted. And maybe this "Max" will be all that he and I hope for.

"Just go out with Max, and if you don't like him, I will tell Uncle Avrom to stop looking," he is almost pleading with me.

"Sure, why not. But please, daddy, if this doesn't work out, let's give it a rest."

"Absolutely," my father agrees emphatically.

Max is leaning across the table towards me, at the same vegetarian restaurant I had gone to with Joseph only two weeks before. He is intense, his eyes are shining. "A beautiful photograph is better than any painting could ever be. A photograph is a perfect representation of the subject. Nothing like a painting!"

"You think so?" I say feeling that Max is hopeless. Unlike Joseph, who was ever so courteous, educated and even deferential in his manner, Max is tall, broad, loud and cocky. To me, he appears to be flouting his ignorance with pride

"I'm not sure I agree with you. A painting is more than a mere representation. It is an interpretation of what the artist sees and feels towards his subject."

"Feelings shmeelings, what I like is reality. I want to look at a picture and know what it is. Like the brochure we just had done for the store. A photographer came and took pictures of the jewelry and let me tell you they were perfect. Each piece looked pure and perfect. Who cares what he feels about a necklace. Representation, true and honest representation is what I call art."

I can't hold my feelings towards Max in any longer. "What are you saying?" I ask disdainfully. "That a snapshot of a necklace on a piece of velvet has as much artistic merit as a painting by Vermeer?" I have just taken a class on the Dutch masters and Vermeer's masterpieces, with their windows casting light on beautiful young girls are clear in my mind. Max says it does, that it's better because it's real. I look at him and I realize that he doesn't know who Vermeer is, has probably never even been to a museum or art gallery.

"The beautiful photographs in our winter catalogue have brought in more money than any paintings I have seen."

"Do you rate art by its monetary value, or by its beauty?" I ask, incredulously.

"Monetary, shmonetary, whatever you call it," he says, "money is what makes the world go round."

No you idiot, I say to myself, it's "Love Makes the World Go Round." I say nothing and continue eating my vegetables while my soul is on fire. What a Plebe, I think. I control myself and do not say what is on the tip of my tongue. It is obvious that I am not going to marry anyone of the "nice young men" my uncle fixes me up with. I think about Naomi and Richard. I'm not going to settle for a loser at the age of eighteen.

Max calls me up on Monday night and asks me out again. I tell him I am busy and that I will be busy for the next few weeks; that I am studying for college exams and won't be able to go out with him.

He gets upset, "I've never heard of a girl who has to study all day long, every day of the week." He tells his match maker, who tells my uncle, who tells my father, who tells me, that Max thinks I am immature, not ready for marriage, that I am only an adolescent.

I have started dating a boy my father totally disapproves of. David is an Israeli boxer who is in this country training for the Olympics. He is being sponsored by some rich Jewish guy who is a boxing fan. I meet David at a school party. He comes along with one of the kids from school. David is a hunk. He is gorgeous, and for some reason he starts lavishing all his attention on me. We dance; he gets way too close to me, but not close enough. He insists on bringing me home when I say I have to leave in time for my curfew. He comes to pick me up for a date on the following Saturday night. My father hates him, at first sight, as soon as they are introduced. When I come home later on that evening, my father is in the living room waiting for me.

"I don't want you going out with that boxer again," he tells me, spitting out the word "boxer."

"Why, what's wrong with him? He's Jewish, he's even from Israel."

"I don't like him for you. I know men like this. He is interested in only one thing. Do I have to spell it out for you?"

"Yes," I say. "You do." I am furious with him for implying that all that a handsome boy could see in me was my sexual availability. "You are so afraid that I'm a tramp that you are scared to even use the word 'sex' with me." I shout at him, "just because he doesn't look like one of the creeps Uncle Avrom calls a 'fine young man,' doesn't mean that I am going to jump into bed with him. And for your information, daddy, sex is what most boys want from girls, even the religious creeps in their old man fedoras."

For a moment my father is speechless. He is shocked, astounded at my reaction. He recovers after a few seconds, "How dare you speak to me like that? I have nothing but your best interest at heart. This is not a man for you. What are you going to do? Marry a boxer?"

"I am not going to marry anyone right now. Besides, David has not asked me and I only went out on one date with him." I resent the fact that my father has set himself up as the guardian of my virginity. I continue going out with David. My father's suspicions strengthen my resolve to do as I wish. In truth, I find David boring after a few dates. All he talks about is boxing, his diet, his exercises and our dates consist of his sponsor's driver picking me up to taking us to the Eastern Parkway Arena to watch David in a preliminary fight. I sit in the front row cringing at the sound of a gloved fist crushing a nose. From where I sit, I not only see blood spurt out of noses but hear bones crunch. I come to hate boxing, the punching, the screaming crowds shouting "kill him, kill him:" men staggering, panting, sweating exposing their bodies to such brutality.

I hate to admit it, but my father was not wrong in his assessments of David's motives. I will never tell him he was right, he needs no encouragement from me to prove his point. After our "dates" are over, David and I sit in the back seat of the car where we make out until I am dropped off. He is so crude. The minute we get into the car he is groping and pushing himself on me. He doesn't make any attempt to talk to me, ask me how I feel, or even discuss the fight he just participated. He never compliments me, even though I take great pains with my appearance before I go to the fight. My friends go out on dates to the Copacabana, the Latin Quarter and to the theater. He has never so much as treated me to a soda. I decide not to tell my father about my feelings for David.

He is so obsessed with the idea of sexual promiscuity on my part that he doesn't realize I've stopped seeing David. It is a Sunday morning and I am waiting on the subway platform in Forest Hills. I'm meeting a friend, spending the afternoon at the Museum of Modern Art. We're doing a paper on Picasso's "Guernica," and having an early supper after that. The trains are running slowly, typical for a Sunday morning. I walk up and down the platform, peering into the dark tunnel hoping to draw the train into the station. Suddenly, I am certain that I have spied my father out of the corner of my eye. I turn around quickly, but only see a large post. My imagination, I tell myself. I get on the train and take out a book to read. I look up for a moment and again I think I have spotted my father. I look out of the window at the black tunnel walls, refusing to let my imagination control my mind. When I get off at 53rd Street, there is no mistaking it. My father has darted behind a pole trying to appear invisible. He follows me onto the street and then I lose sight of him. What is going on? I ask myself. Why am I feeling as if I am being accused of a crime I haven't committed.

"Where did you go," he asks me when I get home, as if he doesn't know.

"You know where I went. I saw you. I told you I was meeting Paula at the Museum."

We continue playing cat and mouse. I can so easily put his mind at rest, if I tell him I am no longer seeing David. But I don't want to give him the satisfaction. Also, I am not sure that he trusts me and I don't feel like defending myself for something I didn't do.

CHAPTER 38

———— ✧ ————

THE SPRING SEMESTER has started. It will be my last one in Music and Art. We are the big shots, wearing our senior caps, maroon and blue, the school colors. My year book, "Con Brio" with the names and photographs as well as special creative writing pieces of my fellow graduates is tucked under my arm. We are seniors walking around the hallways where the walls are covered with the paintings and through whose doors one hears every conceivable instrument. We hug and cry, we don't want to leave Music and Art, but at the same time we can't wait to go to college. Music and Art has been a haven for all of us. This is the safe place to express ourselves, do what we love the most and do the best.

I sit at the piano. I am to accompany my friend Willy Schulsinger for his senior performance final. It is sometime in May and the windows are open. The fluttering breeze is rustling the sheet music propped up on the stand. I can't play and hold it in place so I blow on it every now and then, hoping to keeping in place for the duration of Willy's solo. I wonder for a minute if some eager applicant is walking underneath the window and hearing Willy's voice, just as I heard someone singing only a few years ago. Willy is wearing a navy blue suit with a red tie for the occasion. His arms are spread out and his head is tilted to one side. His voice is beautiful, full throated, deep baritone. He sings one of the German *lieder* by Robert Schumann, *"Lieb Liebchen* (Sweet Beloved)." His German is almost perfect. I coached him and got all the Yiddish intonations out. I am praying that I don't make a mistake and throw him off. I listen to the singing and the words as I accompany, following him. Yes, the German is perfect. The song takes on extraordinary significance for me. He is singing a love song to our school; to my school, to my life. I burst out crying when he finishes. Once again, I am being forced to leave a place I love. Willy understands. He tries to console me.

"We'll all stay in touch," he tells me, patting me on the shoulder. But I know it will never be the same

Part III
Navigating Happily Ever After

CHAPTER 1

I AM SITTING on the living room floor with the classified section of the Sunday New York Times spread out in front me. It is winter break and finals will be held as soon as we return to school in January. College has been a colossal disappointment. I do not know a single soul on campus and with all the rushing and running from one building to another I don't see much hope in meeting anyone. The campus is spread out over many acres and it takes me weeks to become oriented enough to get from one class to another without getting lost. And to make matters worse, the Jewish holidays begin almost as soon as school starts. Before the middle of October, I am forced to take seven days off from school. In college this is a catastrophe. The holidays, which my family has always observed take seven precious days to celebrate over a period of four weeks: two days for the New Year, one for the Day of Atonement, two days for the feast of Tabernacles and two days celebrating the giving of the Torah. I am lost before I even get started and every time I come back to school after a holiday I am far behind my peers. This might not have been an impossible challenge were it not for differential calculus which I am required to take, as a liberal arts major.

The first two years in Queens College are devoted to liberal arts. This requirement provides the students with exposure to the courses offered at the college and an opportunity to try everything before declaring a major field of study in our junior year. I have a chance of catching up in most of my liberal arts courses, English, Contemporary Civilization and Spanish but the math class, integral calculus is my undoing. I, who had trouble with long division, struggled through high school algebra, and almost failed geometry am now learning about rates of falling bodies, theories about the application of lengths, areas and volumes and how they are used in the solutions of differential equations. We spend one hour daily studying changes of mass and slopes, the notion of unlimited sequence and the infinite series to well-defined limits. There is no way on earth that I will learn anything in this class. It is like being taught in a language I do not understand or speak. Moreover, missing so many classes makes the idea of passing the course absurd. I can't face the prospect of failure and then having to take the course again the following semester. I can take calculus for the next four years, but I will never grasp its basic concepts or the need to study them. Who cares if rate of speed accelerates when a feather or a rock is flying out of a window?

I am a realistic person. We are told at freshman orientation that the two years of liberal arts courses we will be taking are considered "elimination" courses, designed to determine whether or not we are cut out for college. We would soon discover where our fates lie.

For me, calculus is just that. I feel that I have been eliminated and that I may as well not return for the humiliation of the final ritual, the granting of a failing grade, taking the course again and lowering my GPA before my freshman year is over. My plan is drop out and not be forced to fail. I am thinking about a job as a receptionist in an office or a salesgirl in a department store.

"What are you looking at?" my father asks innocently when he sees me scanning the employment columns. "Are you thinking of getting a job over vacation?"

"Actually, I am not looking for a job over vacation. I am not going to return for the finals."

"Are you crazy? Of course you'll return for the finals. You spent this whole semester in school and now you're scared of the finals? You have to go to college because *there is no other place for you,* unless you want to work in a factory. College is your only way out of a mediocre life, a life with no opportunities." He doesn't have to add "like my life," but I know it is implied. "You are not quitting!" He turns to leave, "and that's final." End of statement, no room to argue.

There is no point arguing with him, when he makes a proclamation, that's it. This will be the first time I will receive a failing grade and I know that taking the course again will not help me understand the intricacies of calculus. Perhaps I could get a tutor. I know that there are students who tutor other students. They charge $3.00 per hour and maybe one of them might be able to help me get some of the calculus through my head, enough to get a passing grade. It will be my last grasp at an elusive straw.

The minute we return to school I trudge up to the math office and request help. I tell them I must have it immediately, that very day. For one week, for two hours daily, in between my other finals, I meet with Roberta, a pale, shy, homely girl, with stringy brown hair and an advanced case of acne. Roberta, a math major takes great pains to get calculus through my head. I try. All I need is a C and I put all my energy and money in to it. My father has volunteered to pay for lessons with Roberta, a sum total of $30.00!

C H A P T E R   2

———— ✢ ————

THE MORNING OF the math final is bleak, overcast and cloudy. The streets are treacherous, covered with icy patches that have been sprinkled with sand. They are rock hard, slippery and uneven. Slipping and falling on this unfriendly surface would surely cause an injury. The wind whipping my body is relentless, stinging my face and blowing loose sand into my eyes. I am numb from my toes to the top of my head. The moment of doom is upon me and the weather is part of the scripted scene.

Remsen Hall, where the exam is to be given is filled with freshmen, some of them nervous, others, the cocky math and engineering students are joking around, their slide rulers strapped to their belts like badges of superiority. I am handed a blue exam booklet and a copy of the test. I seat myself strategically behind one of the confident math boys and try to recall what the tutor had so recently taught me. My hands are shaking and I can't seem to make any kind of sense from the single question is which is the sum total of the entire test. I try a deep breath, look around the room and notice that some of the students are scribbling frantically in their booklets while others, like I, stare blankly at the equation lying on their desk.

I'm scared that if I fail my father will feel that he wasted all that money on me. I can't deal with that prospect of disappointing him, having him think I am a failure, not worth investing in. I want so much to get his approval, be a source of pride. I know that if I drop out of college he will be devastated. Now I am facing the prospect of this horrible exam and so much of my personhood is riding on it.

I make a decision. I will check my work against the work of the math student sitting in front of me. As if on cue, he picks up his exam booklet and scans it before handing it in just enough time for me to glimpse his answer. I can't copy the entire solution, it consists of several pages in our blue exam booklets, but I can work my way backwards from his answer to the question itself. This is not exactly cheating I tell myself, it is more like "checking" or working the problem backwards. The proctor is sitting at his desk in front of the room, his legs are up on the desk and he is doing a crossword puzzle in the New York Times. He glances up now and then but doesn't catch me. It was so easy that I regretted all the worry and fear I had poured into this. I do not feel in the least bit guilty. I never had cheated before and I know I probably never will again.

When my report card comes in the mail I am rewarded with a C in math, a few B's and some A's. My college career is saved thanks to an irresponsible proctor and the smart math student who sat in front of me.

The following semester is much easier. This time the math is statistics, which although is not a breeze is something I can understand. Nevertheless, I do not like Queens College. Even though I get used to the pressure of having to move all over the campus, it is a cold environment. While many of the instructors are passionate about their specialty, few are invested in their students. They are teaching subjects and not people. I miss the comradery of my high school, the close friendships and the collaboration of making music together. So far I have not taken a single music course in college and probably will not take one until my junior year when I declare my major. There is a band and an orchestra and they are so desperate for French horn players that I am accepted without an audition. The chorus is rehearsing for the annual performance of The Messiah and I am eager to participate. It's a rousing opportunity to be singing with a full orchestra for the accompaniment.

My days are filled with school, homework and studying. In order to maintain a decent grade point average there is no time for a social life at all. At least not the kind of social life I had in Music and Art when there were lots of parties and outings on the week-ends. Occasionally I do run into an old classmate from high school, but we are so busy getting to our next class that we barely have the time to acknowledge each other. I feel lonely and abandoned.

CHAPTER 3

———— ✣ ————

THE TWO YEARS of required liberal arts pass and although they were diffi-cult I am grateful for having been exposed to so many exciting courses; subjects I never knew about and would probably not have discovered were it not for the requirements of my first two years of college. I take a course in anthropology and become interested in pre-Colombian art, ancient Aztec and Mayan culture, old English poetry, taught by a pas-sionate lover of the subject and comparative literature which proves to be most useful critical thinking tool that I ever experienced.

I am able to finally get to my major, music, which is unexpectedly the most challenging subject outside of calculus. I thought that with the four years at Music and Art behind me, music would be a snap. What can they possibly teach me that I don't already know? I am wrong. In addition to my music courses in advanced counterpoint, keyboard har-mony, choral and orchestral dictation, composition and music analysis I must keep up with my practicing and private piano lessons. At the end of each semester the music majors are required to give a recital to prove their proficiency with their instrument.

I manage to meet some new friends at college and connect with other people who went to Music and Art but are not music majors. Judy, a girl I went to high school with but never befriended there is majoring in music as I am and we often commiserate on how much harder Queens is than Music and Art.

My Sundays are almost exclusively spent at the piano. On some of them I don't even stop to eat lunch. The work is so intense. There is music I have to learn to play in every key and compositions that I have to write in the style of Bach, Chopin or Brahms. One particularly difficult assignment is to take an Ode by Shakespeare and set it to music in the romantic style of Schubert or Schumann with a piano part in the style of the German *lieder*. Sometimes my parents leave the house early on a Sunday morning and return after dark to see me still struggling at the piano.

After a grueling week my keyboard harmony class is assigned the task of transposing a Bach Invention into three keys. With all the contrapuntal melodies and repetitions in different keys that weave their ways through the invention I find it impossible to complete the assignment on the day it is due. I call my friend Judy, my old buddy from Music and Art and ask her how she's managing. "Impossible," she tells me. "I can barely play the invention in its original key, let alone three. Let's ask for an extension. We'll each tell Dr. Laufer that we couldn't get it done and when he sees that both of us are overwhelmed he might give us an extension. I'll call Marilyn and see if she wants to come in on the deal. There's strength in numbers."

I come to class on Monday morning, without my assignment but secure in the knowledge that three of us couldn't finish it. Marilyn is absent and Judy comes to school with the assignment completed. I feel betrayed. Now I am the only one in the class who is unprepared and am embarrassed in front of the class. My instructor is not aware of the fact that I do not have the entire week-end to do my work. Saturday is a day of rest and a taboo day for homework. He tells me that he expects the assignment in by the next day or I will be marked "incomplete" and face the possibility of not only getting a lower grade but possible failure.

I confront Judy, "why didn't you let me know that you were not going to stick to our agreement?" I am deeply hurt by Judy's actions.

"Oh, I couldn't sleep all night so I worked from 4 A.M. until I got it done. I couldn't exactly call you at 6:30 and tell you. I was afraid I'd wake up your entire family."

Now I know why she and I were never friends in high school. Her ambition and sense of competition far outweighed her other qualities.

CHAPTER 4

I DECIDE NOT to join a sorority. First of all I am scared that I might be rejected by the sorority. I cannot face that possibility, and prefer not to take the risk. I also hate the exclusivity that is part of the sisterhood, I hate the idea of having to be admitted, voted in or voted out. Moreover, I find the concept of pledging, carrying around every brand of cigarette and gum in order to appease the sorority sisters repulsive. There is the very realistic knowledge that I do not have enough money to pay the dues, buy evening gowns for dances and really be part of the group.

I join what is called a "house plan." The house plan consists of boys clubs and girls clubs made up of young people, like myself, who would like to meet members of the opposite sex but for one reason or another opt out of joining a sorority or fraternity. I am dying to get a boyfriend, meet a boy, or get a date. I feel as though I am the only girl in the entire college who has not had a date since beginning of my college career. Harriett is a fellow student from Music and Art. She is majoring in English literature and we become friends. We join a house plan which consists of about six or seven other girls. Our only reason for being in the club is to go to parties and meet boys. We have no other agenda.

We have a meeting on a sunny Tuesday in November. "There is a boys' house plan in Brooklyn Tech that has invited us to a party on Saturday Night," Myra the leader tells us.

"Where in Brooklyn?" I ask uneasily. Brooklyn is like a foreign country for me. The only place I know how to get to in Brooklyn is my Aunt Sari's house in Crown Heights.

"Well, if we all go together we should have no trouble finding it," Myra tells us.

Harriet and I decide to meet at the Forest Hills subway station and then hook up with the othersa at the party. "I'm sure there'll be several house plans at the party," Myra reassures us. When Harriet and I arrive we find that we're the only girls here. Myra and the other girls do not appear. We wait around for a while but when no other girls show up Harriett wants to go home. "It's not worth it," she tells me. "We're the only girls and I don't feel like dancing with so many of those students from Brooklyn Tech. It's not a good thing," she tells me. I sort of agree with her but feel that there might be some hope of meeting a nice guy if we go in.

"We really have nothing to lose, we're already here," I argue. "We can always leave if it gets uncomfortable. We enter timidly, a room with at least twenty boys.

"Where are the rest of you?" one of them asks.

We shrug our shoulders. "I guess they didn't come."

"Your whole house plan was only able to get the two of you to come?" a crew-cut boy shouts at us.

"Don't yell at us," Harriett tells him. "We're here. It's all the others you should be mad at." Harriet and I exchange glances. We decide that it was not such a good idea to walk in. We slowly back out of the room and run down the stairs to catch the next subway back home.

That was my last experience with the house plan idea

CHAPTER 5

⁌

I WORK AS a counselor at day camp every summer. The pay is good and I love working with little kids. I supplement this income with baby-sitting and am able to save enough money to go to the Catskills for a week end. I am nineteen and very eager to meet a boy, have a boyfriend like most of my friends do. The Catskills are known to be fertile ground for sidestepping the matchmaker and acquiring a romantic encounter. This seems like the safest way to meet someone before committing to a date and going out with a "fine young man," with whom I share not a speck of common interest.

One of the resorts in the Catskills is hosting a Zionist convention for a youth group I belong to. For me, this is the best plan. I can tell everyone I know that I'm going because of my interest in Zionism and not have to come home humiliated if I do not meet a boy. I have only one item on my agenda: meet a boy, preferably good-looking and smart but will settle for only one of the qualifications if I must.

A large bulletin board is perched on an easel in front of the dining hall outlining the agenda for the week-end and the various workshops that will be offered. I look around and realize I am not alone in my plans. The boys, standing in small clusters are sizing up the girls and the girls are doing the same with the boys. I manage to avoid all the workshops and concentrate on my make-up, my hair, my dress and assessing my competition.

I lose no time in my pursuit of my goal. Marvin is from Borough Park in Brooklyn, has curly dark hair and a quick smile that reveals sparkling, straight white teeth. He is a good listener and very enthusiastic when I tell him about my hobbies. By Saturday afternoon I am convinced that I'm in love. He takes my phone number before we leave on Sunday promising to call me during the week. Marvin is all I ever dreamed of: he is Jewish, orthodox, and a math major at Brooklyn Tech. I know he is smart because only smart people are accepted at his school, and best of all, he has the demeanor of a boy and not a man. He picks me up to go out the following Saturday night. He is perfect. He wears a jacket and not an overcoat, and sweeps the *yarmulka* off his head the minute we leave my house. I smile, secure in the knowledge that if we meet someone from school I will look like a normal girl out on a Saturday night.

Before we leave the apartment my father has a few questions for him. "Did you go to Yeshiva?" Yes, he tells him, he graduated from Talmudical Academy, from where my brother got kicked out, and is now a junior at Brooklyn Tech. My father gathers as much information as he can; he is one of four boys, his father belongs to a Hungarian synagogue and works in the diamond trade. He, himself, was born in America but both his parents are of Hungarian background. My father runs all the information he got by my Uncle Avrom to determine the desirability of his pedigree. Uncle Avrom who lives in Brooklyn knows many people from his neighborhood as well as from Diamond Club, an almost exclusively orthodox conglomerate of diamond buyers, sellers and brokers. Uncle Avrom, as always, full of information and if he isn't, knows exactly where to go and get it. He returns the call in less than five minutes. He assures my father that Marvin, indeed, comes from a respectable family, his father, though not a professional man is known to be an honest and reliable diamond broker. The family lives comfortably in a private house in Borough Park and that all three of Marvin's siblings attend *Yeshivoth*. These are all important issues for my old fashioned, European father to know about before his only daughter gets involved with a boy. My father knows all this before I am home from our first date.

I am in love with Marvin and convinced I've found true love, at last. By today's standards, our dates are tame. We never go past petting, reserving sex for after marriage. We continue dating until May when Marvin either chickens out of the relationship or has a consuming desire to join the navy (or as my father later puts it, he probably flunked out of Brooklyn Poly-Tech and had nothing else to do with his life).

I go to overnight camp that summer, as a music counselor and Marvin and I correspond with passionate love letters and promises to be true to each other. As luck would have it this is the summer when the opposite sex discovers me. The guy counselors ask me to go out with them after the campers are sent off to bed. I of course decline. I have given my word to Marvin and inform everyone that I am not available.

Marvin continues writing. He is in Italy, Spain and Greece and he tells me how beautiful it is there and that someday he will take me to see these exotic places. So romantic, until the lastweek of camp. His letter arrives a few days later than usual and I save it to read it in a quiet, secluded place where I can have privacy.

I open the envelope gently and carefully extract the tissue thin air-mail stationery. I don't believe my eyes! What am I reading? Marvin, my true love had gotten drunk with some other sailors and gone to every whore house in Marseilles! He wants to break it off with me. He tells me he isn't ready to stay true to one person. He actually has the *chutzpah* to write me that "it is the only decent thing for him to do: not to waste my time waiting for him."

"What a decent guy," I say to myself sarcastically. "So decent that he wastes my whole summer hoping for what will never come true." To add pain to my sorrow, he writes that life is short and he wants to taste all of it. He feels it would not be fair to plan a future together before he has had a taste of what life has to offer. I cannot believe my eyes as my heart slowly sinks and dissolves. What a bastard! He has to wait until the very end of summer to tell me. He is so decent that he has to make sure I don't date any other guys in the camp, that I don't salvage a drop of pleasure for myself. My self-image is demolished. How am I going to tell all my friends that I am dumped for some whores in the Mediterranean?

CHAPTER 6

I START MY junior year in college feeling as though I've been kicked in the stomach, a clothespin of pain is pinching my heart. The loss of Marvin actually has a physical component. I feel like I have swallowed something I cannot swallow, cannot get to pass though my esophagus. I feel unattractive, cast off, unwanted and rejected. I am afraid that any other opportunities I might get will end just as badly. In my 19 year old mind, I think that love comes to you only once in a lifetime and mine has come and gone. All my old fears come to attack me; what if I have to be alone all my life? Who will take care of me when my parents die? My parents can't stand to see me suffer. "I never liked him," my father says. "I always thought he had something shifty in his eyes. And he is dishonest. Why would a senior from Brooklyn Poly-Tech leave college to become a sailor? Unless he flunked out or did something dreadful, no normal person would leave at the end of his junior year without graduating and getting his diploma. Nah, there's something fishy about him." My father tries to comfort me.

My mother has her point of view as well. "He wasn't a gentleman. He was not gallant, not generous, he was unappreciative. He never once sent you a little souvenir from those beautiful places he went to. Not a handkerchief from Greece, a scarf from Italy, or a scented soap from Marseilles. Any kind of trinket to show you he was thinking of you. You could never be happy with a man who behaves this way while he is courting you. You can only imagine how inconsiderate he would be after marriage. You deserve much better, and," she adds, always the optimist, "You are lucky to rid of him. You will receive much better. You are still so young."

I find myself defending him, which is the last thing I want to be doing right now. "He had no money, you know that," I say. "He was a student, he had no income. How could he afford to send me anything?" I wonder what possesses me to be so charitable and forgiving towards Marvin. He acted horribly towards me and yet I don't want to acknowledge that or give my parents the satisfaction of being right. I hate myself. I feel lonely, unwanted, depressed while defending the person who hurt me so deeply. I trudge around with my eyes fastened to the ground going about my work mechanically.

My father is trying hard to cheer me up. He is sure that a new, serious boyfriend will restore me. He approaches Max Schechter, a wealthy business man whose hobby is matchmaking. Mr. Schechter has recently married off two daughters, aged 18 and 19 to wonderful men and he now prides himself on being a perfect *shadchen*. "I know just who should go together," he tells all who listens.

He is the one who found my old friend Naomi a husband and he has made several other fortunate matches. "I take one look at a boy and into my mind pops a perfect girl for him."

My father is reticent about approaching Max Schechter. He asks our neighbor and fellow Shul member, Mr. Finklestein to ask Mr. Schechter if he knows of any prospects for a nice college girl from a good family. He must stipulate "college girl" because sometimes, in the orthodox community, college is a liability for girls. Some families do not permit their daughters to go to college for fear that it might jeopardize their chances in the marriage market. Many of the orthodox boys study in the Yeshiva and would not consider attending universities and so opportunities for educated girls to be eligible for "good marriages" are significantly reduced.

No self- respecting man wants a woman with more education than he has. Fortunately my father encourages me to finish college, achieve independence So that I will never have to rely on anyone but myself.

Mr. Schechter rubs his hands together and nods. He tells my father he has just the right ma. "He comes from a wealthy family, diamond merchants from Belgium and they have a marriageable son who is a Rabbi in Kenosha Wisconsin. He is sort of isolated in Kenosha where there aren't too many choices of Jewish girls from good, religious families." He tells my father that he will give this boy's father a call on Sunday and get back to him during the week. I know nothing of this arrangement. After Shabbes my father once again calls Uncle Avrom to get information on a male prospect. "See what you can find out about the young rabbi's family." My uncle does not need to make any calls. He knows the family himself and wishes he had been the one to suggest the match. "This is a fine, young man, makes a good living as a Rabbi in the Midwest. He is well educated, plays the piano, speaks fluent French and is good looking." Uncle Avrom is certain that this will be a wonderful match for me and my father is sold. A few days later my father calls me into the kitchen. He wants to talk to me. He hesitates, speaks slowly, remembering my past experiences with arranged matches.

"I spoke to Max Schechter and he and Uncle Avrom know of a wonderful young rabbi from Wisconsin who would like to meet you."

I am skeptical, "why would he want to meet me, he doesn't even know me."

"Well, he's heard about you and he seems very interested."

Marvin has shattered my spirit. I think I am ready to settle for anyone who displays any sort of interest. I am tired of living at home with my parents. I also desperately want to get out of the dating scene, waiting for phone calls, fending off unwanted passes, feeling rejected and alone on Saturday nights. I am willing to marry someone I do not love if he can provide an avenue of escape for me. I inform my father that I am ready to go out with Harvey.

343

CHAPTER 7

HARVEY CALLS ME that very night, long distance from Wisconsin. Long distance phone calls are always important. Few people I know get long distance calls from a boy. Maybe he is rich. For sure, he does not mind spending money on long distance. He is pleasant on the phone, has a slight French accent and we plan to go out the following Saturday night. I look forward to the date, get my hair set in the beauty parlor, something I rarely do, and take great pains preparing for this important date. I wear a rose sweater which my father brought back from work that Friday, check my reflection in the mirror from every angle. Assure myself that this is the best I can look.

When the door- bell rings I am ready. My father insists on opening the door and I am told not to come in to the living room for a few minutes. "We don't want him to think you are anxious. Just be casual, you know, don't act like this is a big deal, remember, act casual. Men don't like to feel they are being pursued," my father tells me this as if I come from another planet.

My mother and I listen to their conversation while sitting on the bed in my parents' room. They discuss the trip Harvey took by airplane from Chicago, the closest airport to Kenosha. My father appears very interested. He only traveled by airplane once and that was from Vienna to Poland. I listen for a few more minutes and I figure it's time for me to make an appearance.

My stomach sinks. Harvey looks like everything I don't like in a man. He is not the tall, lean, casual or the collegiate kind of man I am drawn to. He is short and compact, bordering on dumpy, wears a suit with a shirt and tie, and is so fair that he appears not to have eyebrows. His face is sweaty, shiny, eager and if that is not repulsive enough, he is wearing a brown felt fedora hat. How am I going to get through one evening with him, I ask myself? He blushes so profusely when I enter the room that I feel sorry for him.

"Shall we go out now?" he asks me, probably eager to get away from my father's scrutiny.

I decide to make the best of it. I remind myself that this is only for one evening, I don't have to ever see him again, and, I promise myself, I certainly am not going to end up with him. We go to a small kosher dairy restaurant on Queens Boulevard in Forest Hills where I take another look at him. I analyze his looks and wonder why I am so repulsed by him. He really is not that bad looking. His skin is smooth, his eyes a shade of pale blue and really, he looks perfectly acceptable to everyone but me. I listen to him talk, his voice is gentle but he doesn't stop asking me questions: what do I study, is the college work difficult, are there a lot of Jews in college, do they offer courses in religion? I watch him and the memory appears like a ghost. I am transported to Montelupi Prison a place I haven't thought about in many years. I am standing near my mother, clutching the fabric of her dress in my balled up fist, looking up at the Nazi officer's desk where his hat with the swastika and the eagle are perched. The memory makes my heart flutter. I recall my fear, "will this man take me away from my mother and brother? Will he make us get separated?"

I take another look at Harvey sitting opposite me. He has the same white eyelashes and the same gleaming face as the Nazi officer in Monteupi had. His wrists are exposed and large, pink bones protruding from the cuffs of his shirt followed by chubby hands ending in the same, colorless, shiny polished nails. All I can think of is the lecherous Nazi looking at my mother. They are mirror twins. Their features are almost identical but the emotions they display reflect directly opposite feelings. Both have blue eyes but where the Gestapo's were ice, Harvey's burn with intensity, the Nazi's hands were thin and with colorless nail polish,

Harvey's are short and pudgy but with the same manicured shade of polish. The Nazi's body was rigid, stiff and arrogant. Harvey is bent over the table like a camel with a hump. One is a caricature of the other.

Harvey has taken off his hat and is wearing a yarmulke underneath it. I notice that his scull is an exact replica of the Nazi's scull. I am breathless with the memory of Montelupi where the dreadful toilet and the frightened women wept. Against my will, my mind has taken me to a place I want to forget: the stench, the sleeping mats, the clanking steel doors. I try to take a deep breath, distract myself away from that dreadful place but I can't seem to catch a drop of air. I tell myself that I am being ridiculous. These two men are not in the least bit connected. But my feelings are not to be reasoned with. Harvey the Jew and Georg the Nazi could be father and son.

When I get home that night my parents are waiting up for me. "So, how was it?" my father asks. "Did you have a nice time? Do you like him? Do you think he likes you?"

I cannot answer. I am unable to tell them of my true feelings, my disappointment and disillusionment. I can't tell them what they want to hear: that I had a good time, that he is nice, I like him and that we have much in common. The truth of the matter is that the thought of his touching me makes me think of white worms crawling in a garbage heap and this I cannot share with my hopeful parents. "I'm tired, I'll tell you tomorrow," I say good night and go to bed.

The next day, before I have a chance to speak to my parents there is a delivery of a dozen red roses from Harvey thanking me for a wonderful evening. He returns to Wisconsin on Sunday afternoon and I pray that I never have to hear from him again. Of course that doesn't happen. My parents are thrilled with the roses. "See?" my mother says triumphantly. "This is how you treat a girl. You show her respect, value."

My father is equally overjoyed. "A generous boy, a boy with manners," he tells my mother. There is no opportunity for me to tell them what I think and that is probably for the best. Harvey calls during the week. He will be in New York again in two weeks and would I go out with him? I agree to thinking maybe I should give him another chance. Maybe this time I'll get past my memories.

The two weeks pass. I have school, homework and practicing and I don't give much thought to Harvey. It is December, almost time for winter break and I plan to go out with my girlfriends during vacation. We will be going to Carnegie Hall on Saturday night to hear Handel's Messiah, Radio City Music Hall for the Christmas Show and ice skating at the Wollman Memorial Skating Rink in Central Park.

I am caught completely by surprise when Harvey calls on a Thursday evening informing me that he is in New York again and would love to see me. "How about Sunday afternoon," he suggests. "That way we won't have to rush to get home before it's very late." I think about my friend Naomi of whom I was so very critical not so long ago. I wondered how she could choose security over romance and I realize I am about to do the same thing.

I agree to the date and he says that he will try to get tickets to "My Fair Lady." I know they'll be impossible to get. That show has been sold out for months and besides during the Christmas season it is almost impossible to get tickets to any Broadway show.

He arrives on Sunday promptly at one P.M. and when I ask him where we're going, he digs into his and produces the two tickets to "My Fair Lady." I am astounded.

"How did you ever manage that?"

"My brother has connections," he tells me refusing to divulge more information. The show is spectacular, and Harvey suggests that we go to Seigel's, the expensive, kosher restaurant which I've never been to. He is spending money on me like there is no limit to his funds. I am able to tolerate him much better this time than on our first date and when my parents ask me how my day went, I tell them it was fine. This time a dozen white roses appear with a thank you note. I could learn to love this kind of life if only it didn't come attached to him.

After several more dates, Harvey proposes. I tell him this is too quick, I need more time and that I hardly know him. He brushes my hesitation aside, "Look," he says, trying to sound reasonable, "I know everything about you I need to know. Actually, I knew all about you before I even went out with you. You can't pretend that our families didn't make inquiries to find out if we were suitable for one another. The going out with you is only an American accommodation to the ancient rites of marriage among our people." My cheeks turn to flames, I am so embarrassed. He doesn't even try to pretend that this was a blind date. On top of all my negative feelings for him, I find his reaction arrogant. There is no shred or illusion of romance in our relationship. My first instinct is to say No, I cannot marry you, but something tells me to not be so impulsive. I tell him I must think it over and that I need to discuss this with my parents. I don't dismiss him as I would like to but take all things into consideration. After all, what he said is true, my family approved of him before they had a chance to see him.

On one level he is very kind, generous and thoughtful but physically I find him not only unappealing but downright repulsive. In my heart I feel that I must break it off with him. It isn't fair of me to be taking advantage of his generosity. He wants to get married and so do I, but definitely not to him. I badly want my parents' approval. I want them to be proud of me, to feel that I have accomplished the goals they have set. I want to leave home in a respectable way, but most of all I want to be desirable, to have someone love me enough to marry me. Harvey lacks all potential for romance but I am afraid, that he might be my last chance.

I have a talk with my father and tell him how I feel, that I find Harvey repulsive. Inexplicably, my father displays a side of himself that I have never encountered. He is sympathetic, understanding, "you can't continue seeing him if this is how you feel. This is not how you go into a marriage. You'll have to tell him." I expected my father to be angry at me for refusing such a good prospect and am totally unprepared for his empathy. My father understands, is on my side and doesn't want me to do anything I don't want to do. But then, in contradiction to what he has just said, he muses, as if to himself, "it is difficult to marry off a daughter. You always worry, will her husband treat her well, will he provide for her, take care of her needs? One thing I know about Harvey is that he will always do those things for you. I will never have to worry about your welfare if you marry him." I am back to where I was before our discussion. I desperately want my father's approval, and marrying Harvey would guarantee that. Nevertheless, when I tell my father how I feel, he supports me and then removes his support by interjecting his own feelings.

I make a decision. I am going to break it off with Harvey that very evening, before I chicken out and waste any more of his time. I tell my father and I notice that he is visibly disappointed. He looks dejected and tells me that he does not want to greet Harvey when he comes to pick me up. He doesn't want to face him knowing what is coming. I am going to have to manage this alone. Michael warns me, "be careful what you say to him. He might make a scene. He's been pursuing you like a crazy man. Don't expect him to give up without a fight." What if he puts up terrific fight? What if he begs me to marry him in a loud, loud voice? What if he accuses me of being a gold digger, of taking advantage of his generosity? I am filled with apprehension and with the prospect of the upcoming evening.

We are sitting in a neighborhood, dairy restaurant where I prepare to tell Harvey that I can't continue seeing him. I make up some story about not feeling ready for marriage, needing time out in the world, try to improve my outlook, finish my education before committing to another person, blah, blah…. To my shock and surprise Harvey takes it amazingly well. He is not crushed as I feared he might be. He takes it like a man. For someone who courted me so avidly he is remarkably good natured about it. He understands. "Of course I understand. I'm not a baby. I know that there are chances and risks we have to take in life and although I must tell you I am disappointed, because I really think you are the girl for me but I will get over this." The more he talks, the more reasonable he sounds and though I hate to admit it, I am gaining a measure of respect for him. "I really would like you to give this some more thought and possibly reconsider," he goes on, "don't feel pressured," he adds. "Just promise me you'll think it over. Either way, I'll be alright." He doesn't even look or sound upset. Suddenly he looks like less of a nebbish and more like a man. I wonder if I am making a mistake by breaking it off. Perhaps this is the best way to get out of going on dates with losers and remaining in my parents' home.

I give it a lot of thought. I weigh the pros and cons, consider how wonderful it would be to have my own apartment and my own furniture and then I thinks about Harvey's broad, sweating face, his big belly, his large wrists protruding from his cuffs and his plump, fleshy hands. I really don't want to marry Harvey. The more I think about it the more determined I am to break off with him. I still long for a passionate romance like the one I had with Marvin. As Harvey himself said not so long ago, we all take chances and risks and I will just have to take the risk of possibly being hurt again but not giving up on my dreams. I am only twenty years old and I will finish college, get a job and stop worrying about marriage. I am resolved. And then as if on cue, I hear my father yelling at Michael.

He berates him for not getting up early enough to be in school on time. He has received another phone call from the Rabbi, principal of Michael's school. "Michael is lazy, he cannot get to school on time, is a bad influence on the other boys." The Rabbi tells my father that if Michael doesn't buckle up and get serious, his career at the yeshiva will be over. Poor Michael, I know he suffers from dreadful stomach pains, which will later be diagnosed as Crohn's disease. He lies on the sofa in the morning clutching a hot water bottle, unable to move. My father yells at him telling him that he is lazy, there is nothing wrong with him. All he wants is an excuse not to go to school. "At the rate you are going you will bring me nothing but shame, you have already brought me shame." Michael is nonchalant, he shrugs his shoulders, makes no attempts to excuse his behavior, acts as though nothing my father says or does will bear any impact upon him, as though my father is telling him about some other person, one he hardly knows and certainly does not care about. In the meantime, that old worm of resentment and pain creeps into my heart. It's always about Michael. Never mind that I am dying inside, am in a quagmire of indecision. With him it's always about Michael: poor Michael, lucky Michael, lazy Michael, dishonest Michael. It's as though I don't exist.

And suddenly, I have my answer. I must leave this house. I can't listen to any more of the abuse my father piles on us. I can't bear to watch Michael behaving so passively, acting like the abuse is being hurled at some stranger. I don't want to wait another minute. I feel I must leave this home whether there will be romance or aversion. Nothing can compare to my home life. Nothing can be more upsetting and disturbing. I can't afford the promise of romance. I call Harvey and tell him I've made a decision.

CHAPTER 8

⚜

EVERYONE IN MY family is happy for me. My father feels secure in the knowledge that his daughter will be provided for, my mother is happy that I will have a thoughtful, generous husband, my Uncle Avrom is pleased that our family will be joining up with a very good family who also happens to be in the diamond business, Max Schechter is proud that he was able to make another successful match. I seem to be the only one who is not sure if I am doing the right thing. Before I have a chance to accustom myself to the idea marriage, plans start taking shape. A wedding date is set, invitations are sent out and gifts come through the mail and "thank you" notes are dispatched. I will take my finals for the last semester in January and have already decided that there is no point for me to return to school for the spring semester. The wedding is scheduled for March and I won't be able to finish the term or get credit for the courses I can't complete.

With three semesters left to my graduation, my parents encourage me to finish college in Wisconsin. The only problem is that there are no colleges near Kenosha. There are several community colleges and technical schools, but no college that meets university criteria. There is a university in Milwaukee, but that is a forty mile drive from Kenosha and not only do we not own a second car, I don't even know how to drive. Regretfully, I decide to give up on college for the time being. In a matter of days I have gone from being a B+ college student to an insecure bride.

My mother takes me shopping for my trousseau and I get caught up in the wedding plans thinking of married life with Harvey in a small town in the Midwest, I am reminded of my old Soap Opera, "Our Gal Sunday." The program is probably still trying to answer the question of "whether a poor girl from a small mining town in Colorado could find happiness as the wife of a wealthy, titled nobleman." I wonder if I will find happiness as the wife of an unattractive rabbi in a small town in the middle of Wisconsin.

Harvey flies back to Kenosha. He makes sure that I do not forget him by sending me flowers every Friday for Shabbes and writing often. The long distance phone calls have petered out. Now that he is sure he has me secured we find that we have little to talk about. I love wearing a two karat diamond solitaire on the fourth finger of my left hand, especially when I return to school for that final week of exams. Like several other girls, I have become engaged over winter break. I appear happy to all those around me, and the ring provides me with a good deal of comfort. For the time being I try to put the future out of my mind.

CHAPTER 9

THE WEDDING IS to take place on March 11, 1957 at the Broadway Central Hotel, the place where almost all the orthodox couples I know get married. In spite of my resolve to stop worrying about the future with Harvey, I continue to vacillate. I am glad to be out of the "rat race," but I feel shaky about my wisdom in agreeing to a loveless marriage with Harvey. I know my father would have accepted my decision to call the engagement off, but my confusion and fear overshadow all romantic feelings. I have decided to give up love and passion and chosen safety, security, belonging, being taken care o and, the threat of rejection. Most of all, I know I am anxious to get away from my father's house. I tell myself that I am doing the right thing. I tell myself that it is better to go into a relationship with my eyes open than be blinded by passion and stars in my eyes. Harvey might not represent love and desire but he does represent security and freedom from fear, and for these reasons I agree to a convenient arranged match just as my friend Naomi did not so long ago and as my grandmothers did a century ago.

I spend time with my future in-laws and notice peculiarities about them that make me question everything about them.. Their apartment on Riverside Drive is in an elegant building with a lush lobby and a uniformed doorman. It promises a luxurious interior. When we get off the elevator, even before we enter the apartment I am immediately struck by the odor of mothballs mingled with pungent cooking smells: fried onions, garlic, and spices which I cannot identify. The apartment itself, with its high ceilings and large windows overlooking the Hudson River appears in a state of chaos: jackets and coats are carelessly thrown

across the backs of chairs, newspapers are spread on the sofa and coffee table, and an uncorked bottle of dark amber liquid stands precariously on a pile of books, mail is strewn across the dining room table. I
feel myself recoiling from the disarray.

His parents come to the hallway to welcome me and I notice how
unmatched they are as a couple. His mother wears an old fashioned,
unstyled *sheytl* and her loose fitting dentures shift in her mouth every
time she tries to smile or speak. She is a tiny woman resembling a
pre-pubescent girl, who in spite of having given birth to seven children
has no breasts and no hips and appears to be sexless. She speaks no
English and I have to dig around in my brain to gather enough Yiddish
words to answer her questions. She has a peculiar way of giggling over
everything I say. She sits down on the sofa and motions for me to come
and sit beside her. She seems restless and soon gropes under the starts
to sofa cushion pulling out a dirty sock out from beneath it. She dangles
it in front of me and starts laughing only to stop and run her tongue
around her teeth making sure that they have not become dislodged. I
don't know how to act in her presence. Do I laugh with her at the sight
of the sock, or pretend to ignore it?

Harvey's father is a dapper short man dressed in a carefully tailored
gray tweed suit. He wears a contrasting vest that is clearly designed
to bring out the blues in the tweed suit. His shoes are polished to a
dazzling shine and his shirt is carefully pressed. He moves around the
room like a satyr, light on his feet and always in motion. Unlike his wife,
he speaks a very good, though accented English. Every now and then
he interjects a four syllable word where it is inappropriate. "Isn't this a
lustrous day?" he asks me, referring to the bright, sunny weather, or "do
you mind if I partake of a cigar?"

I can't figure them out. They live in a large, three bedroom apartment
on fashionable Riverside Drive with an unmarried daughter, a divorced
son, a divorced daughter and her two teen aged children: seven adults
in three bedrooms. All the architectural details in the apartment allude
to wealth and artistic taste, the beautifully sculpted molded and the

crystal chandelier are in sharp contrast to the shabby, neglected state the apartment is in now. The wallpaper is peeling, the drapes, once probably purple have faded to a nondescript shade of olive and brown and hang shapelessly in front of grimy windows. Spiders have made their nests in the corners of the ceiling which are now festooned with cobwebs. The sofa and all the upholstered furniture is threadbare and covered with mismatched blankets.

I think about how my own mother decorates our Spartan homes. She buys a mirror at the thrift store to reflect extra light from the windows and offer an illusion of space, she finds a painting in the same store and hangs it on a bare wall, she sews curtains that gracefully frame the windows and embroiders a sheet which she turns it into an elegant tablecloth. "You can never be too clean or too neat," she would tell me when she brushed my hair vigorously until it was shining. She opens the windows on the coldest of mornings to let the fresh air in and dispel any odors that might be trapped in the house. My mother is the queen of clean while Harvey's mother appears to be the exact opposite.

CHAPTER 10

THE WEDDING TAKES off without a hitch. The ceremony, the guests, the music and even the photographs depict a joyous moment but the marriage itself is doomed from the start. We both married for all the wrong reasons, hoping to have wishes fulfilled. I married Harvey because I was tired of dating and scared I might have to face another devastating rejection. I want security and the assurance that someone will care for my needs. I hated living at home where I was criticized, told what to wear and I was desperate to get away from the ever watchful eye of my father.

I marry Harvey to get away from my mother who has sold out to my father, who no longer protects me as she did when we were in Europe, whom I cannot count on as an ally. I marry to get away from Michael who never fails to incur my father's wrath and attention which I somehow equate with love and investment. I hope that with Harvey I will be able to become my own person, make decisions, stop regretting the past and fearing the future.

Harvey marries me because he needs a wife. His congregants are constantly asking him if he has any prospects. He feels that they expect a rabbi to be married and that he is missing the mark by being single. He feels a sense of obligation to his congregation to have a suitable wife. Even though the congregation he serves is conservative, he wants an orthodox bride, one who will maintain a kosher home, observe all the rituals, the prayers, is able to help out by teaching in the Hebrew School as well as the Sunday School. He wants a bride who appears "American" and the fact that I am a "college girl" attests to this. Our hopes and desires are not enough to build a marriage.

Harvey is one series of disappointments after another. I never expected much in the romance department, although our first night together held out some promise, it soon dissipated into a ritual where Harvey gets what he needs and I tolerate the inevitable. It is a love-less marriage and again I blame myself. I keep reminding myself that I knew what I was getting myself into, that I wanted security and willingly traded myself for it. However, Harvey does not deliver on the promises he made. Where I was led to believe that Harvey earned a good salary, was a responsible man able to support me and provide a secure envi-ronment free of financial worries, the very opposite is true.

When we return from our honeymoon in Miami Beach I am dismayed by the bills overflowing the mailbox. Harvey owes money for everything he bought in the past three months. He used credit to send me flowers every Friday afternoon, "easy pay" installments for the several suits he bought before the wedding. He purchases furniture (without consult-ing me) for our apartment on a lay-away plan, he owes money for the laundry bills, for three months of car payments to GMAC, for the car he bought most recently. Harvey owes money to HFC for the airplane tickets to come to New York.

For Harvey all these bills are for "necessities." For me they are stagger-ing. I come from a frugal home where the concept of credit was unheard of, and where no one owed anyone money, where the family motto is "if you can't afford you don't want it." My family was poor but we never borrowed money and never owed anyone anything. These bills are over-whelming, will have to be paid and I have no idea how that will happen.

"Harvey," I entreat him, "why did you ever send me flowers if you didn't have the money to pay for them?" He doesn't understand. To him, credit is just like money. On some naïve level he has not grasped the notion that bills must be paid.

"I'll be getting a paycheck in April," Harvey tries to assuage my fears. "I'll pay the bills then."

"For God's sakes, how much do you earn?" I have tallied the bills and there is no way will we be able to pay the over thousand dollars he owes for all the items he bought. I was told in New York, before I agreed to marry him that he was earning six hundred dollars a month. In 1957, this is considered a reasonable, though modest wage. Suddenly, I am struck by how poor we really are. I am on the verge of becoming hysterical. "How will we ever manage to save enough money to pay these off?"

Harvey tries to allay my fears. He actually smiles and shakes his head in disbelief. "You are so naïve," he tells me sounding reasonable. "Nobody pays their bills off in full. If they did that no one would buy anything and the stores would go out of business. The idea is to keep paying the minimum and keep the owners satisfied. "See?" he points to a bill, "it says 'minimum payment twenty dollars'. I only have to pay twenty dollar this time."

I don't understand. How will twenty dollars satisfy a debt for over two hundred dollars? Harvey acts patient with me, "you are so innocent. Everyone owes money to everyone else. That's what keeps America running." If he is right, I am naïve. If spending money we do not have is the smart way to do things then I am stupid. This is such sharp contrast to my family's values. There is no way I can accept what he is saying.

In May, the following month, all the old bills reappear only this time there is a hefty interest charge attached to last month's statements. This month, instead of owing $2000, our bills amount to the staggering sum of $2067.56. Harvey's salary cannot begin to cover the amount he owes. I am in a panic. Here in Kenosha, there is no one I can turn to for advice or help. I can't possibly ask my parents for financial help, they have already spent a fortune on my wedding. Harvey keeps feeding me fairy tales about owing money not being a bad thing. He appears carefree, content and complacent. I look at him and conclude that it is he who is the innocent, naïve dupe, buying all the stories that the credit companies are out there selling. I realize that I will have to be the responsible partner in this marriage and I do not want that job.

I present an ultimatum. "We are not buying anything but food until these bills are reduced. So far, with every twenty dollars you pay, the bill only seems to be getting higher." But there are things other than food that we have to pay for. We have pay rent, buy gasoline for the car, pay for electricity, phone and for water usage. Regretfully I realize that although I was willing to give up passion and romance to receive security and freedom, I have been cheated and receive neither. Harvey, who promised me security and loving care proves to be irresponsible, childish and stupid. I am forced to accept the fact that he can't even meet his own obligations and responsibilities let alone those of another human being. I was unsure of marrying Harvey. I made a deal to give up my desire for romance and passion for the security of financial independence and a place in my society, I get neither. If anything, Harvey offers less security than my family did. My chronically unemployed father who not long ago told me that marriage to Harvey would free his mind from worry about me was dead wrong.

I am lost in Kenosha. It is a small town in the Midwest where there is not one museum, movie-theater, or public transportation. Harvey's congregation is made up of lapsed Jews, very few of whom observe any of the rituals required of practicing Jews. Most of the congregants are retired, elderly people with a handful of young couples with small children. I have no piano, no friends and nothing to do. The public library is too far to walk to and with Harvey being gone most of the day I have no way to get there. I think I might try to invest some energy into the synagogue. It is a beautiful, old building with gothic details in its architecture. It has been neglected over the years, some of the stained glass is replaced by plain window glass, the pews can use some varnish, and the dull curtain that hangs in front of the ark should be replaced with something brighter. I see possibilities for a synagogue beautification project.

I attend a Lady's Auxiliary Committee meeting and listen to hear if there is anything I might get interested in. I am shy and not eager to make suggestions and so I listen to a treasurer's report, some plans to replenish the prayer book supply, possibly plant a small garden in the front. Everything they talk about is so boring. All the women are either retired or stay at home wives, tending to their husband's and children's needs. They talk about recipes, sales at the small general store, TV shows. Other than living in Kenosha I have nothing in common with them.

When the president asks for new business, and none comes up, I raise my hand timidly. "I think perhaps we might consider a synagogue renovation project. I don't mean anything major. But perhaps we could buy some fabric and sew a new curtain for the ark?"

The response is not encouraging. Sara says the curtain has been there for years and "if it isn't broken why fix it?" The others agree with her. "We love the old tradition that this synagogue holds. Besides the curtain is a gift to the Synagogue in memory of Morris Cohen, the founder of the s*shul*. We do not have enough money in the treasury to take on any new projects." I am disappointed. Now, I understand how my mother feels when she tries to make things pretty and does not have the funds. I know that we can make a new curtain without spending much money.

Foolishly I persist with other ideas. "Would it be possible for us to open a Lady's Auxiliary gift shop? There are plenty of empty rooms at the synagogue, one of which could be converted into a gift shop. We could order everything from a catalogue, maybe even get some stuff from Israel and this way we could make some money and offer a ser-vice to the Jewish community of Kenosha. If someone needs Chanukah candles, a *mezuzah* or a *menorah, a new tallith or a* pretty yarmulke, they would not have to run to Milwaukee or Chicago. We could supply it and make money as well."

"I really don't thinks so," the treasurer informs me. "We are in no position to buy inventory, and none of us would have the time to staff a gift shop open on a regular basis."

At the next meeting I bring up the possibility of planning a show. We could charge money for admission and have fun. We could even make it a dinner show and set up tables for a "cabaret night." I am persistent. I am desperate to breathe some life into this decaying Jewish popula-tion, find a way I might be useful and productive instead of bored.

Every suggestion is met with rejection. I feel embarrassed when my ideas are shot down and I take it personally. I never think that these people may not be eager to have a young girl from New York take charge of projects they have no interest in. There is not one person in all of Kenosha that I can confide in. There is no point in calling old friends in New York since we are trying to save money and even more important than that, I want everyone to think that I am completely filled with happiness.

CHAPTER 11

⚶

I START TO think about getting a job. That way I could bring in some money and find an outlet for all the time I have on my hands. Harvey tells me that I cannot get a job as a sales clerk in Kenosha. It would not look right for the rabbi's wife to stand behind a counter in the small department store selling gloves and scarves to the members of the congregation. I consult the phone book and discover that there is an American Motors plant which manufactures Rambler/Nash cars in Racine. Racine is twenty minutes from Kenosh, and if I get a job there Harvey could take me to work early in the morning and pick me up in the evening. A factory is a big place. I might find something in the sales department or perhaps some small office job.

I talk Harvey into driving to Racine, go to the employment office and inquire about any suitable job at the American Motors Company. I have no typing or shorthand skills so an office job is out. They are only able to offer me work on the assembly line. Even though I don't want to consider that type of work, I tell the employment person that I will think it over.

That evening, a Thursday night, when my parents call to see how my week went, I tell my father that I was interviewed for a job at the American motors which offered me work on the assembly line. Before I get a chance to tell him that I won't consider this his anger is aroused. He flies into a rage. "You're gonna' work on an assembly line? For this you went to college? For this you play the piano? For this we sacrificed so that you could get a profession? Let me speak to Harvey," he demands. Harvey doesn't want to talk to him. He actually cowers against a wall making signs with his hands that he will not talk to my father. I get back on the phone and tell him that Harvey stepped out to buy a newspaper."

Two weeks later, unexpectedly, my parents surprise me by telling me of a trip they'll be taking to see us in Kenosha. They decide on the spur of the moment to come and see us. They have packed a suitcase and food for the trip, and make the long drive to Wisconsin. My parents have come to see for themselves why I would even consider a job. "Anyway," they tell me, "we miss you. It's been a long time and we want to see how your lives are going so we can rest assured that you are happy." I don't believe them for one moment. They want to see what could possibly have motivated me to look for employment on an assembly line in a factory. After a good deal of questioning on the phone, they realize I won't tell them. I have never told my parents about our financial problems but somehow my father senses that something is wrong.

After two days of visiting and relaxing, my father declares that he wants to see our expenses, namely, Harvey's bills. Harvey tries to avoid the confrontation that he suspects is looming. "I have all my bills at the synagogue, in my office," he tells my father hesitating. He is visibly nervous and stutters, "thi… , thi… this is not a good ti…, ti… time to go there. He appears, scared. Worry wrinkles make deep ridges on his bland forehead, and he retreats like a frightened, shrinking shadow. He actually backs away, positioning himself in the corner of the room, leaning against two walls. My father will not be put off.

"Harvey, look, we both know that I will not leave Kenosha until I see for myself why Rita, my only daughter, a college student would consider working in an automobile factory. So why don't we drive down to your office and take a look at them." Harvey hesitates. He does not want to be alone in a car with my father. He goes into the bedroom, to the top drawer in the dresser and produces the statements which are mixed in with his socks and underwear.

Harvey is sweating now, he tries to talk to my father but my father isn't listening to any explanations. He puts on a pair of recently acquired reading glasses and studies the bills. When he finally looks up at us I can see that he is appalled, tears are welling up in the corner of his eyes. He sits down on an ottoman, grabs his head in his hands and wails, "what have I done? What have I done to my daughter?" He pulls his hair, and the unwanted tears come to his eyes. I have never seen my father in such pain. His reaction seems to be out of proportion and although it frightens me I feel a thrill of joy. My father does care for me. He regrets encouraging me to me marry Harvey. He even goes so far as to admit that he was being selfish. "I was only thinking of my needs," he acknowledges. "I wanted to be free of worry about you, wanted to think that I was finding the right husband to take care of you. What have I done?" he berates himself. "You are a competent person, Rita. You could have done everything you needed to do without my interference. I should have never relied on Avrom to get an accurate report. Avrom is old fashioned. He only wanted to see you married and he thought that any family that had no scandal was a good family."

I want to comfort my father, explain that I was compliant. I wanted to be out of the dating scene and be protected from another broken heart. But much as I feel I ought to, I can't take a step toward him. I am moved by his anguish, but my tears are folded like a fist in my throat unwilling to thaw and give me the welcome relief that tears provide. My father berated my tears not so long ago and I find it impossible to let them flow. I feel my father's sorrow and commiserate with it, but feel almost removed from my situation, it is as though his pain overshadows mine.

My father stands up, grabs the front of Harvey's shirt, and faces him. Harvey has shrunken to a shame faced remnant of his former self. He tries to extricate himself from my father's grip but is unable to wrest himself free.

"Don't you see what you've done? You're not a free man. You have enslaved yourself and my daughter to a life of debt. These creditors are not lending you money. They are buying your future, ensuring that you will always owe them more money than you have. At the rate you're going you will owe them until the day you die. None of your payments are being applied to what you owe: it's all going to pay off the interest while your bills are getting higher."

My father stops, takes a time out to thinks quietly. Then, tells Harvey and me that he has saved up some money for his old age. He will lend it to us. We are to use the money to pay off all of Harvey's bills with the proviso that Harvey stop buying on credit and buy nothing that he cannot pay for in cash. He is to make payments to my father in the amount of one hundred dollars per month until the debt is completely paid off. My father will not charge him interest, as that is forbidden in the Torah, and he wouldn't do it anyway to a son-in-law. But, he writes up the agreement into a contract and maybe just for the effect makes Harvey take him to a notary to have it stamped and official looking.

He tells him that he is doing it for me and not for Harvey. He doesn't want to see his daughter so burdened. He tells him that he is grossly disappointed. In addition to the financial debacle he realizes that Kenosha is not a place he wants his daughter to live in. He tells Harvey that he will have to look for another position closer to the east coast, in a town that has a university and opportunities for his daughter to grow. He keeps referring to me as "his daughter" and not as "Rita" or "your wife." I feel the warmth and pleasure cascade down my body. My father has acknowledged me for what I am. He has pride in his heart and for this I am grateful. He looks at me and adds, "just because you are married does not mean I have to give up my hopes and dreams for you."

CHAPTER 12

⸙

THIS TIME MY father does not rely of Uncle Avrom to get him information about Harvey. He does some research of his own and discovers, once more, that Harvey is not who he portrays himself to be. It seems that he did not receive a proper ordination from a reputable Yeshiva or board of rabbis. His family purchased a "Certificate of Ordination" from a scam organization which provides all sorts of documents to people who are willing to pay for them. This one, issued by an association that goes by the Hebrew name of *vad harabonim*, charged $200 and proclaimed Harvey to be a rabbi. My father tells us that in order for Harvey to become eligible for a respectable pulpit, he will have to study and pass a difficult, comprehensive examination. My father finds a highly regarded rabbi in Milwaukee who agrees to study with Harvey and help him pass the rigorous exam. Harvey travels to Milwaukee to meet with him once a week for a three hour study session. In the meantime he reads the "Rabbis Wanted" columns in the Jewish newspapers that arrive weekly. He is following all the strictures that my father placed upon him especially in repaying the money he lent him.

In the middle of July several promising jobs begin to appear in the Jewish newspapers. Harvey replies to several and is invited to visit one in a conservative congregation in the city of Willimantic, Connecticut. He is instructed to bring his wife along. The members want to meet her as well. I buy a tailored new dress for the occasion and a new beret to match. We decide to drive to New York where we will spend two weeks vacationing visiting relatives and friends and from there drive to Willimantic which is less than 150 miles away.

On a summer Friday we set out for the small New England town. Harvey is asked to prepare a service for Sabbath morning and told that on the following Sunday the board of directors will meet in the morning in private and with him in the afternoon. Hopefully, he will have a definite answer by Sunday.

Willimantic turns out to be a charming small town, with a Main Street where all the stores are located. Unlike Kenosha, with its flat, uninteresting terrain, Willimantic is in a hilly portion of New England and has a noisy river bisecting the town. It is a bright day with low humidity and skies unobstructed by clouds. I am enchanted. We check into the old hotel and then rush off to investigate the side streets and locate the synagogue.

That evening we are invited to dinner at the home of the president of the congregation. At first I feel uncomfortable eating at a stranger's home, but they are very welcoming and encourage me to talk about myself. I explain that I am hoping to get my degree and the president's wife tells me that there is a Teacher's College right in Willimantic itself and that the University of Connecticut is a few miles away in Storrs. I should have no problem transferring my credits from Queen's College. Willimantic looks more promising with every passing hour and I hope that Harvey will be able to land a position in the synagogue.

The following day is the Sabbath and it seems the whole congregation has turned out to meet the new prospect. After the cantor leads the morning prayers, Harvey delivers a "home run" sermon. He looks and sounds secure and authoritative. I am surprised at how well he has engaged the congregation; every eye is focused on the young rabbi and everyone seems to listening attentively. After the services we stand on the sunny parking lot, shaking hands, smiling and listening as the members pile praise on Harvey. "I think we did it," Harvey tells me later in the hotel. "This is a young, enthusiastic congregation, they have over seventy-five children attending Hebrew and Sunday school and they are planning to erect a new building. This is a congregation with a future." I am thrilled. I can easily see myself fitting in, not only into the synagogue but into the town itself. After services we are invited to one of the congregant's home for a lunch and afternoon of conversation.

On Sunday morning we walk to the synagogue for the verdict. I am nervous. I so badly hope that Harvey will land the job. Willimantic has everything I want: it is close to New York, has a college in the town itself, and the members are friendly. Several of them have questions for Harvey, like, what was his last salary, what his stand is on intermarriage, how he feels about converts, does he believe in using a lot of English prayers, and then they ask him if he has any questions or if there is anything I would like to ask. I do. I ask if anyone would object to my attending Willimantic Teachers College. The interview is over and the job is his. We are both elated and start making plans before we get back to our car.

When we return to Kenosha to gather up our belongings and inform the congregation that we will be moving to Connecticut an unpleasant surprise awaits us in the letterbox. It seems that one of the congregations Harvey had contacted looks for references and gets in touch with the president of the Kenosha synagogue. When the president of the Kenosha synagogue realizes that we are planning on leaving he dashes off a nasty note telling Harvey that he knows of his treachery and Harvey is fired retroactively to our going on vacation. The congregation is not going to pay him for the summer vacation, money we were counting on. Harvey takes this news much more calmly than I do. "We are leaving this wretched little town and we're never coming back. Let's take joy in this and not dwell on the miserable people who live here." Harvey is enthusiastic while I wail, "What about the money?

Within a few days we rent a U-Haul truck and load everything we own into it, hitch it to the back of our Chevy and drive out of Kenosha without saying good-bye to anyone. We park the truck in front of my parents' apartment because our home in Willimantic won't be ready until the first of September.

CHAPTER 13

WILLIMANTIC, A SMALL industrial town, home to the American Thread Company is surrounded by lush farmlands, poultry farms and fruit orchards. The congregation in Willimantic owns a small house which they rent to the rabbi. It is old and difficult to clean, but it is bright and cheerful and has a pretty yard attached to the property. I have never lived in such pleasant surroundings and sew curtains for the living room, make scatter pillows for the sofa and feel more contented than I have in years.

I enroll in the teacher's college immediately, and start taking education classes. It isn't nearly as demanding as Queens College was and I find that I have time to do all the chores that are expected of a rabbi's wife. I serve on several synagogue committees, take part in the sisterhood show which we will perform for Chanuka, am part of a book discussion that meets monthly and take part in a very competitive Scrabble game. Best of all I meet several women who will become my friends. I am delighted that one of them, Edie Platt attends the college and is in some of my classes.

Edie is a serious antiquer and she invites me on shopping expeditions to the outlying areas where she buys old treasures which she will restore to new elegance. She buys an ancient brass gate post, polishes it, turns it upside down, has it electrified and she has created a stunning lamp. I follow her lead and buy a wooden butter churn for three dollars, sand paper it down to its grain, stain it and make it into an umbrella stand. I go on serious antiquing trips with Edie. It has suddenly become fashionable to restore old objects and turn them into valuable antiques. I see potential in many of the cast off items that the chicken farmers in the surrounding areas have no use for. We find an old rusty weather vane in someone's barn and I buy it for two dollars, scrape it for hours, paint it and mount it on an old coat rack. Edie assures me that it is stunning and I am feeling powerful as the creative energy flows through me perhaps for the first time in my life. Willimantic is wonderful. The congregation loves Harvey and makes us feel welcome and wanted. And I have discovered a few talents I had that had never been revealed to me. I go on serious antiquing trips with Edie. I see potential in many cast off items that the chicken farmers in the surrounding areas have no use for. We find and iron weather vane in someone's barn and I buy it for two dollars, paint it with brass paint and mount it on an old coat rack. The results are stunning. Edie in the meantime buys a wooden bench which she plans to have upholstered and converted to a love seat.

One of the members of our congregation, Kitty, has an old baby grand piano, a Henry Miller, that she wants to sell for $250. That is serious money for me but I am desperate to have it. We strike a deal, I to pay her fifty dollars a month, saved up from my monthly Sunday School salary and the piano is mine!

Harvey is playing a smaller and smaller role in my life and I am becoming aware of the strange turn his behavior is taking. He has always been a late sleeper, claiming that since his job does not start until late afternoon he is entitled to sleep as late as he likes. Whenever I come home from school in the afternoon I notice that Harvey is unshaven and wearing his bathrobe, a discolored old yellow terry cloth that he ties around his ever expanding waist. He looks slovenly and unkempt. I tell him that I am offended at the sight of him in it. I feel that walking around in one's bathrobe all day is seedy and ugly and I ask him to please be dressed by the time I get home. He ignores my requests. "Sometimes I have to work well into the night and no one should expect me to be dressed and ready by eight o'clock in the morning. I have nowhere to go that early and nothing to do should be able to be comfortable in my house." I argue a bit and then accept it as an inevitable fact of our lives. On one particular day when I rush into the house and head towards the kitchen I do a double-take. I notice for the first time that Harvey is not wearing anything underneath his bathrobe. I am repulsed by his nakedness in the middle of the day. Just then the doorbell rings and I realize that Harvey has answered the door in this state of undress. I am appalled. "Harvey, please. How can you answer the door like this? You're a rabbi. You have a reputation to uphold. You're an example of the Jews to the gentile community and a role model to the congregation. You cannot walk around the house much less answer the door in this state."

I notice other strange behaviors. I find a stash of girlie magazines under his bed. When I confront him he tells me that he and several clergymen in Willimantic have been confiscating them from the men's washrooms in the bars that populate the main street. This is a blatant lie and even though I know he is making it up how can I prove it? Who is there to ask? The thought of Harvey reading such magazines is repulsive but I don't want to make any big waves that might result in changes in our lives.

This is the first time I am experiencing any kind of freedom. Harvey demands very little of me. I don't need to answer to any one as to where I am going, where I've been, what time I will be back, how much money I am spending. No one tells me how to behave, what to wear, to keep my voice lower, that I am wearing too much make-up or that my dress is too tight for my big, fat behind. I love living in Willimantic. I love being a student again and going to my friend's house to do homework together.

The congregation consists of mostly young, professional people who are friendly and accepting of me. One of the men even goes so far as to flirt with me. "You know, you look more like a college student than you do a *rebbitzin*," he tells me. "Why did you ever marry a fat rabbi anyway?" he asks in a playful, flirtatious way. I behave as though I am affronted by his comment, but secretly I am pleased. Happy that someone thinks I am attractive enough to flirt with. With the busy life I now lead and the grand piano in my living room, it is easy to overlook Harvey's shortcomings. I enjoy the many compensations life with him offers, and have no one to compare his strange behavior to.

In August we go to New York for two weeks of summer vacation. I visit with friends and family and we make several trips to Manhattan to see his parents. Once again, his father greets us at the door in an elegant, hand tailored suit while his mother hovers in the background like a shadow, in her shabby formless dress with her *shetyl* teetering precariously on her head. I realize that Harvey is a part of both of them. He loves his expensive suits which he wears to the synagogue but languishes in his grubby old bathrobe when he is at home.

When we return to Willimantic, I enroll in my last semester of college and take a full program hoping to graduate by January. I try to attribute Harvey's strange behavior to the pressure he is feeling with the prospect of the High Holidays looming. But it is getting harder and harder for me to ignore it. An elderly gentleman in our congregation gets sick and Harvey spends hours at his bedside. One evening he comes home from the hospital and tells me that Mr. Heller, the old man he was visiting is really his father. I look at him in disbelief. "Are you crazy?" I ask him. "That's not funny," I tell him. "People could start questioning your sanity with such comments."

He is serious. He tries to convince me that Mr. Heller is his father. He informs me that he has been forced to hide all day in a phone booth because Mr. Heller's relatives are Communists and they are after him. I do not know what to thin k. Could he be playing a joke on me?

Soon, thereafter, I come home and find Harvey shouting into the telephone. He is telling the person on the end that I am poisoning his food and that his life is in danger. Harvey is mentally ill. I grab the receiver from him and realize that he is really speaking to another person and this is hardly a joke.

Up until this moment I have been living in a carefree state of denial, reluctant to take a stand, not wanting to change my pleasant life style. Suddenly I stop and start to accept the reality of Harvey's delusions. I'm really frightened. No amount of denial will permit me to believe that Harvey is normal, pretending to be funny. Although I have spent a good deal of my young life in a mental hospital among the "loonies" of Liebenau, I really know nothing of mental illness and the manner it presents itself. All I do know is that we are in trouble and that I have to get away from Harvey. I remember Luther in Liebenau and how violent he got when he was agitated. Harvey might be dangerous and I am frightened. I run to the door, unlock it and make for the street. I have no plan as to where I am headed. I just know that I have to get away from him. He catches up to me. He is driving our car, stops in front of me and orders me to get in. In my rush to get away from him I realize I have lost one of my shoes. "Please Harvey," I implore him, not knowing what I will say next. "It will all be alright. I'll pull myself together."

He appears to be listening to me. "You are sick," he tells me seriously. "You have to go to the doctor right away." I do not argue with him. Getting to a doctor seems like a very good idea. We drive up the street close to the college I attended just this morning when I thought my life was normal. We barge into an internist's waiting room like two mental patients. The patients look at us like we are both crazy and indeed we do appear that way. Both of us are in disheveled states. He is ranting, "I am Rabbi Lederman. My wife is sick." I am standing next to him wearing one shoe, my hair has come loose from its rubber band and is flying wildly around my face. The doctor comes out of his office to see what all the commotion is about. He tells all the waiting patients to make other appointments: this is an emergency, as indeed it is.

It doesn't take long for the Dr. Grove to see who the sick person is, especially after Harvey tells him that he has to get to Times Square because there will be a ticker tape parade for him. He says that he is responsible for the Geneva Conference and that President Eisenhower will be honoring him. He is agitated and tells the doctor that he did what he had to do for the good of the country. Harvey s convinced that he successfully ended the threat of Communism. Dr. Grove nods his head and appears to be listening carefully. He asks Harvey to wait in his office while he takes me into an examining room.

I sit down on a cold steel chair facing the doctor. "I hope you don't mind Mrs. Lederman, but I have to speak with you alone. How old are you?" he asks me in a gentle, soothing voice. No doubt he sees that I have been through a trauma and does not want to frighten me any more than I already am. I tell him and he looks at me with pity. "You are unaware that you are married to a schizophrenic?" I shake my head.

"No," I tell him. "My husband's behavior has always seemed weird to me, but I had nothing to compare it to." I tell him about the incredible debts he piled up in Kenosha, the Playboy magazines, his walking around the house with nothing on underneath his bathrobe, the ridiculous claim that Mr. Heller is his father and that he had to hide in a phone booth from the Communists who were after him. When I disclose all this, it seems that I too must be suffering from a delusion not to have taken Harvey behavior as a confirmation that something was wrong. "But," I tell him, "all this strangeness started gradually and I did not realize what was coming. He seemed normal at first.

Dr. Grove is kind and patient with me and when I start rambling about my experiences with Harvey he interrupts. "With your permission," he tells me, "I would like to confer with a colleague of mine, a Dr. Kinsky. He is a psychiatrist at the Holy Ghost Mental hospital in New London and I know he will be helpful to us." I feel huge relief sweep over me. I am no longer alone, far from home with a crazy delusional man. I have a doctor who will help me with all I have just undergone in the past few hours.

He makes the call. I hear him tell the other doctor about Harvey's behavior and wait for the conversation to be over. When Dr. Grove comes back into the room he asks me if I have a friend here in Willimantic who could accompany Harvey and me to The Holy Ghost Hospital for an evaluation.

"A colleague of mine, Dr. Kinsky who is a psychiatrist will meet you there and take over." He agrees with me that that given Harvey's agitated state, having him picked up in an ambulance or driven there by the police would only upset him further. "Do you think you could find someone to go with you?" He sees my reluctance and tells me that a police car will be following us in case anything happens and that with me behind the wheel and my friend next to me it is unlikely that Harvey will be violent. I call Edie and she arrives with her husband Frank. They don't ask any questions and Frank insists on driving. "We'll pick your car up when we get back," Edie assures me.

CHAPTER 14

A TALL, HOMELY, man greets us in the hospital lobby. He smiles warmly and introduces himself. "I'm Dr. Kinsky," he says extending his hand to Harvey and me. After the usual pleasantries he tells Harvey to follow a nurse to the intake office where she will take a brief history from him and he beckons to me to follow him to his own office. I look at Dr. Kinsky. There is something kind and appealing about his demeanor. In spite of being obese he moves gracefully and is light on his feet. Thick bi-focal glasses are perched dangerously close to the end of his nose and he peers over them to look at me. Everything about him seems to be pointing downward: glasses, chins and belly. His face is creased like an accordion, thick jowls hang loosely under his chins and his eyes disappear beneath the crinkles formed by his smile. He is welcoming, warm, kind and familiar, a sort of man who could pass for Santa Claus. "My goodness," he says after scrutinizing me for a few seconds, still looking over the tops of his eyeglasses. "How old are you? You look like a teen-ager." He nods as if acknowledging a piece of information I am not privy to. "You have certainly had yourself quite a day. Tell me what is going on and what led up to the events that brought you here."

I recite the story I've told to Dr. Grove and will repeat again and again to doctors, congregants, friends and relatives. He listens, interrupting now and then to ask questions. How long had I known Harvey before we got married? Did I notice any strange behavior during his short courtship ? How do I feel about him? Am I physically attracted to Harvey? I mention to him that I had been in love with someone else right before I met Harvey, had been very much attracted to him and had feelings for him that I did not have for Harvey. I tell him how broken hearted I was when Marvin ended our relationship and had vowed I would never allow myself to completely love another person. Dr. Kinsky pays careful attention to what I say and makes notes on a pad of yellow paper. "You married Harvey on the rebound, it's never a good idea." He says this without sounding judgmental. He nods, writes and then tells me that he is going to have a chat with Harvey and it would be a good idea for me to be present so that he won't have to repeat everything to me. It will about twenty minutes.

Strange as it seems, Harvey has calmed down and agrees t o a hospital stay. Actually he seems relieved to be admitted into the hospital. He tells Dr. Kinsky that he had been hospitalized about three years ago at St. Vincent's, a mental hospital in Westchester County, New York. "It was not a bad experience," he tells him "except that I caught chicken pox while I was there. I was as sick as a dog," he adds, stifling a giggle. Just as he begins to appear rational, he adds, "You know that I was the person who orchestrated the Geneva Conference. President Eisenhower is taking all the credit but he knows the truth."

Dr. Kinsky takes off his glasses and bends toward Harvey, nodding as if in agreement. "Has any other unusual event taken place recently?" Harvey replies that nothing extraordinary except for the fact that the Communists are pursuing him. That's one of the reasons he tells Dr. Kinski that he is happy to be where he can relax and feel certain he will be protected. "It isn't easy to be chased after and have to hide. Has this ever happened to you?" he asks Dr. Kinsky.

Dr. Kinsky tells him that he has never been pursued and commiserates with him. "It must have felt awful. The two of them leave while I wait in Dr. Kinsky's office.

When he returns, he tells me not to come and visit Harvey for a few days. "You need to call your parents and inform them of what has transpired. You also need to call Harvey's parents. He is their son and this will surely not surprise them given his history. It is clear that he has a plan and I feel relieved not to have all the responsibilities of Harvey's care on my shoulders. "What I'm going to do is recommend a series of shock treatment s for Harvey and hope we can get him reality oriented. I am going to get in touch with St. Vincent's Hospital in Westchester where he was a patient three years ago. Let's see what we can find out about his previous hospitalization. And, I want you to get some sleep and rest. You must take care of yourself because you have a lot of work ahead of you."

The first thing I do when I get home is to phone Harvey's parents. I speak to his father who acts as though he has never heard of Harvey's illness, knows nothing about his previous hospitalization and appears to be taken by complete surprise. "Nothing like this had ever happened to him before," he insists.

"Please," I say to him. "Harvey himself told me that he was a patient at St. Vincent's Hospital. The psychiatrist who is treating him needs to speak to you and suggested that you call him and arrange to go to Willimantic."

"My dear child," my father-in-law speaks to me feigning patience as though I were indeed an annoying child. "There is nothing wrong with Harvey. He had a bad case of chicken pox and was hospitalized for it. He was cured in a matter of days, even though it was quite debilitating for him." I try to impress him that I am not calling about chicken pox, but a much more serious matter. He seems not to be able to grasp what I am, saying.

"I...., I can't come to Willimantic," he stammers. "It's too far away for me and my heart doctor forbids any travel." I tell him again that this is his son we are talking about, and his serious departure from sanity. I implore him to help me. He is as much their responsibility as he is mine. This is what D. Kinsky told me to say.

His father disagrees. "No, no, my dear child. He was perfectly normal when he married you. I will do what I can for Harvey, but he is not my responsibility anymore. I'm afraid that the major responsibility for Harvey's state is yours." In spite of his denying Harvey's illnesses he sounds upset and stammers. "I h h have to g g et off the phone. The doctor told me that aggravation is very bad f f f for my, my heart. I have a bad heart condition and this conversation is bothering m… m… me. I will have Harvey's brothers Daniel and Louis contact you,." He hangs up.

The next call I make is to my parents. They are dismayed. "No one ever told us about Harvey's condition. With all the research that Avrom and Schechter did, no one knew about Harvey's family, about the mental illness, about the parents being first cousins? How could the family keep such a secret? When I agreed to the introduction I was totally convinced that Harvey had a clean background. I would have never, never permitted you to marry a man with a predisposition for mental illness." My father is frustrated, angry and distraught.

"The whole purpose of getting a *shadchin*, a matchmaker is because they take all the risks out of a marriage. Of course no one uses a *shadchin* anymore, but the people who introduce marriageable young adults to each other supposedly know the families. This is a sacred trust and now I feel it has been violated. Avrom and Schechter do this *shadchin* stuff as a hobby but they are amateurs.. They were less than useless. If I had known what they let pass by I would have done the background check myself. I'm not dumb. I could have looked into the family background, asked their neighbors, members of their shul. Now I see why he was and is spending money like a madman. He is a madman!"

My parents tell me that when they visited in Kenosha they knew there was something about Harvey that was off, but they thought that getting him out of his financial dilemma would help and now they admit they were wrong. They want to come and pick me up the very next day and bring me home. They tell me that they never signed on for me to be a caretaker to an insane person and they insist that I prepare to go home with them tomorrow. "Pack your bags tonight," my mother says.

The following morning when I wake up I feel disoriented. It takes a few seconds for me to realize all that transpired the day before. I am not sure what to do first but I realize that the president of our congregation must be apprised. I know that my first order of business is to inform the synagogue board of Harvey's illness and the fact that it is unlikely he'll be well enough to conduct the High Holiday service in ten days. I call the president of board and he tells me that he will schedule a board meeting as soon as possible. He does not want to make a move without his board. "We will need an interim rabbi to officiate for the holidays and it will be hard to find one at this late date."

I call Edie and tell her all that has happened and that I spoke to the board president. She says she has a great suggestion. "Why don't we ask Michael, your brother to fill in. He went to yeshiva and I think he'll be terrific. Let me call Frank and see what he thinks. The cantor will do all the prayers and your brother can do the responsive readings in English and deliver the sermons. I'm sure he will come up with something good." She phones her husband and tells him her thoughts. Frank is one of the vice-presidents of the synagogue and he agrees that it would be a good idea, provided Michael wants to cooperate. "After all," Edie says, "this is not something requiring a license to practice."

CHAPTER 15

I AM SURPRISED to see my parents in Dr. Kinshy's office when I go to see him the following morning.

"We couldn't sleep all night and we had to see for ourselves exactly what is going on."

Dr. Kinsky loses no time in explaining to them what they came to hear. "Your son-in-law is seriously delusional," the doctor tells my parents. "I saw him early this morning and it looks as though we have a recurring episode of schizophrenic disorder. I called St. Vincent's Hospital in Westchester and they told me that Harvey was indeed a patient there a little over two years ago. He responded well to the shock treatments he received in St. Vincent's Hospital and that is exactly what I am going to recommend."

My father gets right to the point. "What is his prognosis? Will he ever be cured, get better? Will he be able to work? Does he have any future?"

"Mr. Schmelkes, let me try to honestly answer your questions, but before I do that, I have to tell you what I already know. That way I may be able to answer your questions before you even ask them and give you some information you may not have thought about asking." He speaks slowly, patiently, as if he were teaching a class in schizophrenia. "First of all, Harvey's parents are first cousins, and, although we don't know what causes schizophrenia there is one thing we do know, his genetic heritage is not an advantage. Given the close familial ties that his parents have their children are highly predisposed towards having the disease themselves, and passing it down to their own children," he adds. "Should your daughter decide to stay married to Harvey and have children with him they would have one chance in four of developing the disease themselves. Not something I would gamble on."

My father sighs and looks at my mother. "How could any responsible person take a chance on such odds?"

Dr. Kinsky continues. "Will he be cured? No. This is a chronic condition that may reappear periodically especially during stressful times. in its acute phase. In spite of its prevalence, and the fact that it's been around since time immemorial, it is a very poorly understood illness. There are references to schizophrenia dating back to the Roman Empire. As for getting better, that depends on how you define better. Between episodes he will most likely appear completely normal and rational but there is no way of predicting how long a remission will last or how acute the next episode will be. He will be able to work when he is rational but I would strongly recommend that he not have a stressful job. Stress and pressure can hasten episodes and make them more acute. Does he have a future? Of course," the doctor sighs, "it's just not the type of future one would wish for their child. By the way, his intellect and creativity are not impaired when there is a remission. In fact, some very bright people suffered from schizophrenia. Michelangelo was purported to have been schizophrenic, as was Mary Todd Lincoln and Albert Einstein's son."

They continue discussing what might have been the catalyst that brought on this episode and Dr. Kinsky speculates that it could have been the pressure of the upcoming holidays coupled with the hours Harvey spent visiting an elderly gentleman in the hospital who reminded him of his own father.

Dr. Kinsky looks at the clock and tells my parents that he'll have to stop. "Harvey's been handed a bad hand, and unfortunately this illness can be controlled but it cannot be cured."

My father stands up, shakes Dr. Kinsky's hand and thanks him for his time and effort. He walks toward the door and then turns around, "One more question, Dr. Kinsky, what would you do if Rita was your daughter?"

The doctor does not hesitate, "I would take her home, back to my house and have her start her life over again as if this had never happened. She is young. There is no reason for her not to pursue her previous goals. What she's lost in time she has gained in experience." He turns toward me and says, "my suggestion to you, Rita, if you plan to stay in Willimantic for any amount of time, go right back to college here and continue with your life, or you might want to consider moving back to New York and continuing with your educations there.. There is no point in sitting around and waiting for Harvey to get better. He is in the hospital, being cared for and there is nothing else for you to do."

My father nods, "That's exactly what I wanted to hear, Dr. Kinsky."

C H A P T E R   1 6

I RELUCTANTLY SAY good-bye to my parents. It is as hard for them to leave me as it is for me to stay alone scared, and helpless. The only people I feel truly close to are Edie and Dr. Kinsky. My mother is in tears and so am I, but I can't just run out on all of my responsibilities here. I feel so confused and upset. Without planning to, I get into the car and drive around the beautiful New England countryside. The blue sky and mild September day only serves to increase my sadness. I am alone, abandoned and feeling bereft. I never loved Harvey, but I did make a commitment to him and in spite of the anger I feel a sense of obligation and sadness for him. That old sense of duty is tugging at my heart. "How can I leave him after all that he's going through? Yet, how can I stay with him for the rest of my life?"

As I drive, I come to several conclusions: he has awful parents, he is an incredible corner cutter like getting his ordination under false pretense, copying his sermons word for word from books published by rabbis. He is very impulsive spending money that he does not have on things that he does not need. But, I tell myself, he is very sick and will probably never live a normal life. Unwelcome, tears sting my eyeballs. The intense beauty of the turning leaves, the vermilion, orange, scarlet, yellow shades all around me feel like an assault. All this beauty is here for everyone to enjoy, but not for Harvey. Not for him who is in a locked up unit in a mental hospital undergoing electrical trauma on his body. I feel great sadness and pity for him.

I call Dr. Kinsky. I want to know if Harvey is or might become dangerous. He tells me that Harvey is suffering from dementia praecox, paranoid type, which in English means that the type of schizophrenia that is characterized by delusions, suspicion, illusions of grandeur, sometimes great euphoria and sometimes severe depression. "Usually these patients are harmless, but if they think they might get hurt or if they hear voices that tell them they are in danger," he frowns "they act irrationally. Most are not dangerous, but some can be, especially if they hear voices telling them to commit crimes. Every now and then we read in the newspaper about a murderer who claims he heard voices telling him what to do and whom to do it to. But this is very unusual and only makes the headlines because of its rarity." He sees the dismay on my face. "Don't worry," he tells me. "Harvey is one frightened fellow. He is unlikely to cause harm to anyone. Most schizophrenics are harmless, frightened people."

"How do the shock treatments work?" I ask.

"Not really sure," he runs his tongue over his fleshy lips before continuing. "What the electro- shock does is induce a gran- mal seizure that will cause Harvey to have a temporary lapse of memory. When the treatment is finished he will be calm and as I said experience a temporary loss of memory. Picture a cartoon of a jig saw puzzle and all the pieces are scattered all over the screen. The electric shock shakes the brain up and makes the pieces coalesce and form a sensible picture. When you met Harvey he was experiencing a period remission, he appeared normal. We don't know yet how long remissions can last, but given the right circumstances he could stay well for years. Schizophrenia has been attributed to lots of causes and Harvey has the most significant ones. Having parents who are first cousins and both probably carry the gene," he pauses, looking for the right thing to say, "Harvey was just dealt a bad hand of cards. I like him," Dr. Kinsky adds. "He's a nice fellow, too bad about his illness."

CHAPTER 17

I PLAN TO make a decision after all the holidays are over. In the meantime Michael comes to Willimantic to lead the services in the synagogue. He is happy to do it for two reasons. First of all he is getting away from the house and my father's ever present scrutiny and second of all, the congregation will be compensating Michael for his time and travel. He is earning $200 for his service and enjoying every minute of not having to be at home. Michael puts on Harvey's white holiday robe and plays the role of the rabbi. He looks great in the robe and does a credible job with the sermon which he copied carefully from a book of sermons, just as Harvey used to do.

After *yom kippur* the Day of Atonement I drive to the Holy Ghost to visit Harvey. At first he doesn't recognize me and calls me Faye, his sister's name. I had been warned that he would have some gaps in memory but I was unprepared with facing the reality of it. I explain to him who I am and he acts as if he remembers me. We sit and talk and thankfully I feel nothing, not remorse, anger, sorrow or guilt. He appears to be a total stranger and I surmise from his actions that I appear that way to him.

"Are you looking forward to coming home?" I lean towards him and ask.

"Yes," he answers but appears to be confused. "Which home do you mean? Willimantic or New York?" he asks.

He stammers a bit and goes on, "I mean, I like it here. I get kosher food," he tells me not realizing that I am the one who is providing it. "The people are nice and I have friends here."

A nurse, a nun, actually, in a white habit stops me as I am leaving. "He's a very cooperative patient," she tells me, "a nice person, friendly and helpful. But you are so young, and he is so sick. Take your time before you make any plans. You don't want any more regrets than you already have." I don't understand what she means. Is she advising me to leave him or is she telling me to stay? "Give yourself time. Pray about it and God will tell you what to do. God hears our prayers. He has a plan for you and His will is for your good" she is soft spoken and seems very kind. I'm not used to being told to pray to God and accept His will for me.

Dr. Kinsky tells me that Harvey will be discharged the following week. He can't stress enough how important it is that Harvey not go back to the pulpit just yet. "He'll be jumping right back into the fire he just escaped from. The pressure and responsibilities associated with such a position can make a healthy person lose his mind." He speaks kindly and softly. He tells me that he looks upon me as a daughter. He tells me that it isn't too late to rectify things. "I took the liberty of calling his family and they agreed that one of his brothers will come to the hospital and take him home to New York. Harvey was very happy when I told him and he says he is looking forward to going home." Dr. Kinsky delivers this last piece of news proudly. He has accomplished a successful plan for both Harvey and me. He rubs his hands together in anticipation. He has been in close contact with my parents and they all agree that I should return to New York and Queens College.

"I'm not sure I want my old life back. It was not so great when I married Harvey. Why would anyone think that I will be happy to pick up the life I was so eager to leave?"

"Whoa, whoa'" Dr. Kinsky interjects. "I never said that you should make any decisions now regarding your future. You do not have to leave Harvey. You do not have to go to college. The reality is that this could be a temporary arrangement. Harvey goes back to his family and you go back to yours. If after a sufficient amount of time has elapsed, and you decide that you want to give your marriage another try, that will be your decision to make. Going back to college is not an issue now anyway since it is too late to enroll in the fall semester and you have some time before the spring semester starts. The reality of the situation is that unfortunately you have no other place to live. Unless, of course, Harvey's parents decide that you can live in their apartment with Harvey. But honestly, I don't think that is what you want, nor do I think that it's the best route to take."

I am dismayed at the way the events are turning out. The last place I want to return to is the life I led before I married Harvey. I know my father, he is being kind and supportive right now, but he thinks he can control me with the strength of his iron will. He thinks I can put everything past me. That I can return to living with a curfew, being told what to wear, questioned about my comings and goings, and become what I have finally given up: a good, obedient daughter. Life with Harvey was not good but at least I was allowed to be myself. I feel my life is going from bad to worse. I stare at the floor and burst into tears. "I don't k now what I want," I exclaim. Dr. Kinsky pauses before he speaks again.

"I know how this must feel for you. I have a daughter your age and I don't know what I would do if she were facing a similar situation. But slow down. Try to look at this as a time in your life when you can take a break, relax, pursue some of your hobbies. You'll see, life will take care of itself. Whatever is supposed to happen will happen. I realize how domineering your father is and how difficult life with him must be. But try not to think of that. For the first time in your life nothing will be required of you, you'll have no obligations and I'm sure your father will become less demanding of you and more mindful of your needs. I nod and stand up ready to leave.

Dr. Kinsky stands up and walks me to the door. Just as I am about to leave, he places his hands on my shoulders. I turn around to face him he reaches out to hug me. Thinking this is an affectionate, warm expression I hug him back. I am shocked when he tightens his grip on me and suddenly tries to kiss me on the mouth. I don't know how to react. Should I push him away? I looked to him as my friend and protector, a contemporary of my parents, a person who convinced me he had my best interest at heart. I turn my cheek towards him but he clutches me harder making it difficult to breathe. He does not read my message. "No, no," he persists, " I want a real kiss from you."

Oh my God! Not again! The *"glatz kopf"* memory surfaces from nowhere. I haven't thought of *layz kopf"* in years. I feel betrayed by someone I trusted. I disentangle myself and run out of his office. I have lost all trust in him and will never tell anyone about it. People would think I made it up, just as my mother insisted that *"glatz kopf"* never kissed me.

CHAPTER 18

I VISIT HARVEY one more time at the Holy Ghost Hospital. He tells me that his brother Louis will be picking him up and that he will return to New York. When I ask him how he feels about that he shrugs his shoulders and says it's fine. He is cheerful, full of confidence and tells me not to worry about him. "I'll be fine. I'll find another pulpit and get along with my life."

He makes no reference to our marriage but tells me that after a few weeks in New York he will start looking for another position expecting that I will be accompanying him. The president of the congregation visited him and promised to give him an excellent recommendation. He is feeling fine and optimistic about our future together, certain that it will be with me.

The following week, I am driving back to Forest Hills. My mother sits beside. She came to help me pack up my belongings. We arrange for piano movers to move my baby grand to my parents' home, she has sold her spinet piano to make room. She tries to be optimistic. "Everything is turning out for the best. You will start college in January and you do have credits from your year in Willimantic. Before you know it, we'll be attending the first college graduation in our family."

I don't tell her how I feel. I realize and have accepted the fact that there is no other way for me to go. I have no money and no marketable skills. Even my typing is full of errors. I dread the prospect of having to tell my friends and acquaintances what transpired. Suppose they don't believe me, maybe judge me as an unreliable person? I am not strong enough to face their disapproval. I am disappointed in every-thing and everyone. Especially Dr. Kinsky. How can I trust his judgment and competency after that last visit? He seemed so sure of himself, so sincere in his concern for my welfare, and then he behaved exactly as the boys who followed me up the stairs when I was in eighth grade. I even entertain the possibility that he wanted me to leave Harvey so that he could have me to himself. And then, I try to make myself believe that the whole episode was a product of what my mother called "my active imagination," just as she did when I told her about the *'glatz kopf'*"incident.

When we arrive in Forest Hills my father and my brother are wait-ing for us on the street. Michael looks at me knowingly. Only he knows what life is like in our house. "You can have the bedroom," he informs me kindly. "I know it's generous of me, but what are you gonna' do. Everyone has to make sacrifices." He attempts a light, joking mood. We start unpacking the Chevy and carrying my things into the apartment. Everyone is pleased except for me. My father for protecting me, my mother for extricating me from a catastrophic marriage and my brother is getting a cohort back. I feel dismay, failure, sadness and grief.

CHAPTER 19

MOVING BACK IS as difficult as I knew it would be. I hate the little room I sleep in, where I have to remove cushions every night and turn the Castro convertible into a bed. I am uncomfortable and feel like a stranger. I have lost my status, my independence and freedom. Everyone in my house has someplace to go and something to do except for me. Michael is attending NYU and works in the evening as a youth director in a Jewish Center, my mother is busy with her tasks and piano lessons and my father goes to work. I am alone in the house with nothing to do but think.

I want to take piano lessons again with my beloved teacher, Betty Fischer, but I don't have the money to pay for them and will not ask my parents to help. Michael offers to get me a job at the Jewish Center two evening a week supervising teen agers. Life is a bore and I am experiencing one great big episode of depression. I have stopped eating and none of my clothing fits properly. My father stops off at the bakery every evening on his way home from work and buys pastries for me. I appreciate the gesture of kindness, especially coming from him, but I hardly taste anything at all. My father has become gentler with me, he puts his arms around my shoulders and apologizes for encouraging me to marry Harvey, for relying on others to get detailed information about Harvey's family. His kindness is unnerving. It is so unfamiliar that I am uncomfortable with it. I don't know how to respond.

Harvey attempts to get in touch with me but my parents will not allow me to speak to him. They become the filters for everything he tells them and they report whatever they want me to hear. Harvey's family wants to take possession of his car that has been parked in front of our house since I came home. My father does not want to give it up. He is driving it to work every morning. He feels that after all that Harvey's family has done to our family having his car is not such a big deal. One evening, I step out to go for a walk and see that the car is missing. His family must have come to Forest Hills and taken it. I feel relieved. I don't want anything to tie me to Harvey.

Everyone tries to convince me that in many ways I am lucky. My cousin Elsie, whom we all listen to and respect tells me that at the age of twenty-one I would have to be crazy to tie myself to a man who has been diagnosed a schizophrenic, with a genetic history Harvey's "It would be the height of irresponsibility and concern for everyone who loves you," she tells me, "and if you did have children with him, every time one of them did something peculiar or unusual you would question their sanity. Do you want to live like this, always on the alert for signals of instability? Life is hard enough. Don't tempt with fate and jeopardize every chance you may have for happiness. You are young and have everything going for you. Try to get an annulment so that you can take advantage of whatever life has to offer."

Of course, she is right, but I cannot help feeling guilty for abandoning Harvey. Intellectually, I know I can't consider a future with him, his schizophrenia, worrying constantly about who he will be when he returns from the synagogue, the risk of having children with him, the thought of never having children, his bizarre behavior even when he is in remission all convince me that leaving him is the only option I have. After hours and days of obsessing, I decide to broach the subject of annulment or divorce with my parents and they agree whole-heartedly; the sooner, the better.

We engage a lawyer in downtown Manhattan. He will do his best, he tells us. We will go for an annulment because there was "collusion" involved in getting me to marry Harvey. Harvey's family did not disclose his previous illness to me and I married him under the assumption that he was normal. Harvey contests the annulment and that delays the process. I don't care if it's an annulment or a divorce. All I want is to be free of him. Seeing Harvey in court makes me wonder why I ever consented to marrying him. He is bland looking and still as unappealing as he was the first time I laid eyes on him. My lawyer convinces me to plead that I refused to cohabit with Harvey and the annulment is granted.

Now that I have the civil annulment, it is time for me to get the Jewish divorce a *get,* so that I will be free to marry again. This is a ritual which according to the Jewish law can only be initiated by the husband. I start to question the equality of women in the orthodox movement of the Jewish religion. Why should Jewish divorce only be at the prerogative of the husband? That's really not fair, I tell myself. After all, it was my idea to get out of the marriage, not Harvey's. This law seems arbitrary and specious. When I complain about its unfairness to women my father explains that actually the Jews were the first ancient people who recognized the need to sometimes dissolve a marriage and that they are ahead of all others. He makes a good case for the orthodox point of view but I do not buy into it.

At first Harvey refuses to grant me the *get,* the Jewish divorce, and then he disappears. When my father calls his house, he is told that Harvey does not want to grant me the *get,* that he is away and cannot be reached. They will divulge nothing as to his whereabouts. I am furious. Even though I feel contemptuous about this law, I want the *get.* I want to close all the doors to my marriage. Uncle Avrom assures me that I have nothing to worry about. "We have ways of coercing a reluctant spouse." He winks at my father and my father nods.

"We're going to go to find a way. This is not the first time a husband has refused a *get.*" It is not going to be as easy as I was led to believe. Harvey's disappearance has complicated everything. First we have to find him and then we have to coerce him. I cannot understand how my uncle can be so *blase.*

We travel to Brooklyn and consult a Jewish private detective who specializes in finding missing Jewish persons, whether for alimony payments, cheating a business partner, tax evasion, any kind of person who is wanted in the tight knit Chasidic community that shies away from civil authority or the possibility of exposure to governmental scrutiny. Mr. Zatinsky, the detective looks a bit shady. Although on the outside his house looks exactly the same as all the others in the neighborhood, but inside, it is decorated in the most opulent style: thick purple carpets muffle any sound that footsteps might make, maroon, brocade drapes drawn shut and even though it is mid-afternoon and light outside, several ornate table lamps are lit and standing on gilt end tables. Any hint of sunlight or sound has been blocked from the room.

Mr. Zatinsky's jet black hair appears waxed, raked straight back off his forehead. His face is pock marked with acne scars, he wears heavily scented cologne whose smell precedes his entrance into the room, a large sapphire ring on his left pinkie and he is wearing a black, silk smoking jacket. He looks like a character in a gangster movie, possibly starring in a Humphrey Bogart film. His facial expression never changes, he does not smile, frown or show the least bit of animation.

When we are finished talking to him, he looks at us and says, "I don't think you'll be able to afford me. My services do not come cheap and there will be no monetary reward in this venture, not for you, not for me. You look like intelligent people. I'll tell you how do your own investigation." He sits back in the ample chair and speaks, almost in a whisper. "Start by remembering what he likes to do, his hobbies, interests, what kinds of stores he likes to shop in, what kind of food he eats. Ask everyone you know and everyone who knows him and I wish you good luck." He walks us to the door, shakes hands with the men and nods to me.

CHAPTER 20

⸙

I AM FRUSTRATED and dismayed. I am still living in my father's house, under the same rules, same restrictions, constantly subjected to the scrutiny and criticism I thought I had gotten away from when I married Harvey. Somehow the months pass by and I am back at Queens College, eager to I get my bachelor's degree. Because it is the spring semester and many of the remaining music courses are not given until the fall semester, I switch my major to education which will be the fastest route to getting my diploma. The work is easy. I do a student teaching session and realize that I adore teaching. I enjoy the company of little children, their innocence and enthusiasm. I also enjoy the company of the teachers whom I have lunch with. They are all bright, educated women, invested in the development of their charges. I tackle teaching with an interest I haven't felt for anything in a long time. I fell into it by accident, looking for the fastest route to graduation and have found my passion in life. I apply for a fellowship at Yeshiva University, am accepted and receive a master's degree one year after my bachelor's.

There is an important call from Uncle Avrom. He has found Harvey! My uncle paid close attention to the advice from the detective and has done some intensive investigating. He remembered that Harvey is a "Judaica books junky," that wherever he went he would check out Jewish book stores and visits them. Our cousin Moishe Streiz owns a Judaica store on the Lower East Side of Manhattan. Uncle Avrom asks him to contact all the Jewish booksellers he can think of and find out if they had a recent customer by the name of Harvey Lederman.

The orthodox community is small, cloistered and close knit. Everyone knows everybody's business. Many people are connected by family ties or know someone who is connected to the person one wants to contact. My uncle calls my cousin, who calls the Jewish booksellers and Harvey is located in Pittsburg, where, coincidentally my uncle has many relatives who happen to be rabbis.

I hear my father's excited end of the conversation. "You mean to say he's in Pittsburg? You know how to find him?" He tells him that he not only found Harvey, but that but he has already contacted Rabbi Peltz his cousin and that Rabbi Peltz will convene a group of rabbis who will see to it that my *get* is granted. Rabbi Peltz happens to be one of the most respected rabbis on the east coast, he sits on many rabbinic committees and wields a good deal of clout. And the best part of it is that he will see to it that the *get* takes place quickly, probably in one day's time.

"What are we waiting for?" my father asks. "We'll leave tonight. We'll drive to Pittsburg, get there in the morning and request a meeting of the board of rabbis. They'll surely agree. Especially since so many of them are related to you."

At 8 P.M. my brother, father, uncle and I pile into my uncle's Oldsmobile and head west for Pittsburg. We arrive a 6 A.M., check in to a motel, shower and rest and by 10 A.M. we are seated at the desk of the Rabbi Peltz, who is not only the head of the board of the Rabbinical Assembly in Pittsburg, but a leading authority on the laws of *gittin*, Jewish divorce.

"Yes yes," he says. "I know who Rabbi Lederman is. He is new to Pittsburg and he's been visiting all the Jewish establishments. He has a pulpit in the Conservative Synagogue. He's an energetic young fellow. He even got himself a weekly radio spot speaking about the *parsha*, portion of the Torah read each week." Rabbi Peltz checks his watch. "As a matter of fact he is on the local radio station right now. If we hurry we can catch him before he leaves the radio station."

We arrive just as Harvey is slamming his car door, ready to drive away. My father and brother rush to his car, grab the door handle and pull open the door. All this happens so quickly that I barely have a moment to register what I see. Michael and my father strong arm Harvey and force him into the back of Uncle Avrom's car.

"What is this all about?" Harvey asks, looking indignant. "Am I being kidnapped by two *rabbonim*?"

My father tells him why we are there. At first Harvey is annoyed. "You didn't have to come all the way to Pittsburg for that," he says, sounding belligerent. "I would have given Rita a *get*. After all, I also want to re- marry in the future." When no one answers him he continues. "I've only been in Pittsburg two months and didn't have a chance to contact anyone." He remains quiet for a few moments and no one else in the car speaks. I know Harvey and can almost hear what he is thinking.

"You know," Harvey says after a few moments of silence, "It is common for the man to receive payment for granting a *get*. I don 't think I am being unreasonable in expecting compensation."

When no one responds to this comment, Harvey thinks my father might acquiesce and that there might be some monetary reward for him. Encouraged by my father's silence, he goes on, "How much do you think it is worth?" He pauses hoping for an opportunity to strike a bargain. "How important is a *get* to you?" he asks again. My father who does not wish to address such an outrageous proposal rolls his eyes

Harvey does not read my father's scorn. "I actually know some men who received $10,000 in cash," he tells us earnestly. "Since I am the injured party, the one who was abandoned, I believe I am entitled to some compensation."

My father still has not said a word. Rabbi Peltz turns to face Harvey. "We will call a *beth din* and it will decide." *(Beth din* translated means, "house of judgment." Years ago it was the basis of all Jewish law. In modern times it is invested with legal powers within the orthodox Jewish community). Rabbi Peltz continues, "I assure you, Harvey that your side of this story will be heard and carefully judged. If the *beth* finds that your wife left for no good reason, or took part in immoral or illicit activity, then the *beth* will decide in your favor and you may be awarded some compensation. If not, you will have to grant her a *get* if you want to remain a person of good standing in the Jewish community. This is about justice nothing else, not extortion or bribery." Rabbi Peltz has a large following in Pittsburg and is capable of destroying Harvey's career. Harvey is looking uncomfortable. He is not sure how much Rabbi Peltz knows about his past. Instinctively he knows that is will go better for his future if he does not pursue financial gain. I know Harvey. He needs money. He was always in debt, short on cash, but I am outraged at his nerve. The fact that he would demand money from my father after all the lies his family told and the secrets he has kept from us is beyond revolting.

Harvey squirms. He is uncomfortable sitting in the back of the car between my father and my brother. They crowd him and my brother is applying strong pressure to his upper arm. Harvey winces in pain from my brother's grasp. "You can let go of my arm, I'm going nowhere sitting here between you two," he turns toward Michael. "You know that what you and your father did is illegal. This is a kidnapping. You forced me into the car."

"Yeah Harvey, we know. We also know that you are in no position to negotiate. We are four against one here and we have the Jewish law on our side as well." Michael tells him as Harvey tries to shift and pull away from my brother. "I think you are getting off easy. Think of what it will cost you if you get yourself exposed." Harvey who knows exactly what Michael means presses his lips shut and does not answer.

We return to Rabbi Peltz's synagogue, a modern gray building with a huge stained glass Star of David above the doors. He sits at his desk, and I look around the tastefully decorated room. Two large bookcases are stand against the wall holding tall books with Hebrew writing on the back covers. Soft brown carpeting, plush arm chairs and a long, shiny table with eight chairs surrounding it make for a formal yet inviting atmosphere. Rabbi Peltz spins his rolodex, picks up the telephone and proceeds to make several calls. I hear him telling the people on the other side of the conversation that there will be a convening of a *beth din* for the purpose of writing a *get* that very day at 2 P.M. He tells us that he has called a Hebrew scribe to write the *get* as is required by Jewish law and two other rabbis to act as witnesses.

We sit and wait in Rabbi Peltz's office. He asks us if we would like some tea or perhaps something to eat. Uncle Avrom, my father and Rabbi Peltz pass the time talking about their relationship to each other. They discuss the Jews in Pittsburg and my father tells them of the *frum,* religious community that has sprung up in Forest Hills which up until five years ago did not even have a kosher butcher. I sit on a sofa next to a window, trying to read a novel by Frank Nolan, Michael is working on a crossword puzzle from the Pittsburg newspaper and Harvey has asked to be allowed to look at one of Rabbi Peltz's volumes.

A little after 2 P.M. the scribe and the other two rabbis arrive. All three have long, unruly beards and ear-locks like corkscrew curls on each side of theirs ears. They are dressed in identical black overcoats and black hats. The scribe who will write the *get* in Aramaic takes a seat at the conference table in the rabbi's study. He asks Harvey and me few questions, dips an old fashioned quill into the black ink and starts to write while the rest of watch. I am transfixed by the scribe's art, the forming of the letters, each one perfect. As soon as the document is completed, the scribe blows on it to make sure it is dry and passes it over to the witnesses. He then hands it over to Harvey who inspects it and then gives it to me. I am then required to give it back to Rabbi Peltz, the officiating rabbi. According to customary law, he tears it up and files it so that it cannot be used again. What the document basically says is that I am free to remarry and am no longer tied to the marriage with Harvey. It's a "no fault" divorce. We each get a "bill of divorcement" stating that the *get* was granted and that the marriage is over.

CHAPTER 21

———— ❧ ————

ONCE I DECIDED to leave Harvey, I never felt connected to him. The *get* was a necessity, a guarantee that I was free to remarry. How clever I tell myself. We actually did kidnap Harvey and force him to give me a *get*. I can't help but think about all the other young women who are tied to marriages that are over. I ask myself, how fair is it that independent, educated women must abide by these ancient rites, remain ineligible for marriage until their ex-husbands agree to give them a *get*. I start to question the religion I am so firmly rooted in. I am able to accept most of the precepts of orthodoxy, *kashrut,* the special celebrations that mark each holiday with beautiful and meaningful traditions and the many laws associated with the observance of the Sabbath. I realize that this is the way to keep the Jewish faith cohesive, alive while enforcing family unity. I remember the welcoming the Sabbath Queen when I was in camp. So much of it is mystical and spiritual and supportive of serenity, but I cannot accept the arbitrary nature of the rules that orthodoxy imposes on women. How can anyone approve this medieval ritual of the granting of the *get*? There are many practices that are unfair to women. They are excluded from the many rituals and pleasures that men are encouraged to participate in. The separation of the genders in the synagogue, reading from the Torah, leading the prayers during services are just a few of the restrictions placed on women.

We return to our apartment in Forest Hills and everything is restored to the previous status quo. My father still rules with an iron fist, my mother supports his decisions and I find myself in the unenviable position of once again being single in a couples world. The *get* has granted me the freedom to remarry but my status in the orthodox marriage market has rendered me few choices. I have acquired a liability. I am no longer a virgin. Most young orthodox men would not consider marrying a divorcee. In orthodox circles I am considered "used-goods." Even divorced men and widowers prefer virgins and although I am free to remarry there are very few men available that would consider me eligible and could merit my family's approval. I am only twenty-two and I feel as though life has already passed me by.

It is early Sunday morning and I can hear my parents talking to each other in the bedroom. I often eavesdrop on their conversations. This morning they are talking about a conversation my father had on the phone with my uncle. It seems that Harvey's family has started a rumor implying that Harvey was normal until he married me. According to the rumor, I was the one who caused him to lose his mind by my constant demands and complaints. Both my parents are outraged by this blatant lie. "How can we dispel this rumor?" my mother asks.

"We can't," my father tells her. "The only thing we can do is to ignore it. Whoever chooses to believe will believe it no matter how hard we try to convince them to the contrary."

I am aghast. The ugly insect of resentment is churning inside my stomach. Why would anybody start such a rumor, I ask myself? Not only am I the one who was taken advantage of, was deceived and lied to, but now people are saying that I am responsible for Harvey's illness. The injustice is making me feel like throwing up. I've had it with orthodoxy. I tell myself that I will date anyone I feel like and will not be influenced by their observance or lack of it.

For the next few months, while I am teaching first grade in the New York public school system I date several men. One of whom I see on a fairly regular basis. He is Jewish but not observant. His name is Sid and he is an accountant. I have been going out with him for three months and my father becomes impatient. "When is he going to propose to you?" he asks me. I shrug my shoulders in response. I have no idea. I am wondering the same thing but am not about to ask him. Another month goes by and my father tells me that Sid is wasting my time. "What's holding him up? He has a job, he has an apartment, he's 27 years old. You'll have to give him an ultimatum."

"I'll do no such thing," I tell my father. "I'm just going out with him. If someone more interested or interesting comes along I'll stop seeing him."

My father disagrees. "You have tied up all your Saturday nights with him. How are you supposed to go out with anyone else? I tell you he is wasting your time, your youth, your precious years. I will speak to him myself if you don 't."

I have to admit that my father is not wrong. I have tied up all my free time with Sid and he does not seem close to proposing or suggesting any kind of commitment. I am getting impatient, but certainly am not going to confront him. What if he says he doesn't want to marry me? What will I do if he rejects me? I refuse to take a chance.

The following Saturday night, when Sid comes to pick me up, my father tells him that he wants to talk to him in private. "Oh oh," I think. They move into the hallway and I hear my father tell him that he expects Sid to make his intentions known. Sid acts like a fool and asks my father what intentions he is talking about.

I hear my father say, "intentions young man? You don't know what I mean by intentions? *Intentions regarding my daughter!* You have not made it clear if your intentions are honorable." I cringe at the old fashioned phrase. "If you are not planning to ask her to marry you, then you are wasting her time. She has other options."

Sid counters by saying that if he intends to propose it will be done because he wants it. He will not be coerced by an impatient father. "I don't care what your plans are, Mr. Schmelkes. You can't push me around like you do the rest of your family. Rita and I are friends and if I decide to marry her I'll ask her, but not at your insistence." My father is incensed. He tells Sid to leave the house and I am furious. I am angry at my father for pushing his will and I am furious at the rude and disrespectful way Sid spoke to my father. I am also deeply hurt and feel betrayed by Sid who did not say anything more positive about the probability of our getting married. The two men in my life, my father and Sid are discussing my future while I have listen and feel pain and outrage equally at both of them.

I continue seeing Sid in spite of feeling his rejection. I tell myself that there is no one else for me to go places with and but deep inside myself I can't help but hope that things might change; that the next time I see him he will declare that he wants to marry me. On some level I know that Sid and I will never marry but I am not ready to acknowledge that. I keep our dates a secret and start lying as to where I am going. I cannot tell my parents that I am still going out with Sid when he has so humiliated me. I am afraid of my father's anger and fierce temper. I know he will force Sid into a showdown and that is a chance I can't possibly take. I am feeling miserable at this time in my life: sneaking out to meet with a man who does nothing to win my affection. Most of my friends are married and those who aren't are engaged.

CHAPTER 22

WITH THE SCHOOL year coming to an end I realize that I will have two months of summer vacation with pay. Totally free time with no plans. Unexpectedly I receive an invitation from my cousin Miriam who lives in Tel-Aviv with her husband and little boy to join them in Europe for the summer. She writes that they have rented a cottage in Switzerland and would love to have me join them. That way we can spend time together and reunite as a family. My parents are anxious for me to go. They believe that Miriam will introduce me to an eligible man and secretly, I am hoping for the same thing. Miriam promises me a wonderful time in Europe. She has many friends there and we will have a chance to travel together for two months. It sounds enchanting and I take her up on her offer.

When we meet I realize that Miriam has no intention of having me tag along with her. She has other plans. She looks on this trip to Europe as an opportunity to spend time with friends, go night-clubbing in Munich, and leave her little boy in the care of her mother, my aunt Mathilde and me. Spending my days in Europe with a toddler who not only misses his mother, but is frightened of being with me, an unfamiliar person who can't communicate with him because he only speaks and understands Hebrew is not the vacation I was hoping for. I leave my aunt in charge of her grandson and go to Israel where I have many relatives.

In 1960 the country is looking green, busy, civilized and sophisticated. Tel-Aviv is glamorous and filled with young people, all of whom speak English. It isn't long before I am introduced by my Israeli cousins to all sorts of exciting people. One of whom, a young man, is part of a research team preparing for the Eichmann trial scheduled to take place in 1961. He shows me all the sights in Jerusalem and accompanies me on a trip to Bethlehem. I fall in love with Israel, especially Jerusalem, an international, modern city with ancient ruins and religious sites. I promise myself that I will return.

On my way home I stop in London for five days to meet up with a fellow teacher who is spending the whole summer there. London is a magic city for me. All the famous building and events that I only experienced via history books, spring to life for me, Buckingham Palace, Westminster Abbey, the Tower of London.

I love the Brits, their crisp accents, good manners and patience are a grand change from the brusque and impatient manners of the New Yorkers I've become used to. I ask an elderly gentleman coming from church one Sunday morning for directions and he insists on taking me to my destination. Dressed in a top-hat and morning coat he points out all the historic places in London that we pass. I get a new perspective on life, my life in particular.

I make a decision to stop seeing Sid when I return to New York. I think he's too involved with himself and his own world. Like so many of the "me generation" people in the 60's he's caught up with a therapist and examines every action, thought and decision he makes or is about to make, looking for causes and reactions. He is lacking spontaneity and sophistication and I realize that he is not for me. This trip to Europe awakens a desire in me that has been dormant for too long. I want more fun and unanticipated events than Sid is capable of providing.

When I get home I call him and tell him that I met a man who was traveling in London and that we are seeing each other. This, of course is a lie but it is also a test of his feelings. Will he tell me that he's ready for marriage? That he missed me and is happy that I returned?

He tells me that he's very disappointed, that he missed me and waited the whole summer for me to come home. Then he asks me if this new person has offered me marriage. When I tell him that I think this is a serious relationship, he tells me that he is not ready for marriage. When I hang up the phone I feel sadness and relief.

CHAPTER 23

———— ❦ ————

IT IS TIME for me to move out of my parents' house and try life on my own. I find a young woman who has placed an ad in the Sunday Times, looking for a roommate. The apartment is perfect. I have my own room and a new friend. Marie Claire works for Air France as a VIP hostess. She is the person who greets important passengers who arrive in New York from France. We share the responsibilities of the apartment, split the rent and utilities and enjoy each other's company when we happen to be at home at the same time. Now that I no longer live with my parents the pressure to get married and get away is lifted. I am learning that I can enjoy life without being involved with a man. At first my parents are reluctant for me to move away. "How will it look to anyone who wants to date you to see that you are living away from your home?" my father asks. "It just doesn't feel right. An unmarried girl belongs at home with her parents so that she can be protected and taken care of."

"Don't worry," I tell them. "If I have a date with a religious boy I'll tell him I live at home and that he can pick me up at your apartment."

Marie Claire introduces me to her many friends most of who work in the airline industry. They are light hearted, sophisticated, drink a lot of alcohol, and have parties whenever they are not working. This is the first time in my life that I find myself in a group of people who travel extensively, speak several languages, and often drink to excess.

One of the perks of working for the airline industry is receiving free airline tickets to wherever they wish to go after putting in the required number of hours working at their jobs. Marie Claire has scheduled a trip to the Far East with one of her boy friends who also works for Air

France. They are going to Tahiti, Bangkok, Thailand and Singapore; exotic places that I have heard of but never dreamed of visiting. Their life style is completely foreign to me. I can't accept it for myself, but I envy their ease and freedom.

I enjoy their company but feel like an alien. Their casual lifestyle is safe from a distance but taboo for me. Marie Claire is able to juggle several boy friends at the same time. She is open about her sex life and although I listen to her I feel uncomfortable. I know she comes from a different world than I do.

I have applied for and been granted a fellowship in a Master's program in education at Yeshiva University. Twice a week I take the subway into Manhattan and attend late afternoon and evening classes. They are unchallenging and I feel that I am learning nothing. But they will provide me with a diploma and a higher salary in the New York public school system. It's worth the effort. Between teaching my student teaching assignment and attending Yeshiva University, doing homework and hanging out with Marie Claire I find myself occupied all the time;

Teaching first grade gives me a fresh outlook on the world and my place in it. The students are all enthusiastic. Every new achievement for them is a gift for me. "Am I really reading?" an excited little boy asks me after he has put three letters together and formed a word. When I assure him that he is he bounces around the classroom announcing "I can read, I can read!" Where else in the world could I ever get a job generating so much joy? I graduate Yeshiva University in May, take the New York teacher's license exam, pass and am assigned to a public school not far from my home.

Joey is a little boy in the classroom across the hall from mine. His mother died of cancer and he is being raised by his grandparents. He has a sweet disposition, is vulnerable and eager to please everyone he meets. Because his teacher is my mentor and our classes spend many mornings during recess together, I get to know Joey as well as the boys in my own class. He often comes over to where his teacher and I sit watching the six year olds running around the school yard. He loves to talk to us. He tells us that his father is an engineer, a rocket scientist who lives in Philadelphia and comes to New York on week -ends to be with his sons. Every Monday morning Joey comes over to us and tells us about his week-ends with his dad. It is clear that they spend a great deal of time at the different museums in New York and that he is familiar with some I've never been to. The past year has been one of the happiest times of my life. Teaching school, living on my own, meeting many people from different walks of life has convinced me that I am a capable person and that there is much in life that I have to learn about. It is like a new spirit has entered my soul and shown me that the life I have lived, my father's proclamations and mother's conformity are a narrow slice of the world.

On the last day of school my friend and I are in her classroom having lunch when Joey's grandmother comes in to speak to his teacher. I leave them alone, not wanting to intrude on what might be a private conversation and not very interested in what they might be saying. I go into my own classroom and continue packing up my personal possession for the summer vacation.

My colleague loses no time in asking me if she may give my phone number to Joey's father. "Mrs. Ross asked me if you had a boyfriend and about your marital status. I told her that I'd ask you. So, I'm asking. May I give her your number so that she can give it to her son?" I tell her that need to think it over. Dan has two children and I don't want to accept a date with him if the children will be an obstacle to my way of life.

After several days have gone by, I call my friend tell her that she could give my phone number to Dan's mother. I have given it a great deal of thought and decide that based on Joey's personality Dan is a safe bet. He's a good father and cares about his children and I feel that I have nothing to lose by going out with him. He calls me on the following evening and we plan to meet on July 5th because neither of us wants to be stuck in fourth of July traffic.

On our first date, a Saturday night we go to a French restaurant and then wander through a book store in Greenwich Village. It does not take long for me to discover that Dan and I have more in common than anyone I ever met. He has an encyclopedic knowledge of classical music and we realize that we both own identical record collections. He is smart and good looking, with curly black hair that I have always admired in men. He knows more about any subject that most people know about one. He is even a good dancer, something I had not thought about. On our third date he asks me to marry him.

I, joking, reply that I'll marry him if we can go to St. Martin for our honeymoon. The following week he comes to pick me up and tells me he has booked two tickets to St. John and St. Martin for August 1st. After Sid's indecisiveness Dan's assertive pursuit is welcome and appreciated. We plan to get married on August first after only two weeks of dating. My friends question me as to why we are rushing into marriage after knowing each other for such a short period of time. I reason to myself that I already know his son and his mother and that both seem to be well adjusted, kind, smart people, so there should be nothing holding me back especially when I'm in love and anxious to get married and start having babies of my own.

My parents are impressed with Dan. My father tells me that I really "hit the jackpot." My father insists that we get married by an orthodox rabbi. I put my foot down. "Under no circumstances," I tell him, "will I commit to another orthodox marriage contract. Once was enough." My father says that he will not attend the wedding ceremony and while I feel regretful at his stubbornness I am equally stubborn. My mother is once again put into the uncomfortable position of following her husband's orders or following her heart and attending our wedding.

We are married in the conservative rabbi's study in Forest Hills and to my pleasure and surprise my father and mother are there to see us tie the knot.

CHAPTER 24

⁂

WE RETURN FROM our honeymoon in the Bahamas, pick up Joey and Stevie who were staying with Dan's parents and drive to Philadelphia to start a new life. We purchase a beautiful home in the western suburbs, join a synagogue, enroll the boys in the local school and I am pregnant. Dan wants me to legally adopt the boys. We go to orphan's court in Norristown and the boys are ours. After our daughter Anne is born, we have two more children together, Kenny and David and my dream has come true. I am a suburban housewife, mother of five children, owner of several dogs, driver of a large station wagon and member of several car pools.

To say that I lived "happily ever after" would not be telling the truth. We experienced the ups and downs that everyone encounters, especially parents; the disappointments and the victories, the worries and the fulfillments. My life with Dan was for the most part wonderful. He always encouraged me to be my own person, insisted that we buy the grand piano for me which I thought was far too expensive, he was instrumental in getting me to write this book and encouraged me every step of the way.

He passed away on March 3, 2013 after a long, courageous, arduous battle with the complications of radiation therapy. He was a loving husband, father and grandfather and I will love and miss him for the rest of my life.

Epilogue

With apologies to my father whom I painted with a harsh brush stroke.

After many decades of introspection, with the help of my therapist and the gift of maturity, I have been able to forgive my father for taking so much joy from my life. I have come to realize that he was not the giant ogre. He was, in fact, a sad and bitter disenfranchised man. Having come America and starting life over as a factory worker robbed him of his self- esteem. He was totally unprepared to raise two partly grown children according to his standards, yet he took complete charge of us in the authoritarian manner prevalent among parents during his youth in Vienna.

Although not trained for any particular profession or trade prior to the war, he made a respectable living as an insurance agent for the Phoenix Insurance Company, an enterprise with friendly policies towards the Jews. He was a respected member of the Jewish community, having descended from a long line of Talmudic scholars. He, himself was very learned in the Talmud and the other holy books. As a matter of fact, the only reason that he was considered a suitable match for my mother, who came from a wealthy family, was due to his ancestry and his own reputation of being gifted in the study of the Talmud. But though he did value that gift, he was forced to abandon any dream of a secular education and he always felt he was deprived of an opportunity to obtain a profession.

In pre-war Vienna, he enjoyed all the privileges of the Jewish upper middle class. He earned a good living, went to work every day in a suit, made important decisions regarding the welfare of his clients and was able to participate in discussions on secular and religious topics. He was admired and welcomed almost everywhere he went. All this was taken away from him when he emigrated to America. For him, going from an office job to a factory was a serious step down. When coupled with the long and difficult periods of unemployment he lost his last shreds of self-respect and status. Not only did he have to accept the economic under-privilege, he felt he was not accepted as an equal by the temple worshippers because he was unable to contribute financially to the fund raising that supported the rabbi and the running of the congregation.

By the time we arrived in New York, the war was coming to a close. His job as a leather cutter in the war industry was ending and he found it very difficult to find any employment. He tried to open a leather jacket factory and go into business for himself, but there was no call for leather jackets. Nylon was becoming available and most people preferred it to the heavy, stiff coats and jackets that were made of leather. He lost his entire investment when his business failed and he found himself unemployed and unemployable.

This terrible period in his life took away his dignity, earning capacity, and self-esteem; but worst of all was the loss of his place in the Jewish community and all that worked for so hard to achieve. In his Orthodox synagogue in Vienna he was always called to the Torah and given an *alyah*, a special honor reserved for esteemed members of the Jewish community. In the Orthodox synagogues in the United States, *alyot* were purchased, auctioned off to the highest bidder.

There was no way my father could justify taking five dollars from his unemployment check to buy that honor. Consequently, he was never called to the Torah. He felt disrespected, looked down on by the other members of his *shul*, causing him to become bitter towards his religion, and subsequently refusing to wear the *kippah*, a skullcap that would have marked him as a member of the Orthodox community.

As he was struggling with unemployment and religious conflicts, he was furious with my brother, Michael, who seemed to scorn his opportunities for an education. He was frightened that Michael would be forced to accept the same fiscal failure that plagued him. At the same time, while he admired my dedication to my education and my success in school, he couldn't help but wish that my gifts had been given to his son instead of his daughter.

I know that my father loved me more than anyone in the world, but he was frightened of losing me to a secular world, to sexual promiscuity, to becoming too smart to attract a husband, and to spinsterhood. He tried to control my every move in order to do whatever he thought would protect me. His fears and obsessions and even his love for me were expressed through his raging outbursts. And, with the best of intentions, he molded me into the frightened person, who adopted his obsessions as well as his depressions. More than anything else, more than the education, the music, the diplomas, what I wanted more than all of it, was the love, admiration and respect of my father.

By the end of his life, I earned it. After I had gotten a Master's degree, been married to a man with a Ph.D., raised five children to become successful contributing members of society, and after becoming a successful professional in my own field, I won the coveted prize, his admiration.

When my mother came to America she didn't know the man she had married so long ago. By 1945, they had spent more time separated than they did together. The war, the need to be protected and giving up some of her responsibility in raising her children made her anxious to share some of her burdens. She had seen so much suffering and fought so hard to save us that she had no strength left to stand up to my father's outbursts and to protect us. It was easier for her to let Michael and me down than to confront his anger. And so we all appeased the contradictions that lived in my father's soul.

It was hard to forgive her for giving my things away to my cousin. But I have come to realize that on some level she needed to restore some dignity to herself. She felt that the only way to that was to appear rich and successful to her older sister. I don't know whether or not she considered my feelings when she took from me. But on some level, she felt she was safe with me, and that I would always love her no matter what she did. And she was right in that respect.

As for Michael, he did not become the dismal failure my father feared. He was and continues to be a very successful business man:

a CEO in a large global enterprise. He and his wife, Lynne, own three beautiful homes, a condo in New York City with enviable views of the East River and the city's skyline, a beach house in the Hamptons and a winter ski home in the Catskills.

I am a lucky person. Very few children survived the Holocaust and have had the fortunate life I have lived. The older I get the more I realize the profound impact that the Holocaust had on my life. Not a day goes by when I don't feel its terror. I was able to deny the relevancy of my childhood for years but eventually it surfaced and made me aware of where my neuroses came from; obsessive worrying about the people I love, fear for their safety, health and happiness continue to haunt me to this very day. The fear I harbored for my children's safety when they were growing up prompted me to overprotect them and force them to rebel excessively to assert their independence.

My preoccupation with loss and abandonment continue to haunt me to this very day. I have nightmares at least three times a week, where I am being chased in unfamiliar places and have no home. But in spite of all I have lived through I consider myself unbelievably fortunate: I am a survivor. I continue to live in my beautiful home surrounded by many people whom I love and who love me. I have five successful children and seven beautiful grandchildren. My ongoing prayer is for peace and tolerance so that the atrocities perpetrated by Hitler and the Nazis will never again be repeated.

Made in the USA
Middletown, DE
16 March 2019